watsuji
tetsurō's
rinrigaku

SUNY SERIES IN MODERN JAPANESE PHILOSOPHY
PETER A. McCORMICK, EDITOR

watsuji tetsurō's *rinrigaku*

translated by

yamamoto seisaku

and

robert e. carter

with an Introduction and Interpretive Essay by

robert e. carter

STATE UNIVERSITY OF NEW YORK PRESS

RINRIGAKU (Watsuji Tetsurō's *Rinrigaku*)
by Tetsuro Watsuji

Copyright © 1937, 1942, 1949 1996
by Masako Watsuji

Originally published in Japanese by Iwanami Shoten, Publishers, Tokyo
1937, 1942 and 1949

This translation was supported by a grant from the Japan Foundation.

Published by
State University of New York Press, Albany

Printed in the United States of America

For information, address the State University of New York Press,
State University Plaza, Albany, NY 12246

Production by Marilyn P. Semerad
Marketing by Bernadette LaManna

Library of Congress Cataloging-in-Publication Data

Watsuji, Tetsurō, 1889–1960.
    [Rinrigaku. English]
    Watsuji Tetsurō's Rinrigaku : ethics in Japan / translated by
Seisaku Yamamoto and Robert E. Carter, with an introduction and
interpretive essay by Robert E. Carter.
        p. cm. — (SUNY series in modern Japanese philosophy)
    Includes bibliographical references and index.
    ISBN 0-7914-3093-6 (HC : alk. paper). — ISBN 0-7914-3094-4 (PB :
alk. paper)
    1. Ethics. I. Carter, Robert Edgar, 1937–   . II. Title.
III. Series.
BJ1185.J3W372513   1996
171'.7—dc20   96-27890
                                                          CIP

10 9 8 7 6 5 4 3 2 1

contents

foreword

When people in Europe and America remark that the *individualism* to which they are accustomed seems either absent or very much muted in modernized Japan, they are restating an observation made by a Japanese philosopher more than half a century ago and one upon which he based a major work of constructive ethics. Between 1937 and 1949 Watsuji devoted himself to the writing of his *Ethics*, a work many hold to be the major such effort by an Asian thinker in the twentieth century.

Watsuji's critique of the individualism of the West developed only after what had been an early flirtation with it; Byron and Nietzsche were, after all, two of the heroes of his youth. And even when he later concluded that individualism was flawed both in concept and in practice, his criticisms of it were based on decades of wide and informed reading in the classics and major philosophers of the West.

To have been merely *against* the West's individualism without offering an alternative would, however, have been a half-measure. Keenly aware of this, Watsuji prepared his counter-offer by giving close attention to the classics of Asia. In 1927 he published a work on the praxis-oriented philosophy of early Indian Buddhism and, in 1938, a book on Confucius. Both works showed him to be a thinker interested in the impact that theoretical positions had on the ordering and functioning of actual societies. Watsuji's *Ethics*, it is worth noting, was based not only on his analysis of philosophical works but also on his readings in many of the major works in sociology and comparative ethnology of his time.

Even his sharpest critics suggest that Watsuji's ideas, including some of the key ones offered in his *Ethics*, should not be ignored. Because most of these critics want to see more rather than less emphasis on the individual in Japanese society, they understandably find Watsuji accurate about the basic ethical assumption in East Asian contexts, but far too ready to accept the situation that *is* for the one that *should be*—that is, too direct a conflation of description and prescription.

Persons in Japan who champion Watsuji's perspective respond to such criticisms by stating that there is no reason why Japanese, or East

Asians for that matter, need take as universally normative what currently are, in fact, the enculturated assumptions about mankind found in Europe and America. They often go on to suggest that this is *the* work which articulates just why not only Japan but East Asia more generally has been outperforming many modern Western societies in terms of social cohesion, family stability, and even the valorization of work.

It has been more than thirty years since Robert N. Bellah published the first essay about Watsuji in a Western language; Bellah's was a brilliant piece that even then, while pointing out risks in Watsuji's position, hinted at the importance of the *Ethics*.[1] Until the publication now of this work, little has been available to persons outside of Japan in search of translated writings by this Japanese thinker. The only complete book by Watsuji available in English has been *A Climate: A Philosophical Study*, a work which, in spite of being somewhat light-weight,[2] has been that which readers in the West have perforce focused upon in assessing the worth of this philosopher.

Those of us who long knew there were things both much more weighty and interesting in the Watsuji corpus awaited the day when an important writing—his *Ethics*, for instance—might be translated. That day, it is a pleasure to see, has now arrived with this impressive work of translation by Robert E. Carter and Yamamoto Seisaku. Here we have a major treatise by a sophisticated thinker who self-consciously wished to provide a distinctly "Asian" alternative to Western ethical systems—systems he and others saw as conceptually flawed and culturally ethnocentric. Long-suppressed questions about the assumed universalizability of some of the West's most privileged moral modes are posed in and through this work. The study both of comparative ethics and of comparative societies will necessarily be much enriched and enlivened by it.

There may be value here in briefly recapitulating the course of attention to Watsuji in Japan since the publication of the *Ethics*. Conceived and written over the time spanning World War II and the immediate postwar years, the history of this work's composition itself shows evidence of that troubled time.[3] One cannot ignore how controversial Watsuji's ideas have been in postwar Japan. From 1945 until fairly recently he was condemned by Japan's Marxist intellectuals as "conservative," nothing more than a provider of ideological struts for the chrysanthemum throne. Among more conventional academic philosophers Watsuji was largely ignored from his death in 1960 until the early 1980s. During that period these philosophers were almost totally absorbed in discussing the West's philosophical trends—logical positivism and the philosophy of language, for instance. Watsuji seemed irrelevant.

The change came in 1981 with the publication of a bold, fresh, un-nerving study by Yuasa Yasuo.[4] That book both offered searching in-sights into the "warts and all" psychology of Watsuji from the pen of his last major student and also problematized the matter of Asian-based thinkers in a purportedly "international" academy, one in which in fact the only philosophers given the time of day were those who wrote in English, German, or French. That purportedly international academy had also simply assumed that the only questions worth asking were those raised in the cultures where those languages were mother-tongues. Yuasa saw Watsuji's "cultural conservativism" as a goad planted precisely on the rump of assumptions such as those. His close study of Watsuji deftly raised the question of the colonization of thought, a question from which academic philosophers in the West tend to recoil and one that their counterparts in Japan had been repressing— at least since 1945.

Yuasa's 1981 study broke ice. It made Watsuji become newly in-teresting, still problematic but now not so easily dismissible as had as-sumed for decades.[5] Interestingly, this came at a time when, for the first time since 1945, many Japanese, even within the intellectual ambit, were becoming ready to say out loud that there are things within Japanese society that deserved to be preserved at least for the Japanese them-selves and that, in fact, might even have universalizable relevance and value.

Whether what we call "the West" has always been incorrigibly tilted towards a prioritizing of the individual and a neglect of what Watsuji called "betweeness" (*aidagara*) is, I think, an important ques-tion. Nuanced studies such as Alasdair McIntyre's *A Short History of Ethics* suggest that over the millennia "the West" has been far from univocal on a matter such as this. Surely, however, there can be little doubt about this question within modernity. During the recent centu-ries of their intellectual and social life, Europe and America have placed a stress on the individual to such an extent that intellectuals in certain Asian contexts have come to view that emphasis as an imbalance need-ing to be challenged. Watsuji was arguably the best read and the most sharply articulate among the Asian thinkers who addressed this prob-lem. And the *Ethics* is where he best demonstrated that point of view and the challenge to thought implicit within it.

WILLIAM R. LAFLEUR

acknowledgments

In the eight years that this translation has been in the making, many people have provided valuable assistance. We wish to offer them our heartfelt thanks. As well, both the Japan Foundation (through a translation assistance grant and a Japan Foundation Fellowship that Dr. Carter received in 1994) and the Social Sciences and Humanities Research Council of Canada generously supported the translation and the related research that needed to be done.

In Japan, Dr. Jan van Bragt of the Nanzan Institute for Religion and Culture, at Nanzan University, Nagoya, offered valuable suggestions. The Nanzan Institute opened its library to us, as did Kansai Gaidai University, in Hirakata-shi. Matsuko Yoko, a research librarian at Kansai Gaidai, helped with the research of titles cited by Watsuji, as did her counterpart, Linda Matthews at Trent University in Canada.

Involved in the typing and preliminary editing of a surprising number of editions of the manuscript were Erin McCarthy, Jerry Larock, Nicole Bauberger, Sarah Howlett, and Daniel Driscoll, who helped with the diagrams, and especially Kelly Liberty, who meticulously read the proofs. To all of these people we express our gratitude for their dedication.

A former associate of Professor Yuasa Yasuo, Rosemary Morrison, of Oregon, kindly translated several of his letters for this volume, for which we are very grateful. Her translations have a real flow to them, while at the same time remaining close to the literal text.

All of these individuals, and many others have done much to make this a better book than it might otherwise have been.

note to the reader

In an attempt to achieve some degree of gender justice, the translators have adopted the convention throughout the translation of using masculine and feminine pronouns in alternating chapters. While not an ideal solution perhaps, it at least addresses a problem we felt needed attention. The pattern of alternation is not Watsuji's, but the general absence of pronoun specificity in Japanese may help to make this approach at least somewhat plausible. In any case, we thought it the best solution available.

introduction to
watsuji tetsurō's *rinrigaku*

Watsuji Tetsurō (1889–1960) was one of that handful of philosophers in Japan during the current century who brought Japanese philosophy to the attention of the world. Like those in the Kyoto School, he sought to understand the richness of Japanese culture anew, while at the same time distancing himself from it through his study of Western cultural and philosophical thought. The result was both a dialogue with Heidegger and others in the West and a robust rediscovery of the vitality of Japanese ways.

Born in the village of Nibuno, now a part of Himeji City in Hyogo Prefecture in 1889, Watsuji was to become one of modern Japan's outstanding philosophers. As a student at Himeji Middle School, he displayed a passion for literature, especially Western literature, and "is said to have been fired with the ambition to become a poet like Byron."[1] He wrote stories and plays, and was coeditor of a literary magazine. Eventually, upon entering the First Higher School in Tokyo (now Tokyo University), he decided to pursue philosophy seriously, nonetheless "remaining as deeply immersed in Byron as ever and attracted chiefly to things literary and dramatic."[2]

In 1912, Watsuji completed his philosophy concentration in the Literature Department of the Imperial University of Tokyo. Furukawa Tetsushi notes that, "at the time the atmosphere in the Faculty of Philosophy was inimical to the study of a poet-philosopher like Nietzsche. Consequently, Watsuji's *Nietzschean Studies* was rejected as a suitable graduation thesis."[3] In its place he was obliged to substitute a second thesis on Schopenhauer, which he entitled "Schopenhauer's Pessimism and Theory of Salvation." This thesis "was presented only just in time" for him to graduate.[4] Significantly, his *Nietzschean Studies* was later published. It was followed by a study of Kierkegaard. At that time, neither Nietzsche nor Kierkegaard were studied as part of the philosophical canon in Japanese universities.

1

His studies of Nietzsche, Schopenhauer, and Kierkegaard make amply evident that Watsuji was, like so many Japanese intellectuals since the Meiji Restoration of 1868, profoundly interested in learning about the West and its evident intellectual, scientific, and cultural successes. It was a time for looking outward, leaving behind the effects of centuries of isolation, and endeavoring to enter the modern world on even terms. For the moment, however, there was a real sense that Japan was considerably behind because of its past isolation and remaining feudal social structure and that the way forward was to be found in emulating the successes and the lifestyles of Western nations. Front and center in this reassessment was the Western emphasis on *individualism*. It was generally perceived that Japan's feudalistic communitarianism made individual initiative unlikely and that the dynamic economic achievements of the West were equally unlikely given Japan's emphasis on the group with its concomitant cultural uniformity.

Watsuji, too, turned to the West initially for sustenance and then, in his mid-twenties, began to reconsider the place of "creative individualism" in the modern world. Like the novelist Sōseki Natsume, whose lectures he sometimes overheard by standing just outside the window of Sōseki's classroom when he "had no other lecture to attend" while at the First Higher School, Watsuji had begun to abandon his earlier advocacy of existential individuality and was embarking on a critique of individualism and the modern culture of the Western world. Watsuji never met Sōseki while in school, but did meet him in 1913 (and became a member of a study group that met at Sōseki's home), at a time when Sōseki "was turning in his own art from the 'creative individualism' of his earlier period to the more idealistic critiques of cultural modernism and individualism in his late novels."[5] Sōseki died three years later, when Watsuji was 27, and upon Sōseki's death, Watsuji began to compose a lengthy reminiscence of him. His reflections were published in 1918 (in his *Gūzō saikō*), and marked Watsuji's own transformation from advocate of Western ways to critic of the West, turning toward a reconsideration of Japanese and Eastern cultural resources. He began to systematically re-evaluate the ideals and practices of his own culture (by his own admission, beginning in 1917, when he was 28).[6] At the same time, he did not come to reject the ideals and ways of the West, but took from them what he considered to be worthy.

In *Porisuteki ningen no rinrigaku* (*The Ethics of the Man of the Polis*), published in 1948, but dating back to 1932, he dealt with Socrates, Plato, Aristotle, and other major Western thinkers, and in his *Rinrigaku*, published in three volumes (successive volumes published in 1937,

1942, and 1949), he researched the ideas of Descartes, Kant, Hegel, Brentano, Scheler, Schiller, Dilthey, Durkheim, Bergson, Husserl, Heidegger, and others. Rather than abandoning the intellectual and cultural traditions of the West, he critically reflected upon them to illustrate in what ways they are the same or differed from those traditions of the East, which he deemed worthy and correct. The result was an East/West dialogue of high quality, a helpful exercise in comparative philosophy that brought to light similarities and differences in a remarkably subtle form.

Still, the sequence of his published work provides evidence that he was at first Western in his focus, then Eastern, eventually finding ways to combine what he took to be the best of both in his attempts to compare and contrast these radically different perspectives. After his works on Nietzsche and Kierkegaard (as well as his second graduation thesis on Schopenhauer), he wrote *Revival of Idols* (*Gūzo saikō*), published in 1918. This work examined the modern democratic spirit quite critically, then he went on to favor "Nietzsche's *Will to Power* and the 'elite' spirit as well as the poetical revival of the cult of nature as found in ancient Greece." Watsuji adopted an existential *Lebensphilosophie* mixed with Nietzschean stoicism, feeling that, in the world, the problem of suffering was paramount."[7] William LaFleur sees in the *Revival of Idols* (or *Restoring Idols*, as he translates the title) an attempt to re-invest Japanese Buddhist art and iconography, as expressions of Buddhist thought, with something of their original significance.[8] LaFleur interprets Watsuji's rediscovery of the great Buddhist art of Nara, and his lengthy pilgrimage study of it, as a renaissance heralded by a few Japanese intellectuals, in contrast with the "dark ages" of Meiji iconoclastic thought. The Meiji era (1868–1912), in its enthusiasm for things Western, rejected Buddhism as outdated, and as a foreign import. Watsuji, however, saw Buddhism "as the principal cohesive factor in Asian civilization"[9] and more advanced than European Christianity. Watsuji conceived of Nara, the old capital of Japan, as an "international" culture: "It thrived on cultural and intellectual exchange between Japan and the rest of Asia, and as such Nara served as the ideal of a Japan completely open and receptive to all cultures within its reach."[10]

Another work, *Homerus hihan* (*A Critique of Homer*) was written at about this time, but was not published until 1946. As well, his *Genshi Kiristokyō no bunkashiteki igi* (*The Culturo-Historical Significance of Primitive Christianity*) was published in 1926. In this work, he developed a new interpretation of Christianity that took him beyond the critical Nietzschean understanding.

On the other hand, Watsuji studied extensively ancient Japanese culture, primitive Buddhism, and primitive Confucianism.[11] In 1920, he wrote the first volume of *Nihon kodai bunka* (*Ancient Japanese Culture*), which he began to research seriously in 1917, with succeeding volumes published in 1926 and 1934. Furukawa recounts that Watsuji's interest in Far Eastern thought "was first aroused by the question what sort of men it was who created great monuments of art such as the sculptures and buildings of the Asuka and the Nara Eras."[12] In these volumes on ancient Japanese culture he single-handedly rediscovered the importance of Dōgen, the founder of the Sōtō sect of Zen Buddhism, whose works had fallen into total obscurity. Current thought holds Dōgen to be perhaps the only other philosopher in Japan's history who was the equal of Nishida Kitarō. Piovesana observes that in the second volume of this work Watsuji "tried to define the essence of the Japanese spirit, studying it as he did in relation to the adaptation of Buddhist thought and art."[13] *Pilgrimages to Ancient Temples* (*Koji Junrei*), which dealt with the cultural influence of Buddhism on Japanese culture, was published in 1920. In 1927 *Genshi Bukkyō no jissen tetsugaku* (*The Practical Philosophy of Primitive Buddhism*) was published. Watsuji's incredible published output, spanning remarkably diverse subjects of East and West, make clear that, as David Dilworth observes, he "was on the way to becoming one of the great comparative cultural historians of modern times. Influenced by neo-Kantian historiography, by Husserl's phenomenology, and Scheler's value-philosophy, as well as by the theoretical ground in these areas being explored by Nishida Kitarō at Kyoto University, Watsuji went on to explore various cultural/historical intentionalities of the East and the West in a series of influential works."[14] Indeed, he went on to write *Fūdo* (*Fūdo ningengakuteki kōsatsu*, translated into English as *Climate and Culture*) in 1935, his two-volume *Nihon rinri shisōshi* (*History of Japanese Ethical Thought*) in 1952, *Ningen no gaku toshite no rinrigaku* (*Ethics as the Study of Man*), and as already mentioned, his three volume *Rinrigaku* (*Ethics*), a volume at a time, in 1937, 1942, and 1949, of which the present volume consists of a translation of roughly the first half, comprising the first two of three sections.

Appointed assistant professor of ethics at Kyoto University in 1925, Watsuji was sent to Germany in 1927, where for two years he studied in Berlin, and traveled extensively in Italy and Greece. His travels inspired his *Climate and Culture*, a book that may well have stereotyped Western cultural traditions too easily but that, nonetheless, established a vital framework for the comparative analysis of cross-cultural issues.

Japanese interest in Germany and German philosophy was considerable by the turn of the century. Not only was Germany perceived to be the place where the "state of the art" in philosophy was to be found, but Germany itself was thought to be a country with similar aspirations for rapid modernization and industrialization; that is, a country to watch, to learn from, and to emulate. Japanese students yearned after Germany as "the Mecca of philosophy."[15]

Watsuji wrote *Climate and Culture* as a direct response to Heidegger's *Sein und Zeit*, which he thought placed too heavy an emphasis on time and the individual and too little on space and the social dimension of human beings. In Watsuji's words, "from the standpoint of the dual structure—both individual and social—of human existence, he did not advance beyond an abstraction of a single aspect."[16] Watsuji proposed that "it is only when human existence is treated in terms of its concrete duality that time and space are linked and that history also (which never appears fully in Heidegger) is first revealed in its true guise. And at the same time the connection between history and climate becomes evident."[17] By *climate* Watsuji means to include not only weather patterns of a region but the natural geographic setting of a people plus the social environment of family, community, society, lifestyle, and even the technological apparatus that supports community survival and interaction. *Fūdo* or climate is the entire interconnected network of influences that together create an entire people's attitudes (or their ways of going about in the world) and that represents geographic and climatic influences on human society and human interaction with climatic necessities, together with the human transformation of geographic aspects of the environment. Culture and nature are not taken as opposed, as Yuasa Yasuo notes, for "history and nature, like man's mind and body, are in an inseparable relationship."[18] Climate, then, is a *mutuality* of influence, recorded over eons of time as cultural history.

Japanese cultural history represents a confluence of streams of thought that together have formed a sophisticated and remarkably harmonious worldview. The indigenous Shintō tradition serves as the foundation of Japan, but the entire cultural edifice consists of strong influence from Confucian, Taoist, Buddhist, and of course, Western sources. In each case, despite power struggles and instances of intolerance, what is most remarkable about the Japanese is the way in which they welcomed new ideas insofar as they were seen to be compatible with and enriching of the existing Japanese spirit. Watsuji's accomplishment was in laying bare the salient ingredients in this cultural mix to present for the first time an in-depth and coherent account of Japanese ethics. What is more, he did so in a manner that allowed him to utilize Western thinkers in his comparative explication. Plato, Aristotle, Descartes, Heidegger, Husserl, Kant, Hegel, Dilthey, Durkheim, and others are discussed in remarkable detail. The result is a study of Japanese ethical thought and practice that is still unequaled. Twenty years ago, I was told by colleagues in Japan that it was a pity that Watsuji's *Rinrigaku* had not been translated into a Western language, for it was the definitive study of Japanese ethics. Twenty years later, it still is and will no doubt remain a classic of Japanese cultural and philosophical inquiry.

A more extensive interpretive essay outlining Watsuji's philosophical approach is to be found at the end of this volume, following the translation. It includes a bibliography, as well as a detailed elaboration of some of the themes raised in this brief introduction.

Robert E. Carter

part 1

introductory essays

1 the significance of ethics as the study of *ningen*

T he essential significance of the attempt to describe ethics as the study of *ningen*[1] consists in getting away from the misconception, prevalent in the modern world, that conceives of ethics as a problem of individual consciousness *only*. This misconception is based on the individualistic conception of a human being inherent in the modern world. The understanding of the individual is itself, as such, an achievement of the modern spirit and bears an importance that we must never be allowed to forget. However, individualism attempts to consider the notion of the individual that constitutes only one moment of human existence and then substitutes it for the notion of the totality of *ningen*. This abstraction is the origin of many sorts of misconception. The standpoint of the isolated ego, which constitutes the starting point of modern philosophy, is merely one such example.

Insofar as the standpoint of the ego limits itself to contemplating objective nature alone, the misconception does not come to the fore so conspicuously. Indeed, the standpoint of the contemplation of nature is already a step away from concrete *human* existence; it is established as the field in which everyone is made to play, in an exemplary way, the role of a subject contemplating an object. But so far as the problems of human existence are concerned, that is, so far as matters connected with practice and action are concerned, isolated subjectivity has, basically speaking, no connection with them. In spite of this, the standpoint of isolated subjectivity, which abstracts from the practical connections between person and person, is here forcibly applied to the questions of ethics. In this way, the field of ethical questions is also confined to the relation between subject and nature. Within this field, ethical questions are allocated their own region in which to deal with matters of volition, as distinguished from matters of knowledge. Hence, such problems as the independence of the self over against nature, or the sway of the self over the self itself, or the satisfaction of the desires of the self, and so on are of central importance to ethics. In whichever direction ethical theories may be led, however, we cannot solve the problems of ethics from this standpoint alone. Therefore, in the final analysis, ethical principles cannot be posited unless we bring forward such ideas as that of a super-individual self, the happiness of society, or the welfare of humankind. And this indicates precisely that ethics is not a matter of individual consciousness alone.

The locus of ethical problems lies not in the consciousness of the isolated individual, but precisely in the in-betweenness of person and person. Because of this, ethics is the study of *ningen*. Unless we regard ethics as dealing with matters arising between person and person, we cannot authentically solve such problems as the distinguishing of good from evil deeds, obligation, responsibility, virtue, and so forth. We are able to clarify this by having recourse to the concept of "ethics" such as we are now proposing.

The concept "ethics" is expressed in Japanese by means of the word *rinri*. Incidentally, words are among the most marvellous things that we human beings have created. No one person has the privilege of declaring that she alone has created them. In spite of this, for everyone, words are one's own. Words are the furnace by means of which merely subjective connections made by individual human beings are converted into noematic meanings. In other words, words are concerned with the activity whereby preconscious being is turned into consciousness. Now, this preconsciousness is at the same time subjective reality and, as such, cannot be objectified by any means; it is a cluster of practical act-connections. Therefore, when its structure takes form in consciousness, its origin is not derived merely from individual existence, even though its content exists *in* individual consciousness. In this sense, words are also expressions of the subjective existence of *ningen* and open the way toward subjective existence for us. This is why we must first make use of words in an attempt to clarify the nature of the concept "ethics."

The word *rinri* consists of two words: *rin* and *ri. Rin* means *nakama*, that is, "fellows." *Nakama* signifies a body or a system of relations, which a definite group of persons have with respect to each other, and at the same time signifies individual persons as determined by this system. In ancient China, parent and child, lord and vassal, husband and wife, young and old, friend and friend, and so forth constituted "the grand *rin* of human beings," that is to say, the most important kinds of human fellowship. The relation between parent and child is one of these. Now it is not the case that father and son first of all exist separately, and then come to relate to each other in this way later on. But rather, only through this relationship does the father obtain his qualification as father, and the son his qualification as son. In other words, only by virtue of the fact that they constitute "one fellowship," do they become respectively father and son. However, why does one "fellowship" prescribe each member within itself as father or son, whereas another "fellowship" prescribes that its members be considered friends to one another? It is because "fellowship" is nothing but a manner of interaction through which people have definite connections with each other. Hence, *rin* signifies *nakama* (in general) and, at the same time, a specific form of practical interconnection among human beings. From this it follows that *rin* also means *kimari* (agreement), or *kata* (form), that is, an order among human beings. The *rin* are conceived of as ways of *ningen*.

The forms of practical connection, as just noted, cannot itself exist apart from these connections. As specific forms in which human beings act, they exist only together with these practical connections. But when dynamic human existence is actualized repeatedly, in a definite manner, we can grasp this pattern that constantly makes its appearance in separation from the basis of this dynamic sort of existence. This manner is *rin* or *gorin gojō* (that is, the moral rules that govern the five human relations) as transformed into noematic meaning. The term *ri* signifies "reason" and is added to the term *rin* for the purpose of expressing emphatically the aforementioned manner of action or relational pattern. Therefore, *rinri*, that is, ethics, is the order or the pattern through which the communal existence of human beings is rendered possible. In other words, ethics consists of the laws of social existence.

If this is so, then a question arises as to whether ethics is already established and, as a result, has no further implication as to what ought to be. To this question, we can answer both "yes" and "no." Insofar as a group of friends are relationally established, as the phrase *hoyu yushin* ("reliance prevails among friends") indicates, "reliance," as a manner of practical connections, already lies at the basis of the group. Apart from such reliance, friendship cannot obtain. But the group is not a static entity, for it exists dynamically in and through these practical connections. The fact that actions were performed previously in a definite manner does not make it impossible for subsequent deeds to deviate from this manner of acting later on. In this sense, we can say that communal existence contains the danger of extinction on each and every occasion. Moreover, human existence as such infinitely aims at the realization of communal existence by virtue of the fact that human beings are *ningen*. Because of this, the pattern of practical connections already realized serves, at the same time, as a pattern yet to be achieved. Therefore, although ethics is already what is, without being merely what should be, it is also regarded as what should be achieved infinitely, without thereby being a mere law of being.

As can be seen from the preceding, we can clarify the concept of ethics with the help of an analysis of the meaning of the word *rinri*. It is evident that this word carries on its back the ancient history of Chinese thought. The more we pursue the social structure of ancient China in a religio-sociological fashion, the more this history of thought comes to reveal its interesting significance. However, our intention here is not to revitalize the ideology of social ethics based on the social structure of ancient China in its original condition. Our purpose is merely to try to restore the significance of ethics as the way inherent in human relations for the sake of illustrating our contention that, through and through, ethics is concerned with those problems that prevail *between* persons.

Granted the concept of ethics as thus clarified, it is quite evident that such matters as the relationship between person and person, the nature of human existence, the resulting practical interconnections, and so forth, have played an important role in this clarification. We said previously that *rin* means a "fellowship" and is, furthermore, a pattern of act-interconnections that makes its appearance within fellowship. But what is *nakama*, and what is *ningen*? That is not self-evident. To inquire into the nature of ethics is, after all, equivalent to asking about the manner of human existence and to asking about *ningen*. In other words, ethics is the study of *ningen*.

With this in mind, we must now make clear the meaning of the concept *ningen*, which we have used somewhat ambiguously thus far. This task is particularly necessary for the purpose of distinguishing *ningen* from the idea of human being that is prevalent in philosophical anthropology, which is now in vogue. Philosophical anthropology tries to grasp a "human being" as the unity of the drives of life and spirit, as does Max Scheler in his book *Die Stellung des Menschen im Kosmos*.[2] This is nothing more than a new view within a problematics that sees the "human being" exclusively from the standpoint of the unity of body and mind. All that Scheler enumerates as various types of traditional anthropology[3] belong to the realm of this problematic. These types are the following: (1) The idea of a human being inherent in the faith of Christianity. According to it, a human being was first of all created by a personal God, sinned through Adam's Fall, and will be redeemed by Christ. This view constitutes the starting point of an anthropology, whose interest is centred around the problem of body and soul. (2) The study of human being, as possessing reason (*homo sapiens*): (a) that a human being possesses spirit, that is, reason; (b) this spirit forms the world as the world; (c) spirit, that is, reason is active by itself, without dependence on sensibility; (d) the view that this spirit does not suffer change with respect to races, as well as historically. (Only this last point was later overthrown by Hegel.) It was Dilthey and Nietzsche who perceived that this sort of anthropology is nothing more than a Greek invention. (3) The perspective of a human being as worker or technician (*homo faber*). This view is posited in reaction to the second type, that is, *homo sapiens*. No essential distinction is made between human beings and animals here. A distinction is made only because human beings produce words and tools and because human beings have brains that exhibit a special development in comparison with the brains of other animals. This is the standpoint of anthropology, as expounded by naturalism and positivism. (4) The view that a human being is enfeebled by virtue of her having spirit. This view is a new attack against *homo sapiens*. (5) The assumption of a superhuman being. This is the anthropology of the great personality, such as one which lifts the self-consciousness of human beings to a higher level. These five types, without exception, remove (or abstract) the human being from social groups, and deal with him as a self-sustaining being. Hence, the problem of a human being is always centered around spirit, body, or the self. Even though this sort of anthropology is proclaimed as philosophical anthropology, in an attempt to distinguish it from the anthropology that developed as a theory of the body in "ethnology," there is no difference between them with regard to their basic attitude, for they both try to grasp the essence of a human being in the form of an individual alone.

This tendency seems to result from the fact that such words as *anthropos, homo, man,* or *Mensch* cannot denote anything but an individual human being. If we take such a stance, we have no alternative but to explain such things as the relationships between person and person, communal existence, society, and so forth by appealing to terms somewhat different from that of *human being*. But if a human being is, basically speaking, a social animal, then social relationships cannot be separated from her. It must be that a human being is capable of being an individual and at the same time also a member of a society. And the Japanese term *ningen*, that is, "human being," gives most adequate expression to this double or dual characteristic. Therefore, if one takes the position of *ningen*, an attempt to posit the "study of *ningen*" (anthropology) and the "study of society" as somewhat separable from each other would mean nothing more than to have abstracted some single aspect from the complex concrete human being and to let this single aspect stand quite alone. On the contrary, if we want to conceive of a human being in its concreteness, then the two must be one single "study of the human," of *ningen*. At the same time, this study must not be something that haphazardly combines the study of the individual and the study of society but a study basically differing from them both. For the attempt to comprehend the individual and society as the double or dual characteristic of *ningen* and thereby to uncover there humankind's most authentic essence, can by no means be implemented from a standpoint that presupposes a primary distinction between individual and society.

The next issue is to determine in what manner the word *ningen* signifies this twofold characteristic. Does it not, in ordinary usage, have exactly the same meaning as man or *Mensch*? And is not the "study of *ningen*" the Japanese translation of the term *anthropology*? Indeed, that is true; but that is not the whole story. As the literal meaning of the Chinese characters of *ningen* indicate, it is also a word that signifies the *betweenness* of human beings, that is, the "public." Moreover, this is actually the original meaning of the word. In the literature, as well as in those Buddhist sutras the Japanese have adopted from China, the word *ningen* is always used in the sense of "public." In addition to this, during their long history, the Japanese have diverted its meaning to signify an individual human being, as well. This diversion was rendered possible through the usage of certain words that appear in the Chinese translation of Buddhist sutras depicting the view of a human being as involved in *samsara* (transmigration). Because the Indian word that denotes the "world of beasts" was translated, for the sake of convenience, as "beasts," it was regularly used side by side with the word *ningen*. This latter came to mean "humankind," and then "a human being" with the view of distinguishing human beings from "beasts." But what is noteworthy here is not this accidental fact, but the historical fact that the word *ningen*, denoting the "public," was capable of taking in, at the same time, the meaning of "a human being," irrespective of whatever medium might have intervened to produce this result. Various verses, aphorisms, and maxims about human beings were transmitted from China and became well-known among the Japanese people. In them, without exception, the word *ningen* signifies the "public." Still, it was found that, whatever is said there about the "public," also holds good for the individual human beings living within this public. This experience was given expression through an alternation of the word's meaning.

Keeping an eye on this, one had better consider other words that express the whole, as well as the parts, of human existence. The word *nakama* denotes a group, and yet there is also the phrase, a "single *nakama*." The word *roto* also denotes a group, and yet individuals belonging to a group are also called *roto*. This is the case with many Japanese words such as *tomodachi* ("friends"), *heitai* ("soldiers"), *wakashu* ("young fellows"), *renchu* ("a party"), and so forth. These words obviously show that, in so far as human existence is concerned, the whole exists in the parts and the parts in the whole. Judging from this, we can conclude that it is by no means strange that the word *ningen*, denoting *yononaka* (the "public") as the whole of human beings, came as well to signify individual human beings living in the public sphere.

The Japanese language, therefore, possesses a very significant word; namely *ningen*. On the basis of the evolved meaning of this word, we Japanese have produced a distinctive conception of human being. According to it, *ningen* is the public and, at the same time, the individual human beings living within it. Therefore, it refers not merely to an individual "human being" nor merely to "society." What is recognizable here is a dialectical unity of those double characteristics that are inherent in a human being. Insofar as it is a human being, *ningen* as an individual differs completely from society. Because it does not refer to society, it must refer to individuals alone. Hence, an individual is never communal with other individuals. Oneself and others are absolutely separate. Nevertheless, insofar as *ningen* also refers to the public, it is also through and through that community which exists between person and person, thus signifying society as well, and not just isolated human beings. Precisely because of its not being human beings in isolation, it is *ningen*. Hence, oneself and the other are absolutely separated from each other but, nevertheless, become one in communal existence. Individuals are basically different from society and yet dissolve themselves into society. *Ningen* denotes the unity of these contradictories. Unless we keep this dialectical structure in mind, we cannot understand the essence of *ningen*.

It is quite interesting that Dr. S. Yoshida exhibited this dialectical structure by means of the metaphor of one circle possessing different centers within it. But, in my opinion, this circle, which may well have a variety of different centers, cannot be conceived of except as a unity of contradictories. Yet this is impossible, at least insofar as a finite circle is concerned. Therefore, Yoshida conceived of the radius of this circle as being infinite. His view is that each center indicates the individuality of personality, and the circle, with an infinite radius, indicates the infinity of personality. In infinity, all phases of discrimination terminate in identity. However, Yoshida's harmony of identity and difference was applied to the relation between the individual and the infinite, so to speak, and not to the relation between individuals and society with which we have been concerned thus far. Any kind of society is a finite human reality, and therefore, to amplify the metaphor, the circle that represents this fact must have a finite radius. This kind of circle cannot be an appropriate metaphor in this instance, if the possibility of its having different centers is excluded. With this in mind, we can think of a circle with a finite radius, as a determination of a circle with an infinite radius. If the infinite radius turns out to be finite through its negation, then a finite circle is established as the realization of an infinite circle. In this case, the relation of the same circle with different centers, as is the case with an infinite circle, is also materialized in a finite circle. Such a thing may be inconceivable geometrically, but human existence possesses precisely this sort of structure. Here the finite circle, based on the infinite one, exactly specifies a society. Although centers are the negation of a circle insofar as they are points and are individuals separated from each other, they are, as centers, the centers of the same circle. The metaphor of the circle with different centers can have this meaning only when it gives expression to a structure of this sort.

Now, the concept of *ningen* is determined in terms of the dual characteristics of "public" and "individual" human beings, as is not the case with *anthropos*. However, we conceived of what is called the *public* by treating it as a direct synonym of communal existence, or society. Was this procedure appropriate? By raising this question, we approach one of the central problems of modern philosophy; namely, the meaning of *public*.

When Heidegger characterized human existence by means of the phrase *being in the world*, he made use of the concept of intentionality prevalent in phenomenology, as his jumping-off point. He carried this structure a step further, to transfer it to existence, and understood it as having to do with tools. Therefore, we can say that he set the pattern for explicating the subjective meaning of what is called the *world*. But in his philosophy, the relation between person and person lies hidden behind the relation between person and tools. It is obvious that the former relation was overlooked, in spite of his assurance that he had not neglected it. For this reason, his disciple K. Löwith tried to bring to light this hidden element and clarify the idea of "world" mainly with reference to the relationships between person and person.[4] Although Heidegger's study is concerned with general phenomenological anthropology, Löwith departs from this approach and turns toward anthropology. And this latter, anthropology, deals with the relation between oneself and the other, that is, with the mutual relations of persons, instead of with individual "persons." Here, a human being is a person "together with others," and the world is *mit-Welt*, that is, the public, whereas *being in the world* means "to relate with others." Because of this, this anthropology was bound to become the basis for the framing and understanding of ethical problems. The essential feature of life consists in the fact that persons assume an attitude of behaving themselves in relation with one another, and this attitude includes within itself the basic behavior of human beings, that is to say, their *ethos*. For this reason, the study of reciprocal human existence turns out to be ethics itself. Löwith's concern, then, was to analyze the meaning of *world* to include the *betweenness* of persons (the "public").

According to Löwith, then, the German word *Welt* implies a human factor. Its significance is, from our perspective, somewhat similar to that of the Japanese word *seken*, which means "the public." Such words as *ein Mann von Welt* ("a man of the world"), *weltkündig* ("being accustomed to the way of the world"), *weltfremd* ("inexperienced in the way of the world"), *weltflüchtig* ("being aloof from worldly affairs"), *weltlich gesinnt* ("being a person interested in worldly affairs"), *Weltverächter* ("being a person who looks askance at the world"), *Männerwelt* ("the world of men"), *Frauenwelt* ("the world of women"), and so forth indicate, respectively, some definite realm of society. That is to say, *Welt* is not just the world of nature, but of community existence, namely; of a society in which persons are related to each other. Thus, the analysis of *in-der-Welt-sein* must be an analysis of community life.

What has been said of the term *Welt*, applies to an even greater extent to *yononaka* or *seken* ("the public"). Just as the term *Welt* originally meant "a generation," and "a group of people," so *yo*, in Japanese, signifies "a generation," and "a society." That is to say, *yo* transits

temporality and at the same time means something spatial, something
to get away from or wander about in. But when *se-ken* or *yo-no-naka*
are spoken of, what is signified is not only *yo*, that is, *Welt*, but is also
combined with such words as *ken* (or *aida*), that is, betweenness or
naka, in. In other words, what is implied here is the phrase, *in-der-
Welt*. Moreover, the words *ken* or *naka* additionally, as is not the case
with the word *in*, have not only a merely spatial significance, that is,
only a concern about tools, as in Heidegger, but also express quite evidently human relations as well. This is indicated by such phrases as
danjo-no-aida ("the relation between man and woman"), *fūfu-no-naka*
("conjugal relations"), and *naka-tagai-suru* ("to break up relations"),
and so forth.

Incidentally, those human relations now under consideration are
not objective relations that are established through subjective unity, as
is the case with spatial relations between object and object. Rather, they
are *act-connections* between person and person like *communication* or
association, in which persons as subjects concern themselves with each
other. We cannot sustain ourselves in any *aida* or *naka* without acting
subjectively. At the same time, we cannot act without maintaining ourselves in some *aida* or *naka*. For this reason, *aida* or *naka* imply a living and dynamic betweenness, as a subjective interconnection of acts.
A betweenness of this sort and the spatio-temporal world combine to
produce the meaning conveyed by the words *se-ken* (the public) or *yo-
no-naka* (the public). Additionally, these words are used to indicate
something like a single subjective entity, as is suggested by the phrases
seken ni shirareru ("to become public"), or *yononaka o sawagaseru* ("to
cause a stir in society"). There is no doubt that *seken* or *yononaka* here
mean society, or communal existence regarded as a subject. When only
a few friends know about something, we cannot say that it has become
public. Or were a few persons to cause a stir, we could not say that
seken was astir. *Seken*, as a knowing or stirring subject, even though
being an interconnection of acts between person and person, is simultaneously nothing but the community as subject, that is, the subject as
community existence, which transcends the individual subjects involved
in this interconnection of acts.[5]

The "plus value" of the concepts of *seken* or *yononaka* over
against that of *Welt* lies in the fact that the former gets a grip on the
temporal as well as the spatial characteristics of subjective communal
existence. As was said before, the term *Welt* signifies a generation, or
a "group," a sum total of people or the place where people live. But as
time went on, it came to lose this spatio-temporal significance, and

finally came to mean one-sidedly the world as the sum total of objective natural things. On the other hand, so far as *seken* or *yokonaka* are concerned, the meaning of something subjectively extended, which undergoes constant transformation, has been tenaciously preserved. Hence, the concept of *seken* already involves the historical, climatic, and social structure of human existence. In other words, what is called *seken* or *yokonaka* indicates a human existence that is historical, climatic, and social.

With regard to the term *ningen*, which is characterized by *yononaka* and at the same time by *hito* (i.e., an individual human being), we call the character of *yononaka* the social nature of *ningen*, on the one hand, and that of *hito* the individual nature of *ningen*, on the other. To see *ningen* only in the form of *hito*, is to see a human being merely from the perspective of his individual nature. This view, if it be held alone, and even if it is allowed as a methodological abstraction, cannot come to grips with *ningen* concretely. We must grasp *ningen* through and through as the unity of the aforementioned apparently contradictory characteristics.

We described *ningen*, which possesses this dual structure, as something subjective. The implication is that *ningen*, although being subjective communal existence as the interconnection of acts, at the same time, is an individual that acts through these connections. This subjective and dynamic structure does not allow us to account for *ningen* as a "thing" or "substance." *Ningen* cannot be thought of as such apart from the constantly moving interconnection of acts. This, despite certainly producing individuals, also makes them submerge in the whole. This way of being, which is peculiar to *ningen*, or to be more precise, this transformation from being to nothingness, and from nothingness to being (hence, this way of becoming a human being), we attempt to express by the Japanese concept of *sonzai*. Therefore, our concept of *sonzai* is different from *Sein*, *einai*, or *esse*. And our study of *sonzai* is also not equivalent to Ontology.

Why would I, in the present world in which the concept of *sonzai* is used as equivalent to *Sein*, deliberately attempt to oppose this usage by separating the former (*sonzai*) from the latter (*Sein*)? It is because, indeed, the meaning of the Japanese term *sonzai* is all too different from that of *Sein*. The special meaning with which *Sein* has been burdened and which is the central issue of philosophy can hardly be found in the word *sonzai*. At the starting point of Fichte's philosophy, *Sein* consists in a positing that "A is A." As the starting point of Hegel's logic, *Sein* is the direct, undetermined "to be," but this is not the case with *sonzai*.

The key issue of *Sein* lies in the view that the concept of *Sein*, as intended by these philosophers, has the same meaning as the copula of formal logic, but even though functioning in this way, also implies the proposition, "A *is.*" Conversely, out of the fact that the "to be," which signifies that something *is*, functions at the same time as the copula, there emerged the problem of relating thinking and being. Aristotle had already pointed out that *einai* gives expression to the relation of thinking and being itself. Hobbes put special emphasis on the contention that *est* is not confined to being a mere sign of connection but also exhibits the cause of this connection. That is to say, *est* exhibits *essentia*, but not *existentia*. When it is said that the sky *is* blue, something identical that forms the basis of the connection between the sky and the color blue is given expression to by the word *est*. Over against Hobbes, J. S. Mill insisted that *est* also refers to *existentia*. It is true that the copula, as Hobbes pointed out, is a sign connecting subject with predicate. The view that *est*, as the copula, is something more than a sign and refers to *existentia*, is mere mysticism. When a centaur, which is at once a human being and a horse, is said *to be* a product of a poet's imagination, this assertion does not at all mean that there *are centaurs*. Yet *est* does not only operate as copula; viewed from another angle, *est* refers to *existentia*. In other words, *est* refers to "A *is* A," and also to "A *is.*" Now, this affirmation concerning *essentia* and *existentia* occupied the central place in the ontology of the Middle Ages and was based on Aristotle. What happens to all of these problems, however, if we substitute *sonzai* for the term *est*? Is it possible to say that *sonzai* plays the role of copula, or that it expresses the *essentia*? The answer is absolutely no! If this is true, then when you translate the term *Sein* into *sonzai*, you cannot, I am afraid, escape the accusation that you have no knowledge about the issues surrounding *Sein*.

Then what is the original meaning of the word *sonzai*?

The original meaning of the Chinese character *son*, of *son-zai*, is "subjective self-subsistence." It means maintenance or subsistence over against loss. But the self, although subjectively sustained, is thereby objectified and becomes an intentional object, physical or mental. When such words as *sonshin* (the survival of the body), *sonmei* (the survival of life), *sonroku* (the survival of records) are spoken of, a self is maintained in the form of body, life, or records. Because what is thus maintained thereby continues to be, it is said to maintain itself. If the subject maintains the body, the body also subsists. Thus, generally speaking, usage such as *mono ga son suru* ("a thing subsists") comes to be. In this case too, however, *son* (subsistence) is opposed to "loss." *Son*, no matter whether it is asserted in the form of *jiko o son suru* ("the subsisting of the self") or in the form of *mono ga son suru* ("that a thing subsists") is on every occasion capable of changing into "loss." That is to say, it is *son* of *son-bo* ("maintenance and loss") whose essential feature lies in its temporal character.

The original meaning of the *zai* of *son-zai* lies in the fact that the subject stays in some place. Therefore, *zai* is said to be opposed to *kyo* (departure). *To depart* means that what is capable of departing of itself, moves from one place to another. Hence, only that which is capable of going and coming of itself is able to stay at some place. All the usages, such as *zai shuku* ("staying at an inn"), *zai taku* ("staying at home"), *zai go* ("remaining in one's homeland"), *zai sei* ("remaining in this world") show this to be so. Now the place where the subject stays is a social place such as an inn, home, homeland, or the world. In other words, it consists in such human relations as that of the family, village, town, or the general public. Hence, *zai* means that she who acts subjectively, while coming and going in human relations in one way or another, nevertheless, remains within these relationships. Of course, *zai* is also applied to things. But things are incapable of departing from the scene of themselves. Originally, to say that such things stay (*zai*) at some place is an anthropomorphic way of speaking. The determination of place is a human being's business. Hence, to say that a thing stays at some place is only to say that a human being assigns this place to it and possesses it.

If it is tenable to hold that *son* is the self-sustenance of the self and *zai* means to remain within human relations, then *son-zai* is precisely the self-sustenance of the self as betweenness. That is, it means that *ningen* possesses herself. We could also simply say that *sonzai* is "the interconnection of the acts of *ningen*." Hence, in the strict sense of the word, *son-zai* is only applied to *ningen*. The phrase *mono no sonzai* (i.e., "the being of a thing") is nothing but an anthropomorphic expression of "the being of a thing," which is derived from being as a human being.

We Japanese have constructed the concept of *sonzai* in line with that original meaning of the word. If what has been argued so far is accurate, then it is beyond doubt that *sonzai* cannot be equivalent to *Sein*. But just because of this, we are able to use the notion to describe the subjective, practical, and dynamic structure of human being.

In the preceding, we defined four basic concepts; namely, (1) *rinri* (ethics), (2) *ningen* (human being), (3) *yononaka* (the public), and (4) *sonzai* (human existence). Ethics is a way, or the manner of the interconnection of acts that makes *ningen* truly *ningen.* That is, it is a manner of *sonzai* of *ningen.* Hence, the science of ethics is the study of *ningen* regarded as that of *ningen sonzai.* By virtue of the fact that this study probes into the practical basis of "being" and "the consciousness of the ought" and so forth, it claims a basic status over against "the study of being" and "the study concerning the consciousness of the ought to be." Through the basic clarification of *ningen's sonzai,* the problems of how objective beings arise or of how consciousness of the ought to be arises in each age can be resolved. Therefore, prior to questions concerning all sorts of natural beings and idealistic oughts, the clarification of the basic ground must be carried out on the level of subjective and practical *sonzai.*

The problem of the method to be considered in the next chapter is a problem concerned with exactly how an elucidation of this subjective *sonzai* is to be carried out. Assuming that this task is successfully carried out and that the method is thereby established, then the structure of *sonzai* inherent in *ningen* will be clarified from the angle of its unique dual nature, or double characteristics. To have in advance a bird's eye view of the problems of ethics as the study of *ningen,* we will present, in outline, the problems involved as a result of this dual structure of human being.

The first point to be argued is that of the double structure of a human being itself. No matter which topic of the everyday existence of *ningen* we take up, we are inevitably enabled to probe this double structure. A detailed grasp of this double structure will reveal that it is precisely a movement of negation. On the one hand, the standpoint of an acting "individual" comes to be established only in some way as a negation of the totality of *ningen.* An individual who does not imply the meaning of negation, that is, an essentially self-sufficient individual, is nothing but an imaginative construction. On the other hand, the totality of *ningen* comes to be established as the negation of individuality. A totality that does not include the individual negatively is also nothing but a product of the imagination. These two negations constitute the dual character of a human being. And what is more, they constitute a single movement. On the very ground that it is the negation of totality, the individual is, fundamentally speaking, none other than that totality. If this is true, then this negation is also the self-awareness of that totality. Hence, when an individual realizes herself through negation, a door is opened to the realization of totality through the negation of the individual. The individual's acting is a movement of the restoration of totality itself. The negation moves on to the negation of negation. This is the essential feature of the movement of negation.

Now, that *ningen's sonzai* is, fundamentally speaking, a movement of negation makes it clear that the basis of *ningen's sonzai* is negation as such, that is, absolute negation. The true reality of an individual, as well as of totality, is "emptiness," and this emptiness is the absolute totality. Out of this ground, from the fact that this emptiness is emptied, emerges *ningen's sonzai* as a movement of negation. The negation of negation is the self-returning and self-realizing movement of the absolute totality that is precisely social ethics (i.e., *Sittlichkeit* in German). Therefore, the basic principle of social ethics is the realization of totality (as the negation of negation) through the individual, (that is, the negation of totality). This is, after all, the movement of the realization of absolute totality. When seen in this way, it is clear that the basic principle of social ethics involves two moments. One of these is the establishment of the individual as the other, over against totality. What is at stake here is the taking of a first step toward self-awareness. Apart from the self-awareness of an individual, there is no social ethics. The other moment is the individual's surrender to the totality. This is what has been called the *demand of the superindividual will*, or of total will. Without this surrender, there is also no social ethics.

When the basic principle of social ethics is grasped in this way, it also becomes clear that the basic issues of ethics, such as conscience, freedom, good and evil, and so on are all included within this principle. Conscience is the call of the original totality; freedom is none other than the negativity itself of the movement of negation; and good and evil consist respectively in going back into and going against the direction of this movement. Within the purview of this principle, however, these issues cannot yet come to be dealt with concretely, for attention is paid only to the double character of individuality and totality peculiar to *ningen*, and we have not yet embarked upon a study of the structure of a totality inclusive of numerous individuals. Totality is said to arise in the negation of individuality, but it is not able to appear through the negation of one individual alone. Individuals are the many, and the totality as community existence arises at the point where these many individuals become one by forsaking their individuality. But in any totality whatsoever, individuality is not extinguished without residue. As soon as an individual is negated, it negates the totality so as to become an individual once more. In this way, it repeats the movement of negation. Totality subsists only in this movement. Seen from this angle, it is clear that the dynamic structure of the disruption into many individuals, and of their community as well, enables the totality to reappear. The *sonzai* of *ningen* is not only the movement of negation between the individual and the whole. It must also consist in the restoration of totality through indefinite numbers of individuals opposing each other in their disruption into self and other.

The second point to be discussed is the structure of *sonzai* peculiar to *ningen*. How is the *sonzai* of subjective *ningen* disrupted into self and other: What kind of thing is the disruption of subjects? And what does it mean to say that this disruption is negated and brought back to unity? What comes to the fore here is the most basic problem of spatiality and temporality. The disruption of subjects and the reunification of these disrupted ones, that is, the movement of disruption and then of unification, is fundamentally spatio-temporal. All noematic space/time and all formal space/time as the condition through which natural objects arise is, without exception, derived on this basis. In a word, it is the case that space and time are derived from the *sonzai* peculiar to *ningen*, but not that *ningen* is in space and time.

It is not until this basic spatiality and temporality are brought to light that the practical interconnection of acts is disclosed in its concrete structure. In other words, only here can *ningen's* acts acquire their full-fledged determination. From the standpoint of activity, we are truly able to come to grips with that path of *ningen* that is called *trust* and *truth*. For only in *ningen's* acts, does the truth of (*ningen's*) *sonzai* take place or not, and this either/or situation is precisely where trust and truth are located. Against this background, such issues as good and evil, conscience, freedom and justice, and so on can be clarified concretely. The law inherent in the *sonzai* of *ningen*, which occurs spatio-temporally, discloses each of its elements in the form of these problems.

Incidentally, the *sonzai* of *ningen*, whose acts are interconnected by this law, is nothing more than the various systems of social ethics. There is no place in which systems of social ethics cannot be found, so long as the paths of *ningen* are practiced. But the systems of social ethics are not uniform. Thus, we must pay attention to their various forms and particular laws.

The third point to be argued here is that of the structure of solidarity, which inheres in these systems of social ethics. First of all, we shall try to grasp solidarity from the viewpoint of the community of *sonzai*. We can follow it pyramidically, from the simple *sonzai* community connecting two persons up to the complicated one of the national connection. Each stage has its own structure of solidarity, and in this way each of these structures exhibits a particular form of the law inherent in the *sonzai* of *ningen*. Trust and truth and freedom and justice appear here in their special form and by name. Precisely in these forms of solidarity people acquire the definite qualification of *persona* and come to be concretely burdened with responsibility and obligation.

Now, that these forms of solidarity overlap pyramidically means that each *sonzai*-community always has both a private and a public character. By reason of being finite, no finite *sonzai*-community can escape this "privacy." The closer the community of *sonzai*, the more "privacy" is intensified. Thus, on the one hand, "privacy" mediates the unity of social ethics, without thereby ceasing to be private. On the other, it prevents the truth inherent in *ningen* from emerging. This is the reason why *ningen sonzai* makes its appearance in a defective form of solidarity. Here, societies of mutual interest arise (*Gesellschaft*), or what could be called *egoistically connected societies*. These societies, although drawing lessons concerning communal structure from the community of *sonzai*, do not make *sonzai* communal. Here trust, sincerity, service, responsibility, obligation, and so forth are made use of formally but have no substance. That is to say, they are systems of social ethics, without thereby being socially ethical. For this reason, they can be called *deprived forms* of social ethics. But these deprived forms make us conscious of solidarity all the more strongly. It is inevitable, when seen from the angle of the community of *sonzai*, that there should arise an uneven distribution of light and shadow with respect to communal organization, on the ground that the *sonzai* of *ningen* has a spatio-temporal structure. Now, even though the forms of solidarity become conspicuous by abstraction from their actual quality, the communal character becomes a uniformly tightened system without a variety of light and shade. Such is the state, as a legal system of social ethics, wherein each structure of solidarity is given expression in legal fashion and responsibility and obligation are imposed compulsorily. The authority of totality operates here in the guise of the state, and social ethics is protected from destruction by this authority. But the real state includes communities of *sonzai* and societies of mutual interest (*Gesellschaft*) as its substance. There is no state that is nothing more than a mere legal construction. The solidarity expressed legally falls short of expressing the way of *ningen*, if it is not backed up by the community of *sonzai*.

Incidentally, *ningen*'s *sonzai*, which is provided with the preceding structure of solidarity, is essentially spatio-temporal. It forms a system of social ethics in some place, and at some period of time. Apart from land and a specific time period, a system of social ethics would turn out to be a mere abstraction. As Tönnies pointed out, family ties occur in the "home," connections of neighbors in the "village," and links of friendship in the "town." And the home, the village, and the town are all burdened with historical tradition and re-create their history day by day. Or rather, I should say that the connections themselves of family, neighborhood, and friendship together constitute the content of this history. Therefore, the spatio-temporal structure of the *sonzai* of *ningen* must already be a climatic and historical structure when it is materialized in the form of a system of social ethics.

The fourth point to be argued is precisely the existence of this climatic and historical structure. For here the *sonzai* of *ningen* is given concreteness in the full sense of that term. Such a thing as the *sonzai* of *ningen* in general does not exist in reality. What was deemed universally human by Europeans, in the past, was outstandingly Europeanlike. This is understandable. The significance of world history lies in this, that the way of *ningen* is realized in a variety of climatic and historical types. Just as the universal is capable of being universal only through and in the particular, so the *sonzai* of *ningen* can be universal only through its particular materializations. In this way, only where each historical nation aims at the formation of totality in its particularity, do international relations become possible, in the true sense of the word. An approach that attempts to be international by ignoring nationality is nothing more than an abstract illusion.

The last investigatory task leads us to the theory of national ethics. This topic has two aspects: as the study of principles and of history. The former is the theory of national ethics as a part of the system of ethics, and the latter is the study of the history of ethics peculiar to a nation and, hence, for us, of the history of Japanese ethics. These two must not be confounded. Still, even the study of principles cannot be completely separated from the problem of history. As was said before, the climatic and historical *sonzai* of *ningen* is what is here in question. The significance of a "nation" consists in the fact that the totality of *ningen* is formed as particular types. Hence, as a climatic and historical product, *nation* must be clarified through an investigation into its origin. That the investigation of *nation* is usually carried out through its connections with wars against other nations is itself based on climatic and historical conditions. The national communities that emerged because of the disruption of the foundation of the unified Roman Catholic world and those that never achieved anything more than the unity of a nation differ in their climatic and historical structure, even though they may be designated by the same word. Our task here is to inquire into what a nation is, in its various forms, and to clarify what kind of position the realization of national totality occupies in the movement of social ethics, which consists in coming back to a seeming authenticity via a disruption between self and others. Given that the place wherein every form of social ethics dwells is a national totality, the importance of this task will be self-evident.

I hold the position that the business of ethics as the study of *ningen* is to solve the problems noted here by appealing to the basic structure of the *sonzai* of *ningen*.

2 the method of ethics as the
study of *ningen*

In the preceding chapter, we clarified the significance of ethics as the study of *ningen*, and thereby considered the sorts of problems it should be able to resolve. But the problem of how the subjective and practical *sonzai* of *ningen* can be brought to light requires further inquiry.

With regard to the method, we must first of all take notice of the fact that learning in general, that is, "to ask," already belongs to the *sonzai* of *ningen*. Originally, "to learn" meant "to imitate." In other words, it meant to follow another person who already had the ability to do something and learn how to do it by imitation. First of all, it is an action or an activity, but it is not concerned with noematic knowledge. Second, it is transacted with other persons, but is not an isolated person's contemplation. Even in the case where learning is particularly concerned with knowledge, to simply take learning as though already completed and then to memorize it is not to learn. Rather, to learn is to acquire the ability to think so that we are able to think for ourselves. Therefore, if we eliminate for the moment noematic moments, and stick with noetic ones, we are able to say that learning is a relation of giving and receiving, face to face, between person and person. In the same vein, *tou* (i.e., "to ask") means in Japanese also to pay a visit to someone, as well as to inquire about something. In an interconnection of acts such as visiting someone or inquiring about her (as in the activity of asking after another's health, for example), this sense of visitation and inquiry is transacted. To ask after a person's well-being is to inquire about her manner of *sonzai*, and thus about her person. The expression of this relationship is the basic meaning of the inquiry. In this relation, the mutual feeling of two persons is the common concern. Hence, a mutual relationship as such is set up between them. Furthermore, this common concern extends to various tools that are found in this betweenness. As a result, something is asked about these tools, and this "thing" lies between the person asking and the person asked. In this way, a question exists in a communal way, in the betweenness. And this remains so, even when it comes to asking about the meaning of a thing. Seen from this angle, learning as well as questioning is an activity of *ningen* (i.e., a human being, and at the same time, occurs in the betweenness of person and person) and is not an isolated person's contemplation. Learning is concerned with exploring betweenness. A "thing" pursued exists publicly in the betweenness of human beings. That is to say, *to ask* is, essentially speaking, "a question of *ningen*."

This assertion does not square with the convictions of modern philosophy, which takes its start from the *cogito*. But as was said at the beginning of the preceding chapter, this conviction is, in truth, nothing more than an expression of the standpoint of individualistic abstraction. As an isolated ego, a human being stands in opposition to nature. And the relation between them is upheld as the field of questioning. For the moment, let us assume that this position is justifiable. A human being may deal with objects of nature while alone in her study, in separation from other human relationships. But how can she escape from the fact that even this isolated research is, in the final analysis, "a question of *ningen*"? When she submits this question for discussion with other inquirers, she has already posited it in the betweenness of persons, as a common question. Insofar as an assertion is made to friends or in a classroom, through the medium of a common language, even in the case of an assertion of the extremely isolated ego, it is already a question of *ningen* posited among people. Problems of the ego in the history of philosophy have been dealt with as problems common to *ningen* quite beyond the restrictions of time and place, but they can never be problems of the isolated ego alone. As our question is already composed of words or signs, even though we keep it strictly to ourselves, without consulting anybody, then essentially speaking, it is already a question that concerns community. We can have no ideas and, hence, can raise no questions, without having recourse to words or signs. This means simply that the consciousness of a human being is the consciousness of *ningen*. (By saying this, I do not mean to say that consciousness is originally social consciousness. It is true that consciousness occurs socially and there is no such thing as purely individual consciousness. But social consciousness is at the same time individual consciousness. It is because I keep this dual quality of consciousness in mind that I venture to call it the *consciousness* of *ningen*.) Therefore, although we can think alone, yet even in this case, we think alone about a communal problem. This fact is revealed by the very phenomenon of secretly "keeping our question in our heart." We need not keep to ourselves something incommensurable that we do not have in common with others. We can safely disclose our secret before a cat.

As already was noted, any question whatever is a question of *ningen*. That is to say, it is at once a question of the individual and of the community. This dual character of questions make it readily understandable that questions belong to the *sonzai* of *ningen*. The contention that all questions deal with *ningen* indicates that we do not accept the scheme of individual subject *versus* object as the starting point of scientific knowledge. Objects are found, not within individual consciousness, but rather within the consciousness of *ningen*. Hence, the subject itself that is opposed to objects has a double structure and includes within itself connections. The second point to be noted here is that the ground from which questions are raised is that of the practical interconnection of acts. The subject is not something static like a mirror, whose only business is to contemplate objects, but includes within itself the connections between oneself and the other. And these connections operate subjectively and practically, prior to contemplation. Therefore we commit an error if we start from the analysis of a question and then arrive at individual existence. Instead, a question leads us to consider those human relationships that exist between the act of asking and the one asked, that is, it leads us to the practical interconnection of acts. Therefore, it leads us to ethics.

By the way, our question was "what is ethics?" and we found that this question asks about the fundamental structure of the *sonzai* of *ningen*. If so, then by raising this question, we return to the authentic basis of questioning. Questioning belongs to the *sonzai* of *ningen*. And this *sonzai* must thereby be disclosed in a fundamental manner. The activity of questioning here returns to its own basis. Thus, the primary characteristic of the method of ethics consists in the point that the asking activity and what is asked are one.

This can be seen to be immediately connected with a second characteristic. What is sought here is *ningen*, the *sonzai* of *ningen*, which is from beginning to end a practical acting subject, as well as subjective interconnections. If this is true, then in such questions, *ningen* as the acting subject, must be grasped subjectively through and through. This means that the subjectivity of what is inquired into here is the second point that determines the method of ethics. This issue must be assessed from two sides: one, the "subjectivity" of the object of inquiry; two, that this subject is *ningen*.

Kant emphasized unusually clearly that what is asked about in ethics is the subject. So far as his philosophy is concerned, the problem of "knowledge," in which subject and object are opposed to each other, belongs to the theoretical use of reason. What is under consideration here is the position according to which the subject posits objects and their relationships and contemplates them. Hence, the contemplating subject itself cannot come within the field of vision of this contemplation. On the other hand, however, the problem of ethics belongs to the practical use of reason. Here only the practicing subject is dealt with, and what is more, this subject is characterized as *subject* to the very end. The subject is what is not visible for theoretical knowledge. That is, it is the *noumenon*. But the *noumenon* is not a mere *object* of thinking; it is the practicing subject. The "holistic determination of a human being," which Kant posited as the central issue of ethics, consisted in grasping a human being as the unity of dual characteristics, such as the empirical (or phenomenal) and the noumenal (and hence, as objective and subjective). In this way, as the science of the practical subject, ethics is distinguished from the science of theoretical objects. This is Kant's immortal achievement.

However, did Kant comprehend after all that this subject is *ningen*? The position on which he consciously stands is based on Descartes's *cogito* and the individualism prevalent in the eighteenth century. Therefore, the subject was always the ego. Despite this, in describing this ego as possessing the dual characteristics of the empirical and noumenal, he could not prevent the totality as superindividual from coming to the fore of its own accord. What he calls *Menschheit* or *Persönlichkeit* is the only characteristic that renders every individual capable of being a human being. Because of this characteristic, a human being is regarded as a noumenal person, which cannot include differentiation. Yet this undifferentiated entity constitutes the essence of the person as differentiated in an empirical form. So far, the noumenal person appears also under the guise of an individual. Hence, at the back of the dual qualities of the empirical and noumenal, the differentiated/undifferentiated and individualistic/holistic structure of *ningen* was already imperceptively grasped by Kant. It would not be to go too far to say, as Durkheim said, that the super-individual in Kant was, in truth, the community of human beings.

Precisely this structure of the subject that Kant grasped unconsciously is the crux of a problem of particular importance to ethics. Ethics is not only the study of the subject; it is also the study of the subject as the practical interconnection of acts. Given this recognition, the Kantian approach to ethics must appear insufficient. Kant took his departure from the facts of immediate consciousness in the individual, and inquired into the self-determination of the subject practically disclosed in these facts. But the practical interconnection of acts includes the mutual understanding of subjects on a deeper level than is the case with the consciousness of obligation of the individual. On the basis of these subjective connections, obligatory consciousness arises. And what is more, it arises on the ground of a definite betweenness; that is, on this basis, the relations of social ethics are established in the form of self-realization as a way of acting within this betweenness. Therefore, an attempt to start from the ought-to-be consciousness of an individual involves the risk of burying in oblivion human relationships, which are, nonetheless, the basis of this consciousness and letting ethics degenerate into a science of subjective consciousness.

The same risk is to be found in phenomenology. Intentionality is the structure of individual consciousness, and it cannot pass judgment on the betweenness of person and person. Hence, she who deals with ethics from the standpoint of intentionality becomes satisfied with an analysis of the structure of value consciousness. Even when going a step further and paying attention to the person standing at the center of intentionality, as Scheller did, one cannot clarify the relationship between person and person, nor that of the individual person and the whole person, by appealing to intentionality. It is true that Scheller had various insights in insisting on the community of intentionalities, but he failed to penetrate the fact that the betweenness of person and person is something beyond intentionality. Intentionality never becomes an object of intentionality, but in the betweenness, intentional activity itself is determined already as an object of intentionality. Conversely, the intentionality of seeing, for example, is never seen by the object seen. But in the betweenness, one's activity of seeing, is a seeing determined, conversely, by its being seen by the other. Oneself and the other act on each other while being mutually determined by the partner. The various ways of seeing (such as seeing each other, staring, looking angrily at, glimpsing, looking at nervously, seeing while pretending not to see, gazing on in rapture, and so forth) show without exception that the activity of seeing is already determined by the other's seeing. They are not simply one-sided activities but relationships of reciprocal activity.

Nor are they simple activities but the acts of personality. Concretely speaking, we perform the activity of seeing, not merely that of intentional activity. What is called *intentional activity* is nothing more than the product of an abstraction that first of all excludes the relational elements from our acts and then posits the residue as an activity of individual consciousness.

∗ ∗ ∗

With this in mind, I think that all attempts to deal with ethics from the angle of analyzing individual consciousness are unfit, for ethics is the study of the subject conceived of as the practical interconnection of acts. An act is not something constructed out of various activities of the individual consciousness but the movement itself in which subjects, although splitting into self and other, combine in a nonduality of self and other to form a betweenness. Hence, from the outset, an act involves practical interconnection or practical understanding between oneself and the other. Such an act, wherein self and other are connected, must be understood from the practical interconnection of acts itself, instead of from an individual consciousness alone. Our method of ethics must be such as to satisfy this requirement.

However, ethics is a "science," a theoretical undertaking. In an attempt to inquire into "what ethics is," we must elucidate the object of inquiry in such a way as to be able to predicate that "it is this or that." This is exactly what is asked by this question. The practical interconnection of acts itself is disclosed only in the acting. This is practical realization and not a mere theoretical understanding. As a science, ethics must translate practice into a definite proposition, " ... is ... ". In other words, ethics must deal with the subject in a subjective fashion to the very end and yet has to transform it into a precise and definite meaning. This is the third point that determines the nature of the method of ethics.

But the question remains: How is it possible that subjective connections are transformed into the proposition " ... is ... ", which is a connection of noematic meanings? Is ethics, as a science, capable of achieving such a thing? We cannot easily answer yes. Theory is concerned with meaningful objects and cannot directly come to grips with the subject as subject. Hence, so that ethics may translate practical connections into the proposition " ... is ... ", a definite preparation must have been made in advance. What I have in mind here is that inside the practical interconnection of acts is already a practical understanding of *wake* ("meaning" or "reason"). Only through the medium of such practical understanding is ethics able to transform something subjective into noematic meanings.

In an endeavor to distinguish betweenness from intentionality, I have pointed out that the activity of seeing is never one-sided but conditioned by a relationship of mutuality. If this is true, then a way of seeing, such as casting a furtive glance at something, already involves a definite understanding of the partner's attitude. This does not, however, necessarily mean that the consciousness of the latter's attitude is such and such or is somehow clearly established in advance. Before becoming conscious of it, we have already put ourselves into action. Still, this activity is not at all blind but is carried on to establish a definite betweenness. In this sense, we hold the view that the practical interconnection of acts already contains a practical understanding within itself. And this means that betweenness itself is already a practical *wake*. Betweenness consists in the fact that self and other are divided from each other (i.e., *wake-rareru* in Japanese) and at the same time that what is thus divided becomes unified. In order that they may be divided from each other, they had to be one originally; and in order that they may become unified, they must be absolutely separated from each other. Hence, betweenness, as the practical interconnection of acts, consists in a connection of unity/division/union. This is exactly practical *wake*. *And*, insofar as this *wake* is practically understood (i.e., *wakaru* in Japanese), that betweenness arises which is the foundation from which consciousness and language originate. One may comprehend such practical understanding within the vague concept of "instinct." But Marx's dictum that "an animal has no connection with anything" is quite right. An animal's instinct has nothing to do with what we call *practical understanding*. The latter is given expression in the form of consciousness and language and makes progress through these expressions. This is the reason why betweenness, even though it does not arise first of all through these expressions, includes within itself an infinite number of expressions. Not only gestures, facial expressions, demeanor, and so forth but also language, custom, ways of living, and so on are all expressions of betweenness; and they make up the moments that constitute it.

For this reason, we can say that the practical interconnection of acts, as a practical *wake*, are already expressed in various forms within the realm of practice. In particular, they are given the most detailed expression in language, not primarily as theoretical statements but as moments constituting the interconnection of acts. Therefore, already within the realm of practice, subjective connections come to noematic expression through language. They need not wait for a theoretical standpoint to achieve this.

From the perspective of theory, such linguistic expression is already given. That is to say, the subjective has already objectified itself. This is the reason why we are able to subjectively grasp the subjective in theoretical reflection. Reflection does not consist in the fact that we directly turn toward ourselves. Insofar as we remain as a subject to the very end and refuse to become an object, it is impossible for us to turn toward ourselves. The subject objectifies itself so as to become the other and then returns to itself by reacting against that other. This is reflection. In reflection, we are able to transform subjective connections through the medium of linguistic expressions produced in practice into meanings which we have already described in terms of " . . . is . . . ".

This transformation necessarily occurs on the ground that linguistic expression already expresses the *sonzai* of *ningen* as the practical interconnection of acts. Language "expresses something in order to make it apparent." This is *chinjutsu* (the original meaning of this Japanese word is "to expand or enlarge something by giving it expression." It is usually, however, translated as "statement.") It expands the *sonzai* of *ningen* by expressing it and thereby disclosing it. That is to say, it divides (*wakeru*) what it should disclose into a variety of *kotos* (this Japanese word means "a thing" and, at the same time, "a word"), and then connects the *kotos* thus divided. Here arises an instance of "S is P." The form of this statement is usually accounted for in such a way that S and P, which exist independently, are connected by means of *is*. But if S and P originally existed independent of each other, it would be impossible that they could come to be connected, even if the term *is* [as copula] is employed. That they are connected because they were originally one. Hence, prior to the connection of S and P, there must be a disruption into S and P. Here is the fundamental meaning of the word *wakaru* (i.e., "to understand"). When one thing that is to be expressed is divided (i.e., *wakerareru*) into a number of things, it is said to have been understood (i.e., *wakaru*). Therefore, we must say in regard to a statement that priority is to be given to separation rather than to connection. Separation is at once a negation of the original unity and its coming to awareness. In *wakaru*, the unity is brought to awareness. For this reason, together with *wakaru*, what is *wakerareru* (i.e., divided) comes to be connected by means of *is*. The term *is* is nothing more than an indication of the unity that has come to awareness by the disruption. If this is so, then we can say that a statement discloses the realization of *ningen sonzai* through the correlation of unity–division–union.

Moreover, the *sonzai* of *ningen* itself consists of the movement that realizes the original unity through the correlation of unity/division/union. Hence, we are allowed to say that the structure of a statement is the expression given to the structure of *sonzai* of *ningen* in language.

We are now in a position to specifically understand the reason why the subjective connections are transformable into statements such as " . . . is . . . ", as connections of meanings. The *sonzai* of *ningen* is subjective through and through and yet is disclosed in " . . . is . . . ". The theory concerning the *sonzai* of *ningen* comes to grips with this disclosure, and tries to elaborate on it by means of concepts. This is why it is said to be concerned with grasping the subjective connections subjectively, even though it deals with the connection of meanings. Perhaps in other realms of research it is all right to forget that the connection of meanings is a disclosure of the subjective connections, and therefore, it is unnecessary to go back to such things as the origin of meaning and practical understanding. But as the subjective study of the *sonzai* of *ningen*, ethics cannot lose sight of this basic affiliation. With regard to any meaning whatsoever, we must examine its certificate of birth in the realm of practical understanding. Here is a clue to solving the problem of practical science *versus* science as concerned with *logos*. Ethics is not a science that deals only with the objective meaning-content of noematic objects; it is a science that deals with human reality. But insofar as it is a science, it is concerned with theory, not with practical reality as it is. It can be a science only by transforming human reality into *logos*. Nevertheless, we should not forget that the *logos*-like things that are the objects of this science are nothing but indications of subjective realities that are out of reach of any attempt at objectification.

The scientific character of ethics necessarily leads us to the topic of the expression of the *sonzai* of *ningen*. What mediates between the *sonzai* of *ningen* as subjective reality, and its scientific understanding, are those expressions of *sonzai* already carried out within the realm of practice. Because expressions are expressions of betweenness, they include within themselves its understanding. Only through the medium of these expressions and understandings is ethics capable of grasping subjective reality. This is the fourth important point that determines the method of ethics.

If ethics were not an attempt to grasp subjectively the *sonzai* of *ningen*, to the very end, then this sort of medium would not be required. For instance, provided that the objects of ethics consisted of such things as custom, morality, and social systems, all of which are empirical objects, we could afford to collect materials, to compare them, to put them in order, and to bring them to unity in a definite way, without thereby having recourse to an understanding of the medium of expression and understanding. Even if we try to break through that empirical standpoint and pursue ethics as the study of the subject, if that subject is not assumed to be *ningen,* but mere "ego," then we take our departure from the ego as *res cogitans* and, hence, from the consciousness of the ego alone. Also, we would not require expression as the medium. However, it would be possible to conceive of the obligatory consciousness, as is prevalent in everyday life and in the common sense of the people, from which Kant took his departure, as being already some kind of expression. For the noumenal *ego* as the basis of ethics, in spite of its not being a consciousness capable of being an object of study, makes its appearance in the obligatory consciousness of common sense. But Kant himself did not conceive of it as an expression. This is the reason why Kant did deal with the medium of expression as a question to be solved in his practical philosophy.

With respect to theoretical philosophy, Kant tried to probe the basis of knowledge through the medium of the facticity of the sciences, such as mathematics and the natural sciences. The neo-Kantian school, which recognized in Kant's method something of central importance for critical philosophy, applied it to practical philosophy and then tried to return to the basis of ethics by means of the medium of scientific facts, such as the science of law, the social sciences, and so forth. It seems that the question of the nature of the medium is brought out clearly here. But, in truth, this medium is here adopted for the purpose of arriving at the basic concepts of science from the facts of the sciences. Hence, in Cohen, the concept of a human being and in Garland, that of community are respectively grasped as basic concepts. What is here dealt with is not *ningen's sonzai* prior to concepts, but the view that these concepts themselves produce being. With regard to this point, P. Natorp is right in pointing out that the laws of practice must forever be found in and through practice itself.

If this is so, then we must come to the conclusion that tribute must be paid to Kant's attitude, for he looked for the starting point of practical philosophy in the fact of common sense. The only thing that makes us reserve our total acknowledgment of Kant's achievement is that, by *common sense,* he means individual consciousness as ordinarily found, but not that common sense fact which has as much objective meaning as that of the sciences. In the realm of theory, common sense may always be in error. But in the realm of practice, common sense includes within itself the expression and understanding of *ningen's sonzai*. When friends come upon each other, they remark on the weather. This is the common sense of *ningen*. They do not reflect on the reason why they speak of the weather. When they speak of it, they know that they do not concern themselves with knowledge of the weather but only the mutual relationship thereby expressed. Otherwise, these persons are thought to lack common sense. When talk about the weather, as a fact of common sense, is conceived of as an expression of *ningen's sonzai*, then a way is thereby opened to subjective *sonzai*. Why do people talk about the weather? Because the weather is nothing other than a mood of subjective *sonzai*; that is, an expression of one's "state of mind." Moreover, what is here in question is not a feeling without community, as Scheler rightly expounds, but a mood of communal *sonzai*. The climatic character of *ningen's sonzai* is brought out in this way. It is of great importance that the everyday facts of common sense prevalent in *ningen* be grasped as expressions.

With this in mind we can say that there is no mine so rich as that which is called the *everyday experience* of human beings. Walking along the street we can find various goods on display shelves. Common sense already has some knowledge of how to classify, how to use, and why to buy them. In addition, there are none of these goods that does not give expression to *ningen's sonzai* in one way or another. From the standpoint of common sense, no attempt is made to go back to the structure of *sonzai* through the medium of these expressions. Were you to do this, you would be able to draw out the *Gesellschaft*-like structure of *ningen's sonzai* even from but one commodity. And what is more, it is not commodities alone that we come into contact with while walking along the street. There are also transport facilities such as streetcars and automobiles, communication facilities such as postboxes and public telephones, informational and advertisement facilities such as radios, posters, newspapers, and so on. Each provides particularly strong expression to the *sonzai* of *ningen*. Furthermore, also encounters with acquaintances, friends, or relatives are to be included here, wherein various polite compliments are exchanged as well as more serious conversational pleasantries. It goes without saying that all of these are expressions of *ningen's sonzai*.

In other words, as expressions, what we call the *things of daily life* all offer a passage to *ningen's sonzai*. Therefore, we are able to take our departure from "facts," taken in the most naive and ordinary sense of the word. One might gain the impression that what we have enumerated here, as issues to be solved in ethics, takes on an outstandingly metaphysical color. But the passageway that leads to them consists of markedly everyday, ordinary facts. In this sense, our ethics remains in close contact with facts. Here there is no room for methodological doubt. Nobody can doubt the everyday fact that we walk along the street, take a streetcar, go to such and such a place, and perform such and such a task, no matter how we may mistake a falsehood for a truth or how straightforwardly we may pursue truth. What the real truth about these facts is will be disclosed after further investigation. But it is not in accordance with facts to begin by postulating, from the beginning, what is to be scientifically ascertained.

In the preceding we have determined the method of ethics, looked at from four perspectives. As an inquiry into *ningen*, ethics turns back to the person inquiring. Hence, it must subjectively grasp the subjective *ningen*. What is more, the object of science is exclusively concerned with meaning connections. Hence, the subjective grasp must use as its medium "the expressions of *ningen's sonzai*," which expressions are like a melting furnace through which subjective *ningen* is transformed into its meaning connections. These four perspectives necessarily terminate in a hermeneutic method, which tries to understand something subjective with the aid of expressions.

One often associates hermeneutics with strange ideas about the concept of "interpretation." For a time, Marx's proposition that "the only thing philosophers have so far done is to *interpret* the world in a variety of ways, but the important thing to do is to *change* it" was in everybody's mouth. What Marx conceived of as *interpretieren* was the attempt to explain actual human beings, as well as the world, with the help of ideas, representations, and concepts, all from the standpoint of speculative philosophy, and has nothing to do with the attempt to understand the subjective through the medium of expression. Hence, what is here rejected is the view that ideas, thoughts, or concepts produce, determine, and hold sway over a human being's real life but not the view that *ningen's sonzai* is brought to conceptualization through expressions. Philosophers, at the time, had no idea of this method of hermeneutics. That is to say, they lacked a full-fledged realization that a subjective grasp of *ningen's sonzai* requires its own specific method, hermeneutics. Rather, Marx himself unconsciously began to put into practice a method that was hermeneutical in its essence, that tried to grasp those structures characteristic of capitalistic society through the medium of "commodities." What Marx calls the *theory of ideologies* is, at bottom, nothing more than a conceiving of consciousness and ideas as the expressions of *ningen's sonzai*. His position, wherein he is thought to have rejected the standpoint of "interpretation," is already, in fact, extremely hermeneutical.

The crux of the hermeneutic method lies in transforming the subjective into a scientific object with the aid of expressions, which we can by no means directly submit to scientific treatment as an object. For this reason, its business is not to deal directly with concepts used in thinking, but to give priority to the understanding of expressions and their use. Here arises the problem of understanding vis-à-vis thinking. What, after all, is understanding? Does understanding require the same objectivity as thinking? By what right was understanding entitled to enter philosophy as conceived of as the kingdom of thinking?

Indeed, "understanding" is a new citizen in the country of philosophy and was originally the ruler of a literary country. Therefore, it is not the business of science to appreciate a poem. To know the special characteristics, mode, and significance of the beauty of a poem thus appreciated is something that does belong to the ken of science. Now this kind of knowledge is beyond the reach of thinking. It can only be understood. This is why Beck gave the name *understanding* to literary knowledge, as opposed to philosophical knowledge (i.e., thinking), and tried to construct a hermeneutics; that is, a theory of understanding that is opposed to that of mere thinking, that is, logic. For Beck, hermeneutics was at once the basic theory of literature and historical knowledge. During the latter part of the nineteenth century, after Kant's philosophy had been restored and methodology had come into vogue once more and as attention was drawn to the methodology of historical knowledge that Kant fell just short of attaining, the theory of understanding was taken into philosophy. Thus, the hermeneutic method came to be expounded as a basic theory of the cultural sciences as well as of history. The pioneer of this movement was Dilthey.

This development illustrates how the hermeneutic method legitimately entered into the kingdom of thinking. Thinking is unable to grasp historical reality and hence is also unable to grasp the realm of the human sciences full-fledgedly. This is because historical reality is certainly not rational in every nook and cranny but instead has an infinitely deep root of irrationality. It goes beyond the power of thinking to exhaustively grasp historical reality by means of logical thinking alone. Therefore, for a grasp of historical reality we must rely on our "understanding," which is capable of grasping the irrational depths of life. The irrational depth of life expresses itself prior to its being trapped within the net of conceptual thought. It is understanding that, by means of these expressions, is able to come into contact with that unconscious depth of life. Therefore, so far as historical reality is concerned, thinking must give way to understanding, and the logical method must be replaced by a hermeneutic one.

Still, if the same objectivity cannot be claimed in the hermeneutic method as in the logical one, then Dilthey's assertions concerning hermeneutics would appear to be arrogant. Is it possible to think that even in understanding and interpretation, the same necessity is to be found as in thinking? Dilthey endeavors to explore this point by having recourse to the history of hermeneutics. It is true that interpretation is a technique peculiar to specific individuals. But all techniques move toward definite rules. Even thinking was a technique initially, but the rules of this technique were subsequently systematically formalized as logic. In the same way, the techniques of interpretation gave rise to hermeneutics as the formalization of its rules. Therefore, it is certainly not the case that understanding and interpretation are without rules. The thing to be noted here is, however, that they have not so far been dealt with appropriately as matters concerning the understanding of the expressions of life. Here is the task for the theory of historical knowing, which has thus far remained intact. In contrast with the logic necessary for the knowledge of nature, it will be the task of a hermeneutics to elucidate the possibility of knowledge about living connections in the historical world, as well as the means of realizing this possibility. In this way, rules of understanding, which have the same objectivity as those of thinking, will be established in the form of "categories of life" or the "interconnections of the acts of life" that are inherent in the connections of life, expression, and understanding. In contradistinction to logic, understanding will thus be rendered capable of universal validity.

If it is true that ethics must use expressions as its medium, so that it may grasp subjective *ningen* subjectively, then the hermeneutic method will have to be adopted as its only method. However, when Dilthey speaks of this method, he had his eye on only the historical knowledge to be gained in and from art, philosophy, and the various views of life and not on the knowledge to be gained in and from ethics. What Dilthey had in mind with respect to expression is, above all, the work of great artists and philosophers and, with respect to understanding, the grasping of the depth of life by means of the retrospective experience (*Nach-vollziechen*) of these expressions. But expressions are indispensable moments that constitute *ningen*'s *sonzai* even before they crystallize as great works: Understanding is not so much a grasping of the depth of life by means of these works, as it is an immediate understanding of everyday gestures and dialogue. That is to say, what is here at issue are expressions or understanding itself, as moments constituting the practical interconnection of acts prior to their being expressions or an understanding of art, philosophy, and so forth. Hence, understanding is not so much a manner of knowing as the manner of relational *sonzai*, precisely because of its being practical understanding.

Unless they are based on such practical expressions and practical understanding, specific expressions such as works of art or philosophy cannot arise. And as we probe into the matter by going back to that basis, there is no other alternative to the problem of historical knowledge than that it be transformed into a problem about historical praxis and hence about ethics. At this point, we must be aware of our method being different from Dilthey's. In insisting on adopting the hermeneutic method for ethics, we have already moved away from him.

This necessity of our separation from Dilthey lies in his failure to grasp fully "life" as *ningen*'s *sonzai*. It is true that he puts emphasis on "life" as "human, social, and historical reality." But the concept of "life" he uses in an attempt to elucidate the basic connection of life/expressions/understanding, has nothing to do with the grasping of the subjective relations involved in the disruption of life into self and other and their reunion. For Dilthey, society is, in the final analysis, an external system and, hence, is an objective society: It is not *ningen*'s subjective *sonzai*. This sort of "life" is nothing but a thing modeled after individual bodily experience (i.e., *Erleben* in German). But this individual bodily experience takes place only if we live in the betweenness. Even what is conceived of as a unique experience, incommensurable with any other person's, can exist only as a lack of community. Otherwise, there is no possibility of its being brought to expression. Expression is essentially identifiable with being understood. For this reason, "life" must be further traced back to *ningen*'s *sonzai* as the practical interconnection of acts. And "life" has no sooner become known as *ningen*'s *sonzai* than an effort to understand it from life itself comes to take on an ethical aspect. For the connections of life, expression and understanding are none other than the practical interconnections of acts.

Thus, the hermeneutic method as the method of ethics, consists in grasping the dynamic structure of *ningen*'s *sonzai* through its most basic everyday expressions. *Ningen*'s *sonzai*, in its everydayness, constantly manifests itself in the practical connections of life, expression, and understanding; and yet it does not become aware of this as expression. Hence, the effort to realize it as expression is a philosophical activity that assumes the form of a hermeneutic method. What is called *historical knowledge* cannot have a legitimate basis until *ningen's sonzai* is understood. Attempts to select a variety of excellent cultural products as being especially representative expressions and the grasping of the spirit of a historical period through the medium of these expressions are nothing but the application of the hermeneutic method to particular and positive materials. This application constitutes the grasping of the particular forms of *ningen's sonzai.* We will start with the most basic expressions that may serve as the foundation on which this can be achieved.

Expressions of *ningen's* most basic *sonzai* are, as was said before, naive "facts" of common sense for the natural attitude. Apart from all scientific suppositions, we must start from these naive "facts." But our task is to deal with them as such, not to try to discover the relations or rules that obtain between them. The latter task is to be associated with a standpoint that treats facts in only a representative manner. We take advantage of them as a means of grasping subjective *ningen.* Hence, the effort to deal with everyday facts as expressions of the subjective constitutes the most important aspect of this method. We need not ask whether this is possible, for in our daily lives we deal with all things as expressions, although in an unconscious way. An article of clothing with golden buttons is a uniform, and a room in which desks stand in many lines is a classroom. Without relying on judgment or inference, we come into contact with uniforms or classrooms directly. Granted these facts, the hermeneutic method comes to grips with everyday facts and, at the same time, pays attention to their expressive characteristics. It locates itself a step away from the practical act-connections in which we move, as we understand expressions. Here, the hermeneutic method tries to go back from expressions to what the expressions actually express, to *ningen's sonzai.* If we ourselves move in the midst of *ningen's sonzai,* we cannot see it. To separate ourselves by a step and then to see and fixate on expressions as such makes it possible for a *ningen's sonzai* to reveal itself. If it is possible to describe this procedure in terms of reduction, then this is hermeneutic reduction.

All that this reduction can accomplish is something negative; namely, to direct our attention to *ningen's sonzai.* However, to answer the question "what is *ningen's sonzai?"* its structure must be more thoroughly grasped. Because this structure is dynamic, what is demanded here is positive activity. Thus, a practical understanding, inherent in our daily dealings with expressions, must be repeated in a self-conscious manner. It is not enough to separate ourselves a step away from practical act-connections: We must actually detach ourselves from

them absolutely. What is more, we must try to live by the practical connections of expressions and understanding from this position of self-
detachment. In this way, the dynamic structure of a human being's
sonzai is reconstructed as the self-aware connections of meanings. A
hermeneutic structure is sought, not a logical one.

This hermeneutic construction is rendered possible by our moving from expressions back to a human being's *sonzai*. We start with expressions. Expressions are themselves determined by history and
climate. Just as a wooden single-family Japanese house is not the same
as a multifamily brick apartment house or just as family life in Japan is
not the same as family life in Europe, so expressions of daily life vary
greatly, according to differences in time and place. Hence, the
hermeneutic method cannot remove us from the historical and climatic
burden, no matter how we may attempt to make a fundamentally fresh
start of it. Therefore, for this method to be truly basic, historical and
climatic determination must somehow be destroyed. That is to say, what
is inherited in everyday expressions must be traced back to its source,
as constructed, and then must be analyzed critically. It is probable that
what is to be discovered first is the particularity of each human being's
sonzai. But the realization of this particularity is the only way of going
beyond it, thereby overcoming the historical and climatic conditions
inherent in the hermeneutic method. For this method must be situated
in the midst of historical and climatical conditions. It begins with expressions that are determined historically and climatically and yet has
every confidence that it has succeeded in interpreting the universal
structure of a human being's *sonzai* directly. For this reason,
hermeneutic destruction reveals traditions, comes to grips with their
respective particularity, and thereby gains the clarity to reconstruct the
fundamental structure of a human being's *sonzai*.

By having recourse to the hermeneutic method of reduction/con-
struction/destruction, we are able to fulfill the four demands required
by the method of ethics.

part II

the fundamental structure of human existence

3 the everyday fact as a starting point

We have paved the way toward making the most commonsense facts of daily life the means of understanding *ningen*'s *sonzai* by pointing out that there are already many expressions and multiple understandings of human existence. We take from daily life the manner of human existence most familiar to us, and by means of this we try to carry on our investigation directly to the fundamental structure of human existence.

As usual, one who is engaged in contemplating philosophical problems is used to being alone in his study, or to taking a solitary ramble along a quiet road. One deals with things most familiar, such as a desk, a piece of paper, a pencil, an ink box, a book, a window, an outside street, a field, a mountain, or woods. These things exist outside of us, and each of them reveals its own features. We perceive these features and use them in some way. They are considered to have something to do with facts at the "natural level" and to which no theoretical constructs are added. There, what is called *our consciousness* or what it means "to be in the world" becomes a starting point of our consideration. But the question is this: Are these ordinary things really the facts most familiar to us? I now confine myself to this study, alone, and in which I am writing these sentences. This is the same sort of situation in which other philosophers have written about the evidence for the existence of the *I*, from their studies. But they assumed a strangely different attitude to the extent that, even though writing about the evidence for the *I*, they nonetheless did not simultaneously recognize the

49

evidence for the other *I*. Is one justified in holding that the operation of writing has developed without anticipating its readers? To write that "only I am evident" is itself contradictory. For writing is an expression of words, and words are what have come to shape themselves in anticipation of partners who live and talk together. Even though words are written in a foreign language and perhaps with the intention of allowing no one else to read them, this does not mean that these words have come into being without there being partners to talk with, but only that the author is without partners with whom to talk. In light of this, we can say that for us to read books or to write sentences we are already involved with other persons. No matter how much we concern ourselves with the consciousness of *I*, this concern itself implies our going beyond the consciousness of *I* and being connected with others. No philosopher was able to set forth problems without having recourse to such connections.

We are able to claim the same for the reader. I cannot know who reads these sentences. It may be that no one reads them. However, if someone happens to read them, then reading is the event that occurs before his eyes. Even when sitting alone in your study, you have already come into contact with my sentences, insofar as you have read them. In asking what sort of human existence one is most familiar with, one already stands in relation to others. If this is true, then it is legitimate for us to take it for granted that what is most familiar to a reader is that reader's relationship to others. Thus, in assuming an attitude such as that of "reading," we cannot justifiably adopt the standpoint of only *I*.

What I have said thus far is the natural thing to expect, if we reflect on the fact that "letters" are no less the expressions of words than are "sounds." Our words have no essential connections with "voice." They are likewise expressed through visual images. We are able to express the same "thing" by means of the voice and by means of letters. Hence, "reading" as well as "hearing" has something to do with our relationship to others. There is no difference, so far as human relations are concerned, between the fact that one person speaks and another hears or that one person writes and another reads.

For this reason, we think about the same problem, together with each other. We recognize this and have no doubt about this relationship between ourselves and others. If there were room for doubt about such relationships, that is, if it were possible for these sentences to be communicable to no one, then I would stop writing. Then readers could no longer read them. Hence, that these sentences are written and read bears witness to the assured fact that we recognize in each other the relationship of self and other, as established through letters.

If so, then we who are now concerned with a most familiar daily fact stand in a relationship that is somewhere between that of "a writer" and "a reader" and that is regarded as occurring before our very eyes. The same can be said of reading an essay that insists only on the evidence of the ego. The method itself, through which every other thing except the "I" is rendered capable of being doubted, stands within the "relationship of an author and reader," about which there can be no doubt. No matter how the author may emphasize the solitude of the ego, he cannot get out of this relationship, once he has submitted his writing for publication. In the same way, a reader, however much he persistently ponders the solitude of the ego, cannot get out of this relationship with the author, once having embarked upon reading the authored work. This is the destiny from which every philosopher who has written on the ego has been unable to escape.

In this way we are forced to recognize the relation between an author and his reader as a familiar fact, whether we like it or not. For the time being, we must take this as a given of human existence, as evident before us. The contention that this familiar fact is not "the consciousness of I" but rather "the relationship between an author and his reader" is of great significance for us. It indicates precisely that we take our departure not from the intentional consciousness of "I" but from "betweenness." The essential feature of *betweenness* lies in this, that the intentionality of *I* is from the outset prescribed by its counterpart, which is also conversely prescribed by the former. When we write something, how we write is already prescribed by those who read it. The letter form reveals this most conspicuously, no matter who reads it. The distinction that used to be made between published sentences and manuscripts and memoranda is based on this. The latter is negatively determined by readers as "words that have not yet reached the stage where they can be read" or as "words ready to be read." This determination maintains the characterization of being a manuscript or a memorandum. Sentences written to be read positively involve within themselves the determination of their readers. Furthermore, an attitude that lets the matter speak of itself in a seemingly disinterested fashion to the complete exclusion of any concern about readers is nonetheless more strongly determined by readers in comparison with those various gestures that more clearly demonstrate such a concern. For, in the latter, an author cares for himself in the form of caring about reading, whereas writing to be read tries to empty itself so as to let the matter speak of itself to readers. The highest achievement of sentences lies in their becoming as transparent as window glass. Readers are able to see outside as if there were no glass at all. Were this the case, a writer would serve his readers completely. In other words, such sentences would be determined by their readers in an extreme fashion. In the same way, when we read something, its writer determines how we are to read it. Even in cases in which a writer is unknown to readers, as is the case with newspaper stories, the readers have no choice but to read in a manner determined by the writer. One who cannot follow this determination stops reading. That is to say, one ceases to be a reader. Insofar as one is a reader, one follows a series of represented images and treads the path of speculation in just the order determined by the writer.

This is *betweenness,* a fact that occurs before our eyes. A writer is a writer by virtue of being determined by his readers, and a reader in turn is a reader by virtue of being determined by the writer. No matter how temporal and accidental, the relationship between a writer and a reader cannot be established without this reciprocal determination as its essential feature. If so, even in what happens before our eyes, we are already able to find the dual characteristics that are inherent in human relationships. What is termed *the relation between author and reader* is nothing but a relationship that authors and readers construct through mutually depending on one another. What is more, it is not the case that an author and his readers exist prior to this relationship. An author becomes an author only by being determined through his readers, that is, by virtue of having a relationship with them as readers; and readers become readers only by virtue of their having a relationship with the author as a writer. This relationship enables an author to be an author and readers to be readers. By saying this, however, I do not mean that the relationship exists prior to the author and the author's readers. The relationship is constructed, through and through, in the betweenness between an author and his readers. Neither can exist prior to and independent of the other. They exist only by depending on one another.

As a matter of fact, this becomes clearer still when words are not written but spoken by means of voices. In this case, a speaker and a listener exist face to face, and they cannot be unknown to one another. Even if what is spoken about pertains to "the ego," this ego is already something posited in the between between a speaker and a listener. In order to invite people to think about the issue of the ego, Fichte once remarked: "Ladies and gentlemen! Think of this wall. And think of him who thinks of it. That is the ego." Now Fichte, who lured people to pay attention to the problem of the ego, was himself a speaker, and those who are addressed as "ladies and gentlemen" were listeners. Nothing affords more assured evidence of the fact that the relationship between a speaker and a listener exists prior to the issue of ego than these sentences of Fichte, who tried to lead people to confront the problem of the ego.

Fichte made this remark as a teacher, and we too, when teaching a class, are able to speak about the matter under consideration as follows: "Ladies and gentlemen! Near us is a fact that occurs before our eyes. We gather here to pursue questions of ethics together. From a commonsense point of view we recognize this and have no doubt about it. If we had any doubt about it, then to the contrary, we would not come together in this way. For instance, is it not a delusion for me to appear to give lectures on ethics or for you to listen to them? Or is it not the case that we have mistakenly taken these ideas to be firmly rooted in our minds? If so, then I cannot give lectures, nor can you listen to them. Hence, that lectures are given is positive proof that we do recognize each other at this meeting: it is doubtless a fact. There is a possibility that this fact might be overturned in some fashion. It might be that some of you are here not for the purpose of exploring questions of ethics, but with the intention of taking advantage of this opportunity for the sake of some political movement. But the reason why such a possibility is likely to occur lies in this: that you never actually doubt that you are here with the intention of exploring the questions of ethics. If it were possible to doubt this, then an attempt to take advantage of this lecture could never occur."

That we gather for the purpose of mutually exploring questions of ethics is recognized among us as a fact about which there is no doubt. Furthermore, no doubt can be raised from the commonsense standpoint about the fact that you are "students" and I am a "teacher." If you yourselves doubted whether or not you were students, and if I were in doubt about whether or not I am a teacher, you and I could not enter this classroom as we do. It is beyond doubt that we come face to face and stand in relationship as teacher and students. If so, then it is also evident that what obtains here is a relationship between students and teacher. Hence, we are able to set forth holding as an established fact that what happens before our eyes is that "students" and "teacher" come together, and together construct a specific relationship. Were people to come together at random, this specific relationship could not arise. What is called a *school* is a composite of these relationships. A school is represented by the existence of a group of buildings and other facilities. But they are not the school itself. Even when a school is abolished, the buildings that belonged to it can still remain intact. And even without buildings, it would be possible for a school to be established. A school consists of human relationships that are given expression to, by, and within these buildings. And the most basic element constituting these human relationships is the relationship between teacher and student.

We recognize that students and teachers come together in such a way as to constitute a specific relationship. However, we also acknowledge, as well, that it is not we ourselves but the school that sets up specific "capacities" or roles, such as that of teacher and student. To become a student of this school, you are obliged to enroll. I also acquire the status of teacher by accepting a job at this school. It is not only that you indicate your role as student by putting on a uniform, but also by using a student identification card or certificate, in the event that you need to prove your status. That the school prescribes your capacities is here brought to light beyond any doubt. In daily life, you behave yourself in your capacity as student and accordingly are treated as such. To this extent, your existence is determined by those human relationships that are collectively called a *school*. And these relationships consist of relationships among students and teachers. If this is true, then we can say that the relationships that teachers and students are expected to construct by coming together constitute in advance the basis on which such capacities as teachers and students are prescribed.

This fact, which occurs before our eyes, is one in which we are able to find the two relations just mentioned. Without teachers and students, a definite corps such as a school could not arise. In addition, only by entering the school do people actually become teachers and students. This reciprocal relationship is taken for granted and put into practice from the point of view of common sense. One might take this relationship as one of temporal succession. But this does not hold true here. By entering this school you can acquire the qualities of student. To speak of the matter from a student's perspective, the school is given priority. But the question here centers around the already established school. It already consists of the relationship between students and teachers, irrespective of whether one actually entered the school. No matter what stage of temporal succession one may select, the student/ teacher relationship is already established as a reciprocal relationship, as noted previously. Even if we go back to its origin, the situation remains the same. An objection might be raised here to the effect that, before the time when the first students entered, there were no students; in order that students might enter, the school had to be established beforehand. But the school that is open and accepting applications for enrollment, insofar as it is established as a school, already prescribes a definite number of students and teachers in advance and carries through in accordance with a plan to install specific facilities and requirements. It may be supposed that the school, in which there are actually not yet students or teachers, is established only legally or nominally. In other words, it is a school as an abstract notion but not yet a real one in which the pursuit of studies is carried on. Moreover, even an abstract notion of the school has its students and teachers in the abstract. The acceptance of the first students as well as the appointment of the first teachers is nothing but an attempt to materialize what already obtained on the abstract level. If this is true, then before the time when the first students entered the school, it already had students. Nobody has conceived or can conceive of such a thing as a school where there are no conceivable students.

Out of the very facts that have emerged before our eyes, we have provisionally found this same reciprocal relationship. Moreover, the facts that occur before our eyes are not thereby exhausted in content. We have come together for the purpose of exploring questions of ethics. From where? This question is quite easily answered from a commonsense standpoint. Some have come here from their homes and others from their private boarding houses or dormitories. Perhaps no one will insist on the uncertainty of the place from which he has come. If so, it is quite natural that human relationships somewhat different from those one has with the school are what are to be considered here. In your house, you are either a son or an elder or a younger brother. Here a status different from that of a student obtains. And this status is determined by the body called a *family*. Without exception, one gives expression to this different status by assuming a rather specific attitude. One's facial expressions, ways of speaking, and expressing concern vary accordingly, depending on whether one encounters one's parents as a son or a younger sister or brother as an elder, or one's elder brother and sister as the younger sibling. In spite of not willingly prescribing these attitudes, these attitudes are to be distinguished from each other and should not be confounded. Therefore, on the one hand, you may act from the start in a way prescribed by the family; on the other, it is you who, together with your parents, brothers, and sisters, constitute the family and its relationships. What is more, reciprocal relationships obtain even here. Although the roles of parents, brothers, and sisters are prescribed by the family, the family itself is constituted by parents, brothers, and sisters. Such reciprocal relationships are, from a commonsense standpoint, taken for granted as being obvious. For instance, those without children are never called *parents*. They are parents only in their capacity to actually become "parents of a child." In the same way, "a child" is a child only in that it possesses the capacity of being "a child of its parents." A child without parents is actually unthinkable. We can conceive of a situation where a child has lost its parents. Hence, parents and child are capable of being parents and child only on the ground of the familial relationships established among them. Even were you to gather adults and children at random, they would not, as a result, be actual parents with their children or children with their parents. Thus, the relationship of parent and child is constituted by parents and their children. In a situation in which parents and their children are not opposed to one another, the parent/child relationship cannot be discerned. Here again reciprocal relationships are simultaneously established and cannot be dealt with as temporally sequential.

One cannot act out one's role as child or brother while living in a private boarding house or in a dormitory. You are either a resident, occupying a room under contract, or a boarding student subject to the authority of a supervisor, with definite rules in place. The role of resident in a private boarding house is prescribed by the interest relationship one bears to the owner of the room. Therefore, if you pay for board and lodging and do not disturb the other residents, then you are free to assume whatever attitude you wish toward the owner or other residents. In this case, attitudes are not prescribed by specific roles, as in a family. Rather, you are completely free to come and go in the house or to stay in your room as you like. Because these responsibilities are voluntarily constructed through a contract, they lack lasting significance to the extent that they can be discarded whenever you please. But if you were to enter this house at your pleasure, without possessing this contractual right to do so, then you commit a crime. It is obvious that these rights are prescribed by the relationship you bear to the owner. But, on the contrary, this relationship consists of the contractual obligations between the owner and the residents. There is no such relationship where there are no residents. That this relationship is established under a definite contract already clearly indicates it is a relationship that obtains between the partners concerned. What is involved is a human relationship entirely different in kind from family relationships. Still, the reciprocity between the relationship and the members who compose it obtains even here.

In the case where one has the status of boarding student, this human relationship is markedly different from the earlier one. Dormitories prescribe this status because they are bodies originally established in accordance with definite rules for the sake of either those who have the same native place or those who share the same religious faith. Occasionally, such dormitories are established either in accordance with a heritage shared by those belonging to the same clan, not to mention having come from the same native place, or for the purpose of sharing religious practices. What is recognized here are various kinds of communities in which friendly connections are shared by the boarding students. The responsibilities of boarding students are prescribed by these bodies, and these bodies are composed of the students. Here, too, the same reciprocal relationships obtain.

We are able to enumerate various other capacities one may possess, in addition to the one in question. For instance, you may be someone's friend. There is almost no one who does not have a friend. There are a variety of ways to be a friend, such as being an intimate friend, an acquaintance, a childhood friend, a playmate, a comrade, or simply a fellow creature. And granted this variety, there are correspondingly many kinds of fellowship. You carry on your daily life, involved in at least one such fellowship relationship, which is constituted by you in cooperation with your friends. But the capacity to be a friend is prescribed by and exists because of this relationship of mutual reliance. Those who cannot be relied upon or who hate one another are not capable of becoming friends. Such things are recognized by us as a matter of course, and no one would raise doubts about this. Even Descartes was tempted to avoid confronting such doubts by refraining from doubting them in the first place.

We can now confirm an obvious everyday fact, that we always act with a certain capacity and that this capacity is prescribed by something whole, further that this whole is the relationship we construct by means of possessing a certain capacity. Simply speaking, we exist in our daily life in the being in betweenness. Moreover, this being in betweenness is, from the commonsense standpoint, grasped from two angles. The first is that betweenness is constituted "among" individual persons. Thus, we must say that the individual members who compose it existed prior to this betweenness. The second is that the individual members who compose this betweenness are determined by it as its members. From this perspective, we can say that antecedent to there being individual members, the betweenness that determined them existed. These two relationships contradict each other, and yet, such a contradictory relationship is taken for granted as a matter of common sense.

We must now try to come to grips with "betweenness" as a unity of contradictories and from which we must take our departure. This betweenness must be distinguished basically from relations other than human, that is, from relations between object and object or between one item and another. The former is certainly betweenness, but it stands negatively against its members. The structure of betweenness will be clarified, point by point, in the following analysis.

Scholars have devalued common sense time and time again. But the question to be asked here is whether science brings to light this contradictory relationship that practical common sense comprehends, even though in an unreflective fashion. Rather, I think it probable that science has not noticed it for quite a long time. Otherwise, scholars could never have thought it possible to apply to human existence a logic based on the principle of contradiction. Sociology, which has developed since the nineteenth century, seems at first sight to deal with being in the betweenness. But I would question whether the relationship between individuals and society could be probed more deeply than practical common sense is already acquainted with. Nevertheless, we cannot say yes to this question, much as we might regret that answer. Sociology tries to avoid a confrontation with contradictory relationships in its attempt to think in separation from individuals, as though it were possible to deal with "society" alone. This is why the logic of community existence must be reinvestigated. But what is worthy of notice here is that the relationships of communal existence are, as a matter of fact, not to be dealt with by "logic," but by "ethics," whose starting point we recognize in reciprocal relationships.

4 individual moments making up human existence

The everyday standpoint acknowledges that betweenness is constituted as a connection between individual persons. From this standpoint, the being of individual persons is recognized but the question that remains concerns precisely what individual persons are. From a commonsense standpoint, we can say that they have bodies they cover with clothes and that they come and go by their own will. Therefore, persons are said to be determined by their ego consciousness and through their bodies. Psychology and physiology are established on such a basis. The knowledge acquired through these sciences has, in turn, contributed to the reshuffling of common sense. But the question is whether our daily life is actually carried on by individual persons described as we have described them.

To begin with a very simple case, let us first take into consideration the body of an individual human. There is no doubt among us, it seems to me, that the body is an organism of the sort that physiology expounds. This does not mean that physiology has already exhaustively resolved the hidden issues surrounding the human body. Rather, our position is that we need not oppose the attempt to deal with the human body as an object of physiology. This is supported by the fact that, whenever we become sick, we consult a physician. If this is so, then the question to ask is whether in our daily life we actually deal with our body as an object of physiology. Is it true to say, when we meet a friend and exchange greetings, that we take for granted that the greeting of our partner is a movement of our physiological body? Is it true to say, on seeing my friend run toward me while calling my name, that

I pay attention only to such things as the vehement movement of muscle and the vibration of vocal chords? Everyone knows that this is not the case. In the movements of the human body, that is, in its behavior, we catch a glimpse of the expression of an acting subject, rather than the mere object of physiology. Hence, in the way in which a human body exists in daily life, we see not so much a physiological process as expressions of certain practical act-connections. Whether the person whom I asked to help me obtain a job says "yes" or "no" by shaking her head vertically or horizontally is nonsense from a purely physiological standpoint, but it is of great practical significance. Through such practical act-connections, the human body is viewed, as it were, as an individual "person" and not as a mere biological organism.

The strict physiological viewpoint is more readily apparent in a procedure that treats the human body purely as a physiological object. A surgeon treats a patient on the operating table in such a way. Otherwise the operation could not be performed dispassionately. However, for an operation to be undertaken dispassionately, the framework of "the operation" needs to be carefully set up in advance. To plunge a scalpel into a human body is precisely what should be done, even though it is a criminal act in other instances. It should be performed because she who plunges the scalpel into a body is the surgeon, and the one who suffers from this surgeon's knife is the patient. For the purposes of medical treatment, a surgeon must use the scalpel and without hesitation, if it is deemed necessary. She does so because she acts in her capacity as a qualified surgeon. Moreover, the doctor cannot obtain such qualification unless she has undergone a long period of practice, training, and learning beforehand. Even then, the surgeon is not allowed to perform operations whenever she pleases. First of all, she must explain to the patient and to the patient's family members or friends the reasons why the operation is required and she must secure their agreement. Thus, given the agreement of society, or of those who are closely related to the patient, and within a specified period of time, the patient's body is then to be treated as a purely physiological object. What we must keep in mind here is that such treatment is available only at the hands of a surgeon, and all that the patient's family or friends did was to allow treatment to occur. For the family, a "parent" or "child," not a mere body, is undergoing surgery. Indeed, a family member who may observe the operation often falls down in a faint. After the operation, even the physician tries to deal with his patient as a person who is related as a parent or child or whatever.

Therefore, to deal with a human being as a mere physiological object, we must deprive her of various other qualifications in order to construct an abstract framework of understanding. Such abstraction is theoretically very easy, but practically it involves us in many difficulties. From a theoretical standpoint, it is not so difficult to conceive of another person's body merely physiologically and to regard it as an object of corporeal pleasures alone. From a practical standpoint, troublesome facilities are required to be set up.[1] For example, if one has sexual relations with another, without taking advantage of these facilities, the act can never be mere corporeal contact. Even if one person's hand touches another person's hand, it is contact between two persons who possess specific qualities beyond the purely physiological. Facilities within society are set up to function in such a way as to deprive persons of all of their human qualities and isolate sexual intercourse from distinctively human relations. To demand and enter into such constructions is to exhibit one's intention to treat human beings as if they were animals. Such action must be condemned ethically. Within these facilities, however, one is able to abstract from human relationships that which corporeal contact obviously should imply, as well as those obligations and responsibilities that accompany them. Yet, even these facilities cannot operate in the way originally intended, for a mere physical body is itself an artificial abstraction. This abstraction cannot be strictly maintained unless we grant some inhuman compulsion. Thus, even given such an abstraction, people still endeavor to construct some human connections within it, and if they fail to do so, they are likely to die of despair. The committing of a double suicide is itself a practical revolt against the view that human beings are only physical bodies.

If physical bodies already have their own qualities, then it becomes much more difficult to find distinctive individuality in physical bodies alone. Of what does the individuality of physical bodies consist so far as a human body is concerned? So far as physiological bodies are concerned, they can be spoken of as easily as individual trees. But this is not the case with bodies viewed as expressions of the subjective or as persons in their concrete qualities. A mother and her baby can never be conceived of as merely two independent individuals. A baby wishes for its mother's body, and the mother offers her breast to the baby. If they are separated from each other, they look for each other with all the more intensity. Since ancient times in Japan, any attempt to isolate two bodies such as these from each other has been described by the aphorism "to wrench green wood." As is evident, a mother's body and her baby's are somehow connected as though one. To contend that there is no such connection between them, because the link connecting them is not an actual cell is valid for physiological bodies but has nothing to do with subjective bodies. Of course, capacities that inhere in mother or child are also capacities inherent in their bodies. For the child, its mother's body is unique and entirely different from all others; and for the mother, her child's body is also uniquely distinctive. Is it not inevitable to think that this bodily connection is such as to make it impossible to regard these two merely as independent individuals? A mother may go out, leaving her baby at home, but she is all the while attentive to it. Her baby also anticipates its mother's return. This power of attraction, even though not physical attraction alone, is yet a real attraction connecting the two as though one. If it is thinkable that a nucleus, with its electrons circulating around it, constitutes one atom and not just separate individuals, then it is equally permissible to think that a mother's body and her child's are also combined as one. To isolate them as separate individuals, some sort of destruction must occur. That is to say, the connection must be shattered by a power stronger than the connective one. To the extent that this cannot be done, then there is no independence of bodies.

Bodily connections are always visible wherever betweenness prevails, even though the manner of connection may differ. Such connections are readily recognized even among friends, let alone between man and woman, as well as husband and wife. That one wishes to visit a friend implies that she intends to draw near to the friend's body. If she does go to visit a friend who is at some distance by streetcar, then her body moves in the friend's direction, attracted by the power between them that draws them together. If it were previously known that her friend's body was absent (that the friend was away), then this attraction could not possibly operate. That one feels lonely during a vacation because friends are scattered indicates that their bodies are so far away from each other that no contact may be possible. If a relationship between friends allows no possibility for bodily contact, then no phenomena of attraction can be imagined.

With regard to a human body specifically, the incommunicability of bodily sensation is often spoken of. For example, when another person experiences pain we can certainly share in it mentally but cannot actually share the physical pain itself. Indeed, the pain in another person's leg is not my pain. Generally speaking, another person's bodily sensations are exactly what we cannot feel in our own body.

But to conclude that it is out of the question for us to share bodily sensations with others in some sense is a fabrication. For instance, when we stand together, exposed to the scorching heat of the sun, we share the heat. When we are exposed to a cold wind, we can feel the cold together. Therefore, in a life in which we share the same work, we also always share similar bodily sensations. We are far from having even roundabout methods with which to infer another person's bodily sensations from facial expressions alone, to take a single instance (i.e., to analogically infer that it is the same with the other, in comparison with one's own facial expressions, and the bodily sensations they represent). Rather, we assume that we feel the same bodily sensation. Therefore, those who together feel the heat can say simultaneously that it is hot. Or, when one says that it is hot, the other can readily consent without delay.

Were it not for this communicability of sensations, we would be unable to extend even the compliments of the season to another. Difference in bodily sensations can be discerned only on the basis of such communicability and as its determinations. Were this not so and were bodily sensations entirely incommunicable, then how could common words expressing them have emerged? Because we already share pain or heat with one another, we are able to infer, from seeing another person frown, that she is in pain or is experiencing sensations of heat. Apart from this ability to communicate, a facial expression would lose its meaning altogether. Words cannot emerge in a situation where even facial expressions are incommunicable. Therefore, that common words expressing bodily sensations are available to us is already clear proof of this communicability. When another person has pain in her leg, it is true that I do not have the same pain in my leg. I cannot share the actual pain which she has in her leg. However, in the event that both of us are hit on the leg by stones at the same time, we would then share the same pain. The truth is that the incommunicability of pain makes its appearance as a lack of such communicability. But it is not the case that pain is essentially incommunicable. Hence, we ought not to negate the connection between one body and another by appealing to the incommunicability of bodily sensations.

The following objections may be raised: Is it not the case that what I call a connection between one body and another is merely a psychological relation? Is not the attraction between a mother and her child, as well as between friends, psychological rather than physical? To be justified in insisting that there is a connection between one body and another, the existence of the attraction, which is bodily but not psychological, must be demonstrated. However this may be, a human body is a physical solid. The attraction between one physical solid and another is nothing but a physical one. And it is not easy to find this sort of physical attraction between one human body and another. These latter objections seem irrefutable, for attempts to take a human body for a physical solid and to account for a power that sets it into motion as the nonmaterial mind, and then to deal with the relationship between them have for years been the main themes pursued by anthropology. For this anthropological standpoint to be justified, one must, first of all, make sure that a human body *is* a mere physical solid. In reality, this is not so easy as one might suppose. In the previous example, we found a human body transformed into a physical solid on the operating table. To regard a human body as a mere physical solid is nothing but a provisional supposition set up for the sake of medical treatment. Apart from the purpose of concretely curing "a person," this supposition has no validity. Moreover, the reason why the viewing of a human body merely as a material solid has been influential lies in our having become accustomed to thinking of a human body as if it were graspable by merely looking at it, instead of through a variety of practical considerations. A human body, when merely looked at, is nothing but a thing extended in space, like a chair used for sitting. If it is objected that a human body differs in form from a chair, then it would be acceptable to conceive of it as the same as a sculpture or a doll placed side by side with it. After all, is it not the case that human bodies are "material solids" that have the same common form as the latter? The distinction that makes one a living person and the other a doll is recognized only by inference and is, therefore, not something immediately given. This distinctive way of looking at things arises only within a position in which the practical attitude has become completely eliminated and thus is not in accordance with actual everyday reality. When I discover a friend of mine waiting for me beside a bronze statue, the friend is never immediately given merely as a material solid having the same form as the statue. Instead, I discover my friend there, from the beginning. When I shake hands with my friend, it is not that I first touch her hand as a material solid and afterwards come to infer that this material solid is put into motion by my friend's mind. Rather, from the outset, I touch my friend herself. There is no momentary period of time in which a human body is experienced as a mere material solid. (According to Max Scheler, we perceive shame in a blush and pleasure in a laugh. The phrase *first of all, a mere material solid is given*, is entirely false. Only for a physician or an investigator of natural phenomena, that is, only for those who artificially eliminate the phenomena of expressions as primarily given in everyday experience, are such things as purely material solids given.)[2] After I beat another person's body, can I excuse myself by saying that I performed this violence because of my slight dislike of the form of this material solid and that I had no intention of offering an insult to the mind that dwells there? What is more, to speak of the matter in accordance with a merely observing attitude, this observing activity already subjectively involves within itself an element of the human body. It may well be that the agent who looks is a knowing subject. But this subject's looking is an activity performed with her eyes. Therefore, even if someone touches a thing with a finger, for the purpose of observing it, it is, nonetheless, the observer herself who touches it with her finger. This is true even from a merely observational standpoint and even more so from a standpoint of practical action, according to which to say that a subject moves is tantamount to saying that a human body moves. There is no distance between a subject and a human body. Hence, whether considered theoretically or practically, a human body is subjective through and through, so long as it is an element in the activity of a subject.

The viewing of a human body only as a solid material object does not call into question the reality of the subjective human body, although it does focus on the objective one. As a consequence, what is dealt with is nothing more than either a relationship between a subjective ego and an objective human body or a relationship between an objective ego and an objective human body. From ancient times this viewpoint has made it impossible to have a correct understanding of the human body. However, contemporary philosophy requires us to reject this traditional viewpoint, and to return to the facts themselves. (For instance, Scheler insists that, while dealing with the human body as the objective realm of the intentionality of "consciousness of . . . ," it is given independent of and prior to the individual sense organs, sensations, and individual external perceptions, not only as an entirely unified phenomenal fact but also as a subject which finds itself in such and such a specific way (i.e., *Subject eines So-und Andersbefindens*). As a result, the human body lays the foundation of the givenness of the body/soul (*Leibseele*) or *Körperleib*. This "basic foundational phenomenon" is called the *human body* in the strict sense of the term.[3] What is not in accord with the concrete facts of experience is the view that something psychological, accompanied by no bodily events, and a process of the physical body entirely unrelated to bodily experiences subsist in the form of an opposition between body and mind existing independent of each other.[4]

When we are aware of something in our mind, this experience already involves the human body as an element within it. As well, when we put our human body into motion, the movement of mind is already involved as an element in this motion. For instance, let us consider smiling with pleasure. Within the bodily experience of pleasure a human body is already involved as a feeling and moving agent, which produces a smile, which is itself a bodily motion. Hence, this bodily motion is already filled with mind, which jumps with joy. The phrase, a *mind jumps with joy* already indicates the inseparability of mind and body. The grasping of a human body subjectively makes this clear enough. And, from an everyday standpoint, this inseparability is already understood in and through the practical connections involved.

To hold the view that the relationship between one human body and another is a psychological relation, involving an element of bodily experience as well is common enough. To account for this relationship as though it were merely a psychological relationship without giving heed to the relationship between one human body and another is an obvious error. To whatever extent a mental element is involved, human bodies are attracted by and related to each other. These connections are neither merely physical nor merely psychological or physical/psychological. Generally speaking these connections are not objective connections, but subjective ones, which are inherent in human bodies.

Therefore, it is evident that a human body is not, of its own accord, something individually independent. To make it individually independent, we must cut its connections with other human bodies and completely dissociate it from its attraction to others. That is to say, only by destroying or negating the connections between human bodies do we render them capable of being grasped as existing apparently independent of one another. At the same time, this implies the destruction of the capacity for human connections that a human body carries on its back. And this destruction of the capacity is acquired only on the condition that we revolt against the betweenness inherent in existence. A mother can become independent of her child for the first time only when her body revolts against the relationship between parent and child and becomes thereby dissociated from her bodily capacity to be a mother such that her breast swells toward her child. In the same way, husband and wife cut off their bodily connection through divorce, and friends cease to attract each other after a quarrel. The destruction of betweenness results in the birth of opposing bodily tendencies such as dislike, avoidance, and repulsion.

However, human bodies become independent of each other only relatively, yet this does not mean that they become absolutely independent individuals. Hence, for the sake of acquiring individual independence as a body, the revolt against all sorts of betweenness and the destruction of all sorts of capacities is required. You must dissociate yourself even from the capacity as a man of being attracted to a woman. From this extreme vantage point, two examples may be imagined. The first is that of a human body transformed into a mere material solid object which is no longer a person. A human body that is no longer either a parent or a child, not a man or a woman, cannot any longer be "a person." It may certainly be said to be an individual material solid, but this does not exhibit any individuality such as is characteristic of a human being. Individual material solids can never in themselves constitute betweenness. On the other hand, what we are seeking are individual persons who constitute betweenness. Thus, it is to be taken for granted that such persons cannot be found in material solids deprived of their capacity to produce betweenness.

The second example is that a human body that, while carrying on its subjectivity to an extreme, finally dissociates itself from every sort of relational capacity. This body is neither that of a man nor a woman nor is it to be conceived of as a believer belonging to any religious association. A believer possesses one of the capacities prescribed by a betweenness-oriented existence, and hence, a believer's body has a necessary connection with some religious association. Then, is what remains left at the extremity a human body standing before God as one of His creatures? Even she who prays alone in separation from all connection still has her body that kneels and clasps its hands in veneration. But this is precisely a body that is affiliated with God, which is obviously revealed through this prayerful facial expression. Thus, it is not so much an absolutely independent body as an absolutely dependent body. That is to say, in the extremity in which we examine the individual independence of a body, we reach a point at which individual independence necessarily perishes. This is what in Buddhism is described as "the dropping off of body-mind." Even Buddhists who abandon every kind of human privilege in aid of gaining absolute enlightenment and who remain tenaciously engaged with Buddhist truth with a willingness to kill even the founder of Buddhism in order to detach from a connection with all religious association, nonetheless finally end up sitting meditation, which is to a great extent a bodily activity. When they break through this bodily meditation, their body becomes entirely emptied. That is to say, the subjective body terminates in absolute emptiness, when its individuality is carried to the extreme. This is a real feature and characteristic of the individuality of a human body.

At this point a conclusion is reached. Insofar as betweenness is constituted, one human body is connected with another. And insofar as this connection is completely destroyed, then either the human body is a material solid, unable to constitute betweenness, or it terminates in absolute emptiness. To the extent to which we look for a human being's individuality in her body, we have no alternative but to reach this conclusion. Is it possible to look for her individuality in the consciousness of ego?

Modern philosophy took its departure from the consciousness of ego and attained its climax there as well. Even in contemporary philosophy, whether it be phenomenology or fundamental ontology as is expanded by Heidegger, the central question is, in the final analysis, the consciousness of ego. However, it is not easy to consider this issue briefly. Insofar as the question of looking for the individuality in the consciousness of ego is concerned, there is no ambiguity. The reason for this is that by starting from the consciousness of ego, the issue of looking for the individuality of the consciousness of ego does not even arise. I am conscious of myself, therefore I am, but it is not clear whether another ego exists. Only my ego exists with certainty. All other beings are nothing but what is mediated through the thinking activity of this ego. The ego exists as independent from the outset. Whether individual independence is recognizable in the consciousness of ego has no meaning here at all. Rather, the question of greater importance for this discussion concerns how it is possible to know that, in addition to this ego, other egos exist as well. Kant once remarked that it is a shame for philosophy that this question still remains problematic. Even for contemporary philosophy, it is still one of the questions under dispute. (See, for example, Max Scheler, *Wesen und Formen der Sympathie*: "Vom fremden Ich." In this work Scheler considers six meanings involved in this question in some detail, and "the evidence of Thou" is expounded as the key to a solution to this problem. Volkelt, to whom Scheler refers, agrees with this view. They agree in that they reach the same conclusion, but they are divided in their method.)

However, we took our departure from the fact that everyday reality consists of practical connections between one human being and another. There is no doubt about these connections, for they are immediately evident to us. We must ask who are these individuals who constitute this kind of betweenness and whether their individuality is already recognized in the consciousness of ego. This problem is not easy for modern philosophy to resolve, but for us it is immediately evident. The independence of the ego, about which there is no doubt for modern philosophy, must be called into question from the outset, given our standpoint. Thus, the ways of handling this question are precisely the converse of each other. This difference results because, although the one way is concerned only with the relationships between human being and nature, without heeding the relationships between one human being and another, the other begins with human relationships. In other words, whereas the former confines itself to the standpoint of contemplating objects alone, the latter proceeds by investigating subjective practices.

Consider what the phrase *I am conscious of* implies for our everyday practical relationships. As Descartes points out, the *cogito* implies that I perform such acts as seeing, perceiving, imagining, doubting, having an insight into something, affirming, negating, wanting or not wanting, loving, hating, and so on. It is not that what is called *I* exists in separation from these acts, and then performs them. I am I through becoming conscious of something. Consciousness of "I" cannot be isolated from its "objects of consciousness." There is no activity of seeing apart from seeing something, and there is no activity of loving apart from loving something. Therefore, strictly speaking, we must describe the intentionality of consciousness as "I am conscious of *something.*" However, in our daily lives we look at, doubt, or love a *Thou.* That is to say, "I become conscious of *Thou.*" My seeing *Thou* is already determined by your seeing me, and the activity of my loving *Thou* is already determined by your loving me. Hence, my becoming conscious of *Thou* is inextricably interconnected with your becoming conscious of me. This interconnection we have called *betweenness* is quite distinct from the intentionality of consciousness. Activity inherent in the consciousness of "I" is never determined by this "I" alone but is also determined by others. It is not merely a reciprocal activity in that oneway conscious activities are performed one after another but, rather, that either one of them is at once determined by both sides; that is, by itself and by the other. Hence, so far as betweenness-oriented existences are concerned, each consciousness interpenetrates the other. When *Thou* gets angry, my consciousness may be entirely colored by Thou's expressed anger, and when I feel sorrow, Thou's consciousness is influenced by I's sorrow. It can never be argued that the consciousness of such a self is independent.

The dictum that "I am conscious of *Thou*" is a simplified formulation of the consciousness of betweenness. Moreover, the interpenetration of consciousnesses, however different in degree, cannot be got rid of, for it ranges from the most intimate *I/Thou* relationship to a temporary one such as is constituted by passengers on the same streetcar. That there are many passengers on the streetcar determines the consciousness of *I*. Even in the case in which the consciousness of *I* is never directed to other persons, that is, a mode of consciousness in which one finds oneself together with other persons and, yet, has no relationship with them, is nonetheless already codetermined by them. Here we have a manner of consciousness totally different from that in which we find ourselves with persons with whom we are well acquainted. We certainly recognize this difference, however vague the consciousness involved may be. Because of this, the passengers in the streetcar posses a definite attitude toward each other as passengers, and the society formed within it assumes a specific character as such.

The interpenetration of the consciousnesses of self and other is conspicuously recognizable in emotion. (A book that deals with this issue in detail is Scheler's *Wesen und Formen der Sympathie*, vol. 2.) We share the same emotions as others in situations in which the relationship between oneself and the other is quite intimate and in which a sense of community is to a considerable extent realized. For parents who have a child, concern for their child is shared by both. Therefore, were they to lose their child, their grief would be a common grief. They would feel the same grief at the same time. Father and mother know from the start that they are lamenting the same lament, without having to pay attention to each other's experiences. We could enumerate other examples in which disciples have lost their admired teacher or followers have lost a leader to whom they had dedicated their lives. In such cases, the independence of the consciousness of ego is almost completely lost sight of.

What is ordinarily called *sympathy* is not a common emotion as was illustrated previously. It is not that parents who have lost their beloved child are able to sympathize with each other. Instead, true sympathy lies in our ability to feel another person's emotional experiences and to share them. Thus, together with a friend we may lament the death of her child and share her grief. The grief is obviously not the same grief that would be experienced at the death of our own child. Still, it might well be called *grief* nonetheless. Even if I have no reason to lament and find myself in a particularly delightful frame of mind, my consciousness tends to take on a gloomy air overall because I feel my friend's grief. As a consequence, I not only shrink from acting flippantly but even consider it inexcusable for me to find enjoyment, in contrast with my friend who grieves. In this case, my ego consciousness is penetrated by her grief.

Even when intimate relationships, or relationships in which one "feels with" another are not in evidence, nonetheless the interpenetration of consciousnesses still occurs. This is evident in the infectious quality of emotions. For example, one who is seized by melancholia, perhaps due to fatigue, is soon in high spirits once more on entering the company of friends who are engaged in chatting in a silly fashion and on participating in this silly talk for a time. Social gatherings and clubs that developed in Europe were established with the aim of encouraging this infectious quality of the emotions. To escape depression, people attend gatherings and go to various clubs, where they may encounter cheerful faces and listen to funny stories. In such circumstances, no one refers to his or her own pain or grief. Rather, what one does is not to sympathize with others, but to cheer up one another collectively. Moreover, it is recognized that a cheerful mood is regularly occasioned by the interpenetration of one or more consciousnesses. What is called *mass psychology* is frequently carried out by utilizing this infectious quality of the emotions. It sometimes happens that this infectiousness recurs again and again so that the emotions inherent in a crowd of people are extraordinarily heightened. Surely none will assume that the consciousness of ego, which moves in the midst of such emotions, is strictly independent.

The account of the infectiousness of the emotions is found in its extreme form in Scheler, who develops the notion of unified feeling. For Scheler, *I* and another *I* are completely identified. Among the ideal types of unified feeling he expounds is also the interpenetration of consciousnesses, which is not necessarily based on the community of being. Consider, for instance, the pathologically unified feeling that occurs between a hypnotist and the hypnotized person, or the psychology of a child who is absorbed in play or is fascinated by dramatic performances, or a mental state in which someone is charmed by something. Nevertheless, what stands out as an ideal instance of unified feeling is the intense infectiousness of those emotions closely connected to the community of being. To illustrate with a few examples, Scheler refers to the consciousness of identification between oneself and the other prevalent among primitives and recognized in totemism, or *Extasis* as found in the mystic cults of ancient religions, or in sexual intercourse in intimate love affairs, or in that love which terminates in the unity of self and other as found between mother and child, and so forth. These are instances in which the consciousness of ego perishes, so to speak.

To the extent that the consciousness of *I* is grasped as that which intends the other person as its object, then it is not mere intentionality but a betweenness in which the reciprocal penetration of consciousnesses is evident. But the consciousness of *I* also includes an intention of "things" or of "matters of fact" apart from human relations. However, this conscious activity is a oneway intentionality; one not determined by its counterpart. As a result, are we not led to the conclusion that here, only the consciousness of *I* is in evidence?

Even in this case, however, inasmuch as the relationship between self and other persists behind the scenes, the consciousness of ego does not emerge independently. When I see something together with another person, it is not *I* alone who sees the object, I see it together with that person. Therefore, the sense of "feeling with" another is also here instantiated. That consciousness by means of which I feel the beauty of a picture and your consciousness of this picture cannot be said to be entirely independent of each other. We may all "feel" the same beauty. Yet, the differences in people's ways of feeling are likely comparable only because of the existence of this common feeling. An outstanding illustration of a common feeling is the feeling of fright in response to a great earthquake. In this case, our consciousness is not directed toward persons but toward the earthquake itself, and we are all collectively frightened, without having enough time to take into account another person's experiences. Whenever we meet with an unexpected event, our consciousness is clothed in such characteristically communal reactions. For instance, in the event of an electric streetcar emitting fire as the result of an explosion, the passengers who stand up simultaneously feel the same fright. In this event, that they stand up simultaneously is itself an expression of this common feeling.

The same can be said of consciousness becoming conscious of the ego. Fichte, in maintaining that the easiest way to assist people in gaining a clear-cut understanding of the concept of ego, said: "I would like to say to someone the following: think of some object, for instance a wall in front of you, or your desk. There is no doubt that over and above this thinking about some object, you also recognize 'a thinking agent'. This thinking agent is you yourself. In thinking, you immediately become conscious of the activity of thinking."[5] Incidentally, in the case in which the "I" who is teaching and the "Thou" who is taught are together thinking of the wall, then both are also thinking of the ego, which itself is thinking of the wall. Apart from this community of 'I' and 'Thou', Fichte's claim makes no sense at all, and one would be unable to teach another to understand the concept of ego. It can be taught only because the issue of the ego commonly enters into conscious awareness. For this reason, even when we say that we become conscious of the ego, it cannot be a consciousness of the "I" alone, especially at that place where the relationship between self and other is involved.

What is required for us to search for the independent consciousness of the "I" is the positing of the standpoint of the "I" as existing alone, in which there is no one else with whom the "I" shares the same consciousness. This is the case when, while alone, I look at the wall in my study and think of my self that is looking at it. However, in this case if I become conscious of the wall as a wall, then social consciousness has already intervened. What is called a *wall* is that "form" society imprints on clay or sand as a specific tool (that is, as a part of a house). The form does not belong to the consciousness of "I" alone, but rather exhibits a meaning common to all those who are concerned with this tool. Hence, for us to look at the wall as a wall indicates that we are conscious of a meaning that is expressive of this particular thing and indicates that we have already significantly entered the realm of common consciousness. If so, then, to look for that consciousness which exists independently, we must go back to some sort of primitive consciousness in which we do not yet look at the wall as a wall. That is to say, something like the sensation of a stretch of some color must be substituted for the notion of the wall, and an agent possessing this sensation must be posited as equivalent to what is usually called the *ego*, so to speak. In this way, the consciousness of the "I" acquires its independence under the guise of a collection of sensations.

Nonetheless, the results we have just obtained are not in accordance with the facticity of the situation. The consciousness we possess in our daily lives is never a mere collection of sensations. Even when we remain in our study alone, we are still conscious of a wall as a wall, of a desk as a desk, and of a book as a book. It is not that we first possess sensations of color, or tactual sensations, and then proceed to construct a definite thing by bringing them together to form a unity. When looking for a book, we usually already have an eye for a specific book prior to perceiving it; and when looking at a desk, we usually already look at it with the view of writing upon it. This means that from the beginning we must concern ourselves with tools and assume that there is no more primitive consciousness than this concern. The reduction of the perception of objects as tools to sensations is rendered possible only from within a specific psychological standpoint, in an artificial and purposely abstractive fashion.

We can now say that there is great difficulty in grasping the consciousness of "I" as independently individual. As Gabriel Tarde pointed out, even with natural phenomena, it is not that we come to consciousness of them by beginning with sensations. Instead, we perceive natural phenomena as lending themselves to a definite interpretation from the outset. Generally speaking, we directly perceive phenomena as already named by our native language, for instance, *yoake* ("daybreak"), *taiyo* ("the sun"), *seiten* ("fine weather"), *ame* ("rain"), *kaze* ("wind"), *yūgure* ("evening"), *yoru* ("night"), and so on. In the perception of these phenomena, we are already conscious of the communality of identical contents of consciousness. In combination with language, common sense, and those scientific theories prevalent in an age, all play a role, providing a number of prism facets that affect the contents of consciousness. In societies in which sun worship was in vogue, individuals perceived the sun as something divine. For that common sense which is affected by natural science, the sun is perceived as a heavenly body. In either case, the sun is perceived in a specific way from the start, but it is not the case that the same sun is perceived differently as judgment or manners of inference differ. Sun worshippers did not possess the mere sensation of sunlight. Indeed, long before they acquired the capacity of judgment or of inference, even from childhood, people had already been provided with a specific form of social consciousness. This is also true of human desires. Human desires are already characterized by specific social forms. For instance, an appetite makes its appearance as a desire for bread, rice, a meat dish, or seafood specifically, all instances peculiar to the cultural location where this appetite arises. That there are fixed forms of cooking is already proof that an appetite is the appetite of a community, rather than being strictly individual. What is more, were it not for the communal character of appetite, there could be no restaurants, grocery stores, greengrocers, or seafood stores, nor could there be such economic activities as farming, fishing, animal husbandry, and so on. In the same way, the desire for clothing and housing, as well as sexual desire itself, are based on communal consciousness and are socially qualified or modified.

What makes this communal consciousness manifest in a particularly bold form, is the phenomenon of "fashion." Fashion makes its appearance within the modes of clothing, food, and housing already historically and nationally fixed as more detailed common favorites. Even though individuals did not, to begin with, become conscious of a common favorite as their own, nevertheless, they do feel it to be their own favorite to the extent that they are inclined to view deviations from this common favorite as either something funny or ugly. The same is true of spoken language and thought. It is not that words that are "in fashion" cannot express their own unique sort of consciousness, but rather that they are capable of expressing it much better. When an idea comes into vogue, it tends to be regarded as excellent on the ground that it belongs to some majority's way of thinking, and what is opposed to it is condemned as something worthless. No standpoint forsakes the independence of the consciousness of "I" more thoroughly than this one.

Then where should the independence of the consciousness of "I" be looked for? To illustrate with an example, it can be looked for in bodily sensations or in sense feeling. This is where Scheler, who put emphasis on community feeling, looked for independent individual consciousness. It is not that he thought that all bodily feelings leave no room for sympathy. A distinction must be made between sense feeling, which is located in a specific part of the human body, and life feeling.[6] Sense feeling makes its appearance in various kinds of pain or pleasure; for instance, in sensations such as eating food, drinking, touching, the carnal appetites, and so forth. Life feeling is concerned with healthy feeling, or enfeebled feeling resulting from illness, or feelings of vigor or fatigue. Although feeling pain, one may also feel sensations of vigor and strength simultaneously. Similarly, one can feel fatigue, while feeling pleasure. For this reason, these two feeling types constitute spheres that are distinct. What is particularly noteworthy here is that ascendent and descendent tendencies of life as well as health and its deterioration can be felt not only in one's life but also in another's, thereby making the sharing of feelings with others possible. Nevertheless, the pain or pleasure that is felt in a specific place in one's physical body can be neither felt nor directly sympathized with by others. The taste of food and the texture of cloth are entirely peculiar to each individual and leave no room for communally perceived qualities. Commodities corresponding to shared feelings may render possible the connecting of people with each other, but food and clothing specifically must be distributed among them and, hence, may actually separate them from one another. These features are characteristic of bodily feeling.

Were this view tenable, however, then communal eating or fashion could not be understood. Although we may evaluate the same picture together with others, we taste food by dividing it among us.

Its taste depends on each person's peculiar sense of taste. In spite of this, is it true to say that tastes differ from one to another? Do we not enjoy the same sweetness when we taste sugar, dividing it among us? If one person tastes sugar and finds it bitter, we would lose no time in finding her medical care on the assumption that she is sick. We attempt to deal with her as a person who is normally able to taste the same sweetness, although she is temporarily deprived of this ability. Based on the phenomenon that people experience the same taste, "communal eating" has played a socially important role since ancient times. Ranging from sacrificial food in the totemistic period, through banquets in ancient times, as well as the Sacrament in which one takes part in the sharing of Christ's body and blood within Christianity, to the dinner parties so prevalent in the present age, all such activities take advantage of eating as an expression of human interconnection. If it were true that bodily feelings separate people from one another, then such instances could not have occurred. Likewise, a happy family may be associated with such things as dining together or a person's eating at the same mess with others is likely an expression of these people being close friends; these are examples that may well prove that the consciousness of community is based upon a common sense of taste. It is also evident that this sort of community is not based on the communal character of the sense of taste alone. Were it not that the communal character of the sense of taste is an important factor, then it would not have been possible for phenomena such as communal meals to have become such grand-scale social events as they were and are. All that I have said about the communal character of appetite is also true of the cases under consideration. In connection with clothing, the communal character of touch can also be investigated in the same way. And the same can be said with respect to other bodily feelings. I think it correct to say that the economic activities of society are based not so much on the communal quality of mental feelings, as on bodily feelings.

I think it of no use to attempt to find the individuality of consciousness in sensefeelings. Therefore, the only way yet untried is to look within the center of conscious activities, that is, within the personality, which is "the unity of consciousness" or "the point of individuality." It may be that we share with others the sense of taste, the act of seeing, or even the act of thinking. However, the agents involved in these activities are not the same. *I* acts as *I*, and *Thou* acts as *Thou*. Even when all the qualities by which personality is qualified are removed, such as family and friendly relationships, jobs, societal impact, and the requirements of the state, there still remains the *I* that is the agent operating through these acts. This is the deep-rooted point of individuality, which cannot be shared. What illustrates this most clearly is the consciousness of *I* taken as a succession of *nows*. It is only that consciousness originally belonging to *I* that we retain. *I* is not capable of retaining another person's consciousness. For this reason, the unity of retention is entirely individualistic in nature. Even when parents suffer deep grief at the loss of their child, that which renders this experience of grief possible is that which each individual consciousness retains. Unless all the events that occurred in the relationship they bore to their child were retained in the same consciousness in a unified manner, inclusive of her life and possibly her death, then grief could not possibly arise. Behind the various sorts of community must lie the noncommunal unity of individual consciousness.

This assertion is made on the assumption that an act of consciousness consists in a one-directional act of intentionality. Given this, it may well be that the unifying agent of this activity of consciousness is individualistic. What happens, however, if it is true that the conscious acts of an individual are codetermined by another person's acts? What is sought must be a betweenness-oriented retention. In fact, the retention of consciousnesses that interpenetrates into another can and must be communal. For example, suppose that something important is spoken within an intimate relationship between an *I* and a *Thou*. It is never the case that *I*, when listening to a series of spoken words, experiences a mere succession of sounds, that is, a succession of *nows*. Instead, *I* grasps the manner in which an advance on her relationship to *Thou* is made in parallel with what *Thou* speaks. The *koto* of which *Thou* speaks discloses the manner in which *Thou* is concerned with *me*, and at the same time, draws out the manner in which *I* concern myself with *Thou*. Therefore, if words are broken off in the midst of saying something of importance, it is not that *I* hears a mere succession of sounds that are somehow interrupted. Instead, *I* feels a strong tension, that is, an extraordinary continuity of words about to be spoken. Or, if I am impressed by something said and this something is intermingled with the rest of what is spoken, then *I* may pause in my listening at that one thing, even though words continue to flow one after another. The continuity is interrupted. What *I* hear is not a succession of sounds, but the *koto* that expresses the betweenness of *I* and *Thou*. Even though this *koto* is spoken by *Thou* by means of her voice, the *koto* itself is communally retained between *I* and *Thou*.

Only through this communal retention does the betweenness of *I* and *Thou* arise, with its own historical development. A series of spoken words is, in practical reality, primarily an expression of this betweenness and not a mere succession of sounds. For words to be a mere succession of sounds, subjective betweenness must be discarded. Whenever a partner with whom we are intimately related comes to speak to us, there is of necessity an expression of her business or feelings. We cannot listen to a mere succession of sounds without catching hold of the meaning of this expression. If we do not listen to what a partner says because our attention has been arrested by something else, then we do not listen to the succession of sounds either. Let us consider a situation in which we have no intimate concern with anything. For instance, as casual passengers on a train, we happen to hear other passengers talking with one another. Do we hear only a succession of sounds? No, not at all. To the extent that we understand the meaning of their dialogue, we experience bodily the betweenness of others, which may then develop even further. The state of our mind differs depending on whether the dialogue is an expression of good friendship or a quarrel. Were we merely aware of a succession of sounds, such things could not occur. Of course, if the language we happen to overhear is foreign to us—one we cannot understand at all—then only a mere succession of sounds would be heard. This is why the sound of our own language is not as distinct as that of a foreign language. Therefore, when one deals with a series of words as mere successive sounds in an attempt to investigate the consciousness of retention, one is engaging in an experiment to attempt to artificially discard the meaning of the words. We must conclude that what is conceived of as the consciousness of retention is nothing more than an artificial and abstract consciousness.

This is true not only of words, for even when we listen to a melody, we never listen as though to a mere succession of sounds. Instead, we comprehend directly the meaning conveyed by these sounds. To illustrate this with a simpler example, let us consider a fire alarm. It consists of a repetition of three consecutive sounds. But instead of hearing it as a succession of three sounds, we hear it as a fire warning from the outset. And upon hearing it in this way, we immediately stand to open the door and lose no time in getting out of the house. This is so because the fire alarm is a societal expression. Moreover, that it is such an expression rests on the supposition that to retain the succession of these three consecutive sounds is a retention not merely in individual consciousness but also in communal consciousness. Were it not for this communal retention, it could not be established as a kind of expression.

An act of retention may be conceived of as being extremely individualistic, because it is the act that unifies various activities. We so conceive it only because, first of all, we draw out the consciousness of an individual and think of it abstractly. It is not that an act of retention is itself essentially individualistic. The same can be said of a unifying or operating agent of acts. It could also be a communal unifier or operator of communal acts. Only when we deal with it as a unifier of individual acts have we no choice but to conceive of it as individualistic. Hence, although an individual is here presupposed, it is not something revealed here. Whoever insists on the noncommunal character of personality, as Scheler does, while expounding a communal feeling seems to have arrived at the unifier of acts by eliminating every sort of communal character. Yet, Scheler arrived at the concept of an individual only in the sense that the personality as a whole regarded as a spiritual community (such as a church or a nation) is also individualistic. This personality as a whole is a unifying agent inherent in the center of spiritual activities. It performs its activities in the same manner as an individual personality.

In what way do individual personalities participate in the activities of this personality as a whole, and what kinds of activities as a whole are performable, if we exclude from consideration the communal activities of individual personalities? Scheler provides no answer. If we press him for an answer, it would likely be found in the distinction between the social sphere and the secret one that is attributed to individual personalities, as well as to personalities as a whole.[7] If individual personalities are members of the personality as a whole in one way or another, then they are social personalities. They are also secret personalities in their own individuality. The same may be said of the personality as a whole. Insofar as a particular personality as a whole is a member of the greater personality as a whole, it is a social personality. Yet, it is also a secret personality in its solitude. Even if the personality as a whole is itself a secret personality, it is no secret to the member personalities that constitute it. Therefore, an absolutely secret personality can be found only among individual personalities. What is at stake here is the existence of an absolute solitude, or so Scheler thinks. But if personality is described in terms of the unity of acts or as a performer of acts, then where does the distinction between "secret" and "social" come from? The performance of acts as social, is capable of communal characteristics. As a consequence, we are led to conclude that, if attention is paid only to aspects of personality that are attributable to the performer of actions, then the solitude of personality cannot be brought to its extreme. Thus, Scheler insists that absolute solitude is an essentially negative relationship that we cannot eliminate by any means among finite personalities. If so, then personality is individualistic not by reason of its being a center of acts but because it is a negation of all communal characteristics. The essence of individuality lies in the negation of communal characteristics.

Scheler did not possess a complete understanding of the meaning of this negation. But in truth there is no other place at which one can land in one's search for individuality and independence of the consciousness of *I* except that of the negation of this communal character. No matter which aspect of consciousness we may lay hold of, none can be said to be essentially independent. The independent consciousness of *I* is acquired only when isolated from any connection at all with other consciousnesses. Just as we are able to abstractively produce an individual's consciousness of retention by wiping away all elements of betweenness, so our own selfhood is recognizable only at the extreme point where all betweenness is eliminated. What is essentially communal makes its appearance under the guise of noncommunality, which is individuality. Hence, individuality itself does not have an independent existence. Its essence is negation, that is, emptiness.

This becomes evident if we try to conceive of the absolute independence of the individual. In the modern world, philosophers of individualism have pursued the individual reality inherent in individuals to the very end. Where did they arrive by moving in this direction? An individual is regarded as "the unique one." Only the individual is real and the self-existence of the individual is taken as authentic. In Kierkegaard, to illustrate with an example, this "unique one" is rendered capable of being an individual, not out of the human self alone, but only by virtue of the fact that the human self stands before God. It is true that an individual becomes established by being concerned with herself alone, in complete separation from any relationships to others. But this relation of the self to herself arises only within the relationship with God. An individual is said to be isolated only with respect to her relationships with the general public but not with God. God participates in every nook and cranny of the unique one's existence, such that not a single point is independent of Him. If so, we can say that this unique one is not a unique one in the most complete sense of the word. Indeed, the independence of an individual is entirely dissolved in God. This also holds true for the absolute solitude of which Scheler speaks. A secret individual personality is said to be solitary only in the face of God. It is solid only in its relationship with human beings but not with God. The existence of a secret personality is based on God entirely. Incidentally, the idea of the dissolution of individuality also appears in Nietzsche's individualism, which, however, insists on the negation of God. What he describes as "the self" is the will to power as the life of the universe, and his concept of the superman should be regarded as the *terminus ad quem* of humankind's endeavor. Therefore, the self that holds sway over all other persons and subjugates them is, in its true form, a giant self that appears in the entire history of the human world. Conceiving of an individual as the only reality terminates in dissolving individual life and submerging it into the life of the universe.

Further consideration of God or the cosmic self will appear later. What is clearly indicated here is that the pursuit of the absolute independence of the individual terminates, in truth, not with the individual but with the Absolute, where the individual is more than likely to lose its own reality. The dialectical theologians have come to recognize this point most acutely. Therefore, if we wish to make certain of the independence of the individual, then we must separate him or her not only from the worldly community, but also from the Absolute, to speak even more fundamentally. But the Absolute is no longer the Absolute, as standing opposed to the individual. Hence, it is impossible for the individual to be separate from the Absolute. To speak of this in terms of faith, an individual cannot hide anything whatsoever from God. The only possibility of an individual's independence lies in the individual existing in the Absolute and yet in disobeying Him. To borrow terminology peculiar to the dialectical theologians, we can say that we obey God in the form of our disobedience. This indicates that the negation of obedience is also a form of obedience. Thus, the individual cannot get out of the Absolute, however vehemently he or she may rebel against God. It must be that what is not the Absolute is also a manifestation of the Absolute. If this is true, then the independence of the individual is made possible only by not being independent. Here the independence of the individual is pursued only in the direction of negation.

What is meant here is that the independence of the individual is a mode of the deficiency of community. And this view holds true not only of absolute community, such as is established in connection with the Absolute, but also of every community inherent in betweenness-oriented existence. What illustrates this most conspicuously is the phenomenon of "solitariness." We are able to get out of and be separated from human relationships, and thereby to posit ourselves as "solitary," through our own will, through another person's will, or through the force of destiny. This is the negation of community. The negation of being affiliated with a family, or of communal existence, as is described by the terms *friendly, sociable,* and *vocational,* is what makes a human being solitary. However, the problem remains as to whether we can afford to become really independent in such a state of solitariness. Not at all. Solitariness is precisely an independence of no independence. First of all, it can never be that negated being (that is, a family or communal existence) is transformed into something entirely indifferent for solitary persons. She who has lost her family and has become solitary carries on a deficient way of life in just this way. Because of this, the deficiency becomes all the more apparent. For instance, nobody feels more strongly about a child than she who has lost her own child. By disappearing, her child becomes manifest in and through everything else. Not only does all that is left behind point to the child's being but even those things thought to have no connection with the child while alive (for instance, such things as trains, cars, snow, rain, dogs, or horses) and in those things, generally speaking, the child did have interest and that played a significant role in the child's life, now remind her of that beloved child.

If this is true, then, paradoxically, she who has lost her family feels the being of her family most strongly. This also holds true for the solitary person who has abandoned her family voluntarily. By discarding the being of her family, she acquires positive significance for her own being. Her being turns out to be a being that brings a negation into realization. This is the reason why a man's "entering the priesthood by getting out of his own house" holds such great significance. Furthermore, if the supposition is valid that solitariness, as a mode of deficiency, actually manifests that deficiency all the more robustly, then it becomes immediately evident why "solitariness" possesses the same meaning as "loneliness." Loneliness is a feeling of deficiency. Hence, a strong appetite arises for something that is lacking. In the case of entering the priesthood, he who abandons the being of his family is driven by his appetite to appease this lack by appealing to some greater authority and finally to God. If this is so, then the phenomenon of solitariness exhibits not so much that individual independence essentially inherent in an individual as its very opposite. As a mode of being deficient in community, it rather shows that a human being does not desire an isolated and independent existence.

Hegel provides a keen insight into this problem. In an attempt to speak of "love" as the prescription of "family", he draws out a contradictory structure which is, in general, applicable to human community.[8] According to Hegel, love consists, generally speaking, in the consciousness of "the unity of the self and other." A human being (that is to say, we human beings, insofar as we are involved in social ethics-oriented relations) is not merely an isolated and independent *I*, even in her natural and direct state. Only by abandoning independence is it possible for the *I* to obtain the self-awareness of *I*. In other words, *I* becomes aware of itself as *I* only by knowing that it (*I*) is the unity of the self and other. Therefore, the primordial element constitutive of love lies in this, that *I* does not wish to be an independent and unique personality. That is to say, *I* finds itself unsatisfied, and feels that something is lacking in solitude. At the same time, the secondary element constitutive of love lies in the fact that *I* acquires itself in and through the other's personality and the other acquires herself in and through *I*. We can say, therefore, that love consists of the contradiction that the self acquires itself by abandoning itself. In later years, Hegel came to expound this truth by basing on it his arguments on the structure of the family. When younger, he tried to establish his social ethics on this fact. Therefore, for social ethics, *I* can be *I* only by virtue of its not being isolated and independent.

The essential independence of an individual disappears when considered from either side of body or mind. It is obvious that I do not mean by this that an individual actually ceases to exist. What I mean to say is that if we try to grasp an individual in our ordinary life as truly individualistic, it comes to nought. As a result, even though our betweenness-oriented being subsists between one individual and another, we cannot posit this individual as an individualistic being whose existence precedes the already existing betweenness.

By deliberating thus, we are in a position to reject the individualistic view of a human being prevalent in seventeenth and eighteenth century thought. Hobbes expounded on human communal existence from the viewpoint of individualism at about the same time that Descartes lived. Hobbes presupposed the isolated and independent individual that we have sought thus far in vain. He thought that primitive human society or the state of nature consisted purely of individualistically oriented human beings. In the state of nature, people regarded each other as enemies and inevitably waged war against each other. Between person and person only fear held sway. But isolated individuals enter into a "contract" and thereby establish the state for the purpose of escaping this intolerable situation. By means of this contract, the security of life, order, and the law (rights) are constructed. For this reason, the state is only the sum total of atomic individuals, and their connections are nothing more than those deliberately produced by the calculation of personal advantage and disadvantage. Hobbes's view is a typical example of an individualistic view of society. However, where is the absolute individual supposedly to be found? She cannot be found either historically or ethnologically. Thus, we have no choice but to dogmatically imagine an absolute individual based only on the evidence of the ego. Nonetheless, when we take into account practical existence, the evidence of *Thou* is even more fundamental than that of the ego. When we deal with the social existence of a human being, it is a mistake for us to take our departure from the evidence of *I*. Consequently, the supposition of the absolute individual is but an imaginary one, without foundation.

Marx pointed this out most acutely. He made clear that the isolated individual is nothing more than an imagined product, but also that it was worked out in accordance with a definite historical and social situation in mind. According to Marx, the further back one goes in history, the more one discovers that human beings belonged to "a great whole," for instance, to a family, a tribe, or a *polis*. There was no place where isolated persons existed. The same can be said of feudal societies. However, it is not until the emergence of the bourgeois class and free competition had begun to develop in the sixteenth century that the isolated individual first came to be supposed. Thinkers in the eighteenth century, such as Rousseau, tried to conceive this history in a converse fashion. It is the converse of the seemingly factual to think that individuals, who are essentially independent of each other, should construct social relations by means of contracts. Instead, it was out of definite social relationships that there arose the perspective of independent individuality. Therefore, "human beings are social animals (*zōion politikon*) in the literal sense of the word. It is not only that they are social animals, but also that they are animals able to isolate themselves only within a society. It happens rarely that isolated individuals produce something outside of society. For example, production of this kind may occur among civilized persons who happen to be thrown accidentally into an uninhabited region. But even these persons already possess within themselves the force of society as their driving energy. For this reason, to say that a truly isolated individual produces anything at all, is as nonsensical as to say that words develop of themselves, even if there are no partners to live and talk together."[9]

Thus, Marx's criticism is raised primarily from an historical standpoint, and granted this restriction, it is entirely justifiable. The absolute individual has never existed in human history. Therefore, individuals who construct society through contracts or, generally speaking, individuals who precede a betweenness-oriented being are mere fictions. It is acceptable, of course, to think that this view is generally taken for granted.

However, the contention that the absolute independence of an individual does not exist, does not mean that an individual is not independent in any sense. Even though an individual is not individualistic in essence, nonetheless she still stands in opposition to society precisely as an individual. As the negation of communal character, she stands in a negative relationship with the community. Hobbes had clear-cut insight into this. For Hobbes, society and the individual are separate from each other. In accordance with their nature, human beings rebel against communal life. Social aims and individual aims run counter to each other. Hence, coercion is required to ensure that an individual will obey the laws of society. The individual experiences that coercive force which is opposed to and holds sway over her as an individual. Hobbes erred in arguing that isolated persons construct these coercive systems artificially. Still, his insight into the negative relationship between society and the individual as a result of coercion must be held in high esteem. So far as this point is concerned, Marx, who had accused Hobbes of error, was actually mistaken. In the society of which Marx spoke, that is, that Hegel described as "a system of desires," individuals are only cogs in the wheel of a machine and, consequently, have no negative moments such as suffering from the coercive sanctions of society. Individuals, in the materialistic view of history, are mere puppets that inevitably reflect the substantial movements in society. But, is society to be thought of as an organism in which individuals constitute merely its cells?

Gumplowicz's theory of social groups is an elaboration of this problem from a macroscopic standpoint.[10] He rejects the individualistic view of society prevalent in the eighteenth century and attacks the theory of organism in vogue in the nineteenthth century as well. Just as an isolated individual is a fiction, so it is a mere dream to conceive of the "society of humankind" as a single organism. Rather, the truth lies somewhere between. The social world has always persisted only in and through groups. What Gumplowicz describes as a social group is a crowd of people who are connected through various shared communal interests and concerns. At issue here is a conception of community characterized in terms of life, blood relations, vocation, language, religion, custom, common historical destiny, and so forth. For such reasons, even a primitive gathering is a social group; and the proletarian class, full of fighting spirit, is also a social group. These specific social groupings constitute "a society," and there is, in fact, no such abstraction as one single society of humankind that includes these social groupings. Incidentally, a social group is, in this view, an organism in which individuals are regarded as cells constitutive of the group. Gumplowicz says quite frankly that the greatest error committed by individualistic psychology lies in its supposing that it is the individual human being that thinks (*der Mensch denkt*). Because of this error, the ground of thinking was sought within an individual. But the agency that thinks within a human being is not "he" or "she" as an individual but the social group. Not the individual but rather the social group is the thinking, feeling, and tasting subject. All that individuals do is to think and feel as though thoughts and feelings were their own thoughts and feelings, whereas in reality they are the thoughts and feelings accumulated by social groups from ancient times. Hence, an individual's consciousness is a product of the social environment and a reflection of social consciousness. There is no individual independence nor individual freedom. An individual thinks, feels, and acts only in the way prescribed by a social group. For this reason, according to Gumplowicz, morality is a matter of mere necessity but not of obligation. A social group, therefore, implies no use of coercion nor do individuals necessarily rebel against society. Only social groups move in the actual world.

Here we confront a new problem. I think it is justifiable for scholars who try to understand human society to reject taking their departure from "I think" and to look for the origin of individual consciousness within social groups. But, are they justified in wiping out completely the independence of the individual and in wasting no time in expounding, in place of it, the independence of the social group? Do societies that do not stand in opposition to individuals, that is, societies themselves conceived of as thinking and willing subjects, exist prior to individuals, exist in the actual world? Gumplowicz maintains that "groups think" rather than that "a human being thinks." But, what are these groups like that are not "human beings?" Are the communities that we have always confronted in our attempts to locate the independence of the individual actually equivalent to this sort of social group?

5 the element of the whole in a human being

Our attempts to pin down the nature of the individuals who compose betweenness has disclosed that they are, in the final analysis, simply dissolved into community. Is it possible for us to come to grips with something whole that determines individual members composing betweenness just as they are? Can a society or a social group, which serves as that which renders individuals capable of appearing as individuals, be comprehended in its essential features?

No matter how sociologists try to understand a society or a group or how unavailable a definite concept of society may be because its theories are divided into many branches, we cannot deny that something social or related to a group operates actively in the realm of practice. Those engaged in this activity take it as a matter of common sense that a family, a group of friends, a vocational companion, a village, a town, a company, a school, a political party, a state, and so forth are social. Even so, does it follow from this that social relations subsist as something independent of individuals?

Let me take into account *ka-zoku* ("a family") as that society most intimately related to us. As the word *ka* (which means, in Japanese, "a house") indicates, the notion of a family is here expressed in terms of "a house." A house is a definite space, partitioned by a roof and several walls, and divided into a kitchen centering around a cooking range, a sitting room with a table as its center, a bedroom provided with beds, a guest room provided with an alcove in which a picture or calligraphy is hung, and so forth. And in each of these distinctive realms, communal cooking, eating, taking one's rest, or the communal entertainment of guests (that is, the diplomacy of a family) is conducted. Here the "whole" called a *family* makes its appearance. Individual members are also given, within this "whole," their respective roles such as the head of the family, housewife, husband, wife, parent, child and so forth; and the whole of the family is revealed in each of these functions. As with the human body, a hand works as a hand only on the assumption that the whole operates with and, in part, by means of a hand; so it is that a father acts as a father only on the assumption that the whole of a house operates, in part, by means of the father as head of the family. However, in a house, its members are not confined to living things only. According to ancient Japanese custom, every household must have a Buddhist shrine at which one's ancestors are worshipped, and each year on the date of one's parent's death, the family as a whole must observe this event by means of religious abstinence. Even a living parent must behave as a child before the shrine of a dead parent. Therefore, we can no longer say that the head of a house is still the absolute head. Indeed, he cannot decide his family's destiny by his own self-will, for he is also under the control of his ancestors: all that he does is to preserve the "house" he inherited from his ancestors. His obligation is to hand it on to his descendants without having damaged it. We can say that the wholeness of a house is not only more than the sum total of its individual members but also something historical and beyond all of its present members.

The wholeness of a house reveals its nature forcefully when some of its individual members deviate from the path they are obliged to follow as family members. For instance, a father's prodigality or a child's rebellion can plunge the family as a whole into a state of affliction. As a result, the family as a whole concentrates its pressure upon the individual members. It is a force that ties to the whole those members who are trying to disconnect themselves from it. In traditional Japanese society, this kind of force was strong enough to control the members of a family in the name of its ancestors or under the authority of the family name.

Is it possible for us to understand this whole, as something that exists prior to its individual members? There is no doubt that the whole of a house determines its members. Yet, can this whole exist even in separation from its individual members? Certainly not. Even a house as a historical whole becomes extinct, if there are none to inherit it. No house continues to have its existence through its deceased members alone. Only the living maintain the house and worship their ancestors.

They enable the deceased to continue to hold sway over it. Hence, when individual members die or when they are, even if still alive, completely deprived of their qualification to remain members of the house, the entire family perishes. The wholeness of a family does not subsist by itself but rather is dependent on its members.

Consequently, it becomes necessary to conceive of a family as one organism. Although the family as a whole depends on its members, it is not merely the sum total of them but an organic system as well. Here the whole prescribes that each of its members be as they are. Individual members exist only because the whole manifests itself through its parts. Therefore, the family as a whole is to be thought of as an agent that, by manifesting itself in and through its individual members, brings them to unity. Just as Aristotle talked about a similar matter by appealing to the metaphor of the human body, it is the whole that renders individual members capable of living their individuality as they do, at the same time as consisting of these members. But if a family is as we have supposed, then the members of a family are of necessity subject to the whole. Yet it could never be the case that a specific manner of act is compulsorily imposed on its members. A family, as far back as we may go in history, even to a primitive age, involves within itself specific and compulsory kinds of action. Parents somehow know what they ought not to do as parents, children as children, and brother and sister as brother and sister. It is taboo not to do what may or can be expected or required of members of a family. If this taboo is observed, then they are members of the family in good standing. If a parent has sexual relations with his child, then the qualifications required for being a parent, or of the child being the child of a loving parent, are absent. Even in a family in the present, parents and children, husbands and wives have ways of behavior that each must observe. If parents stop behaving as parents, children as children, wives as wives, and husbands as husbands, then the family will be dissolved. Thus, the members of a family do have the possibility of gaining independence from the family. And what is more, even in the event that a family is dissolved in this way, those who were once its members retain the possibility of becoming members of a new family. Members of a family still preserve their individual existence even after they cease to be its members, but the wholeness of a family loses its existence when a family loses its members. This is not the case in relationships between the whole and its parts inherent in an organism.

Thus, we must refrain from conceiving of the wholeness of the family organistically. It is certain that the members of a family are members because they manifest the whole. Yet, the manner of manifesting the whole is entirely different from the manner in which a hand, as part of a body, manifests the whole. Even though a hand is a hand and cannot become other than a hand, in the case of the members of a family, those who have the possibility of becoming something other than a family member, are restricted to specific qualities as family members. For instance, a father has the possibility of being something in addition to a father, such as, an employee, a public official, a merchant, a soldier, a prodigal, a swindler. When he acts in one of these capacities he never acts as a father. Similarly, a mother has the possibility of being a working woman, a daughter, a girlfriend. Yet, only when these persons are determined as fathers or mothers over against their children does the family as a whole make its appearance through these familial characteristics. Therefore, insofar as they are members of a family, they are not allowed to act except in their specific capacities as members of this family. Insofar as a mother is a mother to her children, she is not allowed to behave as the girlfriend of another man. Her way of behaving as a working woman cannot itself be the attitude that she takes toward her children. Thus, the wholeness of the family is a power that actually negates a variety of possibilities attributable to individuals and restricts them to specific behavior. Because of these restrictions, people become members of a family, and the togetherness of its members thereby materializes. It is here that the family-community of human beings is located.

The family-community is a human mode of being, but is not itself something substantial. Even when a family is said to be conceived of as a "whole," it is not that there independently exists "one thing" that is a whole. This is not the case either objectively or even subjectively. A family does not think, want, and feel in the sense in which Gumplowicz claimed that "a social group thinks." The communal consciousness inherent in a family indicates precisely that individual persons are capable of displaying a consciousness not communally acceptable to the other members of a family, yet share with them a consciousness restricted to this family nonetheless. For this reason, the family-community can have a variety of intensities, which differ according to the extent to which its members conform to and, conversely, to the extent to which they rebel against the restrictions of the whole. This variety of intensities materializes in the practical interconnections of actions occurring within a family and hence is likely to be renewed daily. Thus, a family is realized in varying degrees, ranging from an intimate community that is one in body and spirit, to a looser knit community in which members share the same house with bitter enemies. There is no doubt that a family such as this latter one does not operate as one subject.

As was said already, in searching for a whole within the family, which is the society most familiar to us, we come upon those individual elements that constitute it instead. The whole is, then, nothing more than a force that sets restrictions on these individuals. If this claim is valid, then we must conclude that no whole exists in and by itself. However, is this the result of having taken the family as our illustration in the first place? It is often pointed out that a family is not a single unified personality. For us to be able to grasp something whole, we must consider a social body such as is able to act as one personality. The question to ask is whether the whole exists within this social body.

We might take a "company" as another example. A company is a social group that actually conducts trading activities as though a "judicial person." It is a group composed of human beings, but it is conceived of as one judicial subject independent of and in separation from its individual members. Hence, just like a judicial person, a company possesses its own address, expresses its own will, carries on its own business, and has its own rights and obligations. The selfhood of this company is most conspicuously manifest in a "joint stock company." A joint stock company is a social group in which shareholders organizationally combine. But it is possible for them not to step into the place the company occupies. The will of the company is the total will established through the decision of a general meeting of the shareholders and is beyond the will of the shareholders as individuals. Often, a big project that a company launches is beyond the individual shareholders' understanding. The enormous debits and credits of the company are often indicated in figures far from the individual shareholders' concrete experience. Is it not beyond doubt that this "judicial person" is a whole that preserves its existence in itself and independent of the individual members who constitute it?

Be this as it may, a company is a group artificially established and, hence, able to be artificially dissolved. Therefore, its wholeness is none other than what is legally set forth through specific stipulations. In reality, an unlimited partnership is also built on the family bond or lineal relationships. But the essence of the company does not include this bond within itself. The most typical sort of company is the joint stock company. Typically, such companies are "societies established on the basis of a contract." If more than seven investors gather together and draw up various stipulations, offering shares to subscribers, then a company is the result. Or, if shareholders are collected from a wide area, who pay application money for stocks, and then a general meeting of shareholders is called, the end of this meeting coincides with the official establishment of a company. Without a doubt, individuals gather to set up a "judicial person" only under a specific contract. In this example, individuals are those who "invest a specific amount of money." All other qualifications an individual may have are irrelevant here. Therefore, a "shareholder" is not a concrete "person" but the personification of a specific amount of money. The will of a shareholder consists of the right to vote, based on a specific quantity of money having been invested. Therefore, a shareholder is said to be entitled to one vote for each share of stock held. Unless a stipulation is made at the beginning, a holder of 1,000 shares of stocks becomes the possessor of a will 1,000 times stronger than the holder of one share of stock. The total will established through the collective decision of a general meeting of shareholders is a will determined by the number of stocks one holds. A holder whose share of stocks is a majority share is able to make his own will a total one. Such a stock company cannot, however, become a social whole in the true sense of the word. What is called the *general meeting of shareholders*, or its collective decision, is nothing more than a fictitious expression that arises, when one stock is thought of as though it were one individual. The essential feature of a company lies in its not being a group of persons, however, but an accumulation of capital.

An objection may be raised that a company actually carries on its communal enterprise in contradistinction from an individual enterprise. In response to this we must make a distinction between the employees who actually perform the company's business and the shareholders who are involved in the communal enterprise. The phrase *the communal enterprise of shareholders* implies that such persons are mere investors. And those who together constitute a judicial person are those shareholders. In daily business, a director acts as representative of the communal will of the shareholders and operates as the head of the employees. What is more, the phrase *the communal will of shareholders* means only that they demand a definite share of the eventual profit. Hence, most of the various decisions, endeavors, and negotiations that are prerequisite for carrying on business are left for the employees to handle. With this in mind, it is often said that the real power of a company is transmitted into the employees' hands. A company, as a judicial person, is synonymous with the "capital" that places these employees into various activities.

Therefore, we can say that the wholeness of a company is that power which, by abstraction, removes from individual persons all of their human capacities and restricts them to being merely the investors of a specific amount of money. One becomes a member of this company only in one's capacity as investor. Therefore, between one member and another, there is no community of being except with respect to their sharing in the profits in proportion to the amount of money invested. As human beings, they remain entirely separate from one another. We cannot acknowledge this "social group" as being one human whole. This group is created through a relationship in which individuals who wish to earn a profit incorporate their capital as the means of gaining profit. It is a profit-making relationship among individuals. The fiction of a judicial person plays a role only in imparting certainty and continuity to this relationship. This is the same result as obtained in our discussion of the family.

What becomes of the so-called total person? Here we must refrain from dealing with that which common sense allegedly acknowledges as a total person, for common sense knows no such thing. Therefore, we have no alternative but to consider what scholars have understood as the total person. For instance, the total person, or the cooperative person (*Verbandsperson*) of which Scheler speaks,[1] is not the sum total of individuals, any more than it is the result of the reciprocal activities of these individuals. As experienced reality, it is as fundamental as is personality. Such a total person has an independent, intentional consciousness that is different from that of an individual person. However this may be, a total person is not something transcendent of the individual person but rather includes within itself many individual persons as its members. A total person is constituted by the reciprocal experiences of many persons, and these persons, although united into one person, figure as the concrete center of experience or activities of these reciprocal experiences. These activities of a total person are those social activities that find their fulfillment in a possible community.[2] Rule and obedience, commands, promises, praise, sympathy, various kinds of love, and so forth are examples of social activities that make a total person what it is. Hence, the activities of a total person are communal activities inherent in its member and cannot exist apart from them. What is more, these members cannot contain the entire content of experience that the total person has. The latter is always superior to its members in continuity and content, as well as in the realm of activities. Even when members are deprived of their capacity as members, either by reason of death or for some other reason, it does not occasion any transformation in the total person. In addition, individual persons are likely to belong to various other total persons.

The total person is recognizable in a nation, a cultural region, or a church. Hence, it is not a fiction, like the judicial person, but a concrete agent whose reality is likely to be experienced by us. Incidentally, when pursuing the relationship between a total person and individual ones and, hence, the structure of the former in connection with its members, even Scheler himself is led to the conclusion that the wholeness inherent in a total person is difficult to grasp. According to him,[3] the being of a person, as an individual person, is constituted within a person by such individualizing self-activities as self-consciousness, self-respect, self-love, and the inspection of conscience (*Gewissensprüfung*). The being of a person as total person is likewise constituted within a person in and through social activities, as the subject of communal experiences. For this reason, to every finite person belongs both an individual person and a total one. Together, they constitute the two essential and necessary sides of the concrete whole of a person. Within the finite person itself, the individual person and the total one are separated from each other and then are mutually related to each other. Therefore, neither of them alone serves as the basis of the other. If this is true, then, what is "the person" actually like that is supposedly inclusive of them both? The general definition of *person* that Scheler provides in his book runs this way; that it is "the center of activities" or it is "an agent putting activities into practice." In other words, it is a unity looked for on the side of activities that cannot be objectified. These activities are divisible into individualizing activities and social ones, and accordingly, two sorts of activity centers are distinguished. Moreover, Scheler finds this distinction within one person. This is why he says that "to every finite person" there is both an individual person and a total one. We can say that he regards both of these as existing within an individual person. This is clearly seen in his quote on the same issue that "any finite person, whoever it may be, is at once an individual person and a member of the total person."[4] That, within a person, an individual person and a total one are separated from each other reveals that within an individual person is an individual side as well as a side in which the individual person is also a member of the whole. What is disclosed here is not the total person itself, but a characteristic feature of an individual person as a member of the whole. The latter does not differ from what a sociologist speaks of in terms of the social ego. Yet, the wholeness of a total person cannot be grasped here.

If the argument is made that the person is an individual only in the form of an individual person, then the person whose aspects are constituted by the individual person and by the total one cannot immediately be said to be an individual person. Insofar as the person as a total person is regarded as the subject of communal experience, it follows that this subject is a communal subject, but not an individual person. We must conclude that a person is to be dealt with not as "every finite person," (*jede endliche Person*) but as "the person" (*die Person*).[5] The person is a unity conceived of through its activities. This unity is not confined to the individual person. Multidimensional unity consists of its being at once an individual unity and a total one. It unifies the activities to which the term *the person* refers. Scheler did not attain a clear-cut concept of this structure of the person. If one conceives of the person as containing both the individual person and the total one, as Scheler does, then one must draw this conclusion. In expounding the structure of the total person, Scheler himself tacitly recognized this. The total person is a manifestation of the person that is liable to be an individual person, under the guise of this wholeness. Consequently, if we try to grasp the person from the angle of the total person, we must necessarily find many persons as its members, united into one person. That is to say, the person is at once many persons and one person. The total person's wholeness cannot be found except in the unity of many persons. Each of many persons has independence and individuality as the focus of its activities, but these persons come to be unified, even though independent of each other. The significance of this wholeness lies in the negation of this independence of individuals.

Because Scheler did not admit the significance of this "negation of independence," he fell into confusion in expounding the total person as the community of persons. He described the community of persons in terms of the "unity of an independent, spiritual, individualistic individual persons in the independent, spiritual, individualistic total person."[6] By means of this description, even though putting emphasis on the independence of the total person as well as of the individual person, he nevertheless tried to exhibit their relationship. Now, because many independent individual persons constitute the "unity" within the total person, there is no possibility that this unity is something different from the total person. Moreover, insofar as many individual persons are united into one, they must thereby lose their independence. In spite of this, Scheler fails to notice this negation of independence and tries to insist on the relationship of the independent individual person to the total person. As a result, an independent individual person and an independent total person are understood as being in opposition, and the problem concerning the unity of individual persons is left unnoticed. What is further left unnoticed is the structure of solidarity inherent in the community of persons. What interests Scheler is not so much that which centers around the solidarity among individual persons, as the relation between the individual person and the total person. Even though the latter two (the individual and total persons) respectively bear their own self-responsibility, the individual person assumes the communal responsibility for the total person and the latter for its members. The individual person bears communal responsibility for other individual persons, because they are all included in the total person and thus already assume the communal responsibility for the total person. In other words, Scheler assumes that the unity among individual persons is established through the medium of the total person. But what in the world is the total person like, if not the unity among individual persons. He himself does not admit that a total person does not include within itself its member persons. Rather, the total person consists in the unity of many persons. Thus, the self-responsibility of the total person should have been, from the outset, the communal responsibility of many persons. It is idle, then, to speak of the communal responsibility assumed to exist between individual persons and the total one. When the total person takes on the responsibility, then its members already take part in it. Is it not nonsense to insist that the total person assumes communal responsibility for its members?

In all of this, Scheler is overwhelmed by the presupposition that the total person is an independent and individualistic personality. On the other hand, he cannot deny that the total person includes within itself its members. A glimpse of inconsistency appears here. He insists, on the one hand, that the responsibility-assuming relationship between individual persons and the total person establishes the community of persons, and on the other, he describes this community of persons in terms of the total person. How is it possible to think that the total person, as opposed to individual persons, can itself be a total person that includes the relation of these two (that is, the relationship between individual persons and the total person)? I believe that this possibility comes into view because they bear to each other the relationship of being different and at the same time being the same. And what is more, Scheler does not recognize this interfusion of difference and sameness.

Scheler's view of the total person will reveal its authentic features of its own accord, if we understand that it is, in the final analysis, based on "the infinite and perfect spiritual person";[7] that is, a personal God, or the person of God. For Scheler, God is the person of persons (*Person der Personen*). The essential community among individual persons is entirely based on the community between these individual persons and God.[8] For this reason, any relationship between one person and another is mediated through God as the infinite person. For example, a human being's love is based on the love directed toward God, and the latter consists of the fact that finite persons share in the love of God, who is regarded as the infinite person.[9] Every person bears supreme value only when illuminated by the idea of this infinite person. On this point, even the total person is no exception. The distinction between an individual person and a total one is made on behalf of a finite person. But a finite person acquires its personality thanks to the infinite person, and hence the total person that inheres in finite persons is subject to the idea of the infinite person. If so, then, no matter how much the total person may include within itself its members, and no matter how much it may be the "unity" of these many persons, it is one personality to the very end and cannot simply be the negation of individual independence, insofar as it stands under the idea of "the person of persons."

Thus, we must inquire whether the "infinite," as the ground of the total person, should really be thought of as "the person of persons." To the extent that "the infinite" is regarded as something personal, then no matter how great one's conception of this wholeness may be, there is no alternative for it other than to be an individualistic and independent person. In fact, Scheler's concept of the total person is a wholeness that is never completed, to speak essentially.[10] Any total person is likely to be a member of a greater total person. And however far we may expand this, the result is still an individualistic and independent person as a finite person. However, the infinite person who yields a wholeness capable of being a person is not what was discovered by philosophy. Even in Scheler, it is not the business of philosophy to actually posit the idea of God. Rather, the business of positing it is achieved by a concrete person in direct communication with that which is worthy of this idea (that is, a personal God). Hence, the reality of God is based only on the positive revelation of God to the concrete person.[11] All that philosophy has done thus far is to take this God of religion as a philosophical idea. If this is so, then what happens if revelation discloses not a personal Absolute, but rather the Absolute who cannot be qualified as personal? I think that philosophers are entitled to this idea of the Absolute. Or, if it can be said that to make one's choice among established religions allows philosophy to become narrow-minded, then

I think it necessary, generally speaking, for philosophers to resist taking for granted that the Absolute is based on established religions and instead must come to grips with the idea of the Absolute from the vantage point of philosophy itself. By inquiring into the wholeness of a human being, we are able to search after the ground of this idea from within the structure of this wholeness itself. I am convinced that it is not necessary to describe this ground in terms of the total person by having recourse to the idea of a personal God. The issue of whether the wholeness is a person or not must be decided on the basis of the structure of this wholeness itself. The most important thing is to investigate in what way the many individual persons actually constitute the whole. The only way to solve this problem is to be found in the negation of the independence of the individual person.

In the preceding chapter, I attempted to clarify that the independence of an individual person is quite difficult to grasp. The problem of what the essence of "personality" is must be investigated in detail later on. In connection with Scheler's concept of an individual person, I would now like to consider both the individual center of activity and the individual practical subject in particular as individual persons. To negate the independence of the individual person does not merely mean that it perishes. It also means that something which is independent is, at the same time, not independent and hence that something discriminate (that is, different) turns out to be not discriminate (that is, the same as well). If one focuses on discrimination, then there is no community and hence the whole cannot be spoken of here. On the other hand, if nondiscriminateness is considered by itself, then there is no room for speaking of "being together" and hence the whole with its content cannot be found here either. Community consists in different things becoming the same, and the whole consists of difference becoming the same. The one whole, as the community of persons, must be that which results from many individual persons surpassing their individuality and manifesting nondiscriminateness. The wholeness in this whole is the sublation (*aufheben*) of discrimination and the realization of nondiscriminateness. In accordance with the various possible intensities of this realization, the community of persons can also be found in a variety of intensities. The "church" itself realizes itself in a variety of intensities, ranging from the well-organized community such as in primitive Christianity to the conventional church, which is often nothing more than a social club. Yet, to the extent that it brings to light the nondiscriminateness in God, it is still appropriate to call it a *church*.

If this wholeness is the negation of discrimination, then "absolute wholeness," which transcends the finite and relative whole, is the absolute negation of discrimination. Because of its being absolute, it must be that nondiscriminateness which negates the distinction between discriminateness and nondiscriminateness. Hence, absolute wholeness is absolute negation and absolute emptiness. The infinite that lies behind all of the kinds of finite wholeness must be absolute emptiness. Conversely, the unity of difference and sameness that appears in all finite wholeness stands only on the basis of this absolute emptiness. Therefore, every community of human beings, that is, the whole in human beings, can become manifest only to the extent that emptiness is realized among individual human beings.

These results show that the ultimate feature of every kind of wholeness in human beings is "emptiness" and, hence, that the whole does not subsist in itself but appears only in the form of the restriction or negation of the individual. To speak candidly, something whole that precedes individuals and prescribes them as such, namely, such a thing as "the great whole," does not really exist. It is not justifiable for us to insist on the existence of a social group's independence. In an attempt to come to grips with something whole, we are led to confront individual persons who are destined to be restricted and negated, contrary to our intention.

6 the negative structure of a human being

In our previous attempts to come to grips with individual persons who constitute betweenness, we came to realize that they are, in the final analysis, dissolved within a community. Individual persons do not subsist in themselves. On the other hand, we have now come to realize that in our attempts to come to grips with something communal, that is, the whole, what we have encountered is simply the negation of the alleged independence of individuals. The whole itself also cannot subsist in itself. Moreover, when it is said that the whole arises in the negation of the independence of individuals, there is already a recognition of the independence of individuals who are thus negated and restricted. Hence, we must say that individual persons subsist in their relationship with wholeness. Likewise, when it is said that the independence of individuals is established through the negation of community, there is already recognized that wholeness thus negated and rebelled against. Hence, the whole must be regarded as subsisting in its relationship with the independence of individuals. If this is so, then both individuals and the whole subsist not in themselves, but only in the relationship of each with the other.

The relationship with the other that is now under consideration is a negative relationship in both cases. The essential feature characteristic of the independence of an individual lies in its rebelling against the whole, and the essential feature characteristic of the wholeness of the whole lies in its negating the independence of an individual. Hence, an individual is one whose individuality should be negated for the sake of the whole that is to be established, and the whole is that ground against which an individual rebels to establish itself. That the one exists in relation to the other means that it exists by negating the other and by being negated by it as well.

What I have described as a human being's existence as betweenness is that which renders individuals and societies capable of occurring in their reciprocal negations. Therefore, for human beings, we cannot first presuppose individuals, and then explain the establishment of social relationships among them. Nor can we presuppose society and from there explain the occurrence of individuals. Neither the one nor the other has "precedence." As soon as we find one, it already negates the other and thus stands as that which itself has suffered from the negation of the other. For this reason, it is correct to hold that what is here called *precedence* is meant only as negation. However, this negation is always present in the establishment of individuals and society and hence is not to be found separate from them. In other words, this negation itself makes its appearance in the form of individuals and society. Insofar as individuals and society are already established, then society consists of the relations among the individuals constituting it, and individuals are individuals only within society. The view that society is to be regarded as a collection of reciprocal activities or human relationships as well as the view that it is a subjective group existing beyond individuals must be judged to have at least caught a glimpse of a human being's existence as betweenness. With the reservation that such views fall just short of a fundamental grasp of human existence as betweenness, they are all acceptable. Fundamentally speaking, these views arise without exception in negation. Therefore, the reciprocal activities of human beings and the subjective group each reveals its authentic nature only in negation.

On the basis of the preceding two chapters, we can now claim to have reached the negative structure of the human being's existence as betweenness. We must now take the further step and investigate this structure in detail. For this purpose, I think it necessary to pursue the mediation of expressions again. Betweenness as a social fact must be taken into account there as well.

Betweenness, when expressed objectively as a social fact, is the theme sociologists have been dealing with for a long time. A well-known scholar who put emphasis on society as just this "betweenness" was Tarde. In contradistinction to the world of physics, whose primary law consists of the regularity of periodical and oscillatory motions, and biology, whose law consists of heredity, Tarde explored the social world

whose law consists of "imitation." He says that the essential characteristic of society is imitation and that a social group is a gathering of beings who have relationships imitating each other both directly and
indirectly.[1] It is obvious that the society of which he speaks is an "object," just as nature is an object. The difference is that, although the laws
of nature do not depend on the laws of society, the latter do depend
on the former and the imitation under consideration is a psychological
phenomenon; that is, consists of the reciprocal relations of individual
consciousnesses. These relations are not, however, dealt with within
individualistic psychology. Therefore, investigation must be carried on
not about intracerebral (*intra-cerebrale*) psychology but about
intercerebral (*inter-cerebrale*) psychology; that is, the study of conscious
relations existing among multiple individuals.[2] This investigation must
take its departure not from the consciousness of the individual ego but
from the relationships between one subject and another; that is, from
the evidence that consists of the "consciousness of consciousnesses."
This is the study of sociology.

Society is not a substance independent of individual consciousnesses but consists of those psychological relationships between one
individual consciousness and another; namely, as imitation. Just as psychology deals with individual consciousness in an objective manner,
so sociology attempts to deal with imitative relationships in the same
manner. Tarde reduces these relationships to that which holds between
two individuals only, specifically between adults and youngsters. A
youngster learns to speak, think, and behave just as an adult speaks,
thinks, and behaves. Even though this adult has lived a communal life
for a long time and that her activities of speaking, thinking, and behaving have already arisen in and through imitation, this youngster directly models himself after this adult individual but not after the social
group that is independent of this individual. Therefore, the youngster's
imitation is occasioned through the individual adult close to him, and
through such imitation, he, first of all, enters into the society of adults.
Prior to that, a youngster is a living being to be sure but is not yet an
individual within a society. This is also what the adult herself has experienced. The words she teaches this youngster are what she has
learned by imitating an adult. In tracing this string of imitation, we
eventually terminate the series with the persons who originally invented
these words. This is what Tarde speaks of as "the radiation of imitation from the originator." A youngster undergoes this radiation of imitation through an adult. Hence, this adult plays the role of originator
for this youngster. The adult herself is, however, nothing more than a

transmitter of the radiation of imitation. She is a representative of the radiation of imitation, that is, of society. That a youngster can become an individual by imitating another individual, means that society has created an individual. A human being becomes individualistic at the same time that one becomes social.

Tarde takes this relation for granted as a basic fact of a large society. Social life consists of the intersection of an infinite number of radiations of imitation. Just as people in ancient society were puppets handled by prophets, demagogues, their ancestors, and so forth, so it is that even in democratic societies such as are prevalent in the modern world, people nevertheless move under the control of the radiation of imitation initiated through inventors, originators, reformers, and so forth. The only thing to be noted here is that the tendency to imitate is much more heightened in the modern world than in ancient times, because the progress of civilization now consists in rendering the speed-up of reciprocal imitation much easier. People remain rather unaware of such imitation under such circumstances.

This excellent observation of Tarde shows us a side of social facticity in a very clear-cut way. But another important fact is intimately connected with this facticity to which he tries to close his eyes. He insists that a youngster becomes an individual within a society simultaneously with his beginning to imitate. But the question to ask is, in what way does the individuality of an individual result from this imitation? If it is true, as Tarde assumes, that the consciousness of an individual is constituted by imitation, then the reason why this consciousness becomes independent as the consciousness of an "individual," is quite beyond our comprehension. If it is supposed that a youngster speaks, thinks and behaves just as an adult does, then he is, as Tarde argues, "a puppet handled" by an adult, but not certainly a youngster who differs significantly from this adult. If this is true, then we cannot even speak of the relationship between the consciousness of an adult and that of a youngster. Imitation is the communalization of consciousnesses, but not the cause of their individualization. So when Tarde says "a youngster becomes an individual within a society simultaneously with his beginning to imitate," he already presupposes an individual prior to this imitation, that is, prior to a society, and thereby insists that this individual enters society simultaneously with his imitation. Such an individual is, in Tarde's opinion, a biological one that already possesses an innate tendency toward imitation. Hence, in the background of an individual's existence within society lies the biological world. Then, the individuality of an individual is derived only from this biological world, and a society is none other than the communalization of consciousnesses. If so, then the relationship between a youngster prior to imitation and his mother, is not yet a social relationship. Moreover, those pedagogical relationships in which an adult compels, scolds, and disciplines a youngster must be excluded from the so-called social facts as well. For, if the consciousness of a youngster is nothing more than an accumulation of his imitations of adults, then there is no room for negating these imitations and compelling him to adopt another definite way of thinking and behaving. I suspect that this view perverts the truth to a considerable extent.

It can be said that this one-sidedness is generally recognized among sociologists who try to grasp society as betweenness. This is the case with George Simmel. Against Tarde's attempt to reduce all conscious relationships among individuals to imitation, Simmel tried to make it clear that such reciprocal psychological activities make their appearance not only in the phenomena of imitation, but also in such forms of relationship as superior/inferior relationships of obedience, competition, division, the formation of political parties, and so forth. In contradistinction to Tarde's conception of sociology as psychology, which deals with the relationships between consciousnesses, Simmel insisted that "the psychological phenomena" of reciprocal activity should be dealt with, not in a psychological fashion, but in a sociological one. Simmel held that one should derive reciprocal activities or relationships of individuals from their psychological nucleus and consider only the forms of relationships or the types of reciprocal activity. A wider vision appears here than Tarde showed, and the independence of sociology seems to be thereby secured. Nonetheless, there is no difference between Tarde and Simmel as to the point that the forms of reciprocal activities here under consideration are the forms of connection between atomic individuals.[3] This assumes that society consists only in setting up relationships but not in compelling them, and therefore no negative relationships between society and individuals are recognized.

According to Simmel, "society consists of many individuals engaged in reciprocal activities." This is an image of society that "shuns a conflict of definitions as much as possible."[4] In the light of this conception of society, it is evident in Simmel that individuals exist prior to reciprocal activities. In conformity with such impulses as love, faith, social intercourse, and so forth and with such purposeful activities as impulse, defense, offense, play and interest, and so on, individuals join together, behave well to each other, and thereby build relationships.

That is to say, out of many individuals there results one "unity," that is, "society," through reciprocal activity. Therefore, for Simmel, society is social connection (*Vergesellschaftung*). By abstracting the substantial nuclei from social connection, which are referred to as an individual's impulses, interests, purposes, tendencies, and psychological states, he tries to consider only the forms of social connection. They are the forms that bring an isolated existence of atomic individuals to their communal and reciprocal being. By virtue of these forms an actual society comes to be what it is. An actual society is related to the forms, in the same way that a wooden ball is related to the geometrical form of a sphere.

However, in what way are atomic individuals brought together to form communal being? Simmel points out that social connections take various shapes in accordance with the manner and extent of their reciprocal activities. These social connections are distinguished by degree, ranging from the connections one might happen to have with others while taking a walk, up to the various familial connections, or from a temporal social connection such as when we put up at a hotel, to the more intimate connections such as occurred in guilds during the Middle Ages.

Incidentally, I would like to ask whether the manner of connection of reciprocal activities limits individuals' acts to a definite, specified sort. In the connections that occur, when we walk together, for example, we are advised not to behave in too friendly a way to each other; that is, we ought not to assume the same attitude toward mere walking companions as to our friends. Instead, we must confine our mutual participation to the limited realm of the present. Were this confinement shattered, then we could not take a walk together. This is much more the case in intimate connections such as those within a family or a guild, where manners are subject to stricter limitations. However this may be, Simmel speaks of reciprocal activities apart from such limitations and compulsions. Are these reciprocal activities capable of bringing into unity individuals whose impulses are significantly different from each other?

This question concerned Simmel, not as an issue of sociology but rather of social philosophy. The business of sociology is to discover the forms of relationship prevalent in an established society. The question, "how is society possible?" belongs to the theory of knowledge as applied to society, just as Kant's question, "how is nature possible?" has to do with the theory of knowledge.[5] Just as Kant pursued those a priori conditions through which nature is established, so Simmel looked for the a priori conditions that make it possible for society to arise. The forms of subjectivity such as the forms of intuition and the concepts of understanding in Kant correspond to the forms of reciprocal activities in Simmel, which are what render one individual capable of relating with another. The difference between these two philosophers lies in this: whereas for Kant, substantial contents consist of sense data; in Simmel, they consist of individual elements. Hence, the forms Kant identifies abide not in substantial contents but rather in subjectivity itself. On the other hand, the forms Simmel identifies abide within an individual's mind, which is regarded as something substantial. Those mental processes that exist a priori within an individual are the conditions that render society possible.

If Simmel's argument is tenable, then it follows that each individual possesses within herself such social forms as are to be realized in reciprocal activities; that is, the forms of communalization and unification. Yet, how can it be claimed that these individuals exist in an isolated fashion? Only on the condition that we negate the forms of communalization that we have a priori within us can we assume that individuals exist in an isolated fashion. Consequently, for Simmel, the isolated existence of individuals is a presupposition to be acknowledged from the start. He says that "everyone possesses within herself a deep-rooted point of individuality, and is seemingly unable to learn from others whose point of individuality is qualitatively different from hers."[6] According to Simmel, the forms of communalization cling to those individuals. Therefore, an individual's individuality is based on this point of individuality, and the various social forms are responsible for achieving the universalization of individuals. The reason why an individual, with its unfathomable and unknowable point of individuality, can nevertheless enter into relationships with others, lies in our comprehending its individual mind by universalizing it. We obtain a glimpse of a person not in her individuality but as a universalized type. Thanks to this universalization, other persons are recognized as friends, fellows, or comrades; that is, as dwelling together in the same association.

The reason why social forms are capable of bringing individuals into unity lies in their power of universalization. Within an individual this capability of universalization is a priori. Hence, without negating and restricting individuality, an individual can enter into reciprocal activity by putting into effect this power of universalization. What Simmel conceives of in terms of the "manner" of reciprocal activities is not a "manner" through which acts are specified, but the sorts of reciprocal activities that differ from each other in accordance with the degrees of universalization. These specific differences of universalization are recognized a priori. Moreover, he considers the degrees of universalization in connection with the point of individuality. The point of individuality is not a definite secret realm within an individual being but something that refuses to be universalized as reciprocal activities; that is, it is something that exists outside of society. For this reason, an individual who engages in love or friendship can decrease her point of individuality (i.e., those elements that exist outside of society) almost to zero and universalize almost the entire realm of her being. This is the case with reciprocal activity in which universalization is enlarged to its greatest extent. On the contrary, an economically oriented person, who has been produced by the monetary economic civilization prevalent in the modern world, is likely to be universalized only as a mere cog in the wheel of the economic system and place the other sides of her life outside of society. This is the case with reciprocal activity in which there is minimum universalization. In this way, the degree of universalization determines the manner of reciprocal activity.

Thus, Simmel emphasized the possibility of society, without paying heed to its compulsory characteristics. Is it possible, however, to think of such things as the decrease of the point of individuality and the increase of universalization without also attending to elements of compulsion? The reason why beings involved in love and friendship are communalizable without residue is because the manner of acts inherent in them is strictly determined. Community does not arise where acts that betray trust are performed as one pleases. Because love affairs demand exclusive possession, the point of individuality is decreased. This demand of exclusive possession restricts individuals through strong coercive power. Therefore, the increase of universalization and the strengthening of coercion cannot be separated from one another. What is more, coercion's strength increases the individual's possibility of revolting against such restriction. One hates treachery vehemently because the danger of treachery is all the more increased. If this is true, then an increase in universalization is rendered possible only by one's constant endeavor to destroy the point of individuality. Rather, universalization itself must materialize through this endeavor. We cannot speak of universalization (and hence, of social forms) without having recourse to the negation of the individual.

Tarde and Simmel kept their eyes on society only as unifying, communalizing, and universalizing human beings, without thereby paying heed to the negation, restriction, coercion, and so forth society exercises over individuals. Vierkandt, who advanced Simmel's stand-point a step further, and Wiese, who substituted the concept of relations for that of forms, are basically without difference. It is interesting that Vierkandt opened the way toward the utilization of the idea of wholeness and regarded society as consisting of not only the mere forms of reciprocal activities but also as an agent carrying on these reciprocal activities.[7] But Vierkandt's position results in an individual thereby becoming a mere means through which society manifests itself, and the coercion of society against individuals thereby loses its hold to a considerable extent.

It is worth noting that Wiese described the themes of sociology as "the relationship between one human being and another one" (*der Mensch-Mensch-Zusammenhang*) and as "the sphere of betweenness which pierces a human life."[8] In addition, he attempted to comprehend the concept of "social process"; that is, "the acts that connect people with, or separate them from one another." In particular, he argued that attention should be paid to the process; that is, the flux characteristic of human acts. Wiese referred to the temporal state in which human beings are connected or separated through acts by means of social relations and described the building up of social configurations (*das soziale Gebilde*) beyond these social relations as social process. Therefore, social configurations such as the church, the state, the economy, and class possess flowing social relationships as their composite elements and are never something substantial. Hence, individuals are involved in nets of reciprocal relationships and suffer constant change. Moreover, it is not the case that society, which determines individuals in this way, is an unmoved whole. As is the case with individuals, society also "is becoming and becomes in being" (*ist im Werden, wird im Sein*). In this sense, neither an individual nor society is something fixed. Instead, they determine each other, while undergoing transformation.

Therefore, Wiese dissolved society into the flux of human acts and tried to regard society as the "represented total contents" of these reciprocal relationships between individuals and society, when these contents are regarded as one "conceptual unity." However, when he conceives of human acts in this way, he fails to pay attention to the fact that they are confined to specific forms. The reason why social process brings forth a specific social configuration lies in this, that the acts of connection and separation are determined and controlled in a specified direction. Without keeping this point in mind, he expounds the reciprocal determination of individuals and society. Therefore, the individuals with whom he deals, are individuals spotlighted only by their dissolution in society. He writes, "the personal ego (*das persönliche Ich*) is not what we pursue in our sociology as an authentic object of research. Instead, we deal with the social ego (*das soziale Ich*), which interpenetrates various human relationships and owes its character as ego to social configurations. The human products of these configurations are intimately connected with the personal. But the task is not to clarify this totality of a human being (*die Totalitat des Menschen*), but to take pains to analyze the social aspects of this mixture."[9] That is to say, Wiese's task was to consider the notion of society by excluding those aspects in which there were elements of coercion. But by doing so, we must ask whether it is possible to understand "the practical communal life of human beings."[10]

Durkheim strongly emphasized the element of "coercion," in contradistinction to the aforesaid one-sidedness. According to him, the viewpoint that tries to deal with society as reciprocal mental activities or as mental relationships tends to conceive of individual consciousness as dissolved in society. On the other hand, Durkheim emphasized that society stands as the other to individual consciousness. This is what his fundamental proposition of urging us to deal with social facts as "things" (*Règle fundamentale: Traiter les faits sociaux comme des choses*) must signify. Moreover, as the other, society coerces individuals to perform specific sorts of actions. Apart from this, the significance of society cannot be adequately comprehended.

Durkheim discovered this position in the existing characterization of social facts.[11] Just at the place where Tarde found the relation of imitation, Durkheim found that of coercion. According to the former, a youngster imitates an adult's speaking, thinking, and behaving. To the contrary, for Durkheim, adults coerce a youngster into definite ways of seeing, feeling, and behaving. This coercion is already in place, even before a youngster begins to imitate. As soon as a child is born, adults coerce her into sucking milk, falling asleep, and awaking at specified hours of the day. Soon after that, they coerce her to use words, to behave in accordance with specific patterns, and to acquire knowledge. All customs and inner tendencies arise from such coercion. Because of this, a child suffers under the pressures of the social environment from the outset and is thereby situated within the various social roles available. As representatives and mediators of the environment, parents and teachers coerce youngsters into definite sorts of consciousness and actions, instead of merely transmitting the radiation of imitation.

Social facts are, as was said before, the specific forms of behavior, thinking, and feeling, which exist outside of individuals and yet coerce them. Just as words are taught to children from external sources, so the words I now use to express my thoughts exist independently, irrespective of whether I use them or not. If I perform some obligation, I am not actually obedient to an obligation that I myself set forth but to the social order I have inherited from being taught, and such order is thought to be objectively grounded in law and morality. Similarly, religious rites and doctrines, economic institutions, customs, and so forth exist independent of individual consciousness. Furthermore, all of them possess commanding power. Unless individuals obey these specific ways of behaving, they are punished in some way. This is the case even with manners and customs that appear trivial, to say nothing of actions ordered by law and morality. If we dress ourselves by closing our eyes to current fashion, we are surely treated as abnormal persons. She who does not use her native language in speaking to her compatriots is also regarded as an abnormal or disagreeable person. So far, then, it seems that even clothes and words possess compelling power.

If social facts are characterized by "coercion from outside," then we cannot label society universal. Such things as mental processes, which exist within every individual a priori, are not by themselves social facts. Society is not something universal existing within individuals but exists outside of them. Of course, it manifests itself within individuals, but it is able to depart from them as well. For example, customs and morality do not exist as something immanent in the acts thereby prescribed. As expressed through forms independent of these acts, they pass from mouth to mouth, are transmitted to later generations through education, and are preserved by means of words. Judicial or moral orders, maxims prevalent among folk, religious or political doctrines, rules of artistic taste, and so forth are in the same category. It is not that these norms are perfectly and necessarily manifested within individuals. They can exist by themselves, even though individuals may never actually instantiate them.

If this is so, then is it possible for society to subsist in separation from individuals? Can we speak of something as a group phenomenon, without its also being communal (hence, universal), that is, applicable to all of the members or to a great majority of them? Of course, not. Society must be a community that exists in accordance with and among its members. But it is not communal because of its being universal. Conversely, it is universal because of its being communal. The state of a group becomes a phenomenon common to individuals, because it coerces individuals as that which commands. Coercion plays a role in universalization.

Social facts are forms of action (*manieres de faire*). But other forms of being (*manieres d'être*) must be taken into consideration as well: the number of elements constituting society, the principle of ordering them, the intensity of their connection, the geographical distribution of populations, kinds of transportation, forms of architecture, and so forth. At first sight, although they seem outside the realm of action's forms, they are nothing more than the settled forms of action. The political structure of society consists in the ways in which various classes of society traditionally live their lives. The types of architecture are representative of traditional ways of building houses constructed in response to the environment and in keeping with that of the preceding generations. Similarly, traffic routes are people's fixed habits of passage. Therefore, forms of being place no fewer restraints on individuals than do forms of action.

By giving due consideration to these factors, Durkheim defined social facts in the following way. "Social facts are sorts of action, more or less fixed, that are likely to coerce individuals from the outside. They make their appearance universally within a given realm of society and have their own being independent of their individual expressions."[12]

Durkheim came to think that society, as coercive from outside, stands over against individuals. Society cannot be derived from mere individual consciousness. This position is exactly opposite to that which takes imitation or reciprocal activities as constituting society. We can say that Durkheim's position afforded a penetrating insight into one aspect of the relationship between society and individuals. If society exists through coercion, as Durkheim argued, then society and individuals are unified just at the place where they stand opposed to and separately revolt against each other. Unless individuals are able to revolt against society, there is no possibility of coercion. On the other hand, coercion cannot arise unless to make individuals obey society. Therefore, the more individuals revolt against society, the more strongly society, as coercive, manifests itself and, hence, so much the more must individuals obey society's commands. Thus unity in revolt (between society and individuals) is coercion and the reason why Durkheim tried to clarify what is meant by *society* by having recourse to such antisocial phenomena as "suicide" and "crime." The phenomenon of crime shows in an enlarged manner the possibility of individuals revolting against society. What is more, apart from these revolting individuals, there can be no society (hence, no coercion).

In the aforesaid unity in revolt between society and individuals, however, does not society, as that which exists outside individuals, include within itself individuals? Of course it does. Even Durkheim does not deny that society is constituted by individuals. His point is to insist that the whole has a specific reality different from the sum of its parts. Just as an organism is not the mere sum total of molecules, which turn out through their unification to have a life quite different from them, so society turns out to be different from the individuals that constitute it through the association of them with one another. A group feels, thinks, and behaves in a way entirely different from that in which its members think, feel, and behave when they are separated from society. In Durkheim's opinion, the fact of association itself makes the group differ from individuals and is most coercive and obligatory to individuals, as the source of all other obligations. What does Durkheim mean here? How is it possible for association to be the coercion of individuals? What is this association of individuals like?

In an attempt to find the ground of social processes within the structure of inner social environment (*le milieu social interne*),[13] Durkheim describes a living power that sets the material of society in motion as a human environment and investigates it from two perspectives: the volume and the mechanical intensity of society. Mechanical intensity indicates the degree of moral relationship that holds between individuals, of an inner connection in communal life, and hence the degree of fusion among individuals. Therefore, we can say that the inner social environment, when seen from the perspective of its human elements, connects people and allows them to participate in one group-oriented being. Durkheim often thinks of "the nation" in this way,[14] as that which signifies the coercion of individuals. Additionally, society as coercive includes this inner connection in its structure; that is, the relationship that constitutes the fusion of individuals. We can conclude that what he described as the association among individuals has something to do with the relation of fusion but not of coercion. Nevertheless, it must be maintained as well that, when individuals are associated in this relationship of fusion, this association coerces individual members. This relationship of fusion was dealt with earlier through the issues of imitation and reciprocal activities. For this reason, the contention that association among individuals terminates in coercion against them cannot be understood if we stand on the position of regarding society as coercive alone. If there were only the moment of coercion but not of fusion, association would not arise and, hence, an agency that coerces individuals would also not exist. In this way, Durkheim's insight is also one-sided.

By giving heed to society as an objective fact, we can discern that these two aspects (i.e., coercion and fusion) are respectively emphasized in a one-sided way. Insofar as each of these aspects reflects an aspect of society, then these arguments cannot be said to be in error. But both of them err in their endeavor to explain society by appealing to only one aspect. Society must originally be understood to have these two aspects. That is to say, the communalizing and interfusing aspect of association among individuals at once indicates the existence of coercion as well. In light of this structure of society as objective fact, we will understand more clearly the structure of subjective betweenness also expressed therein.

Fundamentally, association and coercion illustrate contradictory states of affairs. From the subjective standpoint, "association" consists of subjects, which as the many, collectively terminate in the one. To cite a familiar example, people who engage in a communal rope pull with sincerity combine to become one subject. It is not that I pull and that you also pull but that "one power" somehow pulls. On the contrary, "coercion" consists of forcing separated individual subjects to subordinate themselves to the whole. It cannot occur except at a place where a subject stands opposed to the whole as its other. This kind of opposition arises when she who pulls the rope takes leave of it, tiring of this activity, or finding herself interested in some other play to which she moves. She who has taken leave of the rope is in revolt against a communal activity, and she stands thereby outside of the power of the rope pull. If the power of the communal activity of the rope pull suppresses this revolt or exerts control over laziness so that the participant returns once more to the rope and the collective pulling of it, then coercion is evident. In this sense, coercion is the power of bringing separated agents back to oneness. Yet, in what manner does association signify such coercion?

Association, in spite of its division into an infinite variety of sorts and degrees, consists in the fact that subjects who were previously separated as the many, come back to the one. Hence, the individuality of individual subjects is discarded in accordance with their respective circumstances, and they become communal instead. In other words, subjective individuals are "emptied" in various ways, and they turn out to be constituents of the subjective whole. However this may be, where did these emptied individuals come from? Individuals are empty in themselves: only the negation of their respective community establishes them. If so, then we can say that before the individuality of the subject is discarded in the associative collectivity, this individuality was already established through the negation of community. Therefore, association is "the discarding of individuality that appears in the form of the discarding of community." This is double negation.

The same is true of what is conceived of as direct association, as is the case of the union of love. The primordial element in the union of love, as Hegel also points out, lies in the self and the other discarding the independence of the ego, but this discarding is performed on the ground of the separation of self and other. Because of this, in love the fear is that oneself and the other will be separated. Hence, a solemn pledge that negates the possibility of this separation must be given in advance. Even in maternal and filial affection, this fear takes the form of a mother's affectionate concern. A perfect union in which there is no danger of the separation of oneself from the other or a unity that becomes as one body, and in which individual members are never conscious of their independence, can never be found within the finite existence of human beings. Even if we bring forward examples of totemistic society with which ethnologists are often concerned, the expression of the whole through the totem already reveals an endeavor to restrain the members from separating from it. In this way, even in what are regarded as direct associations, a double negation is already involved, to say nothing of the particularly conscious interest-oriented association in which separation is already anticipated at the time of establishment and measures preventing it are stipulated at the outset. This shows that the independence those in the association have agreed to discard from the start indicates the recognition that it already consists of the discarding of community.

It should be obvious that the association between oneself and another is already a negation of their separation. Hence, the subjective whole that has emptied subjective individuals appears at the same time under the guise of coercion against the revolt of these individuals. The union of love consists of merely the fact that the self and the other become unified. Its power constantly forces self and other, who try to separate from each other, to continue or resume their relationship. For instance, in the relationship of *I* and *Thou*, the *Thou*, as the agent who accuses and is angered by the betrayal of *I*, retains the authority to end the betrayal from the outset. Truthfully, what is at stake here is not the *Thou* itself, but the "connection" that operates through *Thou*. *Thou* can accuse *I* only through the authority of this connection. Therefore, at a place where there is an *I/ Thou* relationship, there is at work the power that obliges *I* and *Thou*, the power that determines *I* and *Thou* to act in specific ways. The same is true of totemistic society. The totem expressing this primitive connection obligates its individual members through the authority of this connection and thereby determines them to an extremely strict manner of action. Restrictions of the relationships between the sexes are more complicated than in civilized societies, and they also bear more severe significance. Nonetheless, in no society, however primitive it may be, is there no sense of obligation and control over its individual members.

In this way, association is, at the same time, also coercion. If this is true, then we will be able to acquire a more adequate comprehension of the structure of association from an understanding of coercion. The primordial element that coercion indicates lies in this, that an individual revolts against society and is opposed to it as something other than herself. This element signifies the discarding of community. There is no association that does not involve the discarding of community, insofar as coercion and obligation are recognized. Communities, whatever they may be, consist in what empties subjective individuals in their respective ways. To discard the community and revolt against society means to further negate the negation that has already been realized among its individual subjects. Nevertheless, the secondary element that coercion indicates is that society, as standing in external opposition to individuals, nonetheless obliges them to obey in spite of this opposition and thereby negates the independence of subjective individuals. Individuals must empty themselves in various ways, submerging themselves in their respective subjective wholes. Negativity must be instantiated among individual subjects. This is equivalent to discarding individuality, which, in its turn, is discarding community. By keeping our eye on these two elements that coercion implies, we can see that coercion exhibits, in a structure that serves to subordinate those individuals to society who attempt to revolt against it, two directions; that is, the negation of negativity, on the one hand, and its materialization, on the other.

I think that here is where the genuine structure of human association is to be found. If it is argued that association, insofar as it is the connection of individuals, presupposes individuals who discard the community and that these individuals, insofar as they discard the community, already presuppose association, then this is mere circular reasoning. Individuals, no matter what association they may revolt against, turn out to "revolt against," in the sense of negating the negativity as materialized in the association. And this negativity is, fundamentally speaking, absolute negativity; that is, emptiness. Therefore, it can be said that an individual revolts against "emptiness" itself through the medium of her revolting against an association, whatever it may be. In coming to grips with the notion of the individual, we are already brought to "emptiness" as its real feature. An individual becomes an individual by negating emptiness (i.e., authentic emptiness) as her own fundamental source. This is the self-negation of absolute negativity. In addition to that, an individual must be subordinate to society through emptying herself, regardless of how this emptying is performed. This means that emptiness is materialized in various associations to varying degrees. Therefore, an individual returns to "emptiness" itself, through engaging in association of whatever sort. In our attempt to comprehend wholeness itself, its essential feature was also revealed to be emptiness. Absolute wholeness is absolute negativity. Seen in this light, human association, inclusive of coercion, is understood to be the movement of the negation of negation in which absolute negativity returns to itself through its own self-negation. Therefore, for the individual, coercion, even though being coercion from the outside, nonetheless, is self-coercion arising out of the individual's fundamental source.

In this way, the negative structure of a betweenness-oriented being is clarified in terms of the self-returning movement of absolute negativity through its own negation. This is a human being's fundamental structure, which makes its kaleidoscopic appearance in every nook and cranny of a human being. To conceive of the standpoint of a mere individual or of society by itself, while giving no heed to this structure, results in an abstraction that brings to light only one aspect of a human being. Indeed, there are three moments that are dynamically unified as the movement of negation: fundamental emptiness, then individual existence, and social existence as its negative development. These three are interactive with one another in practical reality and cannot be separated. They are at work constantly in the practical interconnection of acts and can in no way be stabilized fixedly at any place. For instance, when a specific association is constructed, it does not subsist statically as a fixed product. The essential feature characteristic of human association is its constantly putting into effect the movement of the negation of negation. When this movement comes to a standstill in one way or another, the association itself collapses. Thus, if an individual, as the negation of emptiness, sticks to this negation in such a way as to refuse to allow the negation of negation to occur as well, then that association disintegrates on the spot. Likewise, if an individual submerges herself in the whole and refuses to become an individual again, then the whole perishes at the same time. Taking a totemistic society as our illustration, this is the extinction of the meaning of the totem. We can conclude that the movement of the negation of absolute negativity is, at the same time, the continuous creation of human beings.

7 the fundamental law of a human being (the basic principle of ethics)

The negative structure of a human being is, as was said previously, the fundamental law that renders a human being capable of continuously forming itself. Were we to deviate from this law, we would cease to exist. Therefore, this law is the basis of a human being. At the outset, we prescribed the ground of human community, namely, the law of a human being, as ethics. Therefore, we can assert that this fundamental law is basic ethics. Basic ethics is the basic principle of ethics. We can describe the basic principle of ethics in terms of "the movement in which absolute negativity returns back to itself through negation."

Objection may be raised that this principle serves as the principle of all philosophy, as with Hegel, and does not serve as the principle of ethics alone. But the principle of ethics is the fundamental law of human beings. Such things as the historical world, the natural world, and logic are all to be found in human beings. A human being, as a part of the natural world, is human existence regarded as a natural object. It exists in an objective way and yet has nothing to do with subjective human existence of the sort that we are concerned with here. Rather, the subjective human being is the basis on which all other objective beings are themselves established. If so, then it is natural that the historical world, the natural world, and so forth, all take the fundamental law of human beings as their fundamental principle in their respective and specific ways. The same may be said of logic as the laws of thinking. These laws are not laws that exist in and by themselves prior to human beings but rather came to be known through human beings themselves. As is indicated by the term *logos*, language has mediated the self-realization of logic. Human beings, in their self-realizing activities, express themselves in and through language. Language expression is the most efficient tool for mediating the subjective and practical connections and promoting the incessant development of human beings. The fundamental law of human beings operates in the form of the principle of language itself. Insofar as language operates as an element within the subjective and practical connections, this principle does not yet reach the stage of self-awareness. Logic is realized as the law of *logos* when this subjective character of practice is abstracted from language, and the latter's principle is reflected on with a casual gaze. Therefore, we can say that logic is the law of human beings when grasped as the law of thinking by means of the medium of language. Once logic is realized in this way, it is correct to argue that it is a law that exists prior to human beings: essentially, logic's law renders a human being capable of being distinctly human. However, when the law of human beings is understood to be the law of *logos*, then it has already been transmitted into the possible world of meanings. Therefore, it cannot be the law of the subjective and practical connections themselves.

The movement of the negation of absolute negativity is, first of all, a law of human beings and not yet a law of either the universe or thinking. The latter will be dealt with later. This law comes from and returns back to the Absolute. However, the view that this law (of the negation of absolute negativity) is concerned with human beings means that this law is closely tied to the practical and active spheres of human beings. The movement of negation sets up the standpoint of finitude precisely by virtue of its being the movement of negation. Due to their negative structure, practical and active human beings are finite beings. The absoluteness of absolute negativity lies in its being in accordance with this finitude. It can have nothing to do with abstractive absoluteness, which stands aloof from finitude. As to where this absolute negativity is to be found, there is nothing for us to do but to refer to an individual or group that presently exists. The negation of absolute negativity establishes the standpoint of an individual. This does not mean, however, that the individual stands in opposition to absolute negativity as his other. This negation always takes place in the form of a revolt against the whole as something socio-ethical. The individual opposes precisely this socio-ethical whole as the other. This whole may appear in various forms, such as family, friends, a company, a state, and so forth. Only when an individual becomes separate from and independent of this whole can individual impulse, individual will, or individual acts be spoken of. Moreover, this finite negation is the self-negation of absolute negativity. Apart from this finite negation, there is no place where absolute negativity manifests itself.

Similarly, the standpoint of the whole is established as the negation of the negation of absolute negativity; that is, as its returning to itself. But this should not be taken to signify a mystical experience in which the individual is immersed in the Absolute. The sublation (i.e., *Aufheben* in German) of the individual's independence that arises as the negation of negation occurs in the form of its subordination to the socio-ethical whole. The individual is immersed in just this socio-ethical whole, which appears in various forms, such as family, friends, a company, a state, and so forth. At any rate, regarding this union of an individual with the whole, mention can be made of a superindividual will, or the total will, or of obligatory acts and so forth. Furthermore, the realization of this finite whole is precisely the return of absolute negativity to itself. The self-return of the Absolute is realized endlessly, and has nothing to do with a static and absolute destination. The place in which this self-returning is exhibited is the socio-ethical whole as finite. This is why the movement of the negation of absolute negativity is said to be the law of human beings; that is, it is ethics.

We claim that both the individual and society are grounded in the Absolute. The law derived from the Absolute is put into effect through the basis of finite society. Hence, the distinction between "closed society" and "open society" and between "closed morality" and "open morality" cannot be allowed here. The socio-ethical whole, which appears even in the form of that which is natural, so to speak, such as family or nation, is never merely biological. When it is argued that, in the course of the evolution of living things, the society of bees or of ants is achieved by instinct, whereas that of human beings is achieved by intellect, and that the latter is evolution's highest point, then it must be that the "society" under consideration has nothing to do with subjective human beings. Therefore, so-called closed society does not yet reach to the socio-ethical whole, in the full sense of the word. Consequently, the socio-ethical unity achieved in a closed society is incapable of signifying the self-return of the Absolute.

At the same time, in what is called an *open society*, each individual is tied to the Absolute, but just because of this, which sphere can be legitimately called *society* remains unclear. From ancient times, "religious organizations" usually have been constructed under this name. However, religious organizations are closed societies that exclude pagans. A society in which all humankind is fraternally united is merely "an ideal," not a socio-ethical reality. In saying this, we cannot go so far as to say that this "ideal" is simply nonsense. If, however, religious organizations, that is, "closed societies," should not have been constructed to attempt to realize this ideal, then from where else could the possibility of achieving and materializing this ideal have arisen? Even if a unity of universal brotherhood were to be constructed within a single nation, it would be an event worthy of surprise and wonder in world history. But from where else should we start other than from just now? Unless we recognize that the finite socio-ethical whole is precisely the place of the self-return of the Absolute, then this ideal would, in the final analysis, fall victim to the charge of meaninglessness.

In spite of this, a type of thinking has prevailed that neglects "closed societies" and attaches importance to "open societies" because, within world religions such as Christianity and Buddhism, the individualistic standpoint of belief has established a direct relationship between the individual and the Absolute. Mystics within Christianity and Hīnayāna Buddhist saints represent this standpoint. Individuals adhering to such standpoints, at least at the beginning, came to exist by revolting against the socio-ethical whole. But this revolt was only a discarding of the finite socio-ethical organization and heed was not given to the fact that the ground of this revolt consisted in absolute negativity. For this reason, the socio-ethical organization was merely discarded. Left behind as well were independent individuals and the Absolute. Clearly, this sort of Absolute is only relative, because it stands over against individuals. Mystics and Buddhist saints, however, did not worry about contradictions of this sort. According to them, the Absolute, although relative to *I*, is yet the Absolute. Because of this, *I* can be immersed in the Absolute as the highest blessing.

It is not that great religious people in ancient times, to say nothing of Jesus Christ and Gotama Buddha themselves, taught us to return directly to the Absolute without thereby going through the socio-ethical whole. It is true that they stood firmly on an individualist standpoint, by leaving behind the palace (like Buddha) or by abandoning their family (like Jesus). Their enlightenment or faith was acquired outside of the socio-ethical organization, in the forest or in the wilderness. When the Absolute was revealed to them, were they satisfied simply with submerging themselves in it? Not at all. Instead, they returned into the midst of the socio-ethical organization, expounded a "new social ethics" or established a society of priests as an ideal yet typical socio-ethical organization. The socio-ethical whole against which they revolted, whether the family or the state, was inescapably grounded in the Absolute. Interpersonal ties inherent in the family or in fraternal relationships were, in essence, instances of that divine love which should connect all persons. And the order of a state based on the law was, in essence, none other than the eternal law. The way back to the Absolute that these great religious figures exemplified lay in realizing divine love and the eternal law within the socio-ethical whole. This is why the enlightenment of emptiness immediately appears in the form of "compassion," and the absolute reliance on God appears in the form of "love." Even if the established socio-ethical organization were to be discarded—nay, just because of this—all the more importance must be attached to the authentically socio-ethical organization. Without the formation of the socio-ethical whole, the movement of returning to the Absolute could not occur. A church or an organization of monks is a fine example of this. We can conclude that worthy religions do teach us not to directly relate ourselves to the Absolute from the standpoint of an individual, but to go to the Absolute through the finite socio-ethical whole. The individualist standpoint adopted by mystics or by Hinayana Buddhist saints has deprived the great religions of their compassion or love.

Therefore, it must be obvious that the negligence of a closed society is unable to do justice to the real significance of a socio-ethical organization. It is also an error to attach excessive importance to a closed society and pretend that it is an ultimate aim. Because the latter view disregards the significance that the socio-ethical organization gains through returning to the Absolute alone, it undermines ethics even though it places emphasis on obedience to the whole. A family or a state, as instances of socio-ethical wholes, has the authority to demand obedience from individuals, but this demand cannot be authorized merely from the standpoint of a family or a state. Where an individual who revolted against a family or a state, finds himself based in the Absolute, then by what right can a family or a state, as finite wholes, demand the negation of this individual? Even the prosperity of a state, insofar as this state is but a finite group of human beings, is not given priority over the dignity of an individual who originates in the Absolute. Likewise, only when a state originates in the Absolute and the negative activity of absolute negativity renders individual obedience to the state possible can the state be justified in negating individuals. Therefore, to recommend obedience to a state without thereby comprehending it as having been derived from the law of human beings will only heighten suspicion concerning a state. It was against such a standpoint that emphasis was placed on "the open society" as a form of counterattack.

By admitting absolute negativity (hence, absolute wholeness) at the base of the socio-ethical organization, we think it possible to avoid both the unwarranted negligence and an overestimation of the closed society. The dual existence of human beings as individual and social is precisely the place where absolute wholeness manifests itself. Because of this, the movement of the negation of absolute negativity turns out to be precisely the law of human beings, that is, basic ethics.

If this is what basic ethics is, then all of the issues surrounding ethics must ultimately originate here. The various concepts with which ethics has been concerned from the beginning are all eventually based on this principle. However, we do not insist that the fundamental principle is likely to provide the full-fledged grounding for every ethical concept. This fundamental principle has come to grips with the negative relationship between an individual and the whole but has not yet succeeded in clarifying the conflictual relationships between one individual and another (and hence, the multiplicity) or the unity among individuals inherent in the whole (hence, the totality). For human beings, it is not that the individual and the whole are something fixed that necessarily exclude each other. Rather, an individual is an individual only in a whole, and the whole is a whole only in individuals. When the whole is considered, the conflicts among many individuals must be recognized; and when individuals are spoken of, the unifying whole must be understood to be that which underlies all of them. In other words, an individual is an individual in its connection with multiplicity and totality, and the whole is a whole in its connection with multiplicity and individuality. Human beings possess this dynamic structure of reciprocal transformation. To describe ethical concepts adequately, a more detailed analysis of this dynamic structure is required; namely, the temporal-spatial structure of human beings. The structure of solidarity built upon the spatio-temporal structure and, further, the historico-climatic structure inherent in this solidarity are all issues that must be investigated, and in that order. But the view that a human being consists fundamentally in the movement of the negation of absolute negativity remains unchanged even to the very end of our inquiry.

One of the basic traditional distinctions in ethics is the value distinction of the good and the bad. In an attempt to deal with this distinction, "valuable things" (*Güter*) or purposes are set up, on the one hand, and moral sentiment or value feeling (*Wertfühlen*) is proposed, on the other. The trend in the modern world lies in rejecting the former and accepting the latter. But can ethical theories of this type grasp the ground of ethics without thereby having recourse to the law of human beings?

The standpoint that attempts to find the ground of ethics in moral sentiment sets up, as in Taylor,[1] at the base of the discrimination between good and bad the sentiment of approval and disapproval and endeavors to derive from it all other moral concepts such as obligation, responsibility, conscience, freedom, and personality. That some event is approved or disapproved of means that it is accompanied by the feeling of pleasure or pain when sensed or perceived or ideally represented by an idea. This is a basic fact of consciousness, which does not yet suffer from a discrimination of the distinction between individual or social. If only we could know in the anticipation of some experience that it is either pleasurable or painful, then we would already have before us a primitive moral judgment, irrespective of asking whether the consciousness operative here is the consciousness of the ego or not. Therefore, the mental conditions prerequisite for the formation of moral sentiment are threefold: (1) the existence of an idea that is felt in one way or another; (2) the capacity to distinguish between past and future, that is, "before" and "after," even if in a somewhat primitive way; and (3) the capacity to feel pleasure or pain by means of the contrast between present experience and an anticipated or remembered one. The structure of this consciousness is prior to the emergence of the consciousness of ego. Thus, a child has the feelings of approval and disapproval before it becomes conscious of its own ego.

These feelings precede social influence. According to the view that insists on the importance of social influence, an approved action is an action that serves society in some way. What is approved is, however, insofar as it is conceived of as mental fact, not necessarily useful. Among various activities approved by primitive tribes are some that do not benefit the tribe. Praise accorded to an excellent hunter include references to something beyond the utility of his technique. One should never underestimate the educational influence of the power of society, but moral sentiment is something apart from mere social influence. And this moral sentiment discriminates between good and bad, with regard to an action, character, personality, and so on.

Yet, in what way are concepts such as obligation, conscience, and so forth derived from moral sentiment? With regard to obligation, the first manifestation of the obligatory feeling is to be found in a self's feeling of dissatisfaction with himself, which is a feeling of disapproval of one's past. A feeling of dissatisfaction already exists at that place where memory and anticipation exist and does not depend on social influence. This feeling is not yet in and of itself an obligatory feeling. Only when it is added to by tribal or clan feelings does the self's feeling of being dissatisfied with himself (that is, the feeling that he should have been something other than he was) become transformed into a feeling of his encountering societal expectations. Here obligation takes its stand in the authentic moral sense of the word.

Now, just because this clan society is regarded as representing God, obligation signifies what God expects from us. Soon afterward, God comes to be understood to be something superhuman and mystical who exists beyond the clan, penetrating into the interior of an individual mind, and thereby the obligatory feeling is internalized. Just as this God is extended beyond the tribal or national boundaries, so the obligatory feeling is enlarged to the extent of its applying to all humankind. The violation of obligation is sin, and the performance of obligation and approval by God is sacredness. But this theological stage does not yet comprehend the distinction between ritual sacredness and moral purification. It is in the ethical stage that this distinction is realized and from which one now understands sufficiently the significance of one's previous dissatisfaction. Then, a human being becomes independent of God. Thus, the obligatory feeling is no longer one of something being expected by God, but turns out to be a feeling of *I* expecting something of myself. This is the standpoint of Kant's autonomic morality. Therefore, the autonomic character of the moral law pertains to a highly developed civilized society but is not a basic fact of ethics. Various stages of obligatory feeling have developed around this impersonal feeling of dissatisfaction.

Conscience is also derived from the moral sentiment. The only difference between conscience and obligatory feeling lies in the former resulting from a more developed process of reflection. Obligation pertains to individual acts, but conscience is concerned with the system of acts. *Conscience* is a general term designating a collection of assurances about obligation. Hence, it is based on the moral sentiment. Furthermore, the concept of responsibility proceeds in parallel with that of obligation. The obligatory feeling relates to the future, but the feeling of responsibility relates to the past. That is to say, the other side of obligation is responsibility. A moral personality is an agent who takes responsibility for his own acts. So far, moral personality is based on responsibility and includes a succession of mental activities (i.e., the memory of one's own past actions and the anticipation of one's future actions) required for the emergence of the feeling of responsibility. Hence, the moral personality is achieved fully when a succession of mental activities connect the memory of one's most remote past and the anticipation of one's future actions. The moral personality brings feelings of obligation and of responsibility into a system. It emerges when individuals or the tribe are developed to their fullest extent. In this sense, the fullest development of the moral personality can be said to be the *terminus ad quem* of moral development. And the educational influence of society is important in this development. Therefore, an individual moral personality can be said to be a product of the tribe.

I have concerned myself with the derivation of moral concepts from the moral sentiment of approval or disapproval. This seems to be a basic standpoint that presupposes nothing more than the temporal structure of consciousness and the feelings of pleasure and pain. But, in fact, this is not so. The standpoint in question already presupposes individual empirical psychology and takes for granted those mental facts assumed by psychology. In reality, there is no independent consciousness for an individual, as was argued in the fourth chapter. Consciousness is at once social and individual. Saying that a child does not yet possess the consciousness of ego, does not imply that its consciousness is not an essential expression of a human being. A child's consciousness develops in connection with its parents, and its memories and anticipations arise through imitation. Therefore, it can be said that the educational influence of society is recognized even in the most primitive consciousness. A child is, from the outset, trained in this way to approve of what its mother approves of.

This social characteristic of moral sentiment does not imply that only what is of use to society is approved. Primitive people approve of accessories that seem to be of no benefit to the tribe. This is because something may be approved of simply on the ground that this particular tribe approves of it. This approval is communal, not based on one member's feeling of approval. The reason why an excellent hunter is praised lies in the fact that a definite standard of hunting technique is existent in this tribe. Apart from such a social background, the sentiment that occasions praise could not occur. An attempt to explain moral sentiment on the basis of the fundamental facts of consciousness, without giving heed to a human being's communal existence, falls victim to being considered an extreme instance of abstraction. The discrimination between approval and disapproval is itself both individual and social and thus cannot be comprehended without recourse to the fundamental structure of a human being.

This is acknowledged by the exponents of moral sentiment theory, when they attempt to derive the feeling of obligation from moral sentiment. The feeling of the disapproval of past actions is the self's feeling of dissatisfaction, which is not yet a feeling of obligation. So that the feeling of obligation may arise, the feelings of the tribe must be added here, and the self's feeling of dissatisfaction with the past must be transformed into the feelings of societal expectation. Here, not only the past is transmitted into the future, but also the relationship of society to an individual intervenes quite suddenly. The emergence of obligation depends on this relationship alone. This is not to say that obligatory feelings are derived from moral sentiment. Those who concern themselves with the theory of moral sentiment presuppose the organization of a tribe or a clan as well as those customs and traditions regarded as the standard of moral action, as distinct from the moral sentiment. Emphasis is placed on the feeling of tribal expectation based on this standard. If so, we can say that some socio-ethical organization and a specific manner of actions are already assumed. What they call a *developed stage of the feeling of obligation* is, in truth, none other than a developed stage of this socio-ethical organization. The feeling of approval or disapproval is simply an experience one has from within this organization.

If the feeling of obligation is derived in this way, then it is clear that the concepts of conscience, responsibility, the moral personality, and so forth, which are based on this feeling of obligation, could not have been derived from the moral sentiment. Thus, there is no doubt that the endeavor to derive the basic concepts of ethics from the feeling of approval or disapproval fails to achieve its objective. But one may attribute this failure to the dependence on empirical psychology.

We now turn our attention to that position assumed by phenomenology, which appeared on the scene as having overcome the weak points inherent in the approach of empirical psychology. Phenomenology places emphasis also on the activity of feeling (*Fühlen* in German). However, the object of feeling is not so much ordinary things as it is essential objects; that is, values. In feeling these values, we appreciate (*vorziehen*) one value and depreciate (*nachsetzen*) another. On the basis of this feeling of superiority and inferiority with respect to values, we seek to attain higher values. The value of goodness inheres precisely in this activity. The aim of this position was to create opposition to that tendency which sought the moral principle only in the formal, to the exclusion of the substantial, as Kant did; to set up a realm of values independent of the latter as something merely tertiary; and finally to discover the moral principle in these substantial values. However, it remains to be asked whether this aim was accomplished without recourse to the law of human beings.

Indeed, credit must be given to Scheler's substantial values-oriented ethics for having rejected traditional *Güterethik* by separating "valuable things" (*Güter*) from those values embodied therein. Values are given in the form of value feelings, and the higher and lower grades of values are found in the feelings of the superiority and inferiority of values. This gradation of substantial values is given a priori for the world of valuable things. Kant's error was his rejection of all substantial values as empirical. As a result, he was left with no alternative but to assert that the realization of a specific substantial value was, in itself, neither good nor bad. However, the a priori gradation of values clarifies the relationship between goodness, badness, and other values. The value of "goodness," in the absolute sense of the word, is value that appears essentially in that activity which attempts to realize supreme value. Likewise, the value of "badness" is that value which appears in the activity of the realization of the lowest grade of value. Goodness or badness, in the relative senses of these terms, is value that appears in that activity which strives for the realization of values regarded as higher or lower.

Because the gradation of values as higher or lower is given in feeling, goodness arises when activity that realizes values is coincident with superior values and is in revolt against inferior ones, in accordance with that value substantiality it intends. Contrariwise, badness arises when activity is brought in line with inferior values and revolts against superior ones. Furthermore, what inheres in activity that realizes positive values at the stage of higher (or the highest) values is the value of goodness, whereas what inheres in activity realizing negative values is that of badness.[2] In this way, Scheler could define the value of goodness and badness on the basis of the higher or lower grade accorded to other values. He tries to describe this result in terms of the following axioms:

A.

1. The existence of positive values is itself a positive value.
2. The nonexistence of positive values is itself a negative value.
3. The existence of negative values is itself a negative value.
4. The nonexistence of negative values is itself a positive value.

B.

1. Goodness is that value in the realm of will which inheres in the realization of positive values.
2. Badness is that value in the realm of will which inheres in the realization of negative values.
3. Goodness is that value which inheres in the realization of the higher (or the highest) values in the realm of will.
4. Badness is that value which inheres in the realization of the lower values in the realm of will.

C.

1. A criterion of goodness and badness is given according to whether or not the value aimed at is in line with superior values or is in revolt against inferior ones.

This last axiom seems to have succeeded in defining very precisely the values of goodness and badness on the basis of the gradation of values. Therefore, it may be said that the moral principle is established only by recourse to the feeling of values or to the feeling of superiority and inferiority of them. However, a little attention reveals that the axis around which an appearance of the value of goodness and badness centers is "the activity of realization" itself; that is, the "will." The feeling of values has something to do with the activity of value cognizance but not with that of its realization. Moreover, the values of goodness and badness arise only in accordance with this realizing activity. If so, then we must assert that the mere position that sets up the feeling of values falls short of actually grasping the value of goodness and badness. This is the major difference between the values of goodness and badness and the other values.

Scheler himself became conscious of this. He says, "the substantial values called goodness and badness could not themselves become essentially the substance of the activity of realization (that is, of will). . . . The value of goodness manifests itself in the realizing of higher positive values given in the feeling of the superiority and inferiority of values. That is to say, it manifests itself in the activity of the will. This is why the value of goodness cannot constitute the substance of the activity of will. It adheres 'to the back', so to speak, of this activity. What is more, this is so essentially and of necessity. Thus, the value of goodness cannot itself be aimed at within this activity of will."[3] An agent holding the value of goodness and badness manifests an activity of will essentially different from "valuable things." But it is not only the activity of will which holds the value in question. Scheler also says, that "basically, the only agent that can be designated as good or bad, that is, which holds the substantial value of goodness or badness prior to and independent of every individual activity, is the 'personality,' i.e., a being of personality as such. Consequently, we can precisely describe goodness or badness from the vantage point of its holder as follows; 'goodness' or 'badness' is the value of personality."[4] He continues, "It is thereby clarified that 'goodness' and 'badness' are essentially different from every kind of substantial value inherent in 'good things' or 'bad things.' This is because personality is not a thing, and it does not uphold the essence of the *Dinghaftigkeit* (thingfulness or thingliness) characteristic of valuable things. As the concrete unity of all possible activities, personality stands confronted with all of the realms of possible 'objects' (physical or mental). Much more is it opposed to that realm of things which constitutes a part of the realm of objects. Personality consists only in performing its activities."[5]

From this perspective, the value of goodness or badness is not concerned with the problem of values given in value feelings but rather with the activities of realization; that is, the will and the personality, which serve to unify these activities. Moreover, neither the activities of realization nor personality are given in value feelings. Instead, value feeling is itself an activity of personality. If goodness or badness are values attributable to personality, then how is it possible that value feeling, as one activity of personality, is able to feel the values that the agent of this activity upholds? How on earth is goodness or badness able to manifest in the activity of the realization of values? Is it possible to comprehend what is called the *being* of personality without thereby having recourse to a law that presides over human beings?

Scheler's main ethical work may be characterized as a substantial valuational ethics. However, five-sixths of its content discusses activities such as willing or feeling and personality. What is more, arguments concerning personality occupy almost half of the entire content in discussing what we have dealt with as the structure inherent in a human being. Scheler's point is that, whereas all sorts of activities are performed and unified by personality, the way of being of this personality must never be allowed to become an object. This subjective personality is unique to itself to the very end. On the other hand, it is both individual and communal as well. Then, the whole personality, life community, *Gesellschaft*, spiritual community, and so forth are discussed in detail, and in these discussions the structure of responsibility inherent in each of these communities is found. We have already discussed such issues in Chapter Five, where we noted that Scheler established the principle of "solidarity that cannot be represented," which inheres in the spiritual community. He makes it "the basic principle of the world of finite ethical personalities." The essential feature characteristic of this principle of solidarity is the view that, in the spiritual community, which consists of "the unity of individual persons within the personality of the whole," both individual persons and the personality of the whole, respectively, assume their own self-responsibility, while at the same time, they bear a common responsibility for each other.

I have already brought to light some defects in Scheler's position. However, Scheler's attempt to seek the basic principle of ethics in solidarity shows that he tried to solve the problem in question by appealing not to value feelings as the one activity of personality, but to the law that preside over human beings.

This reveals that none of the attempts to explain the values of goodness or badness by means of moral sentiment or value feelings could solve this problem without thereby appealing to laws that preside over human beings. Each of these attempts disclosed that the values of goodness or badness are found only in acts, characters, personalities, and so forth, which exist only in human beings.

How is it possible to explain goodness or badness on the basis of the laws that preside over human beings? Even though goodness or badness is found in acts, characters, personalities and so on, we have not yet clarified what acts or personalities are. To clarify the nature of acts requires comprehension of a human being's temporal structure, and to make the notion of a personality clear requires a grasp of the solidarity characteristic of a human being. However, before the structure of acts can be clarified, it must be recalled that we have already described human beings in terms of act connections. Here the subjective movements constituting the betweenness of human beings are vaguely designated by means of the term *act*. And within a human being, who is the agent of these movements, we found individual moments as well as whole ones. However empty their essential features, they retain their role as agents of act connections through their interdependence on one another. We have already described this agent vaguely in terms of personality. To expound further the values of goodness or badness, it will be sufficient for us to refer to act and personality as already described. The problem is to determine what goodness or badness are really like, as inherent in actions and in personality.

The laws presiding over human beings consist of the movement of the negation of absolute negativity. In revolting against one community or another, one revolts against one's own foundation. As an act, the movement of this rebellion is toward the destruction of community as well as being a revolt against one's own foundation. This is why this movement is not approved of by the other participants in the community, any more than it is approved by one's own innermost essence. This movement is called *badness*. Therefore, it is not that the feeling of disapproval gives rise to badness, but that the act itself gives rise to disapproval, by displaying a rebellious character. We are thus able to describe this act as a negating of positive values and an affirming of negative ones or as one that takes leave of the higher values and grasps lower ones. Yet, even in this case, we must presuppose the realm of values as given in value feelings. The problem of values should also be considered from the way of being of *ningen* as an issue of how to deal with the being of things in connection with human beings. Hence, it is related to the issue of how things are disclosed out of a human being. For instance, a flower is said to be beautiful, but that it "is beautiful" is based upon a specific manner of existence of a human being who finds it beautiful. It is the same with all values. Consequently, we must assert that the gradation of values or the positive/negative distinction of values are all grounded on the law that presides over a human being, basically speaking.

What does it mean to reject higher values and maintain lower ones in accordance with this fundamental law? It means that one performs an action that revolts against this law's very foundation. This has been apparent in all of the world religions since ancient times or, to go even further back, in tribal societies. There, revolt against the gods or against the authority of the whole, the isolation of the individual, or the separation from the whole due to hatred or egoism has been proclaimed "evil." Egoism is never, of necessity, accompanied by the establishment of ego consciousness. A primitive person who falls in love with another and in the process violates a taboo is likely to be an egoist, yet without thereby possessing the consciousness of ego. Through practical acts, the ego becomes isolated by revolting against the whole. Only on this basis does the consciousness of ego come to be established.

The law that presides over a human being, however, consists in the movement of absolute negativity returning back to itself. A person who has turned his back on his own foundation in revolting against one community or another may then try to return to his own foundation by negating this revolt once more. This return may also be achieved by recognizing another community. The acts constituting this movement signify the sublimation of individuality, the realization of socio-ethical unity, or the return to one's own foundation. Therefore, it is approved not only by those who participate in the community but also by one's own innermost essence. This is "goodness." Therefore, it is not that the value of goodness comes to be established on the basis of the feeling of approval but rather that the act itself is approved precisely by virtue of its attempting to return to its foundation. Acts such as these can be said to consist of the rejection of lower values and the adhesion to higher ones. The supreme value is absolute wholeness; and an aspiration, or upward drive, or eagerness for it, is "goodness." Consequently, obedience to gods or to the authority of the whole, that is, the abandonment of individual independence, and the manifestation of love, devotion, or service have always been proclaimed as "goodness." This can be illustrated through a simple expression, the Japanese term *nakayoshi*, which refers to the realization of socio-ethical unity.

If badness or goodness is the movement of the negation of absolute negativity, then is the conclusion to be drawn that even badness becomes authorized by the Absolute by reason of its being grounded on it? Certainly so. The movement of absolute negativity, which is a return back to itself, is impossible apart from the moment of self-rebellion. Even though the union of love or self-sacrifice may be taken as goodness, it must be that what is requisite for the arising of this goodness is, above all, the independence of an individual, which is badness. If so, then badness turns out to be that which renders goodness possible, and hence, it ceases to be badness.

Apart from the disobedience to the whole, taboos are unconstitutable; and apart from taboos, an observance of taboos is not possible.

Consequently, the realization of wholeness by means of taboos can be achieved only through violation. Likewise, without the independence of the individual, socio-ethical unity could not materialize. The more strictly the independence of an individual is achieved, the higher the socio-ethical unity is realized. To this extent, the self-awareness of the individual is good, and a separation from wholeness is also good. Insofar as the movement of negation makes a dynamic advancement and does not come to a standstill, there is no badness that does not change into goodness. If badness is supposed to be derived from the Absolute, then this is inevitable. Goethe describes this circumstance vividly with reference to the relation between God and Mephistopheles. A God who stands opposed to a demon is dethroned because; as a relative being, He cannot be Absolute Wholeness.

We must also take into consideration the movement of negation that comes to a standstill in a human being. It goes without saying, however, that this does not mean that the movement of absolute negativity itself comes to a standstill. A human being rises through the movement of negation, yet falls from his essence and degrades to an inauthentic mode of being. Then, a standstill or a fixation occurs within a human being. In some cases, an individual's movement of independence comes to a halt, and the existence of a society as an organic whole results. The movement of independence is the source of all of the evils through its rebellious character and is an indispensable condition for every goodness to the extent that it is an element in the movement of return. But a human being who comes to a standstill without being able to revolt is unable to return. That is to say, he who cannot stand badness cannot achieve goodness. A human being loses his self-conscious essence when he stops the movement of independence and spends hours in idle slumber in a community, falling victim to "the crowd." This justifies an individualism that denies altruism or self-sacrifice as nothing more than a crowd-oriented instinct.

Yet, in another case, there enters onto the scene the sublimation of independence, that is, the cessation of the movement of returning through the negation of negation, and hence individuals that look like atoms existing side by side. Here is a standpoint that stops at the spearhead of individualization and looks back in such a way as to recognize meaning only in the movement of revolt. This standpoint consists in letting the movement of negation come to a stop in its primary negation. And, with this cessation, revolt loses sight of its positive meaning. Although revolt is an element in the movement of return that renders goodness possible, when separated from this movement, it values the source of badness that can no longer be transformed into goodness. This is the fixation of evil, which is equivalent to that which has been regarded as extreme evil from ancient times. When Fichte described badness in terms of inertia (*Trägheit*), he may be said to have had insight into this issue.

In the preceding, the value of goodness or badness can be described by using the law that presides over human beings. The feeling of approval or value feeling operates in accordance with this law. What about the concept of "conscience"? This issue concerns the inside of an individual's consciousness and is loaded with the various qualities of one's own personal experiences. Can it not be said that conscience can be conceived of apart from the social characteristics of a human being?

The phenomenon called *the voice of conscience* consists of our accusing ourselves of attitudes we once assumed or of acts we once performed or in prohibiting ourselves from attitudes we might come to assume or acts we might well perform. It can also mean that we do not feel ashamed of ourselves or that we feel confident of the appropriateness of our acts or attitudes. This phenomenon cannot arise unless we have feelings of approval or disapproval of ourselves and our acts or attitudes. This we certainly admit. It is true that what is called *the voice of conscience* can be heard by an individual only in solitude. Without the self-awareness of the individual, such a voice cannot be heard. For instance, this is the case with the cells that constitute a physical body or with shepherds acting as a crowd.

We should attend to the fact that the so-called voice of conscience is mainly an accusing or prohibiting voice. Not feeling ashamed of ourselves in itself answers the accusing voice. Confidence presupposes fear over against the prohibiting voice. When one does not fear the prohibiting voice, one needs no further confidence to act. Hence, the essential characteristic of the voice of conscience lies in this, that we hear the voice negating us from our innermost parts.

Incidentally, when we separate a human being from all individual/ social connections and grasp him only from the standpoint of individual consciousness, then what should we think of the voice of negation? If it is supposed that an individual is originally independent and that independence is at the core of an individual, then there will be no possibility that the voice heard will have a negative effect. In particular, when an individual acts to preserve his own independence, for instance, when he acts only for his own sake by refusing socio-ethical unity with others or rejects self-sacrifice demanded for the sake of social cooperation, then the voice heard from an individual's innermost parts must be a voice approving of these actions. In fact, this kind of argument is made in individualism, when carried to its extreme. This is the standpoint referred to as the *affirmation of life*. In this case, however, a particularly strong voice is heard that is accusative of one's self. Why? If it is supposed that egoistic acts are disapproved of by other persons or by society, then the accusing voice must be heard from the outside. In spite of this, the voice of negation is heard from within one's innermost place. Even though Nietzsche rejected the voice of conscience as a crowd-oriented instinct, we cannot alter the fact that the voice of conscience is an inner voice. Hence, from the position of self-affirmation, we are afforded no alternative but to assert that conscience is not a basic ethical concept but rather a phenomenon of the degradation of humankind based on hatred.

However, the voice of conscience is heard from the standpoint of the individual's independence and not from that of the animal crowd. This voice was heard in Socrates' mind as well as in Confucius', long before the reversion of values through hatred. We are not reluctant to regard this as a basic ethical phenomenon. Still, what is the source of this phenomenon? If it is supposed that one hears the voice of negation from one's innermost, then there exists a negation at the rear of one's self. This negation is exactly what we have comprehended as the law presiding over a human being. It is the negation that makes an individual an individual. Furthermore, this negation attempts to return to its foundation by negating itself. It speaks as the voice of conscience. Hence, we can say that the voice of conscience is, basically speaking, "a voice invoking absolute negativity." It is little wonder that this has been interpreted as the voice of the Absolute and has been referred to as *God's command* or *the devil's voice*. Thanks to this voice, we do not stop at mere negation but are lured to advance to the negation of negation.

It can be said, therefore, that, just because the phenomenon of conscience is particularly concerned with individual consciousness, it displays the law that presides over a human being so much the better. So conscience, which is particularly concerned with the innermost part of an individual, joins ethical concepts other than conscience, which are affiliated more with a human being's social existence, in being based on the law that presides over a human being.

Ever since Kant clearly set limits to the world of human freedom, as over against the natural world, it has been generally acknowledged that the concept of "freedom" has been a basic concept of ethics. But, the concept of "freedom" eventually was not established in a Kantian manner. The various forms through which the concept of freedom is prescribed are roughly divided in two. One is the individual's emancipation from the whole, which may assume various forms, such as the state, a church, a family, and so forth. This sort of freedom is that with which moral philosophers in England have been mainly concerned. The economical and political position that has been promulgated as liberalism is also based on this concept of freedom. The other is freedom that has the capacity to self-initiate without a cause outside of itself; that is to say, the capacity of self-causation such as our ordinary concept of "freedom" exhibits. This is the control of the self by the self, autonomy. According to Kant's explanation, this autonomy consists of the control of the individual self by the superindividual and authentic self; that is, by the whole self. The first freedom is a negation that enables an individual to revolt against the whole. The second freedom is that negation which further negates the preceding negation. In either case, freedom is the movement of negation. It is clear that freedom is the law that presides over a human being.

This state of affairs further shows that the authentic feature of freedom is absolute negativity. This feature has been long understood. Unrestricted freedom, that is, "to *be* by oneself and from oneself," strictly speaking, can be said only of the Absolute. A truly self-initiating agent is none other than God as Creator. The Absolute cannot stand opposed to anything other than Himself. If something stands in opposition to Himself, then He is not the Absolute. Consequently, the Absolute must be an agent who makes self-negation (that is, non-Absolute being, a relative, or noninfinite being, a finite one) His own self. This means that the free Absolute is absolute negativity. From this it can be understood that freedom is the movement of negation. Thus, the freedom of revolting against one's own foundation, that is, "the freedom of evil," so to speak, can be developed from the foundation itself. The Absolute develops Himself only through this self-negation. In other words, the Absolute emerges only in freedom. The negative structure of a human being demonstrates that a human being arises precisely in freedom.

It is clear beyond dispute that the issues of obligation and responsibility have their place within human interconnections. We have already found that a standpoint which tries to expound obligation by grounding its argument on the moral sentiment only succeeds in explaining the origin of obligation by appealing to socio-ethical organization. Responsibility could give full play to its authentic significance through the principle of solidarity. However, the law that presides over a human being renders socio-ethical organization or solidarity possible.

The socio-ethical unity consists in this: that agents, who become individuals through negation, return to themselves through the negation of negation. Although this unity is a connection among human beings, it involves coercion as well. It is aspiration that initiates the returning movement to the foundation, but as the negation of the standpoint of the individual, it is coercion. Thus, the movement of negation is coercion affiliated with an aspiration for a return to one's foundation. This coercion constitutes the essence of obligation. Because coercion is the movement of absolute negativity back to itself, obligation requires self-negation with an imperative authority, and the thus negated individual obeys this authority out of respect.

Kant endeavored to clarify the basic principle of morality through the everyday consciousness of obligation. The formula of the moral principle he set up in his *Kritik der praktischen Vernunft* runs this way: "Act in such a manner that the maxim of your will may simultaneously be valid as the principle of universal law, at whatever time it may be." This principle clearly includes two elements. One of them is the proposition concerned with several universal prescriptions of the will that exercises control over the various individual acts of an individual subject, termed *you* under a specific rule. This proposition is called *the maxim of will*. Psychologically speaking, it refers to the attitude of mind of an individual called *you*. The other element is the principle that imparts a universally valid law to the will of every rational being, that is, the principle of universal law. The moral principle requires that the former become valid in the form of the latter; that is, that both become congruent with each other. In other words, it requires that a practical prescription for an individual should simultaneously be the practical law for all people and at all times. Based on this possibility, the imperative to act arises. However, exactly what is this possibility? For Kant, it means that the supraindividual rational will lies at the rear of the individual will. Or, it means that at the rear of an individual self lies the superdiscriminative, authentic self as noumenon. It is the foundation of the individual self, so to speak. But, only in separation from the superindividual, superdiscriminative foundation can an individual self be individualistic. Thus far, the individual is not also universal. Because of this, congruence with the universal is again demanded. Incidentally, this congruence is made possible in the returning of an individual to the superdiscriminative at its ground. Kant's principle of practice can be said to consist of the fact that the authentic self sublimates that individuality inherent in the inauthentic and individualistic self. This is exactly what we have understood as the law that presides over human beings. Kant's emphasis on coercion (*Nötigung*) tacitly refers to the negative structure of a human being and that which "ought to be" must also be understood from this perspective.

It would be an overstatement to say that Kant clearly dealt with the supraindividual universal self as the wholeness of a human being. Durkheim points out that, whereas the universal in Kant is, in reality, subjective society, Kant himself failed to see this. It is not our intention to assert that Kant proved self-consciously that the law which presides over a human being is the principle of morality. All that Kant did was to clarify the principle of morality by describing a human being as a whole in the form of a unity of the empirical and the noumenal, he did not go so far as to actually describe the law that presides over human beings. Judging from the essential features of the problem with which he was involved, we can say that Kant came in touch with this law without realizing that he had done so. Hence, his principle of morality is, from our vantage point, the law of human beings, which he tried to express in his own fashion.

Nothing shows this more clearly than the formulation of the categorical imperative, which Kant calls *the principle of humanity as well as of every rational being*. It runs as follows: "Act in such a manner that you do not treat the humanity inherent in your personality and in every other person merely as a means, but also as an end, at the same time." What he here calls *humanity* (*Menschheit*), he often substitutes for with the term *personality* (*Personlichkeit*). That essence which renders a human being capable of being a human being and also renders a person capable of being a person, that is, the noumenal and authentic self that constitutes the foundation of the universal law in the preceding formulation of the categorical imperative, is called *humanity* or *personality*.

The principle of humanity reveals an interesting problem. What does the phrase *humanity in your personality* mean? And what does it mean to prohibit this personality from being "treated merely as a means"? If personality is supposed to be straightforwardly noumenal, then it is out of the question for this personality to assume its essence again as the noumenal self, because it already is a noumenal self. It is also entirely impossible to treat such a noumenal self merely as a means and therefore to prohibit this is nonsense. Even though personality (that is, a noumenal self) makes a person a person, a person must simultaneously be a thing that has an empirical nature. By virtue of its possessing this characteristic, it is required that emphasis be placed on the fact that the essence of this thing as person consists of the authentic self.

It is also possible for this person to be treated merely as a means; that is, in its empirical form.

Now, if one treats "a person" merely as a means, then one is also led to treat "personality," which renders this person capable of being a person, as a means. Because of this, personality, or humanity, which is absolutely not means oriented, can nevertheless be dealt with as a means.

If it is supposed that "a person" possesses the dual qualities of empirical/intellectual, phenomenal/noumenal, and hence, can be both a means and an end in itself, and if the intellectual, noumenal, and end in itself are regarded as aspects of "personality," then it becomes evident why the imperative that calls on us "to act in such a manner as to treat personality not merely as a means but at the same time as an end itself" is called *the law of community*, which presides over "the kingdom of ends." This imperative gives expression to the rational law connecting human beings. Originally, this imperative was not designed to prohibit us absolutely from treating one's own person and that of another as a mere means. If this were so, then the connection of human beings would be entirely impossible. That I assume a benevolent attitude toward you is rendered possible because I treat your person as an end and mine as a means. Conversely, that I receive kindness from you is made possible because I treat my person as an end and yours as a means. Without the means, either in assuming kindness toward others or in receiving it from them, kindness could not occur. Consequently, a standpoint that absolutely refuses to take into account a person as a means must be without any sense of affiliation with the actual connections between persons. There is no possibility, given the standpoint of the isolated person, for the kingdom of ends, as the systematic connection of persons, to arise. This standpoint has nothing to do with what Kant really intended. His point was that, although admitting that it is unavoidable to treat persons as means, he yet pays attention to the fact that this means affiliation is a part of the dual character of personality and emphasizes that persons must not only be treated as means, in a one-sided manner. Persons are to be treated as means and, at the same time, must always be dealt with as ends.

When I receive kindness from you, I actually treat your person as a means, but this state of affairs must be accompanied by the converse in which I treat your person as an end and mine as a means to it; that is, by such an attitude as that in which I hold your person in respect and humble myself in gratitude to you.

Likewise, that I give you kindness is rendered possible by the fact that I treat my personality as a means. But this attitude does not terminate in my making myself your slave. Instead, while serving you, the dignity of my person must also be upheld. In this dual relationship, using another person is congruent with serving another person, and being used by another person is congruent with receiving some service from another person. The content of Kant's principle of humanity is constituted by this double relationship. We can see that this principle is a principle of human connection and based on the original identity of persons as divided into self and other, as well as on the means characteristic of individual personality, understood as the negation of this identity. This is why we supposed that Kant had tacitly grasped the law that presides over human beings.

In the preceding, we have provided a rough outline of the basic law of human beings, that is, of basic ethics. But this is only a formal description. We must now try to instantiate this description by a further analysis of a human being.

part iii

the spatio-temporal structure
of a human being

8   private and public existence

We have found the negative interdependent relationship as the basic structure of a human being. An individual consists of the negation of community, and society consists of the negation of individuality. But we did not lose sight that those who come into being through negation of community are many individuals who were once able to be communal, and that a society consisting of the negation of individuality was once a community constituted by many individuals. Consequently, it was not questioned that subjects, as the many, should possess a subjective extension. But the disruption into many individuals not only yields an objective extension but also a subjective one. Attending to this point, we must embark upon an even more detailed analysis of the structure of a human being.

The various linguistic expressions that describe a human being as something spatially extended in one way or another lure us to grapple with this problem. The original meaning of the word *ningen* is *seken* or *yo no naka*, whose meaning is quite ordinarily understood to connote an extended realm of life interaction. This is clearly shown by such phrases as *seken o wataru* ("to get through the world"), *yo no naka ni de te yu ku* ("to get out into the world"), *hiroi yo no naka* ("the large world"). By saying this, however, we do not mean that the world is here understood as something spatially similar to physical space. When it is said that something is "to be made public" or that "a secret is leaked into the world," the term *world* refers to a realm in which something becomes public or comes to light. When we happen to see our friends in a remote town where they are not expected, we say that the world is small, even though it is actually large. The narrow/large distinction is made in accordance with whether we are known or not. The more we become known, the narrower the world becomes. This extendedness signifies the intensity of our being known. Thus, the characteristic of the world as "a scene in which something comes to light" is described in terms of publicity.

Although attention is paid to the public aspect of a human being, its individual element is revealed to belong to "a private being." This is the being whose actions are not disclosed at some place where they are thought to be destined to be disclosed; that is, a deficiency of publicity. Hence, a private being can also be said, in essence, to be public, except that, in this case, such a person possesses only the mode *privatus*. The case is entirely opposite with individualists in the modern world. For them, publicity is a deficiency of the authenticity of self. Those who stand buried in publicity are referred to as *public figures*. They are deprived of the self and bury their authentic being in oblivion. Consequently, they are not individuals but masses or slaves. This mass-oriented publicity hides a human being's authentic countenance; that is, it hides her deep-rooted individuality. This is a result of the assertions of individualism.

Individualism maintains, however, that the self or the individual is what is disclosed before God, in some cosmic fashion. In other words, whereas the individual self is hidden from publicity, it is entirely public to the Absolute. In individualism, the public aspect of the Absolute is upheld, instead of that of the public, as a human being's authentic countenance. This means that an individual, in essence, is public. The problem here is that the publicity of the public does not truly turn out to be publicity. And this is a correct insight. The publicity of the public is always accompanied by a deficiency and is by no means absolute publicity. Because of this, a human being is public and at the same time private. For one who is entirely isolated, there can be neither a public being nor private being. For an isolated person, as for Robinson Crusoe, there is no longer even private being.

We must now investigate what publicity is, in relation to a private being. The phenomenon generally referred to as *publication*, or the phenomenon that leaks out despite not being published will provide the occasion for resolving this problem.

While keeping our eye on ordinary family life or the company of friends, we can make it clear that such groups possess the characteristic of "a place where something is disclosed." The phenomenon of publication is here indicated by the term *to reveal.*

A storekeeper reveals to her family her decision to finally close her store. A friend reveals to her group her decision to finally leave school. For the family or the group such decisions were not yet public before the information was revealed to them. Therefore, they do not yet share the same pain with her. However, with this information revealed, the pain permeates the whole family, or the whole group.

On the other hand, against an instance of mere widespread publicity, the family or group is still private. Whatever quarrel we may have with our family life and however well we may get on with each other, these affairs are "private," but not yet public, for they are matters that concern the family from within. When we bring our quarrel into the street or reveal our happy existence to the public, then our family life turns out to be an event in the public domain. As is repeatedly observed, in China, a quarrel between a husband and wife is regularly brought out into the street. The wife tries to win the quarrel by speaking out to her neighbors. In this case, a private affair within a family is disclosed to the public, it becomes public.

Further, what is here referred to as *public* is usually a town or a village, which in turn, in a yet wider context becomes a private being. For instance, when the custom of the secret felling of trees owned by the state prevails in a village, the practice is hidden from the public and remains a secret of the village. The same can occur in a meeting whose discussion is not published, such as in privy council or at a faculty meeting. These are public places of an entirely different order for the private actions of members. With respect to the wider public, however, in these closed places the content of discussions is kept secret and hence the content may possibly be leaked.

In contrast with private being, publicity signifies a community that is larger than and exists outside of a private being's limit. Various public beings are, in turn, capable of privacy, in contrast with the larger community, which exists beyond them. Therefore, it is possible that what is already known and disclosed in the "quarters concerned" is not yet leaked to the public. It is also possible that what is leaked to one corner of the public is not yet disclosed to the public at large. We can conclude that the publicity of the public is an index, designating a community that is always larger than the other being in question.

Does the publicity of the public reach as far as humankind in general? There is no doubt that this is not the case, so far as historical facts

are concerned. In periods in which our Japanese ancestors were separated from other nations in the world, people used to describe Japan
as a whole in terms of the word *tenka* ("the world"). The public was
distinctly limited to the nation. Whether one is known outside of the
country, worldwide, had nothing to do with one's being "disclosed to
the public." But what happens in the contemporary world in which
communication and transportation has intensified worldwide? Whatever is today disclosed within a country is likely to be reported outside of it and become known worldwide almost immediately.
Consequently, that something is disclosed to the public is equivalent
to the possibility of its being disclosed all over the world. Thus, we can
say that the publicity of a human being extends to people in general.
Yet, most of what is disclosed within a nation is based upon the communal characteristics of that nation and is not intended to be disclosed
all over the world. Those who are concerned with reporting beyond the
nation pick up on only a small number of events selected on the basis
of international interest and have no intention of informing the world
about all events without exception. Consequently, even among the
people of two nations that have an intimate relationship, they are not
as acquainted with each other's public affairs as might be supposed. It
still remains the case that the sense of "public" is restricted in extent to
the nation.

International publicity bridges the relationship between the possible publicity of humankind in general and the actual publicity that
concerns the nation. It indicates a communality of a sort that is much
larger in extent than national being, which is different in dimension
from the communality characteristic of nations. The latter, however extensive it may be, is established by the communal being that individual
citizens share with one another. It has nothing to do with that
communality that prevails among groups. However, international publicity is not a communality that prevails among individuals but rather
among nations as compactly organized groups. What is called *an international community of individuals* is established among those individuals who are, respectively, representatives of each nation, but it has
nothing to do with the community of cosmopolitans who abandon their
national being. That which is established through the community of
being of cosmopolitans is not available except as a communality pre-
vailing in the nation that arises in the form of a cosmos-polis. Should a
cosmos-polis of this sort be realized, then the publicity of humankind
in general and the national one in particular will merge into one another. It is not in this cosmos-polis that international publicity is called

into question. Rather, it is a publicity that arises among nations. Hence, international publicity, although including as its basis publicity valid for the internal affairs of each nation, nevertheless, must transcend the latter. We cannot help but observe that international publicity is greater in dimension than national publicity.

The phrase *to be disclosed to the public*, no matter how far we may stretch its meaning, can signify nothing but that publicity which prevails inside a nation. This reflects that the meaning of *public* is ordinarily restricted to the limit of nations. Consequently, to express what is intended by *international publicity*, we must replace *the public* with the term *world*. The problem here concerns the scene in which things become disclosed. The disclosure remains unchanged, irrespective of whether the scene in which it occurs is the world or the public. But we must inquire further into this matter. In the first place, when things are disclosed to the public, they need not become known to everyone within a nation or even within a certain community. It is possible that something known to only a small number of people may still display an extremely high degree of publicity. For something to be disclosed means that it is not hidden from the public and that it is open to anyone who wishes to have access to it. Consequently, the extent of publicity must be measured not by the number of persons who actually participate in it but rather by the extent of the possibility of participation. To be disclosed to the public means to impart to everyone belonging to the public the means of the possibility of participation. This is the principal prescription of publicity.

This is clearly evident in the way in which the public is informed. In ancient societies, what was to be communicated was written on a stone or a plate and displayed at important points of traffic flow. Or else, persons were dispatched on foot to spread information to the public. This illustrates the intention of those concerned to inform all possible persons. Incidentally, these primitive ways of communication have lost no vigor even in the modern world. If we go into the streets, innumerable signboards convey, respectively, each vocation to the general public. Often, they may be visible to only a small number of people. However, they were originally designed to be seen by everyone. If something must be hidden from some persons, then we cannot "put up a signboard." Once a signboard is erected, the profession that appears on the board is thereby disclosed to the public at large, regardless of its actual efficiency. Likewise, we can find in the streets today, as in former times, those who walk around to inform others of something, such as, persons wearing sandwichboards or, to go a step further, various public demonstrations. All of these employ the same ways of informing others as in former times and were designed to garner the attention of as many people as possible.

A typical source of public information in the modern world is the press. The notice board that in ancient times consisted of "written words" has today developed into newspapers. Similarly, spreading information by speaking while strolling around consisted of "words circulated through the voice," whose form has developed into radio broadcasting. The press discloses information to the public by means of these two forms of communication. Its aim is to inform as many persons as possible, and that goal is now nearly achieved. The possibility of full participation that was once merely nominal has now become actual. For instance, "the publication" of a judicial judgment means that this judgment is not hidden to anybody, and the possibility of participation through hearing it is given to the entire nation. The actual court itself has the capacity for seating no more than several tens of observers and, hence, the factual distinction between nonpublication and publication depends on whether or not the court actually has the capacity for accepting several tens of observers or not. In spite of this limitation, the court continues to have the reputation of being open to the entire nation, owing to the reporting of the press.

Publicity consists of its not being hidden from the public; that is, of the possibility of everyone participating in coming to know something. If persons are able to participate in existence, and can share (*mit-teilen*) it with one another, then this existence is public. Hence, publicity manifests a deficiency in various forms, according to what extent persons do not want other persons to participate in that existence. We are able to confide only in our intimate friends or lovers about the bitter torment of our inner life but refuse to confide in those who are indifferent to us or are not our friends. We do not want those who are not intimately acquainted with us to encounter our anguish. Furthermore, a family may not want a stranger, with whom they feel it necessary to be on guard or from whom they keep their distance, to enter into the life of family affection. This is because the intrusion of a person with whom common affection is not shared prevents the family from forming an affectionate unity. In such cases, the relationship among friends or within the family is defective in communality and remains private existence, insofar as it does not allow strangers to participate in it.

Generally speaking, we can say that a certain group has the quality of privacy, to the extent that its secret is to be kept hidden. Contrary to public existence, this private one refuses to be disclosed, that is, it refuses the "publication" or "report" of it. Hence, by being published or reported, that is, by being "exposed to the sun," it loses in privacy and gains in publicity.

We do not mean, however, that this kind of publicity keeps the authentic features of things exposed to the sun. Rather, it may even be a place where the authentic features are kept hidden. What a rumor, or a newspaper report repeats day after day is to enter the private sphere that refuses publication, with its own assumptions and imaginings, and brings it to public awareness against the wishes of those who would prefer to keep it private. Publicity thus constructed hides its authentic features by means of a "lie" disguised as authenticity. The phenomenon of "propaganda," which has had an extraordinary rise in free but competitive modern society, takes advantage of this aspect of publicity. It makes it a rule to disclose a certain thing by fabricating support for it. Consequently, if we have skill in manipulating propaganda, then we are able to overcome "truth" by means of a "falsehood" camouflaged as "truth." Falsehood fabricated as truth and that has gained in publicity can no longer be overthrown by the few people who are acquainted with the truth. History advances not through hidden truth but in and through public awareness. Consequently, it can even be said that publicity is rather what Buddhist philosophy of consciousness only tries to maintain in terms of its so-called concept of covering truth.

By saying this, however, we do not necessarily mean that publicity always covers the truth of things. The view that publicity consists of covering the truth is also publicity. If publicity always covers truth, then an attempt to bring truth to light cannot occur at all. In addition, the history of humankind is full of movements that disclose truth and overthrow falsehood. It is in publicity that the "rumor" is disclosed to be a rumor, and "propaganda" to be propaganda. A superficial curiosity is exposed to the sun in rumor, and a tenacious utilitarian-mindedness is evident in propaganda. That publicity that hid Socrates' greatness was also that by which his greatness was disclosed. Thus, publicity covers the truth of things and, at the same time, discovers or reveals it.

The problem here is not in asking in what manner publicity covers or discovers the truth of things. Whether publicity covers or discovers the truth of things, it is certain that publicity arises in publishing and communicating a certain thing by means of words. In the event that falsehood makes its appearance under the guise of truth, no change occurs in that it is still disclosed to the public. More important for us is that publicity arises within "communication." *Mitteilung* in German means "to share with one another," and at the same time, it means "communication."

Thus, that something is published or communicated to the public means that society becomes conscious of it. Hence, publicity is a problem of social consciousness. But the attempt to deal with it as a problem of social consciousness is accompanied by a variety of difficulties.

The attempt to consider "consciousness" by means of epistemology or psychology originates with modern ego-consciousness, which divides the individual into body and mind and deals with the mind separately from the body. Discussion of sensation, perception, thinking, will, feeling, and so forth are all elements of individual consciousness. Therefore, it is unavoidably presumed that an individual mind can be studied in detachment from the body. Even physiological psychology understands the reciprocal relationship between body and mind in this way. Therefore, even after the attention paid by the preceding century to the fact that the psychology of concrete human life has nothing to do with isolated individual consciousness but is actually developed through various kinds of human relationships, all that modern psychology has attempted is to deal with the relationships between individual consciousnesses or with the relationship between individual consciousness and the social environment. These relations are called *social consciousness.*

A position that avoids the term *consciousness* to take into consideration the realm of the unconscious uses instead such concepts as "mind," "spiritual life," and so forth. In this position, one investigates the group-oriented mind or social spirit. Hence, the separation of mind from body one still presupposed.

But the position of the *cogito*, which takes body as mere "matter," should be submitted to severe criticism. The body is not merely the same as any other object but is basically something subjective. As an observer of phenomena, one's eye is not matter as an object but is an observing as a subject. Even the hand of an acting person is not an objective matter but the hand of an acting person. Moreover, apart from the subjective physical body, no human relationships could arise at all. Because a certain movement of the physical body is not merely the movement of matter but an act of a person, a relationship such as agreeing with another can occur. When these elements are disregarded, one keeps one's eyes only on the relationship between one mind and another. To go a step further in this direction, when one investigates the "group-affiliated mind" as an organismic system of mental forces, one considers the supraindividual or group-affiliated mind as entirely analogous to the individual mind.

The same may be said of social consciousness. We cannot say that individual consciousness is entirely emancipated from the difficult question of its connection with the body. On the contrary, social consciousness is treated as pure consciousness which is entirely separated from this connection. If there is such a "mind" or "consciousness," then what does the phenomenon of publication, communication, or disclosing mean? If the relationship between one individual's mind and another's is equivalent to the relationship between one mental act (within an individual's mind) and another, then these minds should be able to be directly connected to each other without recourse to the medium of publication or communication. Otherwise, we could not say that a group-affiliated mind thinks and feels. However, a certain event becomes known to society through communication and thus constitutes the content of the group-affiliated mind. This suggests that the phenomena of communication and publication reveal the structure of a social being that cannot be understood in terms of the analogy with an individual mind. This is why publicity instead of social consciousness should be called into question here.

What does the fact that publicity, as that which becomes known to society only through the medium of communication and publication, show us? To communicate (i.e., *mit-teilen* in German) something means to divide it into many subjects. With respect to the newspaper, a great number of identical things are produced and distributed. With radio, when something is broadcast innumerable receivers are tuned in. Informing divided subjects in this way is something that does not entirely exist in the inherent structure of consciousness. We are led to the conclusion that publicity indicates the spatial extendedness of subjects. Social consciousness also has an intimate connection with the body of society. It is certain that this body has, like an individual's body, an aspect likely to be regarded as mere matter. Although this body of society is basically subjective, we try to describe it in terms of the spatiality of a human being.

9 the spatiality of a human being

We have attempted to understand publicity from the standpoint of such phenomena as publication and communication, whose business it is to enable persons to share something with one another. Publication and communication are, therefore, intimately connected with spatial extendedness. In a primitive form of publication, a notice board was set up at important points where traffic converged. This was done so that what should be conveyed might be shared among as many persons as possible. *Traffic* is a spatial expression of human social intercourse, and traffic patterns gave birth to roads on becoming fixed. Roads stretch out in a spatial manner and are further intersected spatially at certain places. An intersecting point of arteries of traffic expresses intense human social intercourse. For this reason, a notice board set up at an important traffic intersection was designed to have connection with a spatial extendedness as wide as possible. Similarly, to make public an official notice by dispatching a person to communicate it, was also designed to spread information in a spatial manner.

In this sense, to communicate information to the public signifies that the information is spread spatially, in the literal sense of the term. This is true even in the present world. The most outstanding characteristic of the progress of the communication media, specifically newspapers and radio, lies in strengthening and extending the capacity to spread information spatially. Written words are rapidly carried to every corner of the country by the railroad. Spoken words are spread spatially even more rapidly by means of radio waves. Thus, for something

155

to be disclosed to the public is nearly equivalent to its being spread spatially. Here we can find an essential difference between "to be disclosed to individual consciousness" and "to be disclosed to the public."

The spatiality of a human being is known to everybody in an ontic way. People use transportation facilities and behave in a spatial fashion for the benefit of their ordinary lives. It is doubtful whether this facticity is grasped theoretically. Scientific common sense suggests that the world of nature is spatially extended and not the world of subjective freedom. Consequently, it is thought that a human being is spatial as a natural object, instead of being the subject of freedom. If this is so, then several questions arise. Is spatial meaning involved in that relationship in which one person stands at first opposed to and then united with another person? Does the *Thou* who stands beside me indicate that that *Thou*, as a natural object, stands beside me in a spatial fashion? Has this nothing to do with that subjective *Thou* who is related to me and stands beside me? Does the fact that I feel lonely because I am far apart from *Thou* mean not so much that this subjective *Thou* with whom I fell in love is far away, as that this *Thou*, as a natural object, is far away from me spatially?

It is nonsense to raise such questions. It is not that there is a subjective *Thou* who exists apart from *Thou* as a natural object. It is no less true that the former *Thou* is beside me than that the latter *Thou* is beside me. Furthermore, a personality, as the subject of freedom, can also exist outside of and in opposition to me. Notice must be taken, however, that what is here spoken of as *outside* of and in *opposition* to should be taken as being entirely different in meaning from cases in which strictly natural things are dealt with. When *Thou's* physical body is regarded as being merely material, it exists outside of and in opposition to *I*, just as a natural object does. It is never united with me. But, in this case, *I* is merely an agent of contemplation, not the subject of practical action.

On the contrary, when *I* as the subject of practice stands face to face with *Thou*, *Thou* stands face to face with *I* as the subject of practice. One's physical body exhibits personality in every part and, hence, lures another's personality in its every motion. It strengthens opposition through hostility and gives birth to unity through affection. It exemplifies what it means "to be outside" through coolness and draws toward "the inside" through friendliness. In this way, as that which constitutes the subjective connection of acts, *Thou* is capable of existing outside of and in opposition to me. This sort of spatiality is not the same as space in the world of nature. It is not a form of intuition, but rather the manner in which multiple subjects are related to one another. It is not a uniform extendedness, but a dialectical one, in which relations such as "far and near, wide and narrow" are mutually transformed into one another. In a word, it is the betweenness itself of subjective human beings.

When emphasis is placed on the contention that the essential characteristic of *ningen sonzai* is to be regarded not merely as the being of, but rather the betweenness between humans, then we have, in fact, already encountered subjective spatiality. All expressions that indicate the interconnection of the acts of human beings—for example, *intercourse, fellowship, transportation, communication*—can be understood only with a subjective spatiality of this sort. Spatial extendedness, as is evident in publication, communication, and so forth is an expression of this subjective spatiality.

I regard this subjective spatiality as the essential characteristic of human beings. Without it, the systematic relationships between personalities could not be understood. Often, even sociologists who take pains to grasp the essence of society conceive of society without including spatiality in their conception. For instance, they describe human relationships in terms of "the connection of meanings." They used to insist that the relationships in society cannot be understood except by means of the category of spatial representation; it is also recognized that "historical persons" who engage in reciprocal activities with one another are, concretely speaking, united as natural persons with their physical bodies. They continue to say, however, that the essential characteristic of human relationships does not consist of the spatial relationships of physical bodies. For example, they continue to say that the "relationship" between a dog chasing game and the game itself cannot constitute a society; that which renders society a society is the reciprocal activity of minds, that is, the connection of meanings left behind even after abstracting away the spatial relationships of physical bodies. Yet, is it possible to conceive of this reciprocal relationship of minds apart from physical bodies?

Is the reciprocal relationship of minds between a police officer, who runs after a thief, and the thief, established apart from their physical activities? To the extent that this relationship is a subjective and practical one, it is impossible to deprive it of that element which is contributed by the physical body. Only when the practical and subjective characteristics are eliminated from this relationship will it become merely the connection of noematic meanings. This connection of meanings cannot be the practical interconnections of actions inherent in subjective human beings. Therefore, we are led to the conclusion that the aforementioned sociologists had in mind a society understood noematically but not practically existing human beings. There is no doubt that the scientific standpoint deals with noematic meanings. But it is one thing to deal with the nonnoematic being of a practical subject of actions by transforming it into something noematic, and quite another to insist that a society is, essentially, something noematic. The science of practice must include within itself an element that transforms the nonnoematic into the noematic. What renders this transformation possible is the mediation of expressions.

Let us now try to deal with the spatial extendedness of publicity, which is known ontically to nearly everyone. This extendedness seems at first sight to be taken as physical space, but this is not the case. On the one hand, physical space is taken for granted as something entirely independent of the connections between one subject and another. On the other, the spatial extendedness of publicity is connected to subjects by means of mental relationships known as *communication* or news. Thus, space is likely to be eliminated by the cessation of communication or news. What can lead us to this space is a phenomenon that occurs when communication or news is brought to a halt, either artificially or naturally.

When a certain event is prohibited from being described in a newspaper or magazine, the words *reporting* this event are prohibited from being spatially dispersed throughout several millions of copies. This prohibition stops the spread of a report to the public. The means of reporting are not restricted to a newspaper or a magazine. Instead, the telephone, letters, dialogue, and so forth can play a role in spreading the news of this event to a considerable extent. When the telephone, the mail service, and so on are interrupted in their function and even transportation facilities are destroyed, then the report of this event is likely to be limited to a specific locality. Consequently, if a certain area were to be cut off from the services of communication, news reports, transportation, and so forth, then the people in this region would be cut off from the wider public. In this case, so far as physical space is concerned, however, there is no change. As extended, the greater public suffers damage. No matter how distant this region is, whether a remote place in the mountains or a secluded island, it is usually quite removed from the intense contact of communication, transportation, and the like. If this contact is interrupted against the will of the local people, then this event itself comes to emerge as an event of the gravest public concern. The interruption of contact is felt as physical damage by that society, so to speak.

A grandiose example of this is to be found in the Kanto region, where the Kanto earthquake occurred. A degree of communication through wireless telegraphy was available in those days, and communication through traffic facilities was not impossible. However, ordinary communication (such as news reporting) was cut off completely. Hence, in terms of ordinary existence, the society of Kanto was truly separated from the general public. In addition to this, even within the Kanto area, local regions were cut off from each other, and as a result, spatial connection was quite narrowly restricted. Society was temporarily torn to pieces. What played a role in communication to some limited extent were rumors, which were transmitted by word of mouth without an appropriate sense of responsibility in evidence. Such rumors were forcible proof that the ordinary public (i.e., the wider spatiality to which communication extends) had been lost sight of.

For the ordinary public, every event is regularly reported by those who have knowledge of reporting, and such reports become the common sense of society. At the basis of this common sense is a consciousness of the sort possessed by a witness of a certain event, or by a scholar who has specific knowledge of it, or by someone who is concerned with taking responsibility for the reporting of the event. Common sense of this sort could not be established by a society cut off from contact with the outside world. As a result, rumors circulated that an island called *Enoshima* had collapsed, a powder house had exploded, and the Koreans had attacked. Only one who really witnessed the collapse of Enoshima is entitled to make this sort of report. In a society whose communication with the outside world is cut off, the whimsical imagination of an individual, that is, imagination based on knowledge that is inferior by far to that of the natural sciences, circulates and takes the place of current news. This is the phenomenon of rumor. The destruction of communication because of the earthquake was, at the same time, the cutting off of a spatial connection and resulted in the weakening of society as well as in a loss to the ordinary public. That is to say, the lack of connection between one subject and another proved to be a loss of spatial extendedness such as is inherent in publicity. This clearly indicates how spatiality, inherent in human society, is based upon subjective connections.

Thus, we are able to grasp clearly that the public or society is a space connected by such practical forms as communication or the news.

Consequently, all of the facilities of spatial connection, that is, the means of transportation or communication, come to have an especially important significance as the expressions of human beings. Without means of transportation or communication, there would be no society. Metaphorically speaking, these constitute the nervous system of society. Their structure reflects the structure of the social existence of human beings, and the historical development of this structure reflects the historical development of human beings. In this connection, we are able to understand why a vivid description of "a traffic route" in Tōson Shimazaki's novel, entitled *Before the Dawn*[1] successfully bore fruit in depicting the society of that time.

A means of transportation is in essence a "road," where people associate with each other and are united by moving upon it. As to being a means of association, there is no difference between it and the various facilities of communication. The latter are essentially "correspondence," which moves among still-standing persons and allows them to associate and unite. Because both make possible "association," we can say that correspondence is like "a moving road" and a road is "a still-standing correspondence." When persons come into contact and are united, a gesture, or behavior of some sort, or spoken language also play the role of mediator. But, as the connection between persons is enlarged spatially, a road or correspondence is substituted for these less spatially removed forms of communication. We can find in a road and in correspondence socialized gestures of behavior as well as socialized dialogue. Consequently, just as a form of association between one individual and another can be found in the behavior and the words that constitute a greeting, so a wide range of forms of the association of human being can be found in the means of transportation and communication.

In its most primitive form, a road is a track established of its own accord after having been tread upon persistently. Incidentally, that human beings walked along it time and again, indicates that there already was communication. That is to say, this road indicates the existence of connections between human beings, which were established historically, but has nothing to do with that physical thing that is of a certain width and length in merely physical space. A primitive road may still be found among the narrow paths of a village. To take another example, a road that passes along a field and leads through the neighborhood or a road established by having been tread on by a certain number of people is an expression of human interconnection. Another example would be a road or path leading to the guardian god of a village or to the cemetery, which was established by having been tread on by the whole population of a village. These roads give expression to the ordinary intercourse of human beings within that village. For this reason, if "a stranger" happens to walk along this road, the villagers immediately feel as though someone was making a visit from beyond the community and, therefore, pay particular attention to that stranger. These paths exist in compliance with the communal existence of villagers. In addition to the system of paths, there may also be in a village another road that leads to another village. This road was established by having been tread on by the villagers, thereby giving expression to communication that existed between these villages. Furthermore, there is a street that leads to a city and the wider public via these villages. It is a street along which strangers, such as peddlars or travelers, walk, indicating connection with the unknown wider public. When going out into the wider public world, villagers must also walk along this street. But it is not the villagers alone who have walked on it.

In this way, a road gives expression to a wide variety of human communication. Consequently, as the social connections are extended, the road also lengthens. From ancient times, the extension of the political system has run parallel with the construction of streets. As was the case with the ancient streets of Rome, ancient legends in Japan also refer to "four streets" or "eight streets." Even at present, streets are divided into village roads, prefectural roads, and state roads, thus reflecting the structure of the political system. Hence, we can say that a network of roads may well express the infrastructure of society. At the same time, the vicissitudes of traffic routes give expression to that of the social structure. In the Tokugawa era, when communication was usually achieved by means of walking, the system of roads established for the sake of walking indicated clearly the social structure of that time. Thus, a nationwide system of streets converging on Edo, in which the office of the Tokugawa shogunate was located, or a local system of streets centering around the town in which the office of each feudal lord was situated, and a system of narrow paths within each village, each gave expression to the stratified structure inherent in the social connections of that time. Milestones indicated the labors of walking and expressed the extent of the near-and-far relationships within society. For this reason, the local restrictions of society were extremely severe. However, the development of railroads, achieved since the Meiji era, occasioned a fundamental transformation in both near and distant relations. It is certain, even at that time, that attempts were made to connect cities by means of railroads, with Edo as the communication center. But it came to pass that near and distant relations were no longer measured by walking, but primarily by time spent and wages earned. We can say, given that a distance of one day was reduced to one hour, that we have shortened the road to just that extent. A relative who lived one kilometer from us was as remote from us then as a relative who lives ten kilometers from us now. Therefore, the local restrictions have lost their power, and the connections of human beings are now far beyond local limitation. For instance, marital relationships, which were once established within a five or six kilometer distance, have become extended to a distance of fifty or sixty kilometers. As a result, people who live far away from each other have begun to marry, irrespective of where they live.

A region deprived of the advantage of railroads is increasingly distant because of this. On the one hand, a distance of twenty or thirty kilometers is transformed into a half-hour distance, and on the other, the same distance is transformed into a distance of five hours. The latter is, relatively speaking, distanced ten times more than before. Thus, the development of a network of railroads gradually transformed the ways of human communication. The intensity of social connections is given expression to by the intensity of railway lines, as well as by the frequency of trains. I am sure that this tendency will be strengthened even further through the emerging facilities of communication such as the automobile and the airplane. Air travel is completely emancipated from the institutional form of "a road." In spite of this, however, it most typically expresses the essential significance of a road; that is, "a spatial connection."

The next thing to be noted is that correspondence (i.e., in Japanese, *otozure*, which also means "a visit") is a means used when what ought to be communicated by the spoken word is hampered in achieving its objective because of the long distance involved. Therefore, the most primitive form of correspondence consisted in going to one's partner and engaging in dialogue; that is, it consisted of "a visit." To accomplish this, one walked along a road. Hence, the road is the track of an *otozure*, both correspondence *and* visit, so that correspondence is not yet separated from the road. Not until one abandons engaging another person through the spoken word is *otozure* deprived of its meaning as visit, and comes to signify "correspondence." Hence, "to give a verbal message through an envoy" can be said to be the most primitive form of "correspondence." This form is still prevalent in village life and is utilized by large companies, schools, or government offices. In this particular form, an envoy must himself understand the words he is obliged to transmit, for he must speak them, that is to say, he must participate in that *koto*.[2] The messenger is involved in the communication of words as spoken. Hence, "trust" predominated, as was originally indicated by the word *tayori* (which means "news" and at the same time "reliance"). This is why an underground organization, which is particularly built on trust, favors this method of communication. Even a maid who conveys words from one employee to another stands on trust, with respect to this sort of communication.

However, a step forward is taken to a stage in which "written words" are transmitted by a messenger, when he is no longer required to participate in the *koto* thus transmitted. He is entrusted only to transmit the "letter" to the other party. Therefore, we can say that the mediation is transferred from the messenger to the letter. The fact that the messenger is now external to the relationship of communication renders it possible for the message to be carried. When a direct relationship of trust, such as exists between the person who entrusts the letter to a messenger and the messenger thus entrusted is pushed a step further in the external direction, then one gives one's message in trust to him who employs a messenger, without thereby knowing who the messenger is. It was exactly the same with the ancient system of express messengers. But today's advanced postal organization is, in reality, the transformation and organization of this old system into a governmental enterprise. In places where there is a postal organization, the "privacy of letters" is prescribed as being important by law, and this simply expresses the fact that a messenger is external to the affair of correspondence itself.

We can characterize the postal service as an organizational activity of those who externally transmit written words, which mediate between one person and another; that is to say, as spatial liaison agents. In other words, a network of roads or of railways have become something movable; that is, messengers. If this is pushed to the extreme, then there emerges an instrument such as a telephone that replaces the messenger with a machine. That which had previously mediated conversations was gradually forced out of the conversation altogether and has finally been replaced by a machine that is incapable of participating in them. If this method of communication advances to its fullest extent, then we will be emancipated from the restrictions of distance and will be able to participate in any conversation as freely as we wish. And hence, the local restriction inherent in social connection will be likely to almost disappear.

We find that spatial connections vary in accordance with the various ways of communication. It is obvious that a direct conversation and the use of a messenger as a mediator constitute practical connections quite different from each other. In the same way, the latter form of conversation and that achieved through the postal service also differ in their respective ways of connection. Whereas a messenger, whose job consists in delivering letters, expresses only limited human connections, a mailbox, a mail carrier, a post office, and so forth give expression to far-reaching relationships of human beings. For this reason, the development of postal organizations shows an increase in the extent and intensity of human relationships in a society. Under circumstances in which a response to a letter is delivered after a month's interval, we cannot be said to be engaging in a conversation in an active manner. If we receive a response at a time when we have almost detached ourselves from the state of mind we were in while writing the letter, then we are unlikely to share the same state of mind. On the other hand, if and when postal services spare no time in delivering words from one person to another both quickly and frequently, then we shall be able to share pleasures as well as pains. A community of beings would thus be realized. A telephone is designed to strengthen this tendency even further. In this light, we can say that the development of facilities for communication goes hand in hand with that of the nervous system of society.

When communication is conducted with the general public in mind, it is called *news*. It has developed from primitive forms such as notice boards or the transmitting of official notices on foot to advanced forms such as newspapers, radio, and so forth, by virtue of which the general public is able to share in the community of being in various ways.

At first glance, facilities for transportation and communication seem to be objective "things." But they are not mere objects that have nothing to do with subjective beings. Just as gestures or expressions of *Thou*, who stands over against *I*, are neither motions of physical bodies nor mere vibrations of air but are the relationship of a subjective *Thou* with an *I*, so a speeding car, a red mailbox, and a newspaper are not mere physical bodies. For *I* who is in a hurry to leave for somewhere, this car is something that bears *I*'s activity of being in haste. Once all cars disappear from the streets due to a strike, a town is suddenly forced to change its manner of acting in haste. The same is true of the subjective being of *I*, which suffers a great change when *I*'s leg becomes paralyzed.

On the other hand, the moment I drop a letter that is of great importance to me into a red mailbox, there is the possibility that my destiny is determined. Before dropping it into the mailbox, I may still tear it into pieces. It might be that nothing will happen to me. However, my act of dropping the letter into the red box might occasion an extraordinary event. If so, then this red box is not a mere thing. It stands as a turning point in my destiny and is something susceptible to the decisions of my will. That is to say, a car or a mailbox functions as one of the elements constitutive of a subjective human being. In addition, insofar as these physical bodies exert this sort of function, we recognize in them the characteristic of being "a car" or "a mailbox." In this way, all the "things" constitutive of facilities for transportation or communication are things in the same sense that the human body is a thing, and they are also subjective in the same sense that the human body is subjective. This is why we can say that the subjective human being is brought into expression in and through these facilities of transportation and communication. Moreover, spatial connections are expressed here in their various forms. These various forms express social connections based on these forms of spatial connection.

The spatiality exhibited by these phenomena of human transportation and communication is clearly subjective extendedness. It interconnects both subjectively and practically, but lacks the same extendedness as an objective thing. This subjective extendedness arises because human beings, despite dividing themselves into a great number of subjects, nevertheless, strive to constitute a connection among themselves. The subjectivity under consideration is the only one not susceptible to disruption. The practical movement through which human beings communicate with each other by means of the facilities of transportation and communication could not otherwise arise.

On the other hand, the movement of connection cannot occur under circumstances in which subjects remain many and are not susceptible to becoming one. Only because the subject that was originally one, tries to regain this oneness in and through its disruption into many subjects does there arise a movement among these subjects. This practical interconnection of acts establishes *ningen sonzai*. From this standpoint, we can say that subjective spatiality is, in the final analysis, the basic structure of *ningen sonzai*. Our endeavor to grasp *ningen* not only as a human being but also as possessing the dual structure of individuality and at the same time sociality leads us of necessity to this idea of spatial extendedness.

How does subjective extendedness relate to space as objective extendedness? The ego's discovering something outside of itself initiates awareness of space. But this ego becomes the ego only when it gets out of *ningen sonzai*, and hence, it is by no means a primary existence. The evidence of *Thou* arises before that of the ego. It is only through *Thou* that *I* becomes recognized. In addition, this *Thou*, although standing in opposition to the *I* outside of itself, at the same time, is the *I*. Without the *Thou* being *I* and *I* being also *Thou*, the *I/ Thou* relation cannot arise. The subjective being that arises as the unity of contradictories is more primary than the situation in which "*I* finds things on the outside." Consequently, it is not so much that *ningen sonzai* is constructed in space as that space comes to be found in the field of subjective *ningen sonzai*. From this viewpoint we can argue that subjective extendedness constitutes basic space.

Without taking into consideration spatial extendedness, we are unable to give a satisfactory explanation of the personal relationship between the self and other. It is possible to conceive of self and other in terms of self-consciousness. However, it cannot be that the field in which the "other's" self-consciousness is rendered capable of being the other is itself self-consciousness. If the opposition between the self and other remains a merely logical opposition between concepts, then the interconnection of acts cannot arise between the self and other. Furthermore, the interconnection of acts as the unity of contradictories can be established only in subjective extendedness.

It goes without saying that subjective spatiality has nothing to do with space as is evident in a thing's extendedness. Therefore, it is provisionally acceptable for us to exclude space from human relationships. But we must not thereby exclude subjective spatiality. If human relationships, like logical ones, remain an entirely nonspatial connection of meanings, then they remain noematically formed meanings and cannot be features characteristic of practical *ningen sonzai*. The reason why the attempt to understand society in terms of human relationships falls victim to abstraction lies in its having excluded from human relationships subjective spatiality together with space.

If full attention had been paid to this point, then this attempt to understand society in terms of human relationships might have been able to understand society far more concretely. For example, when G. Tarde tried to establish his sociology as a form of a "psychology of cerebral betweenness," he should have gone a step further and pursued the meaning of the term *cerebral betweenness*. Insofar as individual consciousness is thought to reside "inside a brain," the society is located "outside of it" or, more precisely, "between" one brain and another. Society cannot consist of merely those nonspatial "meanings" held in consciousness. Society can arise only between one subject and another in and through practical communication and, hence, through dialogue, communication, and transportation. Tarde emphasizes that a science which concerns itself with the "betweenness" of subjects cannot be satisfied with the standpoint of the *cogito*. If Tarde had stuck with this emphasis, he would have encountered subjective spatiality as the field in which imitational relations obtain.

Questions might be raised about subjective spatiality: that it has not been dealt with previously in the history of philosophy or that it deviates from the orthodox treatment of space. It is certain that the issue of space has always been dealt with as a problem of objective knowledge, as comprehended from the vantage point of contemplation. This was so throughout the entire course of the thought that dealt with this issue, ranging from its objectivist beginning up to its subjectivist turn in the modern era. It is all rather far from the truth that this issue was grappled with as the structure of subjective *ningen sonzai* from the perspective of the practical and the active. As a consequence, space has always been explored in connection with physical bodies or their motion and has never been investigated in connection with the activity of the human subject itself. In spite of this, however, we can insist that the issue of space has always involved within itself a tendency toward subjective spatiality. I think it is necessary to make this assertion clearer, by providing a short sketch of the history of this issue.

When Descartes clearly distinguished between *res cogitans* and *res extensa* at the beginning of modern philosophy, space was conceived of as entirely apart from the subject and turned out to be the essential qualification of the object. This view has held sway over subsequent philosophies. However, we must not forget that Spinoza wasted no time in emphatically denying this position. Following Descartes, Spinoza also distinguished *res cogitans* and *res extensna* or *cogitatio* and *extentio*. For Spinoza, these two do not refer to independent substances but rather to "attributes" of one substance; that is, to God. Therefore, although for Descartes God is not something "extended," there is no doubt that He is something extended for Spinoza. Furthermore, this view is expounded, for Spinoza, in a dual sense. That is to say, God is subjectively extended and, at the same time, objectively extended. God is the cause of Himself and all things as well; that is, as *natura naturans*. At the same time, as the effects that He himself caused, that is, as *natura naturata*, He is extended in the form of *natura naturans* as well as in the form of *natura naturata*.

With regard to the former, we can say that, because extendedness is regarded as an attribute of God and because an attribute is His way of acting, then God himself, as *natura naturans,* creates, gives birth to, and acts while existing in the form of something "extended." Hence, this something extended is, basically speaking, God himself but not His creatures. However, God is also, in one respect, something created; that is, *natura naturata.* The attribute of extendedness makes its appearance here as a *modus.* This *modus* is concerned with the fact that every physical body extends in three dimensions.

"Extendedness," which is possessed by this physical body is the substantial essence of all physical bodies, and therefore, things do not differ from one another in their substance. But they are physical bodies that differ from each other in accordance with their *modi.* Thus, we can argue that extendedness as an attribute is concerned with extendedness as inherent in the active Creator, while extendedness as a *modus* is concerned with that which is inherent in created physical bodies. Extendedness in Descartes referred to only the latter.

For Spinoza, the extendedness of the former sort is more basic and, hence, is of greater importance. We can see that subjective spatiality is to be grasped in connection with the Creator. If we free Spinoza's concept of God from the tradition imposed on it by the philosophies of the Middle Ages and associate it with the authentic feature of absolute totality, then that subjective spatiality advocated in Spinoza will coincide with what we have said so far.

In Kant's philosophy "the conversion toward the subject," which began with Descartes, reached its climax. The subject of knowledge is central in Kant's philosophy. Kant substituted it for Spinoza's concept of the Creator. That "extendedness" by means of which Descartes characterized the essence of the physical body was made an attribute of the subject of knowledge (i.e., the form of intuition) rather than an attribute of God, as in Spinoza. Extendedness was thereby also transferred from the physical body to the subject.

However, what is extended is not the subject itself but rather the physical body. The point is that only in that space regarded as a form of intuition is the extendedness of a physical body possible.

Consequently, space is, according to Kant, a form of intuition but not a subjective extendedness. This is the point to which we should pay particular attention. Kant's attempt to deal with space as a form of intuition tends to subjectify space. Why did he fail to achieve the concept of subjective space?

Because intuition is in Kant the receptivity of the subject, the form of intuition is also none other than the manner in which the subject operates as a way of reception. Furthermore, this subject cannot be allowed to become an object from the standpoint of theoretical knowledge, but from a practical standpoint, it comes to manifest itself as the subject of activity. If so, then it follows as a matter of course that the subject whose way of operation proceeds through space as a form of intuition also operates in the same way as the subject of practice. That is, there is no alternative for us but to assume that space itself turns out to be the subject's manner of operation. Nevertheless, Kant does not entirely recognize this. In his opinion, intuition as receptivity is merely concerned with the establishment of objects. It cannot be involved with the realm of practice. As soon as the function of intuition is ended, space also loses its place. Why?

It does so because Kant pursues the relationship between a human being and nature, not that between one human being and another. The first characterization of space that *I* posits is something before me as existing outside of me, keeping its eye on objective things only, but it has nothing to do with other persons. Personality is that which is not likely to be seen. Yet, do we not allow other persons to stand in opposition to us, as existing outside of us? Can we say that what stands opposed to us is not so much another person as another human body? It is evident that the opposition under consideration differs from a mere opposition between physical bodies. An opposition between one person and another is such that no sooner do they oppose one another than they become one. In saying this, however, we cannot mean to exclude the possibility that one person lets another stand as opposed; that is, outside of himself. To this extent, space must also be seen as the subject's way of operating. From this perspective, we can say that, in Kant, space remains a manner of intuition and was not pursued to its subjective extendedness, because his concern was confined to the relationship between a human being and nature alone.

German idealism, which rejected the duality of receptivity and spontaneity and tried to explicate everything from the standpoint of spontaneity, takes space as a product of the subject, as activity. In Fichte, the ego posits space as a product of imagination. In Schelling, it is an activity of intelligence and an external sense organ transformed into an object. Furthermore, in Hegel, space is the first moment through which *Geist* as the absolute Idea negates itself so as to become nature; that is, it is its most abstract and universal way of being outside of itself (*Ausser-sich-sein*).

Throughout these suppositions, space is always dealt with as a manner of a subject's objectification or externalization. Hence, it is not so much the essential quality of a physical body as it is the manner in which a subject operates. Here, we can say that the subjectivity of space is clearly recognized. What is more, it is by no means an extendedness inherent in the subject itself. The way in which a "subject devoid of extendedness" lets an "extended object" arise, or even produces it, is itself in space, and here it is not asked whether the subject itself is spatial or not. This confirms that the field dealing with the issue of space is still to be discerned in the relationship between a human being and nature and is not yet transferred to the practical relationships between one person and another.

The historical period that followed retrograded rather than promoted issues concerning the subjectivity of space. That the subjectification of space had always presupposed homogeneous space; that is, the "unique and infinite space devoid of qualities," occasioned this backward movement. This conception of absolute, homogeneous, and unmoveable space was peculiar to Newton. Whether we regard space as the form of intuition or the objectification of the subject, this notion always calls into question "uniform extendedness."

Is there any place for such homogeneous space? To do justice to this notion of homogeneous space, Kant tried to separate space from sense qualities. But, was this separation justified? This was again called into question, after which war was waged against the subjective notion of space.

One of the positions to reject absolute space was that of Brentano.[3] He argued that, because sense qualities cannot be separated from space, there is no "space" but only "something spatial." In his opinion, we have no intuition of space such as was proposed by Kant. Rather, the intuition of space we possess cannot be separated from sensible qualities. Qualities cannot exist except in physical bodies, and the latter cannot exist apart from the former. In addition, there is no self-sustaining place that is not permeated by physical bodies, no empty space. Space and qualities are in themselves abstract things. Concretely speaking, there are only physical bodies that, although having extendedness, differ in quality from one another. As a consequence, something physical is something spatial and apart from that there is no space as merely extended. In this way, Brentano relativized space and brought it back to physical bodies, thereby restoring the ancient view of space.

On the other hand, there was another who held the position that affirmed unified absolute space, while raising objections to Kant's concept of space as devoid of qualities. According to Anton Marty,[4] space is not something that inheres in some other thing, but is something absolute that exists per se, and at the same time, it is something unreal

(*Nichtreales*, something inactive). He accepted that there is no space devoid of qualities, as Kant held. From an intuitive standpoint, what is given is only the representation of space as permeated by qualities. Except in abstraction, the moment of spatiality and that of qualities cannot be separated. As a result, the intuition of space as devoid of all qualities does not exist for us. And the quality of infinity of the intuition of space is not something immediately given to us. Our intuition of space is extraordinarily confined. Nor is the uniqueness of space immediately given. There are various spaces such as the visual and tactile. Therefore, we can say that Kant's description of the intuition of space is false. Hence, his attempt to claim, as based on it, the a priori nature of spatial representations is also doubtful.

One of the reasons why Kant regarded space as an a priori representation lying behind external intuition was that he held that a representation of the nonexistence of space cannot be conceived and that it is quite thinkable for objects not to exist in space. The truth is, however, that this thinkability is warranted as an abstraction based on thinking. We cannot represent space as devoid of objects. Our intuition of space consists of the unity of spatial and qualitative elements, in which unity these two elements are based on each other such that it is impossible to give precedence to either one. Consequently, if sense qualities are empirical, then space is also empirical; and if space precedes experience, then sense qualities must also precede experience.

However, what is here subject to doubt is not only the a priori characteristic of the representation of space. Of greater importance is that the subjectivity of the representation of space is not yet ascertained. Even if the representation of space is admitted to be a priori, the subjectivity (i.e., phenomenality or ideality) of space cannot be derived from it. If our intuition of space adequately corresponds to reality in some ideal manner, then this intuition is not subjective but objective. Then there is no problem in calling what corresponds to this objective intuition space. Hence, the objectivity of space must be affirmed. The only thing to be noted here is that this space is not an object that bears a causal relation to intuition. Consequently, it is neither real nor a substance. It is an object through and through.

Furthermore, although Kant tries to maintain the subjectivity of the intuition of space on the ground that this intuition involves within itself only mere relations, Marty holds the view that the determination of places cannot consist of mere relations. Without being based on sense qualities, a relationship of togetherness cannot be conceived of. In this way, Marty posits objective space that exists in and per se.

It can be admitted that these criticisms have brought to light a defect in Kant's theory of space. It is not our question at present to ask whether or not a vital aspect of Kant's theory of space rests on homogeneous space, but we can say that these criticisms are justified, so far as homogeneous space is concerned. On the other hand, to exclude homogeneous space does not directly mean to push space away to the side of things. There can be another perspective that comprehends the inseparability of space and qualities and insists on the subjectivity of space just on the ground of this comprehension.

Bergson's[5] attempt to discern fundamental space in concrete experiences indicates a move in this same direction. On the basis of reality as immediately given to consciousness, Bergson tries to bring to nought the distinction between the extended and the nonextended and between quantity and quality. Pure external intuition consists of indivisible continuity. It is concrete, continuous, and differs in kind. At the same time, it is an organized extension that is not the same as homogeneous space. In other words, it is a living continuity filled with sense qualities and has nothing to do with a space that is infinitely divisible.

However this may be, this direct intuition is disrupted or divided to correspond to practical concerns or the demands of the social life, in the direction of pragmatic usefulness. There then arises a "togetherness" of elements. Because we break down the unity of fundamental intuition, we feel ourselves compelled to construct again the external connections among the separated elements. What is constructed is an artificial unity called *an empty frame*, rather than a living unity based on inner continuity. Just as separated elements are already dead, so the frame including them is also dead. This frame is none other than homogeneous space. Therefore, it can be said that space is a scheme of divisibility derived from the demands of practical life. By means of this scheme we divide the continuous and fix becoming, thereby making it possible for our activity to manipulate matters.

Without paying attention to this vital concern, Kant tried to attend to homogeneous space from the perspective of contemplation only. This is why homogeneous space was conceived of by him as relating to scientific knowledge, without investigating its basis, and thus was established as a form of intuition.

However, fundamental space must be sought out before being deformed by the demands of practical life. There is that immediate intuition in which qualities belonging to various dimensions are seen to have something in common, and in which all qualities take part in extension to varying degrees. That is to say, every sensation is extended, and concrete extension consists in different kinds of sense qualities. This concrete extension is by no means a field in which real movements are carried on, but is an extension that occurs on the ground of real movements. Practical concerns reverse this authentic relationship. Thus, in an attempt to intuit the real features of reality, we attempt to come to grips with that concrete extension which is antecedent to practical deformations and to discern the fundamental unity of spirit and matter, body, and mind by keeping our eye on the indivisible continuity of this extension. In Bergson's thought, space is fundamentally attributed to the subject. Furthermore, this attribution is made possible by tracing back to the basis of homogeneous space.

The insight that homogeneous space is not the real feature of space was certainly gained because of the progress that the theory of space made after Kant. This was not necessarily progress toward the subjectivity of space. To preserve the subjectivity of space by sticking to the inseparability of space and qualities, we must go so far as to presuppose a subjective extendedness such as is found in the concrete sensation of extension that arises in movement, as is evident in Bergson. We can argue that this gives clear evidence of our assertion that the issue of space always involves a tendency towards subjective spatiality.

However, even Bergson could not carry this all the way to the interconnection of acts among subjects. He stops with a position of intuitive knowledge concerning reality. It is a standpoint of mere "contemplation" but not the philosophy of "practice." Consequently, the practical activities he speaks of are not so much concerned with personal relationships that occur between one person and another, as with those activities through which a human being holds sway over things. This is why Bergson recognizes them only as activities of transforming concrete extension into abstraction and homogeneity. In this light, we can say that Bergson still moves on the plane of the individual subject versus the objects of nature and that he does not, fundamentally speaking, abandon Kant in this respect. We cannot truly reach the origin of space unless we assert that actual movements conceived of as lying behind concrete extension are not what are immediately given to consciousness but rather have something to do with the practical activities of subjects antecedent to consciousness.

The same can be said of Heidegger, who definitely dealt with "the spatiality of the subject itself."[6] He speaks of "an existential spatiality" (*existentiale Räumlichkeit*) of "a being there" (*Dasein*), which is regarded as "being in the world." For Heidegger, who conceives of "a being there" as more fundamental than the opposition between subject and object, space is not inside of the subject nor is the world within space. "A being there," despite existing in the world, finds space in its concern with what is at hand. Tools are "at hand," or in their region (*Gegend*) and occupy their place (*Platz*). Space such as an environmental region implies that it is itself in the world but is not a field that renders possible the world within itself. For this reason, the ontological subject is itself spatial, as a being in the world. Thus, in his attempt to make spatiality constitutive of the being of the subject, Heidegger advances a step forward over Bergson.

In spite of this, however, the spatiality inherent in "a being there" is, in the final analysis, attributed to the relationship of concern between *I* and tools and has nothing to do with the relationship of communication among human beings. It is certain that the practical concerns Bergson devalued, in Heidegger, were significantly restored under the guise of *Sorge* ("care") and that fundamental space found its place there as the structure of "concern." Hence, for Heidegger, space is probed, not by a contemplative approach, but in a more fundamental way. But the concern of *I* with tools is the very ground out of which the relationship between an individual subject versus the objects of nature emerges immediately as soon as its abstraction is carried a step further. The practical relationship between one human being and another is not a major element constitutive of the "concern" he tried to expound. Or rather, it should have been its major element, but this he failed to grasp. This is why spatiality, even though it was conceived of as that structure which is characteristic of the existence of the subject, still stopped short of being a spatiality inherent in the practical interconnections of human beings. This is why he considered temporality to be of far greater importance than spatiality.

Scheler,[7] who tried to find the spatiality of the subject without having recourse to "the concern with tools," exhibits this state of affairs in an exaggerated way. He regarded spatiality as the "essence" of space. That is, what makes a somewhat formed space to be space is spatiality. Spatiality is given prior to sense data and hence cannot be derived from the space of sensation, which is, in fact, an artificial product of the laboratory.

However, we do not mean that spatiality has, in Scheler, something to do with intuition or receptivity, as Kant had thought. Rather, it is "a bodily experience of power exerting its influence on spontaneous movement." Consequently, spatiality is, to begin with, merely the subject's capacity for self-movement or living movement. In other words, "a human being's drive for movement" is spatiality. When this drive fails to be realized, then the phenomenon of a spatial void appears as a mode of nonbeing. In this way, Scheler tries to grasp space as spontaneity instead of as receptivity.

What, then, is the self-movement of the subject? Is it possible without the subject having any relationship to anything at all? If a human being's drive to movement is conceived of as arising from the ground of life alone, without having relationship to anything, then we must say that such a human being is an artificial product of a laboratory. On this point, Heidegger's exposition is much more concrete, for he tried to grasp "a human being" as a "being in the world," precisely through our intimate concern with tools. However, provided that the self-movement of the subject is already associated with the concern for something because of its being a movement of life, is it possible to think that this movement is concerned only with "things" but not with "other subjects"? We have already recognized that *ningen* is fundamentally individualistic and social and that a mere solitary person is only an abstraction. As a result, the self-movement of a solitary person who is concerned only with things, is also an abstraction. The self-movement of the subject is the spontaneous movement of *ningen* and hence must be an activity affiliated with human relationships.

We have thus far given a historical account of the issue of space. It can be said that the subjectification of space has been one of the major trends of modern philosophy. Note that, because the subject under consideration is a subject contemplating nature or is only an isolated individual, in no adequate sense of the term did subjectified space become a spatiality of the subject. Now, this subject has been prescribed as *ningen*, that is, as possessing the double characteristic of individual and social. The spatiality of this subject must consist in the subjective betweenness of human beings. The spatiality that constitutes the structure of existence of a "being there" as expounded by Heidegger, must be based fundamentally on that meaning of spatiality presently under consideration. A subjectivity based on a concern with tools is possible only if tools are already established in human relationships. Only when we extract the element of the individual from these human relationships and keep our focus on this individual while considering his human activities are we able to come to grips with the concern with tools.

For example, as Heidegger frequently suggests, only the labor and organization of handicrafts as active relationships among human beings causes concern with handcrafted tools. An organization of this sort essentially consists of the subjective interconnections of human beings, but mere contemplation is not its objective. Furthermore, Heidegger places emphasis on the proposition that it is only through the medium of these tools and their products that other persons manifest themselves. He refuses to see the pivotal point that these tools have already emerged out of those human relationships involved in collective labor.

For the time being, let us suppose, as does Heidegger, that the aforementioned procedure complies with that of ontology. Why does he depart from the concern with tools instead of from the concern with other persons? This question cannot be solved by attending only to the structure of "being in the world." Only in the concern with other persons do we find tools. It is not that a shoemaker finds other persons only through the medium of the shoes he produces but that he makes shoes as ordered by other persons. It is not that a scholar finds other scholars only through the medium of his desk or books but that in thinking through his problems—and it is not necessary to exclude problems of mere ego consciousness here—in terms of those human relationships collectively called the *academic world*, he comes to need books. Heidegger did not heed such self-evident matters of fact. In my opinion, the reason for this is because his ontology of "being there" also follows in the wake of Descartes's conception of the *cogito* and Heidegger, from the very beginning, presupposes individual existence without social existence. As a consequence, it is vital to attend to whether or not a thinker has come to comprehend the double characteristic of *ningen*.

Even though the position of the *cogito* is still an influential one, it is inevitably subject to various difficulties if only in connection with the issue of space. I have already considered the view that homogeneous natural space is not what is immediately given. Together with this consideration, it is also the case that attempts have been made by various persons, including Heidegger, to derive such a space from concrete space. Heidegger maintains that only a contemplative standpoint, in abstraction from that existence which is associated with the concern of a "being there," leads to the abstract transformation of a concrete, environmental space into a homogeneous one. However, environmental space retains its own characteristic perspective in spite of having been determined by concern. Space never becomes homogeneous, even from a "contemplative" standpoint, where the elimination of concern fixes this characteristic perspective. If thinking transforms it into homogeneous space, then homogeneous space becomes a mere thought.

With regard to this problem, Litt's view or Becker's is much more instructive. Litt[8] emphasizes the perspective structure of space; Becker[9] speaks of "space with its positions fixed." Both of these spaces are environmental spaces with the ego as their center, from which we cannot emancipate ourselves, insofar as we stand on the standpoint of *I*. In order that homogeneous space may be constructed out of space of this sort, Litt requires the reciprocity of perspectives. Becker requires the relativization of positions by means of the movements of *I* and hence the transference of feelings in which *I* places himself in the position of another *I*.

In this way, emancipation from the standpoint of *I*, in which positions are fixed around one center, makes possible homogeneous space as the intersubjective world. If so, then homogeneous space cannot be derived from the standpoint of the *cogito*. It is made possible by reciprocal relationships or the transference into another *I*'s feelings, through the standpoint of a human being's social existence. This is what Durkheim emphasized.

To inquire into the origin of space, we must comply with *ningen*'s dual existence as individual and social being. The history of space leads us in this direction, and it is not an arbitrary decision on our part. Thus a new position on space is firmly established. Space is not a merely theoretical or contemplative issue, but must be comprehended in connection with the individual subject. It is called into question in subjective practice, yet not in individual practice such as the concern with tools, but rather in those practical activities inherent in human relationships. Subjective extendedness, which is inherent in the activities of *ningen*, is exactly the characteristic of spatiality of *ningen sonzai* from which originates all other kinds of space. This extendedness is a "tension" within the interconnection of the acts of subjects, which changes its strength and degree of inclusiveness in accordance with the multiplying and unifying of subjects. Such phenomena as communication and transportation, which do not allow themselves to be contemplated, express this. Consequently, the spatiality characteristic of *ningen sonzai* is subjective through and through. It cannot be objectified. However this may be, the nonobjectification of basic space was already taken for granted in the attempt to regard space as the manner of the externalization of subjects, but it need not be accounted for just now.

We clarified earlier that subjective spatiality is inherent in the structure of *ningen sonzai*. But by saying this, we have no intention of departing from the attempt to regard space as the form of externalization or of objectification. Rather, we intend to insist that the ground of the possibility of the objectification of subjects lies in the spatiality of the subject (see p. 165). Only the spatiality of the subject renders possible the opposition between *I* and *Thou*, for example. And, only the opposition between *I* and *Thou* can establish "an object as *Thou*."

What is at issue here is the primordial element through which things can be found as objects. Therefore, the natural environment, consisting of such things as mountains and rivers, grass and trees possesses a "*Thou*" characteristic in its primitive features. This has been recently clarified by research into the consciousness of primitives and children, but it is also a matter that can be proved ontologically in the actualities of human existence.

For instance, when we love or think fondly of a double row of maple trees, we deal with them as *Thou*. Hence, it is not that we first find mere "things" about us, infer another ego existing among them, then apply the relationship between *I* and another ego analogically to that which exists between *I* and trees, and finally reach the stage in which we actually love trees. Instead, when we see trees, they are already trees that are characterized on the basis of our human existence as a double row of trees. When we find a double row of trees, having already socially constructed such a thing, we do not try to infer other egos from it. Instead, whatever things we may apprehend as objects, we have already, prior to objectification, found them to be *Thou*. In this sense, the spatiality of the subject is already at work as the form through which something is found as objective. In other words, that subjects stand opposed to *I* by becoming *Thou* or *He* or *She* is, in general, the result of that primordial element that renders any object capable of coming into being.

The stages through which the world of objects (as the natural world) arises out of this primordial element correspond to those stages through which environmental space, or space with its positions fixed, or homogeneous space, and so forth come to arise. Environmental space arises when one eliminates the tension spread over subjective spatiality and then stands on the standpoint of the individual. In this case, the tools at hand occupy this sort of space.

To go a step further, an individual's departure from the concrete relations of concern to a "contemplative" standpoint establishes a perspective space, with its positions fixed. Natural things detached from tool characteristics occupy this sort of space.

The negation of subjective spatiality, that is, the standpoint of the individual, establishes these sorts of space. In spite of this, the origin of space lies in the "betweenness" of subjects, that contradicts the standpoint of the individual. Then, through the negation of this latter standpoint, perspective disappears and homogeneous space arises. This homogeneous space is the abstraction of subjective space carried to its extreme. At issue here is the natural world, which arises in an intersubjective way; and hence, it arises within consciousness in general.

We can trace the stages through which the subject is externalized. Space consists always in the manner of externalization, which, however, is possible only by virtue of the fact that space is, in its origin, subjective spatiality.

10 the temporality of *ningen sonzai*

In the preceding chapter, we considered only the spatiality of *ningen sonzai*, but this sort of spatiality cannot subsist apart from temporality. That *ningen sonzai* is spatial at once means that it is also temporal. This is what I want to clarify in this chapter.

We considered the phenomena of transportation and communication and made approaches to an understanding of the spatiality of *ningen sonzai*. I will now return to these phenomena and will reflect upon them further.

It is certain that transportation and communication consist of spatial connections. What is important in these phenomena is that spatial connections give expression to the activities of the human subject. If the latter moment is absent, you can certainly discern the motion of physical bodies there but the phenomena of transportation and communication disappear. We remarked that a "road" is correspondence[1] at a standstill and that "correspondence" is a moving road. A moving agent or an agent at a standstill is, however, not merely a physical body but rather the human subject itself. A "road" is at a standstill, while allowing a walking agent to appear upon it, and "correspondence" is itself moving, while allowing an agent to appear to be at a standstill. At the place where the connections between human beings occur, in accordance with human subjects moving and standing still, the phenomena of transportation and communication appear for the first time. Indeed, moving and standing still are exactly the temporal developments of human communication. If so, it will be possible for us to approach temporality by coming to terms with these phenomena. This seems to indicate beforehand that a correspondence exists between spatiality and temporality.

To begin, let us reconsider the various phenomena of transportation. Its most primitive form is walking. We walk along a road to our workplace or to visit a friend. For this reason, the phenomena of transportation are dealt with as expressions of the extendedness of human existence.

It was maintained previously that the reason why these phenomena refer to basic spatiality is not because a road is extended spatially but because human existence, and human communication in particular, is established in such subjective activities as walking along a road. But these subjective activities have nothing to do with the mere movements of physical bodies. While walking along a road, we can change direction, speed, and so on, in whatever ways we please. Furthermore, what is now under consideration is not mere indeterminacy. When we begin to walk, this walking activity is already determined by a definite "place to go." That is to say, going to our workplace or to a friend's house and so forth exist beforehand as directions for our walking activity.

Hence, in taking one step after another as we do in walking, there exists beforehand a place that is not yet reached. In saying this, however, we do not mean that a representation of the place of destination exists persistently as a content of consciousness. As an example, we can cite Toan Tejima, who writes that "when you leave your house, with the idea of returning there, it may be that you think you have this idea always in mind over the entire journey. But actually, you do not remember whether you have had the idea persistently. But if someone suddenly prevents you from going there, then the fact that you had wanted to realize this idea by any and all means will come to your mind."[2] That is to say, it is all right for a walker not to ponder her destination, while being preoccupied with what happens before her eyes. In spite of this, the direction of one's walking is already determined beforehand. Beyond the present consciousness of the walker, this "already beforehand" has the significance of being the manner of her present existence. For this reason, it can be rightly said that walking is not the mere motion of a human being, but has to do precisely with the transportation of a human being.

I think that a clue has already been given for reaching an understanding of the temporality of *ningen sonzai* through the phenomena of transportation. It was observed that walking, as a means of transportation, is already determined beforehand. First of all, we would ask what the term *beforehand* means. For a walker who is preoccupied with cars or bicycles on the road, her workplace or a friend's house are places not yet reached, and various relationships that are expected to occur there, do not yet occur at all. Moreover, the place as the *terminus ad quem* determines the present walking, regardless of whether she is conscious of it at the present moment. What supposedly takes place there, as one's work or life concerns, determine one's present walking to such an extent that the latter is made to be a means to this purpose, whether or not one becomes conscious of it in the present.

If so, then those human relationships that are supposed to occur at the place to which one is going already exist within the present walking, "beforehand," in spite of not yet having actually happened. In other words, the essence of this walking consists in the realization of possible human relations. This walking is determined by this possibility. Rather, the walking itself is the possibility. In this way, those human relationships that determine the present walking beforehand are the authentic "future"; that is, "the destination to which to go." It is "a place to go" for a person who pays a visit. At the same time, for a person who awaits a visit, the person who is expected "to come" has "not yet come."[3] Thus, we can say that the "future" is, in every kind of practical activity, the possible betweenness that gives this activity its direction; that is, its possible *ningen sonzai*.

Then what does the term *already* mean? Those human relationships that exist within the present walking beforehand cannot determine it, unless they *already* subsist in one way or another. One goes to one's workplace or pays a visit to one's friend, only because a definite state of labor or of friendly relationships "already" somehow exists. Hence, it is not that the past betweenness that obtained until yesterday is now gone, having somehow perished: it exists in one's present attendance at the office or in one's visit to a friend and in turn determines ones' present walking in the form of those relationships about to occur. Even if one pays a visit to achieve a working relationship or a friendly relationship for the first time, this "for the first time" is determined by that betweenness that exists in the "already." That is, it is established in the betweenness of our having had no relationship thus far, but wishing for one. And this fact gives this visit a special flavor.

Thus, we find ourselves burdened with human existence in which what is possible "beforehand" is "already" determined. The already established human existence that belongs to the future is its authentic "past"; that is, its "bygones." The present walking is determined by the future that exists in the form of the past and thereby reveals the manner of transportation characteristic of *ningen*.

Human relationships, which the simplest types of transportation exhibit, do not remain only to be subjectively extended but also possess a temporal structure in which the past and the future are unified in the present. This established possible betweenness determines the direction of one's present activities. But this determination does not mean that the past betweenness is repeated just as it is in the future. It is possible for a walker to destroy entirely the betweenness of yesterday in her destination. However, this sort of destruction is possible only because she is nonetheless burdened with this past betweenness. Only those who shoulder a burden are able to relieve themselves of it. The difference lies in the fact that the established betweenness determines, in this case, the present activities in the negative. But there is no difference in that the past still determines the present. Even she who is going to her friend may intend to proclaim a breach of friendship on arriving at her destination. However, this makes no difference to the characteristic of "beforehand already" that inheres in the act of walking.

We have examined a person's walking as an illustration of the simplest type of transportation. But what was found there can be applied just as it is to more complex phenomena of transportation. For instance, when starting from Tokyo station, an express train is already bound for Kobe or Shimonoseki beforehand, and relationships in the Kansai area, involving a great number of the passengers, have already served to make them passengers on this train. Therefore, we can catch a glimpse of the transportational interconnection of collective human beings in the form of an express train.

On the other hand, from the vantage point of a much more intuitive vision, we refer to a scene peculiar to a crossroads in a megalopolis. Here roads simply cross, but countless numbers of walkers, bicycles, cars, and streetcars come and go, like a stream of water. The stream is given birth to by the activities of countless numbers of people who are going to various places for some purpose and become entangled in this complex way. Even if we single out any one of these activities, there is no difference in their exhibiting of a unity between the established betweenness and a possible one. For example, a delivery boy riding his bicycle at full speed to take something home to a customer, or a business executive in her car on the way to a meeting or a trucker carrying materials to his factory—these countless movements, although determined by an already established betweenness, also lead to the construction of certain new betweennesses. That is to say, these movements, in their various ways, give expression to the dynamic structure of human relations. And even in comparison with the case of a single walker, there is no difference in that they are *already* determined in their present movement *beforehand*.

Provided that the social phenomena of transportation express the dynamic structure of human relationships as we suppose them to do, then the characteristic of "beforehand already" differs from "anticipation" and "memory," which are reflected on from the standpoint of individual consciousness. The already established betweenness is not merely the memory of *I* but rather socially established *ningen sonzai*, and the possible betweenness is also not merely the anticipation of *I* but socially possible *ningen sonzai*. The "customer" to whom the delivery boy brings a package, exists outside of this delivery boy's memory, in definite relationship with his shop. And the anticipation inherent in those business relationships within which he hands over the package is likewise beyond this delivery boy's anticipation and lurks behind the social business relationships that transform this shop boy into only one element in these relationships.

In this way, that human relations are already socially determined beforehand can be clearly observed in that transport facilities, for instance, move in accordance with plans prescribed beforehand and within a definite budget. A budget or a plan can be set up only in "anticipation" of the possible movements of human beings. And, what is more, the anticipation in question is not an anticipation within individual consciousness alone but is also a social one. A railroad schedule is a scheduled plan of traffic services and expresses an "anticipation" of the movement of people. This anticipation is a social anticipation of possible human relationships. Hence, anticipation of the future exists not only in individual consciousness but also within society itself.

Now, plans or budgets for transport facilities can be set up only by being determined through the established relational traffic patterns of human beings. Even though a new plan is formed, this term *new* can here be used only because it has been determined by the established relational traffic patterns. If this is so, then the burden of the past still exists within society itself. The phenomena of transportation exhibit exactly this social fact of being predetermined as "the structure of *ningen sonzai*."

What is observed in the phenomena of transportation can similarly be observed in those of communication. To write a letter is to attempt to establish a connection with a person who is at some distance, far or near, from us. This activity of setting up a connection shows that, although determined by the betweenness already established in one way or another, we try to comprehend the possible relationships beforehand. Even though this letter may give rise to a great change between the two correspondents, this change remains a mere possibility before the letter is sent. Consequently, the letter, once on its way, can be said to be possible betweenness itself. From this standpoint, we will be able to comprehend a mental state of expectation that a person may exhibit, when she receives and then opens the letter. Indeed, this psychology is displayed even more pointedly at the moment when one receives a telegram. The fact that a message is a possible betweenness can arise only on the basis of established betweenness. At a place where betweenness does not obtain in any way, the phenomenon of communication does not, generally speaking, result.

The phenomenon of communication also demonstrates the dynamic social structure of *ningen sonzai* in the form of communication facilities. The intensity of a communication network expresses the established social relations in their intensity, and the plans involved in the lines of communication established express a social expectation concerning possible human relationships. In this way, communication facilities that were thought to express the spatial connection of *ningen sonzai* can, at the same time, be said to express its temporal structure.

We can approach the temporality of subjective human beings through the same phenomena of transportation and communication that have exhibited subjective spatiality. *Ningen sonzai* is subjectively extended. On the other hand, as a subjective connection, this extendedness must possess a structure that, although shouldering the established betweenness, aims at achieving a possible betweenness in and through its present activities. That is to say, subjective extendedness is temporal in structure.

If the preceding argument is tenable, then it becomes clear that the temporal structure of *ningen sonzai* is, in fact, the basic structure of *ningen sonzai*, which was dealt with in the preceding chapter. As was remarked earlier, *ningen sonzai* is an incessant movement in which one becomes an individual by departing somewhat from the communal and then negating this individuality and bringing to realization the community in one way or another, so as to return to one's authenticity.

Now, *ningen sonzai* is characterized in terms of the incessant movement from an established betweenness to a possible one. An established betweenness is the community from which an individual separates herself, and a possible betweenness is the community to be realized. If so, then what was grasped as "the movement of negation" in *ningen sonzai* makes its appearance here in the form of temporal structure.

Just as the movement of negation was, in its extreme, the self-activity of absolute negativity, so temporality is precisely the manner in which absolute negativity exhibits itself. That is to say, an established betweenness is, in its extreme, the absolute wholeness that consists of the nonduality of the self and the other; that is, the authentic countenance prior to the birth of one's parents, as is said in Zen Buddhism. In other words, it is authenticity as the ground out of which we, fundamentally speaking, come forth.

At the same time, possible betweenness is absolute wholeness, which also consists of the nonduality of the self and the other. By bringing to realization the nondual relationship between self and other, we return to our authentic home ground. This ultimate ground out of which we come is the ultimate *terminus ad quem* to which we return. Here lurks what authenticity *sive* futurity signifies. The temporal structure of *ningen sonzai* is, in the final analysis, the exhibition of this authenticity.

That the basic structure of *ningen sonzai* is grasped as temporality is because *ningen sonzai* is subjectively extended. From the standpoint of subjective spatiality, an individual cannot simply be a disconnected point. Of course, an individual obtains her individuality precisely through the negation of community, and precisely because of this, she cannot have an independent subsistence. That she is established through the negation of community means that she finds that other individuals exist and she distances herself from them. This gives rise to the opposition between subjects, such that the self stands opposed to the other, and there appears also a "tension" that spreads over these subjects. The self and the other are distanced from one another, so it does not follow that they are self-subsistent without connection. Rather, the truth is exactly the contrary. It means that they become relative to one another. For this reason, this distance turns out to be, at the same time, a field in which the movement of the connection as well as the unification of subjects, takes place. What was grasped as subjective spatiality is exactly the connection between subjects who stand opposed to each other in the form of self and other. This subjective spatiality is the movement of subjects in which they become communalized through their attempt to individualize. Therefore, the view that the structure of *ningen sonzai* is grasped as subjective extendedness, plays an important role in bringing this movement of subjects into full relief. As a result, this dynamic structure comes to be seen as temporality.

It is not that the daily life of human existence is concerned with gaining one's authentic countenance. Just as was understood through the phenomena of transportation and communication, all that we do in our everyday concerns is to proceed to a possible betweenness, while shouldering the betweenness of the past. Trifling movements occur, for the purpose of sending goods home or to see a friend or to attend a meeting and so forth.

However this may be, why does a human being move incessantly in these ways? Why do we constantly head for a possible betweenness? In a word, why are we determined "already beforehand?"

If this "already beforehand" bears no significance here, then one can discard it. However, for those who look forward to a friend coming from a distant place or who promise to see a lover, determination "beforehand" is of great significance. That is to say, regarding the possible connection of human beings, people show a concern so great that it is beyond imagination. This is so because the direction of this possible connection is, in the extreme, the direction in which a human being tries to return to her authenticity. The present concern is not with "one's authentic countenance"; nevertheless, this concern does lurk in the background in the form of possibility. The reason why people look for connection of whatever sort is because absolute wholeness is authentic possibility for a human being.

Therefore, we can say that a *ningen sonzai* who acts in her mode of being in which her self and the other stand opposed to each other, to achieve unity and community in one way or another, develops this authenticity. As the unique possibility of *ningen sonzai*, this authenticity gives every human existence its own direction. Herein lies the basic *terminus ad quem*.

This *terminus ad quem* is, for a human being, an "authentic" place—the term *authentic* is here taken at face value—the ground out of which she comes forth. With the home ground in view from which she comes forth, a human being also returns to it. Consequently, it can be argued that the negative movement of *ningen sonzai* is an act of returning to one's home ground.

This is what the phrase *already beforehand* basically means. In this authenticity we catch a glimpse of the basic unity of *ningen sonzai*. One can be whole only within this authenticity; that is, within absolute wholeness. This wholeness reveals its basic unity in the movement that realizes the "identity" inherent in the nonduality between the self and other through the standpoint of the "difference" imminent in the opposition between them. Therefore, "to return to the home ground" occurs from within the standpoint of nonduality between the self and other but not in that of the mere "self."

The standpoint of the "self" is that of the opposition between self and other that has departed from authentic wholeness; that is, it is a standpoint of inauthenticity. This sort of inauthenticity "presents itself" on the scene in the very movement of "returning to the home ground." Hence, *ningen sonzai* who seeks to realize the nonduality of the self and other through their opposition has the structural unity of "returning to the home ground in the present."

It is not inappropriate that to "return" to the home ground, understood in this way, is called the *future*. Authenticity, although realized in various communities of human beings under the guise of "alreadyness," has not yet come. As "futurity," it always lurks behind the present opposition between the self and other and subsists there as the direction of a nondual relationship between them. This direction can never disappear, no matter what tightly organized community may be actualized. Rather, to the contrary, we can say that this direction is strengthened as the tight organization of community is increased. Consequently, as futurity, authenticity signifies an infinite direction. Only in infinity, that is, in the absolute negativity, can a human being be whole.

Likewise, it is also not inappropriate for us to call the "home ground" out of which we come forth, the *past*. This "home ground" is certainly our authentic countenance, but it is, at present, something that demands realization from us infinitely and, hence, is something that does not yet exist. If this is true, then we have completely lost that authenticity which was once existent and which is none other than "the golden age that was gone." If the meaning of the past lies in its having once existed and now is nonexistent, then authentic wholeness is the past. Even though being the authentic countenance of a human being, it is precisely the "past" because of its being the "future."

It is also appropriate in terms of the "present" to call a place where the future and the past are unified a field where one is "about to come" to the "home ground," which is the past. It is *ningen sonzai* existing in the present that, although being associated with absolute negation in the past and in the future as well, reveals this negation in the present under the guise of the opposition between the self and other. Because *ningen sonzai* exists, it is said to be inauthentic if seen from the vantage point of authentic countenance, which is absolute negativity. On the contrary, because of its deprivedness, as characterized by the *in* in the term *inauthentic*, it also exhibits a process through which authenticity, as absolute negation, unfolds itself.

Therefore, it is never inappropriate to grasp *ningen sonzai* as the unified structure of past, present, and future. To put this another way, the structural unity of *ningen sonzai* "comes to the home ground in the present." Despite suffering from the opposition between the self and other, it realizes the nondual relationship between them. It "comes" to authentic wholeness in nonduality, in the direction of the future. As well, it comes from wholeness in the past, in that it, too, is the "home ground" of *ningen sonzai* in its authentic countenance. The present discloses the movement of coming to the home ground, in the present opposition between the self and other.

Ningen sonzai clearly exhibits this structural unity through the phenomena of transportation and communication. The activity of the present consists of the unity of the possible betweenness, as well as the already established one. The possible betweenness is the direction in which agents who stand in opposition to the self and other come to human wholeness, in whatever ways that may be, in a nondual manner. Whatever human connections are here envisioned, they constitute a direction toward connections that, each to its own degree, realize the whole.

The already established betweenness indicates that what is at stake in the opposition between the self and the other was once authentically a whole, in one way or another. Whatever kinds of connection might be at issue here, the whole was already realized in them, to some degree. That direction that has already been realized is now aimed at. This movement in the now aimed at direction is a finite form of the movement of "coming to the home ground." As the unity of the two, the activity of the present manifests authenticity. However trifling *ningen sonzai* may be, without exception it bears such authentic significance.

We grasp the basic unity of *ningen sonzai* as temporality. As was observed previously, there is no such "thing" as "space" but rather "spatiality" as the existential structure of *ningen sonzai*; so similarly, there is no "thing" called *time*, but rather, there is the temporality of *ningen sonzai*. Moreover, it is not the case that *ningen* exists "in time," but on the contrary, time emerges from *ningen sonzai*. Because what exists in a spatio-temporal fashion is basically the human being, we must again consider *ningen sonzai* in our attempt to come to grips with the essential features of space and time.

And, quite the reverse, we can now follow up on just how many concepts of time have been derived from this basic temporality. Every concept of time is derived from subjective temporality, whether this derivation is scientific or not. The concept of "time" most commonly used refers to each moment of a human relationship, which aims for the future while shouldering the past; for instance, the time when one was born, the time of marriage, or that of death, and again, the time of seeing someone, or of departing, or the time when one left one's house. Such "time" is not something measured. Instead, it is an "occasion," or an "opportunity" present in human relationships. Therefore, even when a phrase is used such as *to open one's mouth with timing*, this timing has nothing to do with measurement but rather is the choosing of an opportunity.

In addition, this choice is made when we keenly anticipate the future, while determined by our past relationships. It can sometimes signify a critical occasion, called the *crossroads of destiny*. Out of such "times," we can select a time that repeats itself most frequently; that is, a time without a destinylike crisis: the time of waking up in the morning, or the time of eating, the time to go to bed, or to put the matter on a somewhat larger scale, the time to seed, the time of harvest, and so forth. Due to its homogeneousness, this sort of time is fixed publicly in human existence.

In particular, human labor relations are prescribed through public "time" of this sort. Here, "time units such as hours, minutes, and so on" appear on a small scale and "seasons" on a large scale. Because of being public, time units are often manifested by a bell or a whistle. Seasons are likewise manifested by festivals, ceremonies, or national holidays. Measurement takes place for the first time within such time units or seasons. What served as the standard of measurement in ancient times was the sun or the moon. (To speak truthfully, a watch can be said to have been constructed on the model of the motion of the sun.)

Now, together with this sort of measurement, time units or seasons began to be conceived of not only as indicating each occasion of public life but also as constituting a continuous stream.

Nevertheless, time units and seasons cannot exist apart from human existence. Time units are measurements, because they are fixed publicly. For instance, to ponder the approach of noon by looking at the sun, is to measure the "interval" before the public "time" of eating. Or to become aware that one must hurry after looking at one's watch is to measure through public time units the "interval" until the "time" when some human relationship, as prescribed or promised beforehand, is expected to occur.

Moreover, this "interval" begins as a duration of activity but not that which is called *time*. When "there is no interval, or no time," we control our activities to suit the situation in such a way as to "shift gears" by speeding up our activities or by refraining from doing work that demands great effort. Consequently, the measurement of time units signifies an adjustment on the part of *ningen sonzai*. This is the case with measuring an "interval" of "time" for dining together or meeting someone. Therefore, even if time units are conceived of as flowing successively, this is not the case with time that runs away homogeneously and quite independent of human relationships. Hence, the time under consideration sometimes passes more rapidly and sometimes more slowly. The same time interval is sometimes long and sometimes short.

Similarly, seasons began being measured by public farm chores and cattle breeding. Therefore, without exception, to bring days into unity by means of the moon's waxing and waning as well as to bring months to unity by means of the positions of the sun's rotation occurs as a result of the perspective of social labor. Therefore, "years" were admired among primitive human beings as bearing something of the somewhat mystical. This is a very old and universal phenomenon. Gods of years are born, grow, prosper, lose vigor, die, and rise from the dead once again. Through these gods, those who were believed to sustain a society's labor came under control. Hence, the measurement of seasons described by primitive religion signifies the control of *ningen sonzai*.

This tendency becomes more intensified as years, instead of seasons, are measured. As Beck has already pointed out, only in compliance with a tightly organized social ethics-oriented association such as a state are years counted. This was a way of counting the years that have passed since the reign of some ruler began. Consequently, the standard of measurement was unique to each state. The present Christian era was constructed, as the phrase *Anno Domini* indicates, after the model of the ruler's era. A way of counting years without reference to any state or any religious association has not appeared on the scene in the entire history of humankind. The various ways of counting years, such as the ten calendar signs or the twelve hoary signs (as was carried on, first of all, in China and then in Japan) seems to have been closely connected with the aforementioned mysteriousness surrounding "years."

"Time" as an occasion, public "time units," "seasons," or an "interval" of time for a purpose, or the years of such and such a ruler are all types of time that do not run away homogeneously. When we extract human relationships from these types of time and measure them by means of the sun or a watch in an abstract fashion, then "natural time" will arise for the first time. Even from this standpoint, however, we cannot yet say that homogeneous time is established in a full-fledged way.

For instance, in a period in which time is measured by the sun, there occurs expansion and contraction, as far as daytime and night-time are concerned. A time unit at night is short in summer and long in winter. As we divide the interval evenly, with sunrise and sunset as our basis, we are not immune to the seasonal fluctuations of time. What is more, this manner of measurement is quite natural for countries in which farm labor is predominant. Thus, time is not yet extracted from human subjective existence and, hence, is not yet a homogeneous stream in the true sense of the word. Only when time is entirely separated from *ningen sonzai* does it come to be conceived of as something divisible and measurable that flows homogeneously and independent of human beings. Such time is a medium in which not only human activities but also all other phenomena take place. This concept of natural time has already been established as the standpoint of common sense from ancient times.

It should now be evident how the concept of time, inside of which every phenomenon occurs, was derived from *ningen sonzai* in an abstract manner. It is appropriate to discover the origin of this sort of time within subjective *ningen sonzai*. However, the problem is to determine whether such subjective temporality is itself justifiable, if we view it from the history of the issues surrounding time. Here, we want to make sure that such a view of temporality is not abruptly called into question by the history of the issues surrounding time, and that the development of these issues does in fact move in a direction favorable to this view.

The problem of time takes its departure, as a general rule, from natural time. Therefore, from the beginning, this problem was extracted from practical activities. From a contemplative attitude of "only looking at," an attempt is made here to extract and grasp time from something's motion. However, the attempt develops in two contradictory directions. One of them arrives at physical time by carrying abstraction to the extreme, and the other traces physical time back to concrete time, which has served as the ground of this abstraction, finally grasping subjective temporality. The latter direction can be said to have already returned to that extremity to which a contemplative standpoint allows itself to be carried, that is; to such temporality as the structure of individual consciousness or of individual existence.

With respect to the traditional concept of time, Aristotle is said to have already mentioned something essential in an exhaustive fashion.[4] Ancient philosophy regarded time sometimes as "something which is" (οὐσία) and sometimes as "that which is not" (μὴ ὄν). Aristotle sided with the latter. Time consists of the past that "is no longer" and of the future that "is not yet" and what is, is the present "now." Moreover, it is not that the sum total of these "nows" gives rise to time. "Now" is only "this now," which immediately turns out to be what is not now; that is, the other. There is no selfhood in "nows," which, therefore, cannot be said to be "what is," that is to say, which is "what is not." Thus, provided that the past, the future, and the present are all of them that which is not, then time cannot be "what is."

Then, what is time? One may say that the motion of all things is time. But Aristotle does not side with this opinion. A "motion" exists in the midst of "something moving" and, hence, exists only at a place where "something moving" exists. But time is everywhere, even beyond "something moving" and, hence, exists at the side of "something moving." Therefore, time is not a motion.

However, Aristotle does not try to grasp time in separation from motion. Even for him, time does not exist apart from motion. That is, time is not κίνησις (motion) but κινήσεώς τι; that is, something in motion. Then, "what" is in motion time? To this question he gives the answer that, at first glance, seems strange: "Time is a number of preceding and subsequent motions."[5] That is to say, time is what is counted as being in motion in accordance with "before and after movement." But what counts as being in motion? Motion is a transition (μεταβολεή) from one locus to another or from some thing to another. This structure of motion is called μεθοδος, that is, magnitude or extension. Therefore, motion exists in accordance with ἀκολουθί (or extension), and time exists in accordance with motion.[6] What is counted as being in motion is here made clear. That is to say, the transition from one locus to another is counted as extension, as is being in the order of "before and after." What is so counted is none other than a series of "nows." Time is a series of "nows."

This concept of time seems to have been an attempt to grasp time by means of a spatial schema. To the extent that the motion of something "conforms to an extension" as it transits from one locus to another, then this extension may be thought of as "a road of motion" from one locus to another; that is, it is a line. As "something unmoving," it constitutes the basis of this motion. "Something moving" passes individual places located on this line, one after another. Hence, a motion that "conforms to an extension" is conceived of as a transition among individual places; that is, a spatial transition from one point to another.

Therefore, just as space is divisible, so motion is also divisible. And just as a line is a sum of points, so motion is, so to speak, a succession of moving points. By the way, because time is that which is "in accordance with motion," the divisibility of motion turns out to be that of time and a moving point turns out to be a temporal point, a "now." Just as a line is a succession of points, so time is a succession of "nows."

Understood in this way, the concept of time does not differ, in its essence, from that prevalent in modern science.[7] What modern science has chosen as representative of time is a motion that some moving physical body T discloses along its moving track. Let us refer to points that evenly divide a moving track successively, starting with T_0, T_1, T_2, T_3, . . . When T passes along points such as T_1, T_2, T_3, . . . , we can say that time units 1, 2, 3, . . . , have elapsed.

Now, what is counted here are spatial points but not the stream of time itself. The stream of time is here transformed into a spatial line. Consequently, even if the track of a moving physical body, T, including those parts that have already passed as well as those parts that have not yet passed, is given once and for all, this makes no difference so far as a scientist's eye is concerned. This means precisely that no heed is given, in this conception of time, to time regarded as a "succession as its special characteristic."

Bergson pointed out with acuteness an abstract characteristic of this concept of time. He found "a cinematic mechanism of thinking" at its basis.[8] What is directly given in experience is "pure duration." But the practical and technical demands of life tend to fixate the purely enduring reality, because of the necessity of setting up goals on behalf of which one must act. This is the role the intellect plays. The intellect thinks of "something moving" with the aid of "something unmoving." It fixates a flowing duration of reality into discontinuous images.

The cinema exhibits this sort of mechanism in a concrete fashion. The cinema is, basically speaking, nothing more than a series of momentary snapshots or a togetherness of unmoving images; all motion is thereby transformed into stills. That which allows these still images to move is not within the visible photographs themselves but an invisible motion within the projector. An actor on the screen displays various kinds of motion, which is actually the result of the rotation of an abstract and simple machine. A mechanism of this sort describes, just as it is, the mechanism of our knowledge or thinking. We try to fix reality that is incessantly flowing and construct from it a becoming again in an artificial manner. The motive force of this reconstruction is practical action. In this way, our thinking, without focusing on pure duration or the indivisibility of motion, tries to control this flowing reality under the presumption of homogeneous space or homogeneous time.

In this interpretation of Bergson, a human being's intellect is merely a "controlling intellect," which supposedly makes invisible the true features of reality and, hence, time as well. The controlling intellect presumes homogeneous time. As a result, the concept of time that took its departure from Aristotle and has been inherited by modern science can never come into contact with the true features of time as pure duration. I would like to express regret at Bergson's interpretation and its failing to subject to a full-fledged analysis the "demands of the practical life," which uses the controlling intellect as its means. But I am in complete agreement with him when he points to the abstract quality of homogeneous time.

However, the above discussion presupposes that Aristotle's concept of time comprehends time by means of a spatial schema. Nevertheless, his viewpoint can also be interpreted in an entirely different way. This is the case with Heidegger.[9] According to him, we need not understand spatially the phrase *a transition from one thing to another,* as found in Aristotle. "Transmutation" or "becoming different" (ἀλλοίωσις) of the sort that occurs in the change of colors is yet another example of transition. Aristotle calls the structure of "motion" in this sense an extension (μεϑοδος). Therefore, this extension has, fundamentally speaking, nothing to do with spatial extension. It is but a "stretch," and spatial extension is merely one of its modes. This interpretation is different from Bergson's.

Second, the term *to conform* in the sentence *a motion conforms to an extension* must be understood not to have anything to do with the relation of an ontic being but rather with that relation involved in ontology. When the structure of motion is understood ontologically, an "extension" lurks behind "motion" in the order of construction within this ontology. Therefore, when it is said that time conforms to motion, this means exactly that "a motion" and, hence, an extension are together experienced as basic layers of the experience of time.

Aristotle's position can be applied not only to spatial transition but also to "the becoming different" of colors (i.e., to qualitative changes). The suspicion that Aristotle has grasped time with the aid of a spatial schema disappears completely.

Third, let us, for the moment, think only of the transition of loci. What is collected in this transition is not points such as "here" and "there" but rather "from there" "to here." The phrase "from . . . to" in-

dicates that we, despite preserving something antecedent, still anticipate something subsequent. This is exactly what Aristotle wants to say,
according to Heidegger, with the phrase in accordance with "before and
after." No matter what locus we may pick in this transition, there are
none which do not involve the connection "from" something "to" another. Even in the case of a transition of loci, a transition from one point
to another does not occur.

Fourth, what is counted as being in accordance with "before and
after" is "there" inclusive of the aforementioned structure of
"from . . . to." Because "theres" are counted as "now here" and "now
there," this *now* also includes the connection of "before and after," as
involved in "from . . . to." Consequently, even though time consists in
a series of "nows," this series differs from that of spatial points. Rather,
it is a continuity of "nows," which extends over before as well as after.
If so, then time is not a sum total of "nows." On the contrary, only
within "now" can a "stretch" of time be clarified. "Nows" are not parts
of time but rather time itself.

As was noted, Aristotle's concept of time, which regarded time
as something "stretching," can be interpreted without reference to spatial schema. However, what does the statement that time is "numbers"
mean? Because "nows" include within themselves a transition, they cannot be counted as "points." Nevertheless, what is counted as a motion
in accordance with "before and after" are "nows." What kind of counting is in question?

"Now" turns out to be "what is just gone," when it is said to be
"now," counted in motion. Yet "now" is always one as "now." The togetherness of "nows," such as now, now, now, . . . , is not at stake here.
For this reason, we can say that "now" is the limit of "what is just now
gone" and "what will come now" and that time is tightly controlled
by these. Even though one may say that these "nows" are "numbers,"
the term *numbers* differs from the sense of "numbers" by means of
which points are counted. It refers only to the essential feature which
a number possesses as a number. In other words, a number is not concerned with the entity or with the way of being of that which is counted.

Similarly, when we count a motion by means of "nows," this
counting is also not concerned with a substantial entity or with the way
of being of what is "moving." This is the reason why time is said to be
numbers. This view gives birth to a characteristic of time Kant called
the *form of intuition*. However, just because time is numbers in this
sense, we can measure that which renders time capable of being numbers (i.e., motion). In other words, time is "that which counts"; it is "a

measure." But if we measure motion by means of time, we do not count it by breaking it into pieces, as in counting points, but rather grasp motion through those characteristics of its being in transition. In other words, "nows" are not points but become measures of motion because of being transitions. To measure motion by means of time is to measure a duration, which appears in the form of "from . . . to." This measurement is what is meant by the phrase *being in time*. This is also what Kant meant when he said that time is a container (*das Worin*) on the "order of before/after."

Aristotle's definition of time, as indicated by the phrase *numbers of motions counted by means of before and after* can be, according to Heidegger, interpreted in this way. Provided that time is of numbers and measures in the aforementioned sense, then this cannot exist apart from "mind." Without mind, neither the counting activity itself nor a counting agent is possible. Hence, neither what is to be counted nor what is counted is independently existent. If this is true, then time must be subjective. What is mind? And what is the subject? These questions are concerned with the basic locus of time. Aristotle's concept of time had just arrived at the gateway to these questions.

Whether the explanation provided correctly interprets Aristotle's conception of time is not the issue here. At any rate, his concept of time is understood to be the same sort of attempt to grasp time spatially as is prevalent in modern science, on the one hand, and goes so far as to affirm the subjectivity, of time on the other. And these two sides are representative of the two great trends that surround the issue of time.

Now, if we side with the latter interpretation, it is evident that the issue of the subjectivity of time, as is noted by Kant, has been a trend in the history of philosophy ever since Aristotle. Already in ancient times, Plotinus spoke of the subjectivity of time. He insisted that time does not exist outside of the mind and that it is a qualification of mental life itself, as well as its extension. Furthermore, Augustine, keeping his eye on the fact that time steps exist within the mind and hence that time is measured within consciousness, developed a theory of time in connection with anticipation, attention, and memory. In the philosophies prevalent in the Middle Ages, Aristotle's definition of time was repeated again and again, and the influence of Plotinus and Augustine were also to be found there. In the modern world, too, the subjectivity of time is spoken of, especially in English philosophy. Berkeley and Hume represent this view. Seen from this angle, Kant's view of the subjectivity of time is but a guideline for these trends.

Newton's idea of absolute time shone brilliantly before Kant's eyes. This absolute time is homogeneous and entirely spatialized. Therefore, Kant, too, adhered to a conception of time from which all phenomena are derived; that is, the one and only infinite time. Moreover, Kant could not help but conclude that time is "the manner in which we intuit ourselves internally" or that time is "a form of intuiting ourselves or our inner state of mind."[10]

What does the phrase *to intuit oneself* mean? In Kant, intuition is a representation (*Vorstellung*) of a phenomenon. It is not concerned with what exists in itself but posits before us (*stellen vor uns*) something to which we are related receptively. Consequently, *pure intuition* represents only the "relation of being affected." If so, then to *intuit oneself* means only to represent that relation whereby I am affected by myself. What occasions this self-effect is the activity of the self in which something is posited within the mind; that is, the self-activity of representing something. For instance, in my exercising the activity of seeing something, I am affected by myself. Furthermore, what represents this relation of self-affectation is self-intuition. The "inner sense organ" of which Kant speaks is not a function of receiving something from the outside but of receiving from oneself. That agent which represents what is thus received through the inner sense organ is self-intuition. Kant grasped the manner of this self-intuition through the form of time. There is no doubt that time belongs entirely to the subject and that it comes to nought if regarded as independent of this subject. What is more, as a form of self-intuition, time belongs to the essential structure of subjectivity. This is why the united structure of transcendental apperception is expounded in and through the schema of time.

Kant's achievement lay in developing that influential trend of orthodox philosophy which consisted in transferring the issue of time to the realm of bodily experience or consciousness. So, in contradistinction to the standpoint of science, which adhered to natural time, this trend developed in an entirely different direction. Whereas the former arrived at a new concept of time through mathematical physics, the latter arrived at temporality, regarded as the structure of consciousness, by taking a route from psychology through phenomenology. Here one attempts to grasp basic time, from which natural time as well as physical time can be derived. As well, that state of affairs which regards the issue of time as the basic problem of human existence arises here. I would like to trace, in brief, the history of this view.

As time began to be investigated as an issue of consciousness, "homogeneous time," as in Kant, had soon become an object of criticism.

In Brentano, who is a forerunner of phenomenology, special emphasis is placed on the issue of time.[11] Time is said to be neither an intuition in the Kantian sense, nor something a priori or infinite. The same may be said of space. The intuition of time we possess is inseparable from qualities and quite limited. For instance, a succession is something qualitative, such as a continuity of sounds or a change of colors, and an intuited time representation is psychologically present time, which lasts for only a few minutes. Time, as expounded by Kant, is not intuition but a universal concept extracted from it.

Kant is also mistaken in regarding time as only the form of the organ of inner sense. When one perceives a melody or a dance, the sounds or colors themselves transmute temporally, but this transmutation does not originate in the organ of inner sense. We are able to perceive something temporal even externally. Strictly speaking, "time" does not exist, but what does really exist is "something temporal." And this something temporal is perceived only as "the present."

In saying this, however, we do not mean that there is no discriminatory structure in the present. The present is, to a variety of degrees, distanced from the *before* because of its being the *after* and from the *after* because of its being the *before*. Though everything is now existent, it is, nevertheless, recognized as what is, more or less, distanced in either of the two contradictory directions.

For Brentano, "something temporal" is substituted for time. But he goes a step further and recognizes the temporal modi of representation (*die Temporalmodi der Vorstellung*) as lying at the basis of the temporal.[12] Just as the basic modi of judgment are approval and disapproval and those of emotional relationships are love and hatred, so the basic modi of representation are the present, the past, and the future. The difference between these modi is not a difference in the objects themselves. When we represent a certain external object as being at a standstill, it is the same in its *before* and *after*; and when we represent it as moving, it occupies different places in the *before* and *after*. The object is the same, only the manner of representing it differs. Moreover, this difference is determined relative to *I*, who is a presently existing agent[13] such that it is either contemporary with *I* or precedes *I* to a greater or lesser extent. The continuity of sounds such as in a speech or a melody moves through a relation of this sort.

Incidentally, *I*, as an axis of this difference, is straightforwardly (*in modo recto*) represented by means of a modus of the present, and something temporal determined relatively to it is represented in an oblique way (*in modo obliquo*). Here the phrases *in modo recto* and *in modo obliquo* are also concerned with the modi of representation of which Brentano speaks. For instance, when we represent "a lover," the person loved by this lover is also represented. The latter is referred to by the term *in obliquo*. When I represent myself as a perceiving agent, I am referred to by the term *in recto*, and what is perceived by me is referred to by the term *in obliquo*.

Thus, insofar as the axis is lying with the modus of the present, we have no alternative but to think that the present, the past, and the future, all of which are modi of representation, are modi always involved in the representation of the present. Standing in the present, I feel that some sound is present, another has passed away, and a third is even more distant. The past, the future, and the present are respectively the past of *now*, the future of *now*, and the present of *now*. The present entirely limits the evidence of inner perception.

In this way, Brentano found basic time in the structure of representation in the form of *now*. And precisely because basic time is an aspect of the structure of representation, he came to the conclusion that judgment and emotional relations based on this representation also possess their own temporal structures.

By interpreting temporality in terms of the modes of representation, Brentano connected all of our mental concerns and mental attitudes with the consciousness of time. Although Marty fiercely criticized Brentano's theory of time, insisting on the absolute, unactual, and independent qualities of time,[14] he emphatically agreed with Brentano about this sort of connection. The only difference is that Marty attempted to grasp temporality as a mode of judgment rather than as one of representation.

Marty insisted that we originally acquire the concept of time by reflecting on the way in which we relate ourselves to objects mentally. These ways of relating cannot be intuition, however. For instance, "a past sound" is not a sound nor a sense quality in general. The same can be said of "a future sound." We do not intuit it but only think of it. Therefore, consciousness of time must be regarded as belonging to a conceptual construction. It is no accident that words expressing judgment take the form of the present, past, and future and that the verb and the copula are called *Zeitword*. Temporal modes belong to judgment. They are a species of judgmental quality. The present manifests reality or straightforward facticity, and the past and the future manifest unreality or transformed facticity. The distinction between the past and the future arises only because of the differences in objects. Thus, temporal difference is fundamental and essential for judgment. We must assume the temporality of all things on which we pass judgment. We must also think that "eternal truth" is not something timeless but rather applicable to all sorts of time.

Marty's opinion is tied to his objection to Kant's theory of time.[15] Kant recognizes the temporal characteristic in inner intuition alone, but Marty recognizes it even in outer intuition. Kant insists on the infinity of time intuition, but Marty insists on its finitude. We have, according to Kant, pure time intuition, but Marty maintains that we intuit only fulfilled time, that is, only "the temporal."

On these points, Marty followed Brentano. Furthermore, he was even decisively opposed to the notion of the subjectivity of time, taking instead the position that time is a mode of judgment. The ordinary form of contradiction, that it is impossible for something at the same time both to be and not to be, includes within itself the temporal qualification of *at once*. In arguing that it is unjustifiable for the mere basically logical proposition to stand under the condition of time, Kant attempted to eliminate this temporal qualification. However, from Marty's perspective, this attempt is futile. All that exists or is factual is qualified by temporality in one way or another. Consequently, from the statement that a proposition takes into itself a moment of time, it does not necessarily follow that this proposition ceases to be a purely logical one and turns out to be an a priori synthetic judgment valid for phenomena alone. Apart from a moment of time, the law of contradiction simply does not come into being. Time is a universal condition of all sorts of factuality, and the proof of the existence of something factual results in the proof of the existence of time. Time exists in itself, independent of the subject.

Thus, Marty distances himself from Kant in various respects. Yet, in conceiving of time as a mode of judgment he is close to Cohen, who is said to have carried Kant's critique of reason to its conclusion. For Cohen, time is also the basic form of judgment and the category by means of which pure thinking produces its content. Apart from time, there is neither multiplicity nor content.

The essential feature of time as such a category, is as "anticipation." Therefore, there is, first of all, the future, from which the past stands out in full relief. From this perspective, Cohen abandons Kant's view that time is the form of pure receptivity. On this point, he deviates from Kant to the same extent as Marty. Nonetheless, it can be asked why Cohen upholds the subjectivity of time, while Marty opposes it? The reason is that the significance of subjectivity differs for each.

For Cohen, time is consciousness as pure spontaneity. This consciousness is pure apperception regarded as consciousness in general, which Kant referred to as *the subject*. For this reason, time as a form of judgment is still the form of the subject. In this sense, it can be said, as Natrop pointed out, that time exists within consciousness but consciousness does not exist within time.

Incidentally, Marty, insofar as he regarded time as a mode of judgment, cannot consistently reject the subjectivity of time. But, unlike Cohen, Marty adheres to the contention that judgment is objective not subjective. Consequently, time simply could not be subjective insofar as it belongs to judgment.

All theories of time that have attempted to improve on Kant have allowed time to belong to the structure of consciousness, whether they regarded time as a mode of representation or as a mode of judgment. Hence, the development of the study of consciousness necessarily gives occasion to an advancement in the theory of time. Bergson's philosophy reflects this trend precisely, as does phenomenology. These are thought to represent a theory of time typical of the modern world.

As was said earlier, Bergson develops the concept of homogeneous time through recourse to a cinematographic analogy of thinking. As is the case with homogeneous time, the commonsense concept of time is a spatialized, abstract, and symbolic one, which fails to come to grips with genuine time. He strictly distinguishes this commonsense time (*temps*) from the genuine one, expressed as *durée*. Our own existence exhibits this "duration" directly, which we are able to perceive inwardly at the deep bottom of ourselves. Our existence suffers moment by moment from unrelenting transformation. No matter what one may choose from among sensation, representation, emotion, and volition, there are none that do not transform at each moment. What seems to remain unchanged is the seeing of an object at a standstill. Yet even in this case, a visional image of "now" is distinguished from that of a moment ago. Because images thus distinguished remain in the same state, a phenomenon referred to as being at a *standstill* arises for the first time. Therefore, no essential difference exists between the transition from one state to another and adherence to that same state. No doubt, transition as well as duration are involved in something's remaining in the same state.

This is even more the case with our psychological existence, which is in an incessant stream. It is a concrete duration in which the past advances while plunging itself into the "now," thereby encroaching upon the future. Consequently, the past is not something gone that is occasionally recollected. Instead, it accompanies us in its totality every moment. What we have felt, thought, and desired since childhood, exists "there now." It interpenetrates the present. Of course, when we think, we are concerned with only one portion of the past. But when it comes to our entreating, desiring, or acting, we involve necessarily the totality of the past.

In other words, even though we can recollect only a very small portion of the past, we nevertheless manifest its totality in our activities. Our personality is precisely this "survival of the past," and manifests continuous growth. Consequently, every moment is "something novel" and comes to be added to the whole past. But this is not the whole story. Every moment is not only new, but also "what cannot be discerned in advance." Generally speaking, prediscernment lies in projecting past perception onto the future. In reality, an artist's creation cannot be discerned in its completion beforehand.

To prediscern is to produce something before it is produced. Therefore, it is an entirely self-contradictory assumption. We must admit that we create our existence incessantly, as is the case with an artist's creation. The self creates itself. Here we gain a glimpse of our "action," through which we create ourselves as that which has never been before, although determined by what already has been. In this activity, we depend on what already has been, but nonetheless, we are just what we act.

With respect to Bergson on this point, we can say, without thereby falling into error, that he already depicts in outline Heidegger's idea of thrown project (*geworfener Entwurf*). By referring to the temporal structure of personality, Bergson clarified that the *now* each person faces possesses the characteristics of being a spearhead of history, which is unique for each person. Further, because of this he went so far as to suggest why this problem of *now* cannot be resolved except by the person concerned.[16]

Time as production is called by Bergson "the authentic life of things" or "basic reality," out of which any reality whatsoever is derived. Hence, there is no alternative but for it to be superindividual cosmic life. This does not, however, alter that basic reality is "a life" or "consciousness" such that it is susceptible to being internally intuited. Consciousness lurks behind the origin of life.

Intuition and intellect are the two contradictory directions of consciousness. The former invigorates the meaning of life itself, and the latter kills it. For this reason, intuition is said to be spirit itself and even to be life itself in a sense. The basic structure of this life or of consciousness is time as duration.

Bergson conceives of this life as belonging to the psychological order, on the one hand, and having the significance of activity and practice, on the other, because of its incessant self-creation. Practice cannot be identified with a practical attitude that fixates duration by using intellect as its means. If this is so, then as "intuition," life cannot remain contemplative but must be practice in the most basic sense of the word; that is, it must be practice as a creative activity. Hence, as pure duration, freedom must further reveal its authentic nature as practical freedom.

Moreover, we leave as a great issue yet to be tackled the problem of clarifying the relation between cosmic life and personal life. However, Bergson did not pursue the issue of time to that extent. For this reason, despite the emphasis in his ethics on the control of society over individuals,[17] he failed to introduce time into the structure of society itself. He inquired into the problems of society by standing on the position of "creative evolution" in which cosmic life, whose structure consists in time, that is, as "flying jump of life" (*élan vital*), is investigated primarily within the biological realm. Human society is, like insect society, precisely the *terminus ad quem* of the evolution of life. Consequently, the phenomena of "society" are not something different in order from other natural phenomena. Instead, as the phenomena of one life, they can be recognized, for instance, even in an individual, which is actually "a society of cells."

Originally speaking, life itself is "a co-ordination of controlled elements which are in charge of a work. That is to say, something social lurks behind something vital."[18] The manner in which life uses tools to deal with materials is twofold: instinct and intellect. In instinct, tools are part of the ingredients necessary for living things. In intellect, tools are apparatuses existing outside of the organ of self, which a human being must invent, produce, and learn to use. In this way, the paths of instinct and intellect take different evolutionary directions. At their culmination, one turns out to be a society of ants or of bees and the other a society of human beings.

Therefore, the phenomena of "society" are not only confined to human society. We can say that a society of ants or of bees is the completion of instinctive society. Here, individuals blindly serve for the benefit of society. If we keep our eye on the "order" alone, we can say that this is a perfect society.

Contrariwise, the society of a human being aims not so much at order as at "progress," which the initiative of individuals promotes. Only in the society of human beings is independence and the freedom of individuals recognized. Consequently, individuals continuously carry on the activities of human society. Human society has developed to the greatest extent in the direction of this form of evolution.

As was said previously, in Bergson, life, which is social in its origin, gives impetus to the formation of human society in the direction of intellect, on its way to evolutionary progress. Hence, the temporal structure of life he has emphatically expounded in terms of "a flying jump of life" contends only that evolution occurs by means of a discontinuous leap. Obviously, we can here discern that Bergson confines his idea of "a flying jump of life" to the biological realm. Provided that life, structured by time, is something internal and, hence, is dealt with mainly in subjective practice, we must assert that a flying jump of life comes to the fore, for the first time, within subjective human society. The structure of human existence itself, in which personalities, while standing opposed to each other, come into unity, must reveal the genuine feature of "a flying jump of life."

The structure of pure duration, which brings heterogeneous agents into unity in the form of a leap, was first discovered in the fact of an individual's direct consciousness and then attributed to the basic structure of life. Judging from this approach, we must assert that the structure of pure duration should be deepened not so much in biological phenomena, as in the subjective dimension of human life. If a flying jump of life is superindividual, then it must take the form of a jumping unity of lives inherent among heterogeneous individuals. There is no comparison between this and a society of ants or of bees.

Even though one personality performs her self-creative activity in entirely her own way, she consists, nonetheless, in the creative activities of a superindividual life. The past, which we understand in the sense that we manifest the totality of the past in our activities, is both the past peculiar to our personality and, at the same time, the past of a superindividual life. This means precisely that we possess the past in betweenness. We grasp this fact through the existence of *ningen*.

Because he tried to conceive of society biologically, Bergson failed to heed the jumping unity of heterogeneous agents that inheres in human existence. Furthermore, he thought little of the idea that the structure of human society is precisely a flying jump of life itself and that "a closed society" is precisely the place in which cosmic life manifests itself. This error can be attributed to Bergson's attempt to find basic time within the structure of life that immediately turned to biological phenomena, without thereby being deepened to take into consideration the subjective bottom of human existence.

Bergson's understanding of time as the structure of life comes to a standpoint only a step away from regarding time as the structure of subjective human life. However, time and again the philosophy of life has been subjected to doubt concerning whether it ought to be considered a strict science or not. For this reason, we will consider phenomenology, which professes to be a strict science. Even here, however, we will finally arrive at the same conclusion after taking almost the same journey.

Husserl's "Phenomenology of Internal Time Consciousness" attempts to resolve the question of the construction of time consciousness by appealing to the intentionality of consciousness.[19] Because this attempt analyzes time consciousness phenomenologically and, hence, also analyzes the phenomenological content of time experience, first of all, objective time must be excluded from this analysis and then only time experience as the absolute phenomenologically given must be left to be explored. As a matter of fact, objective time is what is constructed as an object of experience in and through this subjective time consciousness.

The question to be asked next is, in what way is time consciousness itself constructed, which serves here as the ground of construction? Husserl expresses this question as an inquiry into "the origin of time," and he looked for a clue in Brentano's theory of time.

Psychologists prior to Brentano confused subjective time with objective time. Hence, they failed to distinguish between the duration and succession in sensation and the sensation of duration and succession. In other words, they thought that, just because sensation endures, duration is perceived. In his theory of the modes of representation, Brentano rejected this view of the sensation of duration and insisted that sensation itself productively constructs representations accompanied by time-moments such as "the past," "the present," and "the future."

Brentano dealt with objective psychological experiences, and his position belongs to the realm of psychology. However, his observation has a phenomenological nucleus as well. As a matter of fact, consciousness inclusive of the unity of the present and the past is something phenomenologically given. This point must be further developed.

What is to be noted here is that Brentano does not recognize the distinction between an act and its content. As a result, that time moments belong to both remains unclarified. According to Brentano, there is no discrimination among the acts of representation, and there is a difference of intensity only in their primary content. Time moments are added to them in a parallel way, and these moments are conceived of as stratified durationally.

If so, then it must be concluded that contents do not pass away but always remain present, and that the past, as a time moment, constitutes one element of present experience. This does not clarify what time moments are. So, Husserl tried to clarify time moments in accordance with the distinction or connection between an act, its contents, hence, between an act and its grasped contents, and its grasped objects. He constructs objects of time (i.e., objects inclusive not only of the unity of time but also of time extension) in the succession of acts in memory, perception, and anticipation. Husserl also analyzed in detail the objects of time and the succession of acts in their reciprocal relationships and, by going a step further, solved the problem of how the succession of acts are constructed by appealing to intentionality. At least, this is what he tried to achieve in his works.

To begin, Husserl comes to grips with the immanent objects of time in their manner of manifesting themselves. For instance, a sound begins and then comes to an end. After the sound has ended, the durational unity from beginning to end gradually sinks into the past. In this sinking back (Zurücksinken), one still retains the sound. Insofar as the sound is retained, it may be said to be the same sound, and the duration of a sound is also of the same duration. But when we attend to the manner in which sounds are given, they, as well as their duration, constitute a constant stream. Any point or any phase (Phase) of this duration of sounds is brought to our consciousness as the "now," and a continuity of these phases is brought to consciousness as the "already." That is to say, a portion of the time duration, ranging from the beginning to the "now," is brought to our consciousness as the already passed duration.

In this way, the same sound is manifested as passing. Thus, we are able to distinguish between "durational and immanent objects" and "objects in their mode of passage." In this latter mode, one object turns out to be the other, moment by moment. This is illustrated in Figure 1.

An object in its mode of passage is not necessarily conscious. "Consciousness" and "experience" are related to their object in this passage through its medium of manifestation. This is intentionality. This consists precisely in that "phenomenon" which constitutes the objects

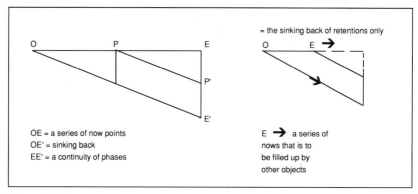

Figure 10.1

of immanent time. If we say this in compliance with immanent objects, then we refer to their "passage characteristics." And, as the phenomenon of time-constructing consciousness, it is "the passage phenomenon" or "the mode of temporal positing time." This passage phenomenon consists of a succession of incessant transformations and the point phases of this succession constitute the indivisible unity.

On the one hand, the objects of immanent time begin with their originating point, "now" and endure in the form of a continuity of passage phases. On the other, each of the passage phases is a continuity that constantly enlarges itself; that is, it is a succession of the past. In other words, the continuity of passage of an enduring object is a continuity whose respective phases are constituted by a succession of passage modes at various time points of this object's duration. Therefore, each moment of concrete continuity modifies the mode of passage at this time point. No sooner has a new "now" appeared than it passes away, and the entire past continuity of bygone passages sinks into the depth of the past. This "double continuity of the modes of passage" constitutes the structure of the passage phenomenon.

Now, in this double continuity, we pay attention not so much to the objects of time as to the continuity of their phases. We retain an original impression, as the originating point, of something past at the succeeding moment. However, this retention occurs in the "now." So in the following moment, this retention is itself retained. In this way, a continuity of retentions arises in which a subsequent point retains all of the preceding ones. The consciousness of impressions flowingly transforms into a new consciousness of retention. From this perspective we can say that a sinking into the past also takes place in and through retention, as is the case with the succession of original impressions.

This modification of retentions is clarified as one of the unique intentionalities, for retained contents are not contents in the basic sense of the word. For instance, a perceived sound is different from a sound moment constitutive of retention. A retained sound is not in the present, but is rather a "sound recollected primarily in the *now*." For this reason, it does not "really" exist within the consciousness of retention. Obviously, an original impression must precede any intention toward such a sound content. With the original impression as axis, retentive intentionalities are likely to arise, like the tail of a comet. Besides this, both of them are entirely different from each other. And for this reason, retention or recollection differs from the original impression or perception.

The intention of retention constructs "the past," and original impressions construct "the present." Adding primary anticipation (i.e., protention) constitutes the activities of time construction. As usual, the perception of a melody is an activity consisting of these three moments. But, this the perception of present intention, considered against past intention and future intention, transits continuously and melts into nonperception. The "now" is only an ideal limit. It is an abstraction incapable of sustaining itself and can exist only by being mediated by the nonpresent.

When time constructing activities are thus accounted for, it is clear that Husserl gives special priority to the intention of retention. He tackles the intention of retention frontally in an attempt to describe how these activities are further constructed in absolute subjectivity. This is because the ultimate unity of the constructive stream of consciousness becomes known through our having as a clue those double characteristics inherent in the intentionality of retention.

Retention is, for instance, the retaining of sounds, on the one hand, and the retaining of the very retention of elapsed sounds, on the other. The latter constitutes the unity of retentions in the stream of consciousness. Each phase of the stream of consciousness is a continuity of retentions unified in such a way that "bygones exist simultaneously" (*Vor-Zugleich*). As the stream goes on, this continuity undergoes change with respect to retentions. Whenever the new "now," that is, a novel original sensation, makes its appearance, a modification of retentions transforms the preceding original sensation into a retention, and this latter retention is further transformed into the retention of retention. The unity of retentions, which undergoes modification every moment, Husserl called *vertical intentionality* (*Längs-Intentionalität*). An intentionality of this sort constructs a succession of a series of retentions with a new and original sensation as their spearhead.

Contrariwise, the retention of sounds is called *horizontal intentionality (Quer-Intentionalität)*. In this case, a new and original sensation is the sensation of the sound of "now," and its retention is not the retention of retention but rather a retention of bygone sound points. Therefore, horizontal intentionality constructs "enduring sounds" rather than a continuity of retentions.

The two sorts of intentionality are inseparably connected. Nevertheless, horizontal intentionality constructs immanent time, and vertical intentionality constructs the semitemporal order of phases constituting the stream of consciousness. The stream of consciousness builds up its own unity as a one-dimensional semitemporal order. As a result, it is argued that "this prephenomenal, preimmanent temporality is intentionally constructed as the form of time constructing consciousness within this consciousness itself."[20] This means that vertical intentionality solves the problem concerning basic temporality that is inherent in the consciousness of retention.

Time and again it has been noticed that Husserl's thought fails to attach importance to future intentionality, which appears in "anticipation." This failure is attributable not so much to his stopping short of giving due consideration to anticipation as to it being the inevitable result of his fundamental standpoint. As is shown by his repeated attempts to take into consideration sounds or melodies as examples, he tries to analyze time consciousness in compliance with the objects of immanent time as given in original impressions and then tries to find the basic layers of this time consciousness. His problem is that he calls into question only conscious activities that passively follow after what is given while retaining it and leaves spontaneous and active experiences entirely out of consideration. This means that phenomenology is, from the outset, the study of contemplative consciousness and therefore excludes both practical and active attitudes of living. It stands to reason that the anticipation of the future, which manifests its superior significance, particularity through practical activities, does not receive adequate treatment.

But what happens if future intention is given due consideration as a central problem to be dealt with? Original impressions are involved in the intentionality of retention like the nucleus of a comet. But, what is its equivalent in future intentionality? Indeed, is it ever possible to solve the problem of the anticipation of the future by means of intentionality?

Further, one additional question must be raised here. Can the stream of consciousness, on which basic temporality is grounded, be itself nontemporal? Husserl argues that basic temporality is precisely the intentionality of consciousness itself and that this intentionality is constructed within basic consciousness. Therefore, basic consciousness is itself not temporal because it is the ground of temporality. That is to say, in the nontemporal stream of consciousness, the primary contents and experiences (i.e., "consciousness of . . . ") are discriminated from each other and the intentionality of these experiences turns out to be prephenomenal temporality that serves to construct phenomenal time.

The ordinary meaning of the phrase *to be temporal* simply means to be in time thus constructed. If so, then basic consciousness must be beyond all time. From the standpoint of phenomenology as based on individual consciousness, however, how can the stream of consciousness or experience be nontemporal? Husserl's stream of consciousness is at each phase a continuity of pre-coexistent retentions and, at the same time, constitutes itself as a succession of these phases. Hence, although the stream of consciousness includes within itself retentional modifications within vertical intentionality, it flows from one phase to another. If this is so, then we must suppose that the stream of consciousness, which should be beyond time, already possesses a structure equivalent to the schema of time.[21]

Heidegger, while subjecting such problems to further reflection and giving central priority to the moment of anticipation, tried to locate temporality at a ground deeper than intentionality. Starting from spontaneous and active experiences, instead of from the passive consciousness of givenness, he endeavored to locate basic temporality not in the intentional structure of contemplative consciousness but in the structure of human existence as "care" (*Sorge*). However, even in this attempt, Heidegger upholds Husserl's inheritance in that he clearly distinguishes basic temporality from both time "derived from" this temporality and the temporal in the sense of our being in such time. Furthermore, Heidegger is in accord with Husserl in that he inquired into the origin of time at the utmost foundation of his philosophy, and hence the "systematic place" of his time interpretation is at the very basis of his philosophy. Moreover, Heidegger transformed his philosophical position from a phenomenology of pure consciousness to that of a hermeneutic phenomenology of self-conscious existence. By virtue of this transformation, the origin of time is more likely to be probed in greater depth in the direction of the basic structure of self-conscious existence itself, rather than in that of the mere structure of consciousness.

For Heidegger, to regard "now" as a point and to take time as "a series of nows" is to base one's interpretation on the traditional concept of time. Husserl's notion of a series of "phases" is exactly the same as this. Aristotle's definition of time can be clarified, when interpreted from the existential standpoint, as that which comes to grips with time in our everyday concerns (i.e., as time prevalent in the everyday world). But, insofar as "nows" are thought of as constitutive of time, then Aristotle's concept of time can be understood to be the source of the traditional notion. Now, this traditional concept of time levels basic temporality and covers its authentic features. Human existence allows traditional time to arise in and through the loss of the self, as evidenced by its falling victim to finitude. Consequently, traditional time is inauthentic temporality as a modus through which temporality comes to the fore.

In what manner then, does Heidegger make clear what he means by authentic temporality? He takes his departure from the ontological analysis of being there (*Dasein*), as explored in terms of "being in the world." According to him, the average everydayness of being there consists in a being in the world in an abandonedly disclosing and a thrownly forethrowing way. Thus, although being together with others in the "world," *Dasein* concerns itself with its own possibilities (i.e., its "can be"). At stake here is the whole structure of *Dasein*, which is interpreted as care through the medium of anxiety (*Angst*).[22]

To begin, *Dasein* is concerned in its being with this being itself. This "to be concerned with . . . " consists of freely projecting in a forethrown manner toward those possibilities peculiar to the self.

Incidentally, "to be free" with respect to the possibilities peculiar to the self means, ontologically speaking, that *Dasein* is for itself and in its being always and already ahead (*vorweg*) of itself. In this sense, *Dasein* always already exists "beyond and outside of itself" (*über sich hinaus*). Moreover, it is concerned not with beings other than itself, but rather exists toward its own possibilities. This is exactly what the phrase "to be ahead of itself" (*das sich-vorweg-sein*) means.

However, this *Dasein* is not a subject without a world, but rather a being in the world. Hence, *Dasein* is burdened with its being in the world. In other words, *Dasein* is always already thrown into the world. If so, then "to be ahead of itself" must be further qualified by this new prescription. That is to say, it "is ahead of itself in its already being in the world" (*Sich-vorweg-im-schon-sein-in-einer-Welt*).

Dasein, as usual, falls victim to its concerns within the world, and escapes from the possibilities peculiar to *Dasein*'s authentic self.

Consequently, to the prescription must be added the essential characteristic of *Dasein's* being abandonedly in and alongside inner worldly objects of concern. In this way, the whole structure of *Dasein* is understood to "be ahead of itself in already being in the world as being alonside what it encounters in the world" (*Sich-vorweg-schon-sein-in-[der-Welt] als Sein bei [innerweltlich begegnendem Seienden]*). This is precisely what Heidegger calls *care.*

Because a distinction between practical attitudes and theoretical ones appears later on the basis of this "care," we cannot characterize care itself as practical. Volition, desire, attitudes, impetus, and so forth are all modes of "care." Care constitutes the whole structure of *Dasein.* It possesses a clearly articulated structure. Where in the world is the basic unity of this structure located? The answer is this: it is in "temporality."

To interpret the ontological significance of care in terms of temporality, Heidegger uses the phenomenon of death as his medium. His analysis, which begins with a being in the world and ends with a clarification of the structure of caring, is not yet, according to him, carried to its completion. For this account remains somehow satisfied with inauthentic being as deprived of its wholeness and fails to clarify what is meant by possible authenticity or by wholeness.

For this reason, the total "can be" of *Dasein* (*Ganzsein Können*) must be questioned. Insofar as *Dasein* exists, what can be or what will be is left unfinished. In this unfinishedness exists the "end" itself. The end of a being in the world is death. This end, as inherent in a being, sets limits to and determines the possible wholeness of *Dasein.* By employing the concept of death ontologically, we can examine whether *Dasein* is at its end in death (*das Zu-Ende-sein*); that is, the whole being of *Dasein.*

Then, what is death? It belongs to *Dasein* in the form of "unfinishedness" or the "not yet" (*Noch nicht*). To come to an end by finishing it means that it is no longer there, that it is no longer *Dasein* (*nichtmehrdasein*).

Now, to come to an end in this way is a way of being proper to *Dasein* and for which no one can find a substitute. Therefore, death is a way whereby *Dasein* actually exists. Although existing actually, *Dasein* is already "not yet" (*schon sein nochnicht ist*). Despite existing actually, *Dasein* is, at all times, already its end. Hence, the end that death signifies is not meant to be *Dasein's* "being its end" (*Zu-Ende-sein*), but rather a "being with its end" (*ein Sein zum Ende*); that is, a finitude. (The German expression *Zu Ende sein* means that one, while aiming at that which is her end, has come so far as to reach her end.

But, on the other hand, the term *zu* is also used, as is clear in such phrases as *zu Hause, zu Berlin, zu Fenster,* to denote the meaning of "in" or "at," as in a state of standstill. The German phrase *Sein zum Ende* takes advantage of this use of the term, signifying a being at its end. This also shows that *Dasein* is already its end on all occasions.) Death is a way of being that *Dasein* is obliged to bear just as soon as it begins to exist. *Dasein's* structure, which is here brought to light in terms of care, is, as a matter of fact, a structure inherent in "a being with its end" (i.e., finitude).

Consequently, the phenomenon of death comes to be clarified with the aid of the fundamental structure of *Dasein.* Death's possibility inheres in one's own being. No other person has anything to do with it. One cannot outrun this possibility. It is based on the disclosure of *Dasein* in the form of "being ahead of oneself."

Conversely speaking, "a being with its end" materializes fundamentally this structural moment of care as "being ahead of oneself." Now, *Dasein* is already thrown into this possibility, when it comes to its own being. That is, it shoulders death. This is fundamentally disclosed in "anxiety." This thrownness unto death constitutes the moment of "to already be." But in daily life, people live in oblivion of death; that is, they flee from and cover their own "being with its end." As an abandonment to the world, this matter constitutes the moment of "being by the side of . . . " *Dasein's* everydayness is thus abandoned blindly to the public (*das Man*). One loses the possibility proper of one's self among the public. Therefore, one dies, but one does not think that one dies. Death, which belongs to everyone, is hidden, and we speak of death only as something to do with the public and that takes place as a happening in the world. Hence, the certainty of death—that it is possible at every moment, as well as the indeterminacy whereby we cannot know when it comes—is hidden from the public. Thus, the three moments constitutive of the care are interpreted to consist of the possibility of death, the thrownness unto death, and the hiddenness of the possibility of death.

But if *Dasein's* everydayness is an abandonment to the inauthentic position of the public, then how is it possible for one to come to grips with authentic "being with its end"? This is possible because *Dasein,* although factually thrown away to the abandonment of its authenticity, yet escapes from it ontologically. This moment of the ontological "getting out" is recognizable in "forerunning" (*Vorlaufen*). To possess possibility means to forerun into it. To possess the possibility of death at every moment means to forerun into it at every moment.

In this way, this forerunning discloses to *Dasein* its abandonment of the self and brings to possibility proper its own self. And more than that, it discloses the self under the guise of the freedom unto death. Precisely this "voice of conscience" gives evidence of this ontological "fore-throw" from the side of existence itself. Conscience calls *Dasein* forth to its own self. The calling agent and the one called are the same *Dasein*. Even though experiencing anxiety in its thrownness (i.e., *Schon-sein-in . . .*) toward its own possibilities, *Dasein* becomes a calling agent. It is the same *Dasein* that is called to its own possibility (i.e., *Sich-vorweg . . .*). What is more, this *Dasein* is called forth from its abandonment to the public (i.e., *Sein-bei . . .*). Thus, conscience discloses itself in the form of the calling voice of "care." Precisely through conscience *Dasein* comes to understand its authenticity, in spite of its being abandoned to everydayness.

What content does the voice of conscience disclose? An answer to this is given in the self's own "being indebted to" (*Schuldigsein*). As debt is ordinarily understood, something is owed and must be paid off. This means that a debt causes a lack in other persons. But what is here in question is not other persons but *Dasein*'s way of being indebted. Understood in this way, indebtedness is the ground of a lack. To speak in a formal manner, indebtedness consists in its being the ground of being as determined through the nothing (*Nicht*); that is, in its being the ground of *Nichtigkeit*. This fundamental indebtedness renders possible every kind of sin or debt.

However this may be, this ground of *Nichtigkeit* is found in the structure of care. First of all, *Dasein* is thrown, and this being thrown is not (*nicht*) what it brings forth by itself. And what is more, a thrown *Dasein* constitutes the ground of the possibility in its own being. For this reason, for *Dasein* to be in its way of being thrown signifies that *Dasein* is "the ground," on the one hand, yet that it cannot hold sway over its own possibility on the basis of this ground, on the other. This *not* (*nicht*) constitutes the ontological significance of thrownness and, hence, establishes the being of *Dasein*. Second, so far as the "fore-throw" (i.e., the project of freedom) is concerned, *Dasein*'s possibility is "determined" by means of the fore-throw as the thrown; that is, by the nothing (*nichtig*). In addition, the fore-throw itself has essentially the characteristic of *Nichtigkeit*. Third, that thrownness, as well as the fore-throw, has the characteristic of nothingness sets up the basis of the possibility of nothingness that inheres in an inauthentic *Dasein* in its abandonment.

In this way, care is, in its essence, pierced through by nothingness. It is essentially the ground of nothingness (*Nichtigkeit*). This is why *Dasein* is said to be indebted to (*schuldig*) as *Dasein*. That which the voice of conscience discloses is none other than this indebtedness.

That *Dasein* is essentially an "indebted being" renders morality possible in a general way, as its ontological condition. For the self to listen to the voice of conscience is to undertake the fore-throw toward the possibility of its own authentic indebtedness, that is to say, to choose without restraint its own possibility of being (and hence death). This is "to will to have conscience" (*Gewissenhabenwollen*). And this disclosure of *Dasein* in its self-understanding comes to the fore under the guise of "preparedness" (*Entschlossenheit*).

Preparedness signifies an authentic self-being that does not, however, separate *Dasein* from the world, but rather brings the self into the midst of its being with care. The reason is that, because preparedness consists in calling the self back from its self-abandonment to the public, the fore-throw in preparedness has itself the characteristic of thrownness, which is achieved only toward a definite factual possibility. This factually defined being is called the *situation* (*Situation*). Therefore, the situation is the being of *Dasein* disclosed in preparedness. The voice of conscience has no alternative but to call forth *Dasein* into the situation.

Incidentally, preparedness is precisely "to forerun toward death" in its disclosing of the possibility of the authentic self. Hence, the preparedness evidenced ontically is "a forerunning preparedness" (*vorlaufende Entschlossenheit*) and thus also gives witness to the authentic and comprehensive possibility of *Dasein*. Here we have acquired a situation that is fundamentally adequate for interpreting the meaning of being which is inherent in care.

What I have so far mentioned paves the way for making clear that the ontological meaning of care lies in temporality. A question that invokes this temporality is the following: what is that which gives *Dasein*'s authentic total being as the basic unity of its structure as a whole? The answer is as follows: forerunning preparedness possesses its own possibility of being (that is, death). This state of affairs is rendered capable of realization, because *Dasein*, in general, is able to come to itself in its own possibility and it holds within itself the possibility of having itself come to itself (*Sich-auf-sich-zukommenlassen*) as such. This having itself come to itself constitutes the fundamental phenomenon of the future (*Zukunft*). A being that includes death within itself is possible only in the form of *zukünftig* ("futuristic"). For this reason, the basic future has nothing to do with "the now that is not yet actualized but is about to be so," as is ordinarily conceived. That is to say, it has nothing to do with the "future" taken in the literal sense of the word. Instead, the basic future has something to do with the arrival (*Kunft*) through which *Dasein* comes to itself in its own possibility; that is to say, in the "self-aware arrival."

Second, forerunning preparedness understands *Dasein* in its essential indebtedness. That is to say, it shoulders its thrownness. This means that *Dasein* is in its having been mode (*Gewesen*). *Dasein* can be in this mode when understood as self-aware arrival. Insofar as *Dasein* is, in general, in the form of "I have been" (*ich bin gewesen*), it comes to itself in a self-aware arrival manner through which it "comes back" (*Zurückkommen*). Consequently, *Dasein*'s forerunning is a "coming back" to its own having been.

And third, forerunning preparedness discloses a situation inherent for *Dasein*. When *Dasein* acts, it engages itself with the objects of concern that are factually conditioned. This means that *Dasein* allows what presents itself (*Anwesendes*) in the environment to encounter it (*Begegnenlassen*) through that thing's activity. This is possible only when "a thing" emerges and presents itself (*Gegenwärtigen*). Preparedness is capable of being itself only in the form of the "present" (*Gegenwart*), in the preceding sense.

These three moments clarify preparedness in that, "while coming back to itself in a self-aware arrival mode, *Dasein* brings itself presently into the situation." The unified phenomenon of "a having been present self-aware arrival" (*gewesend-gegenwärtigende zakunft*) is called *temporality*. And here, insofar as *Dasein* is qualified by temporality, is its total possibility as forerunning preparedness rendered possible. Temporality here discloses itself in the form of the meaning of authentic care.

In the preceding, the structure of care was grasped in the form of "*sich-vorweg-schon-sein-in . . . als Sein bei.*" The fundamental unity of this structure of care consists in temporality. *Sich-vorweg* ("being ahead of oneself") is based upon this self-aware arrival. *Schon-sein-in . . .* ("to already be in") gives expression to the having been. *Sein bei . . .* ("to be by the side of . . . ") is rendered possible in the presenting. This has nothing to do with the future, the past, or the present when understood in their ordinary senses but constitutes precisely the unified structure inherent in the care of *Dasein* and on the basis of which *Dasein*'s various modes of being are rendered possible. Therefore, any being whatsoever has its source in the fact that temporality discloses itself (*Zeitigen*).

This temporality shows itself to be fundamentally "outside of it-self" (*Ausser-sein*) in these three moments. This is why the phenom-ena of the self-aware arrival, the having-been, and the presenting, are called *Extase* ("self-detachment") of temporality. The essential feature of temporality consists of time coming to fruition (*Zeitigung*) in the unity of self-detachment.

This is what Heidegger tried to bring to light in terms of authen-tic, basic temporality. This temporality makes the distinction between authenticity and inauthenticity in *Dasein* being possible and, hence, ren-ders impossible time interpretation in inauthenticity. With the aid of inauthenticity, it is possible to make clear all of the modes of the ordi-nary concept of time.

The development of the issue of time as pursued by phenomenol-ogy has reached as far as this fundamental temporality. This indicates that the attempt to grasp time in and through the subject probes con-sciousness gradually in search of the place where time lies, finally ex-tending to the ground of being that lies even deeper than consciousness. From Brentano's perspective, which understood time as a mode of rep-resentation, we can conclude that this was quite rapid progress. But a limitation that results from sticking to the standpoint of phenomenol-ogy is left intact to the very end. That is, phenomenology from begin-ning to end analyzed individual consciousness only. Even after attention was deepened from consciousness to being, it was still con-cerned with "individual being."

Although Heidegger's departure from being in the world is al-ready based on *Jemeinigkeit* ("to be myself on each occasion"), this *Jemeinigkeit* must be further disclosed as "an agent suffering from death" from the perspective of total possibility, to enable interpreting the unified structure of care inherent in being in the world as tempo-rality. That being which manifests its totality by means of death is an individual through and through and not *ningen sonzai* (that is, a be-tweenness-oriented human being).

With regard to the phenomenon of human death, Heidegger him-self was able to deal with only individual death. Even though such events as one's last moments, the deathwatch, the funeral, a tomb, a Buddhist service held after forty-nine days in which a bereaved fam-ily, relatives, and friends participate all belong to human death, he omits them. If so, then the totality grasped through the medium of the phe-nomenon of death is the totality of an individual being. The totality of *ningen sonzai* has escaped his hands. Hence, what Heidegger did was to dig down to individual being in pursuit of a field in which temporality lies, but he could not go so far as to inquire into *ningen sonzai*. For Heidegger, the self-realization of an isolated self through the preparedness for death takes place in the future, the already established finitude of the self-realized self in the having been, and its specified location in the situation in the present. And the self that is said to come back to itself in the unity of this temporality is utterly isolated. Even when said basically to be "outside of itself," this self is still isolated. The temporality expounded as the unity of self-detachment is entirely an individual temporality. As a result, this temporality fails to materialize in the form of historicality. Instead, it only plays the role of basically grounding "what is," as the object of individual consciousness. That Heidegger's main theme was concerned with "being and time," but not with *ningen sonzai* and time, reflects this from the very beginning.

I pointed out earlier that Bergson's theory of time, although dealing with time as the structure of life, was unable to deal with it as the structure of *ningen*'s life. If life, as elan vital, is superindividual, then it must be that vital unity to which the lives of heterogenous individuals give birth. And what is more, falling victim to the biological concept of life, Bergson failed to recognize that the vital life of *ningen* is more fundamental still.

On this point, Heidegger takes a further step. The biological life, of which human life is only one phenomenon, is only based on the "being" of "what is." *Ningen sonzai* is the ground on which this sort of "being" is established. For this reason, *ningen sonzai* is more fundamental than the life of any living thing. Thus, Heidegger probed a step further into the ground of time in that he had paid attention to *sonzai* (that is, existence). But the question remains: what became of the issue of the vital unity of heterogeneous individuals? His attempt to clarify only the structure of individual being under the guise of the unity of having been presenting self-aware arrival, falls entirely short of solving the issue of the vital unity between one individual and another. This results from the onesidedness of his approach by which he tried to grasp *ningen sonzai* only in terms of individual being.

What I have argued gives expression to a trend theories of time have manifested up to the present. Time has been inquired into as consciousness, life, or the depth of being, and its theories have been pursued to such an extent that no issues concerning such matters have been left undiscussed. In spite of this, why do they remain so onesided, as was indicated previously? It is because time was forced to be separated from space, while the tendency to look for time on the side of the subject became intensified. Bergson's pure duration was developed in an endeavor to rescue time from its spatialization. Husserl's basic time had something to do with the stream of consciousness and was not related to space. Heidegger's temporality constituted the basic structure inherent in being in the world and possessed a dimension that was different from that spatiality which finds itself within the world, as based upon the structure of this temporality.

However this may be, the vital unity among heterogeneous individuals cannot arise apart from basic space. The togetherness of one *Dasein* with another can arise only with that space in which our relational concerns with such things as tools takes place. What is the field in which two *Dasein* coexist? This field must also belong to the basic structure of *sonzai*. As we turn eyes to this basic spatiality, we must simultaneously consider that temporality that breaks through the confinement of individual being, and turns out to be constitutive of *ningen sonzai*.

11 the mutual relation of spatiality and temporality

Through the medium of the various phenomena of transportation, communication, and so forth, we grasped the spatiality of a human being; and through that same medium, we grasped the temporality of a human being as well. We also made clear that both are constitutive of the structure of *ningen sonzai*. The interconnected acts of human beings establish spatiality. Hence, it depends on their temporal structure. On the other hand, temporality, as the movement that unites human beings as they stand opposed to one another, cannot arise apart from their spatial structure. Consequently, the structure of *ningen sonzai* is spatial because it is temporal and temporal because it is spatial.

The structure of *ningen sonzai* as betweenness thus consists in spatiality, when viewed statically. *Ningen sonzai* spreads out subjectively as the subjective realm in which things manifest themselves. Now this spreading out is the movement of negation through which authentic unity is negated so as to result in the opposition of self and other and through which this latter negation is itself further negated to result in a nondual unity between self and other. For this reason, when viewed dynamically, the structure of *ningen sonzai* is a temporality that allows past authenticity to arise nondually as the future, in and through present dualistic activities, and that consists of the self and other. Oppositions and unities that are spatial, motivate time to arise. Space and time are the two ways of grasping the same structure and do not subsist independent of one another. This is why we succeeded in interpreting both of them out of the same phenomena of transportation, communication, and so forth.

I am convinced that we can clarify the structure of *ningen sonzai* only by appealing to this mutual relation of spatiality and temporality. The opposition of the self and other cannot be conceived of apart from the subjects standing in opposition to one another spatially. On the other hand, this opposition between the self and other is possible only through the subject's disruption, by becoming two temporally. Only what was once one can stand opposed to itself in such a way that the opposition between the self and other may arise. Only what is capable of becoming one is divided as self and other. If so, then the ground that renders the self and other opposed to each other is a spatial totality that serves as the ground of spatial opposition, as well as possible totality that allows the self and other to develop themselves in a coming back to unity manner. Consequently, there is neither a merely static totality nor a dynamic one. Totality is static and, at the same time, dynamic and conversely is dynamic and, at the same time, static. It is also something possible and, at the same time, something that actually presents itself. This totality is, at bottom, subjective "emptiness."

Because of his emphasis on the total possibility (*Ganzseinkönnen*) of individual being, Heidegger focuses on the phenomenon of death. But his endeavor to gain access to totality through the medium of the phenomenon of death indicates that he stuck fast to an atomistic individuality in defiance of the spatiality of *ningen sonzai*. We cannot have access to the totality of *ningen sonzai* only through death as an end. This totality is, first of all, to be found beyond the totality of individual being and only in and through the infinite oppositions and unities of these latter totalities. Therefore, the totality of *ningen*, although inclusive of "being in its death," is also that totality that goes beyond death.

Insofar as it is the totality of *ningen*, it is a finite totality through and through but not yet an absolute totality. On the other hand, insofar as it is a totality, it is possible only as that which manifests an infinite totality; that is, the absolute one. Absolute totality, whose essential feature lies in the negation of negation, manifests itself only as the totality of *ningen*, not somewhere outside of and in separation from the totality of *ningen*. Hence, the total possibility of *ningen sonzai* must be found not in "being in its death," but in the nondual relationship between the self and other as disclosed in the direction of absolute totality. This nondual relationship cannot properly be called into question unless we give heed to subjective spatiality in a basic way. However, Heidegger puts this subjective spread between the self and other entirely outside of his field of vision and keeps his eye focused on the total possibility of the "self" only as comprehended with the aid of the phenomenon of death. This derivation entirely converts his view of the authenticity and inauthenticity of *ningen sonzai.*

It is ordinarily taken for granted that if you cut off the subjective spread (i.e., the spatial interconnectedness of people) between the self and the other and side with the position of the "self," this "self" turns out to be that authenticity inherent in a human being. And, then, the loss of the "self" is declared to be inauthenticity.

However, that the essential characteristics of a human being lie in the "self" is a view upheld by modern individualism of the kind that found expression in Cartesian abstraction and Hobbes's hypothesis. I am convinced that such views are not in line with the reality of *ningen sonzai.*

When the "self" is grasped as such, it is already the "self" as opposed to the "other." Hence, the negation of *ningen*'s totality is already involved. Cohen is entirely just in his insight that the medium of the other establishes self-awareness. One can contend that *I* becomes aware of itself only through the medium of *non-I,* by making a detour of nothingness only on the ground of the subject in which the self and other are not yet disrupted. In holding this view, we must assert that the self and the other come to be opposed through negation only on the ground of *ningen*'s authenticity. This authenticity is the source of the "self," and at the same time, the "self" comes to be established only as the negation of this authenticity.

The negation of authenticity is inauthenticity. What Heidegger calls *authenticity* is, in reality, inauthenticity. And when this in-authenticity becomes further negated through the nondual relation of self and other, that is to say, when the "self" becomes annihilated, only then is authenticity realized.

Looking backward from this perspective, we are now able to call this totality of *ningen* the *authentic self.* But the authentic self in this case is the superindividual subject, as in Kant, and not an individual self that becomes a totality through death, as in Heidegger. The authentic self, is the negation of the inauthentic self (equivalent to Heidegger's authentic self) and hence the negation of any inauthentic "other" whatsoever. For these reasons, the authentic self must consist in the nondual relation of the self and other.

The annihilation of the "self," taken in this sense, is the negation of the negation of authenticity and constitutes the basis of every selfless morality since ancient times. The loss of the "self," as expounded by Heidegger, does not at all imply the aforementioned negation of negation. What is given by Heidegger's position merely buries selfness in oblivion and is far from being capable of establishing self-conquest, sacrifice, self-denial, and so forth.

What he describes as the public (*das Man*) is simply the "loss of the self," in the sense that the authentic "self" loses its characteristic feature of being a self and stands under the sway of the "other," an averaged individual deprived of his unique characteristics. He falls victim to finitude as a manner of individual being. This has nothing to do with the realization of an authenticity that goes beyond an individual in a nondualistic way. To regard self-negation only as the "loss of the self" is the result of his having identified the "self" with authenticity. Here Heidegger loses sight of the important significance of "self-denial" and any way of understanding it.

This upside-down version of authenticity hindered Heidegger from gaining a sufficient understanding of the significance of the "preparedness for death." The original countenance that makes its appearance in Heidegger's "preparedness for death" is concerned through and through with "an individual" but not with *ningen*. Only in the relationship between self and other that the preparedness for death gives full play to its genuine significance. As a spontaneous abandonment of the self, it paves the way for the nondual relation between the self and other and terminates in the activity of benevolence. Because of this, it reveals for the first time the original countenance of *ningen*.

Yet, if one is concerned with only individual being, then how significant can this preparedness for death be? The self-realization of the finitude of an individual being is of no significance by itself. It acquires its significance only when it paves the way to the supraindividual.

Moreover, even without reference to a supraindividual totality, Heidegger recognized the great significance of the preparedness for death and tried to include within it all of the significance belonging to "conscience" as well as of "indebtedness" that was implied. This was necessary, for he tried to explain the phenomena of conscience and indebtedness from the perspective of individual being alone. In his opinion, that public which has lost the self also loses sight of death. Falling victim to the public renders the preparedness for death impossible. The voice of conscience that calls *Dasein* back to the "self," out of this betrayal of "selfhood," and makes it aware of its own death. Consequently, conscience is concerned with only the preparedness for death and has nothing to do with *ningen sonzai*, which consists in the relationship between the self and the other.

In addition, in an attempt to describe indebtedness, Heidegger obtained an ontological description of indebtedness by entirely excluding social relationships from the phenomenon, which ordinarily appears under the guise of something social. As a result, indebtedness is not a description of *ningen sonzai*. All that is implied is that an individual being lies at the ground of every "nothing." The reason why it is the ground of "nothing" is that an individual being is finite (that is, it is determined by nothing).

However this may be, the question remains, how is this finitude of individual being capable of becoming the ontological condition for morality? What is ordinarily called *indebtedness* constitutes the ground for the lack from which others suffer. Heidegger's ontological description of indebtedness eliminates others and merely takes the finitude of self-existence as the ground of all lack. Because this description excludes the connection of the self with others, there is no possibility of a relationship with others arising.

For indebtedness to involve others, the relationship between the self and other itself must be added to the description. This means that subjective spatiality, which arises as the relation between the self and the other, must be taken into consideration. Only when this is done can the finitude of an individual being be said to be the possible ground for indebtedness to others. In this case, however, the finitude in question is no longer a finitude appearing in "being in its death" but is rather a finitude of an individual that stands in relation to others. Because of this limitation, that is, because of the opposition between the self and other, due to the negation of the authenticity of the self, an individual being takes on itself something that it ought to accomplish in the presence of others. That is to say, it must further negate the negation of its authenticity and come back to its own authentic infinity.

Viewed in this way, indebtedness is, fundamentally speaking, a prescription of *ningen sonzai* and not only of an individual being. What "ought to be accomplished" here is the totality of *ningen*, as realized in a nondual fashion, and not just an individual's death.

Be this as it may, despite arguing that "what ought to be accomplished" is merely an individual's death and that *Dasein*'s being is called forth to the possibility of indebtedness through the voice of conscience is equivalent to *Dasein*'s being prepared for death, Heidegger maintains that these constitute the ontological condition of morality. But, this is an abstract way of thinking that results from the elimination of God from the standpoint characteristic of the Middle Ages, which expounded morality as the relationship between God and human beings. It has no ground from which to access the real features of morality. The realization that individual being is the ground of all sorts of evanescence is not enough to elicit a morality that commands an individual to act in accordance with the supraindividual will. To the contrary, the realization that the ground of individual being is emptiness renders it possible for an individual being to become the ground for nondual fulfilment of the self and other (that is, the realization of totality), which also brings about the possibility of morality. Thus, it is clear that the voice of conscience calls *Dasein* back from the falling victim to the "self" and toward the authenticity of going beyond it, and thus it awakes *Dasein* to the truth that the ground of individual being is emptiness.

We can perceive that Heidegger's description of a human being as individual is entirely burdened with all of the defects involved in trying to comprehend temporality, in complete defiance of subjective spatiality. The source of this error lies in his attempt to take *ningen sonzai* into account by confining it to something individual from the very beginning.

Contrariwise, we took our departure from the view that *ningen* is not, fundamentally speaking, merely individual, but consists of the unity of the duality of the individual and the social. For this reason, we must investigate the temporality of *ningen sonzai* in line with that subjective spatiality in which the self and other, although opposed to each other, are nonetheless brought into unity. From this standpoint, the basic unity of the structure of being inherent in *ningen* cannot be conceived of apart from the community of *ningen*. To come back to authenticity as self-aware arrival is precisely to realize the nonduality of the self and other, which is established as the negation of negation. Only the nondual relationship between the self and other renders coming back to the authenticity of *ningen* possible, but the mere "self" cannot do this. Not only the mere "preparedness for death" makes this possible but also "death" as self-transcendence, that is, as the negation of the self or as self-denial. This death is, however, the having been (i.e., essence) of *ningen* in its authentic countenance. Hence, to "come" to authenticity is to come back to one's authentic countenance. Because this "coming back" is possible only in an inauthenticity in which the self is opposed to the other, the inauthentic standpoint of the "self" "presents" itself as a field in which this coming back is materialized. For this reason, *ningen sonzai*, even though disrupted into an opposition between the self and other, still realizes the nondual relationship between them, thereby possessing that structural unity which "comes back in the present."

Comprehension of the mutual relationship between temporality and spatiality seems to enable us to grasp them, respectively, in their genuine features. It leads us to the possible totality of *ningen sonzai* by going beyond the total possibility of individual being and discloses the structure of this totality which arises as the future in the form of a coming back to authenticity. This structure of totality consists in the negation of negation carried on spatially as well as temporally.

Remarkably, Hegel had understood the negation of negation as "the living soul of totality"[1] and succeeded in obtaining a clear grasp of the mutuality of time and space as well. To be certain of the connection between negativity and time/space, I think it useful here to subject our deliberations to further scrutiny by meditating on his ideas.

In Hegel, the negation of negation is the essential feature of the "Spirit" as the ultimate totality. Therefore, Spirit realizes itself through the path of negation. Spirit, which manifests the negation of negation in its in-itself mode of being as *Idee*, turns out to be "Nature" in its for-itself mode as the negation of *Idee* itself. Furthermore, Spirit comes to itself as "Spirit," that is, as the real feature of Nature, in the negation of negation that arises through the sublimation of self-externalization.

Now, in this process of development as a whole, the self-externalization of *Idee* itself constitutes an important moment through the medium of which absolute negativity is materialized. Although the Concept (*der Begriff*) possesses in Nature a completely external objectivity, only when the concept comes back to itself from Nature, that is, only when this objectivity and the subjectivity of concept are brought into self-identity, is absolute negativity realized. The systematic field that time/space occupies consists precisely in the moment of the self-externalization of this *Idee*. From this perspective, we can say that time/space in Hegel is the most conspicuous place in which Spirit makes its appearance through its "negation."

In Nature, *Idee* is said to be "the negative of itself" (*das Negative ihrer selbst*) or to exist in an external way over against itself. This is externality (*Äusserlichkeit*), as the essential definition of Nature, is called *space* in its in-itself mode of being. Therefore, all the descriptions of space are derived from abstractive and universal "externality" (i.e., to be outside of itself, *Aussersichsein*). To begin with, because space is external, it consists entirely of ideal togetherness; that is, of mutual externality. Next, because this mutual externality is entirely abstractive

and does not include any definitive discrimination, it is entirely continuous. Even though "here" is spoken of, it is not yet a place but its
possibility. Hence, many "heres" are entirely identical. The term *externality* signifies this abstractive multiplicity. Even though a distinction
is made with respect to many "heres," these distinctions fall short of a
genuine division.

As soon as division becomes genuine division, space is negated
to become "points." Insofar as the negation of space is itself spatial,
points develop into lines and planes. But, if the negation of direct externality (that is, space) establishes space as made up of lines and planes,
then it is an inner negation of itself. Hence, the real feature of space
lies in the self-sublimation of the moment of space. When this constant
self-sublimation possesses a definite being (*Dasein*), it turns out to be
time. Hence, points possess their actuality in time. Points divided are
removed from space.

As was stated previously, because space is direct externality and
time is the negative unity of externality, then time is the negation of
negation and is the real feature of space. Space itself is transformed into
time. But space and time are not opposed to each other.

We are forced to see how nicely the negativity of Spirit is grasped
in space/time and how strictly it is brought into connection with the
concept of objective space/time. Further, the latter argument results in
the systematic placing of space/time at the apex of the philosophy of
Nature. Hence, the negativity space/time exhibits is also confined to
externality as the negated mode of *Idee*. This sort of externality can have
no other meaning than that of the primary category of mathematics or
of physics.

But for we who have pursued the subjectivity of space/time and
have finally come to grips with it in the form of the subjective structure of *ningen*, objective space/time can no longer be a basic issue.
Hence, Hegel's theory of space/time is not worthy of being further dealt
with here. Nevertheless, the negativity of space/time he emphasized
still does not lose its significance. In accordance with his position, we
cannot help but think it inevitable that, for Spirit, as "the true reality
in which *Idee*'s development resulted," that is, for Spirit as "subject,"
subjective spatiality and subjective temporality are called into question.
Nature, which is sublimated in Spirit, is the object identified with the
concept and therefore must be subjective Nature, so to speak. Time/
space, as appearing in subjective Nature, can no longer belong to the
category of physics.

When subjective Spirit becomes "externalized" through its self-negation, this externalization is not, it seems to me, an externalization like the other of *Idee* but rather must be a subjective externalization or the subjective opposition arising from the disruption of self and other. Even with respect to this subjective externalization we can judge that Hegel's description of space is equally true, just as it is. In other words, space consists of the togetherness of subjects; that is, the mutual externality of subjects. Moreover, because it does not involve any definitive discrimination insofar as it is direct and abstractive, then space is straightforwardly continuous; that is, directly nondualistic.

This subjective externality, which is at once discriminatory and nondiscriminatory, is simply equivalent to our so-called spatiality of *ningen*. Subjective *ningen sonzai*, despite being subjectively in mutual externality, is straightforwardly continuous. The self-awareness of this discrimination consists in the negation of spatiality and, hence, in the negation of the community inherent in the nondualistic relation between the self and other. Nevertheless, it turns out to be precisely "the self" instead of "points." Thus, because *ningen sonzai* is the self, the nondualistic relation between self and other is further rendered possible as the negation of the self.

This inner self-negation involved in spatiality is precisely the real feature of spatiality and thus is the temporality of *ningen sonzai*, as well. In this temporality, that is, in the movement of coming back to authenticity through the opposition of the self and other, the self acquires reality for the first time. The discrimination inherent in the self gets out of spatiality, which is indifferent (*gleichgültig*), due to its being discriminatory indiscrimination, and comes to acquire the meaning of uniqueness that negatively takes part in an authentic totality in two directions.

As the negation of spatiality, temporality is the negation of negation in which we, although divided between the self and the other, come back to ourselves in a way in which the self and other are related nondualistically. In this sense, we can say that temporality is the negative unity of externality (that is, the disruptive opposition between self and other). From this we can say that the negation of time/space, even when seen as the subjective structure of *ningen sonzai*, does not lose its significance.

To interpret Hegel transformatively in this way, however, we must demand that the concept of "Spirit" be subjected to a basic modification. For Spirit is, in its basic feature as subject, provided with the structure of temporality and spatiality. Heidegger makes reference to this, but only insofar as temporality is concerned. In Heidegger's opinion, the negation of negation as the essence of Spirit cannot be conceived except as being based on temporality. When *Idee* is said to come back to itself through negation, temporality imparts significance to this coming back.

However, we must raise the further question, is this "coming back" rendered possible only through temporality? Originally, division or separation made the coming back (*Rückkehr, zurrükgehen*) possible. And this division/separation is fundamentally based on the spatiality of the subject. The division/separation in the world of *Idee*, which has nothing to do with spatiality, is in reality a noematic expression of the spatiality of the subject and, therefore, cannot be established by itself alone. If this is so, then what makes the coming back possible is not temporality alone but temporality and spatiality. Hence, the negation of negation, as the essence of Spirit, is based on temporality or spatiality. Spirit, which also demands spatiality as essentially constitutive of its structure, cannot be *Idee* in its in-itself mode of being. In other words, the standpoint of Spirit is not idealism. We must modify the concept of Spirit to this extent.

In spite of this, we do not intend to argue that Hegel treated *Idee* only as idealistic. Instead, *Idee* was for him a "subject/object" and hence the unity of the idealistic and the realistic. Or, it is a possibility that possesses reality in itself. In other words, it is that whose essence (nature) can be grasped only as something existent.

Nevertheless, this *Idee* is essentially "reason" in the philosophical sense of the word and in its essential feature is nonspatial and nontemporal. Therefore, "the real" in *Idee* is not yet temporal or spatial. The negation in *Idee* is not yet inclusive of spatial opposition or the temporal coming back. Only when *Idee* becomes "Nature" in its self-negation, does time or space first make its appearance.

However, we have found spatial opposition and a temporal coming back in the basic structure of Spirit. Hence, the fundamental significance of negation lies in disruption and unification carried on spatially and temporally. Even in its in-itself mode of being, this Spirit cannot be a nonspatial and untemporal *Idee*. It is certain that it can be said to be nonspatial and untemporal, if it were to be judged from the standpoint of objective space or time. But from a standpoint of subjectivity, Spirit is spatial and temporal. The standpoint of Spirit cannot be idealism. And insofar as Spirit is, generally speaking, opposed to matter, the term *Spirit* is not appropriate here. This is why we must call it *subjective ningen*.

We have transferred the systematic field of time and space from the beginning of the philosophy of Nature to the most basic and ultimate field. At issue here is the subjective structure of an agent, as coming back to itself through the negation of negation. Hence, we cannot completely deal with the relation between spatiality and temporality only by transformatively interpreting Hegel's view that the real feature of space is time.

On the one hand, certainly a real feature of spatiality is temporality. Once we realize that subjects are in nondualistic unity, while standing in reciprocal externality, it is equivalent to their coming back to authentic unity through the opposition between self and other as the negation of betweenness and, furthermore, through the nondualistic connection between them as the negation of that opposition.

On the other hand, the real feature of temporality is spatiality. The subject comes back to itself through the opposition between the self and other, just as it realizes its authenticity through self-negation. This realization is possible because the subject remains as itself in its negation (and, hence, the other). The subject, despite standing in opposition between the self and other, yet is nondualistic. Here identity and difference are brought into harmony, as discrimination or indiscrimination.

This dialectical structure we called *spatiality*. *Temporality* is a dynamic manifestation of this structure. Hence, it can be said that the real feature of temporality is spatiality. What is conceived of as a phase in which temporality "gets outside of itself" results from the subjects being in a mutual externality in which identity and difference are immediately brought into harmony. Only this mutual externality establishes the dynamic structure in which the subject comes back to itself in a presenting itself to the other way.

The interdependent relationship in which the real feature of spatiality is temporality and the real feature of temporality is spatiality expresses precisely that spatiality and temporality are in accordance with each other. This accordance enables us to secure the subjective materiality available for an agent's coming back to itself through the negation of negation. Mere temporality falls short of enabling us to grasp the individual/social dialectical structure of *ningen sonzai*. Hence, it is impossible to genuinely grasp the act interconnection of *ningen sonzai* as well as the historicality arising out of this interconnection. To bring temporality into accordance with spatiality is the most important standpoint, and it enables us to eliminate these difficulties.

We have here acquired the basis with which to grasp *ningen*'s acts to a fuller extent. All of the endeavors to solve *ningen*'s acts, without appealing to subjective materiality, consist of either changing them into merely psychological acts, dissolving them into noesistic acts, or presupposing them as already taken for granted. None of them probed deeply enough into the real features of acts. We are now in a position to overcome these deficiencies.

12   the acts of *ningen*

From the outset, we have described the *sonzai* of *ningen* in terms of the practical interconnections of acts. We have done so to indicate that *sonzai* has nothing to do with the "being" of an objective thing, nor with the logical "to be." We have also indicated that this *sonzai* is the subject's dynamic relationships but has nothing to do with the ontical relations between one objective thing and another nor with relations in the noematic sense of the word. I am sure that I could have given expression satisfactorily to what I had intended, without describing clearly what an act is.

Incidentally, an analysis of the spatio-temporal structure of *ningen sonzai* shows precisely what the interconnections of acts are. Interconnections of acts consist of the subjects launching the movement of coming back to themselves through their extendedness, that is, through the countless disruption/oppositions between the self and other. Hence, the act is, first of all, an interactivity between subjects. No act occurs in a place where the opposition between self and other does not occur. Second, the act, shouldering established human relations by itself, nonetheless operates in the direction of possible human relations as well. These are the two indispensable elements of an act.

Let us consider the first element: that an act is an interactivity between subjects. This means that it is not the act of an independent individual. We have already been assured that an individual's independence cannot subsist in itself but rather arises only in the negation of any community of whatever sort. And the negation of community results precisely in the opposition of many individuals. For this

235

reason, an individual's act stands necessarily in relation to other individuals, because it is an act of individuals who oppose one another. Insofar as this is the case, then an individual's act has significance as an act.

What is meant by the term *okonai* ("personal doings") or "*mimochi*" ("behavior") is indicative of such an interactivity of subjects. Just as with the term *Verhalten, mimoch* seems to mean essentially static behavior, not dynamic activity. But the Japanese phrase *mi no mochi kata* ("the way in which one behaves oneself") is a mode of relationship one assumes over against another subject but has nothing to do with the morality of a merely independent individual. What is meant by the term "*taido*" (i.e., an attitude) is not merely something static, but has something to do with positive activity towards other subjects. For example, we listen to what others say in earnest or we are engaged in consultation with another person with sincerity. The attitudes involved in these cases are the most efficient elements by means of which we interact with our counterparts through conversation. Likewise, *mimochi* ("personal doings") have usually been conducted as that which indicates how we go about forming personal relationships. When it is said in Japan that one's *mimoch* is good or bad, this means that the way one has of relating to others is good or bad. I think that an ontical understanding of an act has already been taken into account here.

If it is tenable to claim that the act signifies our relationship to other subjects and, hence, arises within human relationships, then activity directed toward objective things is not yet sufficient for it to be considered as an act by itself. For instance, I see food before me, have the will to eat it, and use my hand with a clear conscience to put it into my mouth. These are the motions of eating food, but it is not yet an act itself. As far as this eating motion is concerned, it makes no difference whether I eat with my fingers or perhaps make a noise while eating.

As for our daily meal, however, we carry on in accordance with one prescribed form or another, and therefore, our eating cannot be mere motion. The manner of our eating is socially prescribed, beyond our own arbitrary will. If one eats something with one's fingers instead of with chopsticks, by choice, then this is itself an expression of some attitude already directed toward other subjects. If it happens at a table to which one is invited as a guest, then this will be taken as an expression of contempt toward the host; or if it should happen at a table at which only friends are present, then it will be taken merely as having fun or as directed toward the participants in an attempt to create a caricature of oneself. To give less extraordinary instances, at a dinner in which one gives expression to definite human relationships, as when dining with one's family or with friends, even a manner of eating in which one finishes eating ahead of others expresses an attitude that refuses to allow a relationship with others. These are all acts and not mere motions. Thus, human relationships, but not mere volitional relations with things, make eating an act.

The same can be said of motions performed under circumstances in which no other persons are present. The motions of taking and eating fruit growing ripe on the tree is not an act when taken by itself. But if this fruit is cultivated in a field, then this motion turns out to be an act of theft. In this decision to eat is involved an implicit relationship with the cultivator of this fruit, and hence one commits an act that violates another subject. The motion of eating a fruit is not merely a relation to things, but it is also a relationship with another subject. This makes the motion an act.

Examples of this sort are countless. In addition to a meal, one might imagine, according to Spencer's illustrations for instance, setting fire to something, or reading a newspaper, or opening a window to let in fresh air, or wearing an overcoat when it is cold. To set fire to something is a mere motion, just as it is. But, setting a fire in a place where there is danger becomes an act by virtue of its relationship with other persons. To read a newspaper is a mere motion. But to read it while being negligent of what one should do, as when one reads in front of a guest as if taking no notice of her at all, is clearly an act. To open a window is not a mere motion, if it occurs in a place where one has a relationship with others, for example, on the train or in a café. Even wearing an overcoat turns out to be an act that should be done in accordance with strict etiquette, when one stands in relation to others.

So, clearly, to define an act in relation to objective things is not in accordance with the actual facts. On the contrary, it is self-evidently easy to grasp an act by giving heed only to the relation of one person to another apart from that of a person to things. What we have in mind here, in terms of *okonai* ("personal doings") or *mimochi* ("behavior") is usually just this sort of personal relationship. However, even this personal relationship is mediated through a gesture, a motion, language, and so forth and, hence, is not merely a direct relationship between one subject and another. Nevertheless, that this personal relationship is achieved through various expressions as media is entirely different from a motion a person performs merely on a thing.

Accordingly, as one detects a specific motion in the body of one's counterpart, one puts one's own body in motion in a specific way as well. In such cases, the human body is not dealt with as "matter," as in physiology. And the movement of the body during this interval of time is not mere physical relations nor biological ones. Instead, it involves as well the relationship between one subject and another, as distinct from the relation between a person and a thing, even though such movement uses physical expressions as its medium. We are sure that what is here discerned is the place where the act is grasped concretely.

If so, then attempts to describe an act by means of volitional choice or decision and by referring to characteristics such as being conscious, volitional, and intellectual, while keeping an eye on its relation with objective things, are all beside the point. Even a motion in accord with such conditions falls short of being an act, if no element of human relationship is involved. This is evident from the example of the meal.

In general, techniques used by human beings who are concerned with things involve such characteristics as were mentioned. The same can be said even of the motion of a primitive human being who chases game. It alone is not enough to constitute an act. Technical motion acquires the meaning of an act, not by mere technique alone, but only insofar as they are established within the context of human relationships.

To state the matter differently, all human technique has been established socially. Hence, to comprehend technique in isolation from human relationships is itself already an abstraction. A primitive who chases game was, concretely speaking, performing an act. As a member of her tribe, she acted to acquire food for it. The mere technique of chasing game may be abstracted from the whole context, as when we deprive her action of the tribe-oriented relationship. In other words, the mere technique is, originally speaking, conceived of as "what is not an act." In addition, insofar as it is a technique, it cannot fail to have such characteristics as the conscious, the volitional, and the intellectual. (Socrates's view that "virtue is knowledge" was originally entertained in reference to technique in general. Hence, *virtue* must be understood to be "excellence" in its original meaning. A carpenter's virtue lies in her being more excellent than those who are not carpenters in the techniques of building a house. And such excellence involves the knowledge of how to build a house.)

Furthermore, we must note that even a motion that possesses no characteristic of consciousness, volition, and intellect may still turn out to be an act, if it is a moment constitutive of human relationships. The phenomenon ordinarily called *being at fault* bears evident witness to this. If we mistakenly tread on another person's toes on a train, we apologize for this mistake. By apologizing, we take responsibility for treading on another's toes. Moreover, precisely because it is a mistake, it is not an act done consciously, as a volitional decision. Rather, we were simply careless. We take responsibility for the carelessness of our act, in spite of its not being consciously chosen by our own will, but because of a lack of care; that is, by nonfeasance.

Why does nonfeasance possess the characteristics of an act? This can be understood only because of its having a definite "station" within human relations. Even the passenger in the train already stands within a definite station or place as a passenger. To this extent, she is already burdened with various forms of activity. The prohibition against inconveniencing other passengers is one of them. A lack of care is the result of a lessening of one's determination to stick to the aforesaid way of acting. Therefore, we can say that nonfeasance is also an act. This sort of problem cannot be resolved if one tries to describe an act only in terms of a choice or decision of the will. In addition, not only mistakes but also acts of nonfeasance are oftentimes called into question in our daily lives.

What can be said of the motion of an infant? An action can never be ascribed to an infant. This is because there is some difficulty in speaking of its motions as being conscious, volitional, and intellectual. But the infant always stands in a relationship with its mother and with other people. If it is supposed that such relationships are constitutive of the essence of an act, then is it inappropriate to speak of an infant's act?

To this question we are able to give the following answer. An infant does not stand in opposition to its mother or its baby sitter, as an individual. Even when it is fretful, an infant does not assume an attitude of acting contrary to its various connections with its protectors. What is recognized in the infant is the possibility of becoming an individual but not its actuality. For this reason, even though motions as well as the attitudes of the mother and other protectors who are concerned with the infant bear the meaning of act, the infant's motions corresponding to them are not to be regarded as acts. This is constitutive of those special characteristics peculiar to our mutual relationships with an infant. It is certain that even an infant is, in its turn, capable of moving itself consciously, volitionally, and intellectually. But this is not enough to allow us to admit an infant's motions as instances of an act.

In the preceding, we have attempted to clarify that it is not the elements of individual consciousness but the spatiality inherent in *ningen sonzai* that establishes the act. This is the primary element constitutive of an act. On the other hand, as the dynamic relations of *ningen*, the act is not dependent merely on spatiality. We must therefore pay attention to a second element.

If it is supposed that the act is an interactivity of subjects, is it possible to say that this interactivity is not at all burdened by the past? For instance, is it possible that one can work with other persons without thereby being determined by the past? Let us consider the simplest action in which one speaks to another person. In daily life, this "speaking to" is necessarily carried on in accordance with definite manners, for instance, speaking in a friendly way, or uttering a polite expression, or acting with a stiffened attitude. As systematized ways of speaking, these forms are used according to our past relationships with one another, which we assume in our interactions with our counterpart. If one were to use a polite expression in speaking to an intimate friend, instead of employing a more friendly way of speaking with which one is ordinarily accustomed, this would be a joke, or else we would suppose that something unusual has happened to the relation between the two.

Our manner of speaking is determined by the past as strictly as in the preceding illustration. And, in addition to specified ways of speaking, there are no other entirely undetermined expressions. Even when one speaks to a person with whom one has had no contact in the past, the past in which there was no contact determines her way of speaking even more strongly than in any other case. This is evident in the way in which we speak on the occasion of a first meeting.

What is more, that one did not have a direct relationship with the other person does not mean that she stood in no relation to this person. As soon as one is born, one is involved in a definite social system. To this extent, one always stands in some relationship to other persons. One's social status or vocation exhibits this relationality objectively. Consequently, one decides how to speak to others in accordance with these relationships. Even when one's status or vocation is not clearly recognized, one still infers from their appearance, and speaks to them accordingly. These various ways of speaking are subtly formed, just as human relationships are subtle. Therefore, a novelist who tries to describe the concrete features of a human life brings subtle human relationships into full relief by appealing to the ways of speaking of the characters in the novel. The way of speaking is more important than its content.

If even the simplest way of speaking cannot be exercised without being burdened with past mutual relationships, then there can be no doubt that the content of this speaking, along with the various gestures and motions that accompany it, as well as activities that have been exercised for a long period of time as the compound of these moments, are strictly determined by the mutual relationships of the past. The exceptional past in which one fell in love with another or in which one felt hatred for another influences one's activities in the same exceptional way. A friend who comes to an amicable settlement by saying "let bygones be bygones" is capable of this settlement just because she shoulders the very past that must be let go. And bygones do not perish but rather determine present activities in a very specific fashion as the modified past. Human relationships that were constructed in the past, even though these relations are not as exceptional as one supposes, nevertheless reflect upon activities of the present without exception. This is not only the case with relationships in which "one bears a grudge against another" but also with relationships in which "one does not adhere to the past obstinately." These two cases are different from each other only with regard to the way in which they are determined by the past but have nothing to do with the distinction of whether they are determined by the past or not.

If it is supposed that the act is an interactivity of subjects and that each of these activities is determined by the established relationships between these subjects, then it is obvious that the act is burdened with the mutual relationships of the past. But this is not yet enough to establish the act. The interactivities of subjects, no matter whether they move in the direction of revolting against each other or in coming into unity cannot be activities unless they involve in advance relationships that do not yet exist.

In line with the preceding example, consider the example of one who says something to another to elicit some kind of relationship with this person. Even a mere greeting, when expressed with this purpose in mind, gives birth to something different from an instance in which it is not expressed. This is much more the case when an activity of speaking has an important meaning content. In this case, even a word is enough suddenly to change the interrelation of the participants. Therefore, the speaking activity must aim at this novel result in advance. Accordingly, because such speaking aims at novelty, there is no difference whether the speaking activity aims at nothing more than the preservation of the established interrelationship. That this established interrelation is preserved arises from the speaking to; and if this speaking to did not take place, then the established interrelation might break down. For example, if I come upon a friend on the street and turn my face away from her, then the resulting disruption between us is expressed. However, even a simple greeting is likely to avoid such disruption. From this perspective, it is obvious that a speaking to is pregnant with the possible interrelations to be realized.

What is illustrated by such activities of speaking to another is also valid for all of the complicated "working to" activities. These are "working to" activities precisely because they aim at a potential betweenness. If a gesture, a motion, a conversation, and so forth are predestined to be unable to elicit any relationship with one's counterpart, then they cannot be "working to" activities. To bow in greeting to an electronic pillar or a stone wall is not in the same category as these activities. But, if a potential relationship with a spirit is aimed at in and through bowing to trees or stones, as is the case with primitive people, then there is no doubt that this bowing is a "working to" activity and, hence, an act of worship. Thus, the direction toward which the subjective relation is to be brought about in the future is an indispensable element of the act.

The future direction of the act is similar to what is ordinarily referred to as *motivation* or *purpose*. But, as was argued previously, an activity that works on objective things is not yet an act by itself alone. Moreover, this activity of working to is already provided with a motivation or a purpose. Even a motion such as eating food is an activity that aims at eating. Seen in this light, we can say that an activity which simply aims at something falls short of being an act by itself alone. The act occurs in the full sense only when it aims at some specific relationship with another subject and hence at some possible interrelationship.

However, this potential interrelationship is also determined by the past, and therefore, one cannot aim at it simply as one likes. Just as the desire of a child to take stars in its hand cannot be said to be the purpose of will, so the desire of a propertyless person to obtain a credit loan amounting to a million yen from the bank cannot be considered to be a genuine purpose of the will either. Insofar as a relationship with another is the aim, purpose exists only in relation to another subject and does not arise only within the consciousness of *I*. A business person who sells goods with the aim of profit already stands in such a relationship with a customer. Conversely, a customer qualifies as a customer insofar as she acknowledges that a business person aims at a profit for himself or herself.

From this perspective, motivation or purpose, as discussed from the standpoint of individual consciousness, is not by itself enough to become a constitutive element of an act. An act, which is described by means of the psychology of the will, is something from which a future element inherent in its relationship to things is eliminated. To grasp an act concretely, we must grapple with it as a movement that, although determined by past interrelations within the field of human relations, advances to future interrelations.

From this perspective, we can say that an act is occasioned not only by the spatiality of *ningen sonzai* but also by its temporality. In absence of either of these elements, the act cannot be. Now, let us turn our attention backward. The phenomena of transportation, communication, and so forth, by means of which we have tried to grasp the spatio-temporality of *ningen sonzai*, were all, in the final analysis, expressions of acts. To go to one's office somewhere, or to deliver some goods to a customer, or to inquire after a friend's health, or any of other countless motions combine to form the phenomenon of transportation. And to worry about a friend's safety, or to make contact with comrades, or to deliver a receipt for money paid, or any of other countless relations combine to form the phenomenon of communication. Among these phenomena, there are none that are not the expressions of acts. Ordinarily, we are in the very midst of acts.

If such examples are all acts, then they are related to each other manifoldly and inexhaustibly. There is no such thing as an isolated act. For instance, to go to one's office is an act already distinguished from not going to one's office out of laziness. However this may be, this act arises from countless other acts, such as walking along the left side of the street, behaving in such a way as not to cause trouble to other passengers in the train, crossing an intersection in accordance with the signal, and so forth. And, moreover, this act in itself is only an element among the many constitutive of the social activities at one's place of work.

Certainly we can cut off one fragment from the systematic relations of these acts and consider it separately. An attempt to deal with motivation, purpose, decision, accomplishment, and so forth, as a series of conscious activities is ordinarily carried on in compliance with such fragmentation. But it is an abstract way of dealing with an act and, hence, not its concrete feature. When I happen to meet and greet a friend on my way to my office, only the relationship with this person comes to the surface of my consciousness. In this case, it may be that the purpose of going to my office disappears from my consciousness. When I decide to cross the road, while keeping an eye on the signal and attending to the comings and goings of the cars, the whole of my consciousness is ordinarily occupied by this act. In spite of this, the act of going to my office is carried on through the nexus of these acts. If an interruption of electric current occurs or a prohibition of intercourse is ordered while I am but halfway there, the purpose of going to my office instantaneously comes to the surface of my consciousness once again.

Let us consider that I put into practice at my workplace a decision I had decided to carry out a month earlier. It may be that this decision was nearly obliterated during the intervening period. But a slip of paper or a fellow worker's utterance provides the occasion for allowing this decision to come to the surface of my consciousness once again. The act arises after an interval of one month. This sort of act is intermingled with the act of going to my office as well as with various other acts of my fellow workers and cannot be a single, isolated act. But the relationship here referred to is only a fragment. Concretely speaking, a manifold and inexhaustible number of connections are involved here.

We live in the midst of acts. And each act stands within the context of manifold and inexhaustible connections. Even when we extract a fragment and investigate it, we must not forget that even this fragment arises from the aforementioned connections as its inexhaustible background.

The ordinary description of the act in traditional ethics proceeds in such a way: to extract a fragment or a horizontal section from the systematic relation of acts, thereby eliminating human relationships, and then to deal with it as an activity of individual consciousness, simplified as much as possible. Consequently, an act is characterized in terms of rational activity, inclusive of the consciousness of purpose, the knowledge of means, and the choice or decision of will. Or else it is characterized in terms of volitional activity such as when one aims, plans, makes a decision, and carries onward toward specific goals of accomplishment. But I am doubtful whether *ningen*'s act can be described in terms of psychological activity in such a simple manner as this.

In the preceding, an eye was kept on the distinction made between so-called instinctive action and the act itself. But this distinction is emphasized only because one stands in the position of *homo sapiens*, according to which one tries to describe *ningen* differently than an animal. This puts the interrelational structure of *ningen sonzai* completely out of sight. Hence, what is dealt with as an act by those who try to describe it in this way is, in actual fact, something far beyond this description.

In order to illustrate this thesis, I want to consider an example of an act to which Kant referred in his book *Grundlegung zur Metaphysik der Sitten*.[1] It is a classic example of an act. But more than that, it also shows that Kant, who placed great emphasis on the will in connection with an act, had to consider many other elements in his attempt to deal with a real example.

When he tried to give his clearest description of "the act as derived from an obligation," Kant considered four examples of an act. Here his argument points out two things. First, he indicates that in an action that is in accordance with obligation, on the one hand, and yet is based on physical attachment, on the other, it is difficult to discern whether it is genuinely derived from or is based on obligation. Second, an act can be said to be derived from obligation only when it is put into practice in accordance with obligation, even in cases where the element of physical attachment is entirely eliminated. Hence, it is not his intention to fully describe what an act is like. But the act illustrated for the sake of the preceding argument indicates clearly what he thought an act was. This is exactly what is called into question here.

One of Kant's examples was that of a retailer selling goods. To sell goods to an inexperienced customer by making undue profit, or to sell goods at a fixed price so that even children may buy in safety, or to sell goods honestly under the conviction that one should not make undue profits are all counted as acts. If so, then what is here called *an act* includes the selling of goods to individual buyers, or the management policy of a retail shop, or the attitude of this retailer to business activity in general. It may be that to sell goods at a fixed price is the management policy of a retail shop, but it is not something decided on each occasion of business activity. Furthermore, the preparedness to do business honestly is this retailer's attitude toward life but has nothing to do with the techniques of business per se. From this perspective, we can say that the act here considered is an activity of business or an attitude of conducting life that this particular retailer exemplifies throughout the whole of her life.

In this way, if a business person's biographical life as a whole is called an *act*, then it will be obvious that this act is established through countless other individual acts associated with one another complexly and inexhaustively. An act is not a simple structure in which one "aims at some end, sets up a project, decides to do it, and then accomplishes it." More than that, the aforementioned business person's life is possible only because of his or her being determined by the age and by society and cannot depend only on his or her own will. Whereas Kant took for granted the presupposition that not to gain excessive profits is to act in accordance with one's obligation or that one is obliged to sell goods honestly, nevertheless, the problem of what constitutes excessive profits or honesty can be resolved only socially.

Within a society that allows one to have the freedom of commercial pursuits, one can acquire profits by circulating commodities in accordance with one's social function. The profit rate is determined socially, and a social criterion decides the problem of whether one gains excessive profits or not or whether one is honest or dishonest. Society expects a retailer to circulate commodities on the basis of this criterion. If she tries to acquire more profit than the acknowledged rate allows and expects, in defiance of this expectation, then she betrays the social trust. This is why she is said to be dishonest.

Kant's argument presupposes that human relationships are inherent in business, and yet he hides this presupposition. For commercial pursuits to take place, however, a definite socio-ethical system must already have been established, and for a retailer to perform her business activities, a definite procedure of trading must already have been prescribed. What Kant simply called the *acts* of a retailer are those human relationships which one forms with one's customers on the basis of the preceding procedure of trading, throughout the whole of one's life.

Kant's second example is concerned with "the preservation of life." He regards various painstaking efforts that many people make to preserve life as acts. Hence, works done to gain daily food are all acts. Or, when she who dislikes her life due to unhappiness or pain and thus desires to commit suicide finally overcomes this desire and continues to persevere in her unfortunate destiny, then this is also an act.

If so, then an act is generally associated with the living of our lives. It has something to do with that feature of a human life is established as the relationship of complex individual acts. It is not to be identified with a simple act that one "aims at, sets up as a project, decides upon, and then accomplishes." Much less can it exist apart from human relations in general.

Living a life is possible only within the complex system of economy, and much of our unhappiness and misery is the result of human relationships. If so, what is discussed here under the guise of acts are the acts of a subject that are associated with one another in a complex and inexhaustible manner. Kant advances his argument by presupposing that to preserve life is itself an obligation, but this presupposition cannot arise apart from the social relationships that already inhere in the act of preserving life. In one's being, one has a position that is determined by various forms of the whole. By virtue of this, one is obliged to preserve one's life. Apart from this position, it would not matter at all to ethics whether or not one preserved one's life.

Kant's third example is concerned with "benevolence." One is affectionate toward another who suffers from pain. It may be that one takes pity because one likes to see the other person pleased or that one loses interest in another person's destiny due to one's own pain and yet one retains an affectionate feeling for the other. Or it may be that, although she who is born to be apathetic acknowledges her fortitude in persevering in pain, yet she takes pity on others because this is her duty.

Incidentally, to be benevolent and to show mercy is impossible without a partner. Hence, it is obvious that this act necessarily refers to human relationships. Even though it is also presupposed here that to be merciful is a duty, this sort of duty cannot arise at all in a society in which the equality of its members is already actualized. In such a society, to show mercy is rather an insult. In this light, we can say that the duty of showing mercy arises from a perspective that regards the fairness of distribution as morally right in a society in which there exists the strong and the weak, the rich and the poor, and in which the weak and the poor do not yet think it shameful to be shown mercy. The issue of distribution has something to do with human relationships and cannot be dealt with only from the side of an individual's will. If the purpose of being merciful—the decision, the accomplishment, and so forth—can be spoken of, then this is possible only under the circumstance in which the act of mercy as indicative of a proper relationship among subjects has already been established.

Kant's fourth example is that of "assuring oneself of one's happiness." All movements that try to acquire happiness are dealt with here as acts. These include the pleasures of the table, love affairs, the pursuit of health, and so forth. Now, the problem of what happiness is, as Kant himself points out, is still left unresolved. If happiness is to fill up something that is deficient, then socio-ethical connections must always be regarded as conducive to happiness. The pleasure of the table lies not in the tongue alone but with the partner with whom one shares it, and the happiness of health cannot be conceived of as happiness for an isolated person. Thus, we can say that the act of looking for happiness is also an activity of forming human relationships.

Each of these examples by which Kant illustrated an act, is a movement that develops under complex connections in human relationships. Despite shouldering the past as the relations between self and other, it nonetheless turns toward the future. The trading business of a retailer, the labor of workers, the benevolence of the rich, and the enjoyment of pleasure are, without exception, all concerned with the *sonzai* of *ningen* that unfolds temporally between one person and another. They are already actualized as the activities of "working to" of *ningen*, even before they are represented as the temporal activity of consciousness that "aims at, projects, decides, and accomplishes." A definite pattern inherent in these activities is realized as duty, but the self-awareness of duty does not prescribe the pattern of the act from the outset.

Kant's categorical imperative is formed by means of the word *act*. It may be that Kant tried thereby to give expression to the meaning of the imperative, "Thou shalt prescribe your will." However, if it is supposed that the acts with which he illustrated this refer to one's attitude of living one's life throughout one's whole life or to the spatio-temporal formation of human relationships, then we can perceive that, behind the categorical imperatives that orders one to "act," there is hidden a way of forming human relations that is the law of *ningen sonzai*.

To indicate the universality of this categorical imperative through an analogy with natural law, Kant subjected four examples of act to further investigation. His point was to demonstrate that unless a maxim is valid as a universal natural law or unless it is desired as such, then this maxim conflicts with the supreme principle of duty. Hence, the swerving from a duty characteristic of an act is here demonstrated from the content of the maxim alone, without recourse to human relations. But, was Kant's attempt successful?

The first example attempts to demonstrate that the act of suicide is an act that swerves from one's duty. The maxim of this act is this: "If life promises less pleasure than pain, then it shortens itself." This is the principle of self-love as the pursuit of pleasure. However this may be, the essential feature of the feeling of self-love lies in promoting life. That this same feeling gives birth to the destruction of life is, therefore, a self-contradiction. For Kant, nature cannot allow self-contradiction to be its law. Hence, the maxim cannot be a law of nature and the act of suicide deviates from one's real duty. This is what Kant demonstrated.

Yet, if the law of nature consists in the unity of contradictories, then this demonstration turns out to be meaningless. At the very least, the view that the law of life consists in the unity of contradictories has been frequently proposed in the contemporary world. It is certain that to produce is to accelerate life. But at the same time, it is the consumption of life, its destruction. The enjoyment of life, in which self-love reveals itself most conspicuously, is at once an enhancement of life *and* its consumption. If this law of life is taken for granted, then it can be said that the self-contradictory nature of suicide accords with this law. It does not follow, however, that suicide is in harmony with duty. It is still antiobligatory. For whether or not one does something in harmony with duty does not depend merely on whether it is self-contradictory but is determined by whether one is faithful to one's workingplace as prescribed by the totality.

The second example is that of the act of borrowing money by making a false promise, when one is in need of it. The maxim of this act runs something like this, that "one borrows money by making a promise to pay it back, in spite of one's knowing that it is beyond one's power to do so, when one is in need of it." Should this maxim turn out to be a universal law, then a promise becomes, in general, quite impossible. This means that such a law would terminate in self-contradiction. Therefore, it cannot be a universal law. This is why the act under consideration also is antiobligatory, argues Kant.

Still, the question remains, is a false promise said to deviate from one's duty because it is self-contradictory? What if we make a false promise, while supposing all the while that this promise will turn out to be impossible. In this case, the maxim of my act is, "I want to have a society in which no promises are made; I engage myself in a false promise, insofar as there are persons who are involved in false promising, and I look forward to the time when the phenomenon of promising is extinguished." Even if such a wish were to become a universal law, there is no self-contradiction. But this conclusion does not allow us to conclude that a false promise is an act in accordance with duty. Consequently, it is not the case that the self-contradiction inherent in making false promises is a decisive element to condemn it as antiobligatory. Kant implicitly presupposes that a promise must be rendered possible.

Incidentally, a promise arises, when, in human relations, we formulate a future connection, while shouldering past trust. We do not engage in a promise with one who has before betrayed a trust. Once a promise is made, we take it on trust that something which has not yet happened will necessarily happen. For this reason, the issue of promising is most evidently based on the spatio-temporality of *ningen sonzai*. No promise is possible without a partner. No promise is apart from the relationship with the past and with the future as well. To formulate the future unity in advance, while shouldering the past; this is a promise. A false promise lies in this, that one intends to betray the promise, while accepting the aforementioned promise structure as a presupposition and pretending to engage in a genuine act of promising. The breach in duty arises here.

The third example is the case in which a talented person is immersed in various pleasures, while throwing away her given talents.

Even were the maxim of this act to become a universal law, there would be no self-contradiction, and so nature could be established. But is she able to will that this maxim of idleness become a natural law? No. Because, as a being provided with reason, she wants necessarily to develop her ability. Hence, the act of idleness and the immersing of oneself in pleasure is a swerving from one's duty.

The desire for self-development on the part of those who are provided with reason is presupposed in Kant's argument. But what happens to those who do not have this desire, as is supposedly the case with the natives of the South Seas, to whom Kant referred as clear example of idleness? Is there not room for us to take the position, as Herder argued, that their peaceful and happy life may be of high value, when considered from an ethical point of view? Let us illustrate with another example. What happens when a talented person hides her talents and lives quietly as a mere farmer?

Kant should have brought to light, as the *ought*, the development of ability and the progress of culture as well. But his *ought* was established in the unity of the intelligible and empirical characteristics of the will. Therefore, no room is left for him to presume the development of abilities as *obligatory*. Here again, unless we comprehend an act by keeping our eye on the spatio-temporal dynamic structure of *ningen sonzai*, we cannot clarify the swerving from duty as a characteristic inherent in the act of idleness.

The fourth example has to do with an attitude of mind in which one neither does damage to nor envies another's happiness nor does one exercise one's power for the sake of this cause either. Even if this attitude were to become a universal law, human beings could easily maintain themselves. Indeed, people can manage their own affairs better when they do not meddle in each other's affairs. However this may be, it is impossible for us to desire that this principle become a law of nature. For we do not wish that state of affairs in which we are completely hindered from having another's affection or sympathy, no matter how we may hope to have it. In this procedure of argument, Kant presupposes that human beings are in need of the affection or sympathy of others. This bears witness to Kant's recognition of human relationships to be something essential to human beings. If so, then the attitude that people neither interfere with nor extend help to one another deviates from this essential characteristic. It results from a fixation of the direction of revolt against the community. Only from the standpoint of human relationships are we able to demonstrate that this attitude swerves from duty. If you do not think this way, and if you establish your standard of judgment only on whether or not you are able to will that this maxim become a universal law, then you can insist from the standpoint of individualism, which considers all affection or sympathy as something shameful, that "I desire this maxim, and hence, the afore-mentioned attitude does not swerve from duty."

We cannot demonstrate that a revolt against duty characteristic is inherent in such acts as suicide, the making of a false promise, the indulgence of idleness, or the abolition of reciprocal aid merely by keeping our eye on the maxim. However, because these acts are originally movements involved in human relationships, the characteristic of revolting against duty is predestined. Hence, it seems as if even insufficient demonstrations suffice to explain this point.

But so far as acts of suicide or false promising are concerned, they are actually put into practice as a series of many acts of complex human relationships, and so they do not simply depend on one purpose or one decision. Consequently, if we affirm that the maxim of the act of suicide is this, "If life seems, in the long run, not so much to promise us pleasure, as to cause us pain and damage, and I decide on the basis of self-love to shorten this life as my principle," then this maxim has nothing to do with the countless acts of suicide committed in front of us day by day. The real act of suicide is usually committed with an awareness of the bankruptcy of life, because suicide cannot be based on a principle. Accordingly, a suicide note is filled with excuses offered to one's family, friends, and sometimes, to the nation as a whole. A self-murderer feels that her suicide is something "inexcusable." While endeavoring to pluck up the courage many times to do it, she finally succumbs to the temptation of death on some specific occasion. She does not recognize that suicide is a revolt against duty simply by comparing a maxim allowing suicide with some universal law, because suicide cannot fall under a definite maxim, as Kant argues. The same may be said of a false promise.

As a matter of fact, a maxim such as the one upheld by Kant could not be thought of as valid except for a swindler who borrows money from others by deceiving them. Despite being aware from the outset that such an act is a crime, this swindler dares to do it. One ordinarily borrows money from another on the assumption that "things will improve," because it is nearly impossible to be sure that future payment will not be remitted. Were there a clear prospect that future payment was absolutely impossible, the creditor would also know that. Further, if one is so desperately in need of money that one is forced to make a false promise, then one's poverty will be discussed among one's relatives and friends, and eventually various forms of assistance will be offered. Hence, before one succumbs to becoming a swindler, various previous stages must have been involved. A simple act such as Kant discussed could not even be thought of. Kant's intention was to compare the maxim of an act with a universal law and not to grasp the act itself. But to describe the maxim of the act in terms of a simple proposition led to a misunderstanding, on Kant's part, of what is entailed by an act as concretely grasped.

By reconsidering the examples of acts of which Kant made use, we have made it clear that an act is always oriented toward human relationships beyond the qualification of its being a volitional activity, on the one hand, and that Kant attempted to shed light on it only by having recourse to the principle of determining the will, on the other. Now, the will in Kant is, strictly speaking, practical reason, not just individual conscious activity. It is also qualified as an individual's will, but this qualification has to do only with its empirical nature. The will in Kant is, then, in essence, supraindividual and universal spontaneity; that is, creativity.

We may argue that Kant's categorical imperative, which demands a correspondence between the subjective principle determining the will (i.e., the maxim) and the objective one (i.e., the moral law) simply requires a correspondence between the individual and the universal wills. This correspondence is precisely what we had in mind by means of what I term the *individual/total* basic structure of *ningen sonzai*.

The categorical imperative that orders us "to act" implies that this correspondence is materialized in and through an act. To put this another way, in Kant, an act is grasped not as an activity of the individual will that "aims at, projects, decides, and accomplishes" but as the movement in which this individual will is united with the total will. Even his attempt to test the revolt against duty characteristic of an act by means of the criterion of whether its maxim is likely to become a universal law was, in truth, made to examine whether the individual will is unified with the total one. It was not made to search out the logical consistency of the maxim. Moreover, because Kant could not adequately come to grips with the act as a characteristic feature of *ningen*, the maxim had came to be shown by him to fall short of being unified with the total will through that self-contradiction in which the maxim terminates, when carried to its extreme as the universal law.

Cohen's ethics, which itself is said to be Kant's standpoint carried to its extreme, advances the act significantly as a characteristic feature of *ningen*. For Cohen, the act is an activity that pertains to reason as fundamental spontaneity. Consequently, it is concerned not only with will but also with thinking. As for the latter, purpose and content are its objects, and the act is the means that produces these objects.

As for the will, however, acts constitute its content and purpose, and objects are a means through which to produce these acts. The act of thinking contains those problems to be solved, and hence, it aims at objects indefinitely. But the act of will by no means aims at objects. In other words, the latter concerns itself not with "beings" but only with *oughts*. The will has acts as its purpose and as problems to be solved. Therefore, it is never the case that these acts transform something internal into something external. Instead, the will performs its internalization so much the more through its turning out to be acts. That is to say, something internal moves into something external and thus enlarges its internal self through this externalization. Here is the difference between thinking and willing.

An act of this sort displays what is termed *the unity of activities*. The unity of activities is the unity of will and, hence, the unity of personality. This unity is precisely the final purpose at which ethics aims. However, this unity has nothing to do with that unity (*Einheit*) which is regarded as the "one" and which makes its appearance in Kant's scheme of categories. Rather, it should be called *individuality* (*Einzelheit*). Individuality belongs to multiplicity (*Mehrheit*), and multiplicity acquires its unity in totality (*Allheit*). Therefore, unity makes its most evident appearance in totality. The unity of act lies not in individual activities but in the nexus and connection of activities under the guise of their totality. "It is not one hand that enables the act to be performed. Rather, many hands must be connected with each other for this purpose."[2] In this connection the unity of act as well as that of will is established for the first time.

The multiplicity presupposed in this unity, that is, many hands, refers not to things but only to personalities. Hence, the connection of individuality/multiplicity/totality is, in the final analysis, the individuality/multiplicity/totality of personalities. This hinders us from conceiving of an act and the will as that which is concerned with individual consciousness. "The unity of act, and hence that of will, presupposes much more than the willing and acting individual, that is, the merely specious individual. A separate individual cannot will, or act, but is able only to desire and to put itself in motion. In order to will and act, the separate individual must be emancipated from the limitation of individuality."[3] To say the matter in a single phrase, the act is the movement of bringing into realization the unity of *ningen* in the connection of individuality/multiplicity/totality. Cohen discovered this in his attempt to carry Kant's position to its consequence.

The reason why the feature of act that is characteristic of *ningen* was proposed in such a full-fledged way, by standing upon Kant's position, lies, I think, in that its embryo was already present in Kant himself. However, not everyone understands Kant in this way. Some interpret him as having dealt with only the volitional activities of separate individuals, and others as having kept his eye only on the will, while overlooking the act. Still others explain that the will, with which Kant grappled, was not the will we are able to experience, but something extraordinarily metaphysical. In line with these various interpretations, a variety of objections were also raised against Kant. By picking up on a few of them, we will attempt to observe to what extent anti-Kantian critical standpoints lose sight of the feature of an act as characteristic of *ningen*.

A. E. Taylor's *The Problem of Conduct*, to which I referred earlier, attempts to refute metaphysical ethics that centers around the autonomous personality, the will, freedom, and so forth by explicating moral facts through experimental psychology. For this reason, "we do not make use of 'the will,' 'decision through motivation,' or 'freedom,' until we ascertain the real facts concerning the ethical aspects of human behaviour. What we have before us, are countless mental processes. . . . It is only after we describe these processes in detail by means of the method of experimental psychology that we can pass judgment on whether hypotheses indicated by such terms as 'the will,' 'motivation,' 'freedom' and so forth are subservient or offer hindrance, to the clear and adequate description of facts."[4]

Now, what sort of mental process did Taylor have in mind, when he spoke of "act"? Surprisingly, in no place in his book does he describe the act (i.e., conduct) itself by means of "the method of experimental psychology," in spite of the book's title, *The Problem of Conduct*. It is precisely through the moral sentiment that he grappled with the basic facts of morality. It is certain that moral sentiments are liable to be described psychologically. But what happens to the act, which is, after all, the central point?

One of the issues with which he deals under the title of "the psychological investigation of human conduct" is the analysis of motivation. He uses the term *motivation* in two senses. One refers to those sentiments that accompany the earlier stages of an act, and the other to the purpose or the effect aimed at by the acting agent. For the analysis of motivation to serve as the basis of the scientific study of ethics, motivation must be conceived of in the first sense. He understands motivation in this sense. That is to say, the sentiments that accompany the act but not the purpose or effect aimed at is the determinant of the distinction between the goodness and badness of an act. Such is his alleged investigation of the act.

Taylor illustrates his position with examples of acts. A person performs righteous deeds throughout her life but from unjust and coarse motivation; or a politician takes advantage of her party or her country for the sake of her own well-being. These are among the examples cited by him. Is the treatment of such acts as performed over an entire lifetime, able to come to terms with experimental psychology? Thus, a person took care of her neighbor throughout her whole life, she accomplished all of her duties without mistake, she kindly helped those who suffered from unhappiness, but she did all of this for the sake of her own self-complacence. But, is it possible for an experimental psychologist to possess the knowledge that the motive behind these countless acts is always and necessarily self-complacence?

Such judgments ought to be the business of a biographer, a historian. A historian does not deal with a person's acts as her own psychological events alone. Rather, her acts are the various relationships formed with those with whom she has been involved. While shouldering the past, these acts develop into the future, and thus incessantly create novel perspectives on life. That the author of *The Problem of Conduct* upheld this complex nexus of acts, on the one hand, and proposed a method suitable to experimental psychology, on the other, gives evidence of his failure to cope with the problem of just how to investigate conduct itself. Moreover, the acts he illustrated are, in reality, not mere mental facts but acts of *ningen*.

In comparison with such objections, Max Scheler's critical comments on Kant are filled with brilliance. However, his comments were made possible by eliminating from the act the significance of "*ningen*'s act." For him, Kant's theory of volitional activity cannot be refuted because it is metaphysical but rather because Kant committed an error resulting from his lack of an analysis of volitional phenomena. This lack is particularly evident with respect to the substantiality of the will. Because he prohibited the substantial from becoming the determining principle of the will, Kant overlooked that the act directly aims to realize some definite value. To describe this point in detail was Scheler's purpose.

According to Scheler, the act arises in various stages as follows:[5] (1) first, there is the presence of the situation including the objects of the act; (2) then the content to be realized through the act; (3) then the willing of this content and its stages, that is, the preparedness of mind, purpose, deliberation, one's project, and eventual decision; (4) then those various activities attributed to the human body, which lead to such motion as that of two hands and two legs ("the will to do"); (5) then those perceptions and states of feelings connected with these activities; (6) finally, the bodily experience of the realization of the content itself (accomplishment). These stages are followed by those states or feelings posited in and through the realized content, but these states or feelings are not what are experienced in the act. The act is realization.

The basic question that arises here is, what is the relationship between the content of the will and that of the accomplished deeds, and furthermore, what is the relationship between the content of the will and those objects dealt with by the act, that is, as "practical objects"? Regarding this point, Kant presupposes, first, that the content of the will is based on that of effect, and second, that the content of effect, which provides the state of pleasure to an agent, is likely to become the content of will once more. In this presupposition, Scheler found Kant's most conspicuous error. Scheler's analysis of the elements of the act was offered for the purpose of bringing this error to light.

With respect to the objects of an act as the primary element, that is, as "practical objects," Kant has already committed an error. In Kant's opinion, practical objects are perceived things (hence, are the contents of representation). However, in the act, what we are concerned with are value things or value stuffs but not with mere objects of perception. Consequently, behind practical objects already lie such activities as value feeling, the superiority and inferiority of value feelings, love and hatred, and so forth. If so, then values are the a priori of practical objects but not effects of the act. Kant overlooked these a priori values pertaining to the substantiality of will.

The "content that is to be realized through the act," as the second element, is of a state of value (*Wertverhalt*) that exists in accordance with value objects; that is, as a valuable matter of fact (*Sache*). Because it makes its appearance only under the guise of the object of will, in contrast with the objects of knowledge such as the contents of perception, it is something standing over against the will (*Widerstand*) and is different from an object (*Gegenstand*). In this case, the term *object* indicates only represented objects, whereas value objects become something standing over against (*Widerstand*).

Ordinarily, *Widerstand* means something like a sense of resistance, but in fact it is that phenomenon directly given only in an endeavor of the will. Hence, that matter of fact (*Sache*) stands over against the will. It is obvious that the content now under consideration is by no means mere feelings affiliated with a state, that is, *Zustand*, as Kant implies. It becomes evident here that the view that the contents resulting in imparting a state of pleasure to an agent are likely to become the content of the will is in error.

The third element concerns the desire for the aforementioned content. Originally, the phenomenon of will consisted of striving, in which something desired (*Gewolltes*) is given as that which should be realized. A wish, which is an endeavor that does not aim at the realization of a specific content, must be distinguished from the will. Here the option of adoption or rejection, made on the basis of the bodily experience of "can do" (*Tunkönnen*), comes to take on an important significance. If what is desired lies in the "cannot do" realm, then it cannot bear the characteristic of that which is to be realized. Hence, this desire becomes little more than a wish. The realization of content by means of the will is possible only in the "can be" realm, and in this case alone the will becomes the "will to do," which can be counted as the fourth element.

The desire for content is taken into consideration at various stages. First of all is the "preparedness of mind" (*Gesinning*). Because the content of will is a value state, as was already argued, and various activities such as value feeling, the superiority or inferiority of value feelings, love and hatred, and so forth can be at work if the value state noted earlier is to become the content of will, then values permeate the volitional preparedness of the mind. Hence, in the preparedness of mind, the a priori value consciousness is said to be congruent with the nucleus of the will. Then, various stages subsequent to it are to be considered developments of the preparedness of mind, so to speak.

"Purpose" arises when the willed value-state and the particular quality of *Widerstand* determines the content of will. That is to say, it is the will to do a specific thing. "Deliberation" is required to examine those conditions determinative of the content of will. However, this content is not a real matter of fact, or "a thing." When *Widerstand* is found standing against the established contents aimed at, a real agent standing against it, that is, "a thing," appears in connection with which we are able to grasp the "project" (*Vorsatz*) or "decision" at subsequent stages. And also because this novel content (i.e., the content of the project, to begin with) is formed, the impact of phenomenal things on our states of feeling occurs. (It can be said that purpose is *prospect* and that project is *design*.)

This establishes "the will to want to do something" as the fourth element. In a "project," that the will comes into direct contact with empirical reality, that our body engages with the immediate object of an action, and that its motion is determined in place and time has already been brought to light in "planning." "The will to do" arises at the place where this is set in motion in the activity of a human body. It is here that we are able to grasp clearly the intentional structure of the will.

The intention of will is twofold. Fundamentally, it aims at the realization of a value state. Then, the intention "to want to do something" is added to it secondarily. For instance, when one takes a hat from a hatrack and puts it on, what is basically intended is the state of a hat resting on one's head, not the motion of a human body. The motion prerequisite for wearing a hat occurs when the fundamental intention is accompanied by another intention to want to do something. This distinction will be understood clearly when compared with a situation in which the motion itself is fundamentally intended.

For example, a jealous farmer sets fire to her rich neighbor's house. This farmer intends to bring this gorgeous neighboring house to nought; that is, she intends to destroy its value. To this intention, to set fire is added as another intention to achieve it. That is, it is not that the action of setting the fire is what was basically intended. On the other hand, when an incendiary maniac sets fire to something, the fire setting itself is what is aimed at from the outset. These two cases are clearly distinct.

This clarification of the intentional structure of willing provides accessibility to important prescriptions pertaining to an act. "What is called an act in the strict sense of the word, is an experience in which the aforesaid state is materialized in and by a real doing. That is to say, it is the unity of such particular experiences, which subsists as a single phenomenal unity entirely independent of every kind of objective causal process pertaining to an act as well as of its consequences."[6] The state aimed at and the real doing of it are grounded one on the other but not as purpose and its means. It is quite out of the question that the pleasure expected from a deed is aimed at as its purpose. The objects of will constantly arise anew, independent of whatever results may come out of past activities. The consciousness of "can do," which selects and chooses these objects, is given phenomenally as a special kind of consciousnesses of endeavor, without thereby being mediated by past experiences. Thus, it is entirely false that pleasure is the determinant of the will, as Kant claimed.

The fifth element is concerned with sensation and the state of feeling affiliated with the activity of the human body. They must be distinguished from that feeling or state occasioned by the realization of an act. The latter no longer constitutes an element of an act. The sixth element, which is an experience of the realization of the contents themselves, brings the act into completion.

Thus Scheler rejected Kant's presupposition by understanding an act as an experience of the realization of a state of value. He attempts to fill up a crevice left behind by Kant's failure to adequately prescribe the objects of desire. This is evident in Scheler's idea of environmental "things" (*Milieudinge*). Presupposing the influences of things on the sensitive faculty (*Sinnlichkeit* in German), Kant insists that the will of morality determines itself independent of these influences.

However this may be, what are the things or objects of which Kant speaks? Are they things in themselves? Or are they things that make their appearance in a representative experience? Or are they objects of the natural sciences? Kant deals only with these three sorts of "things." However, the things dealt with in an act are none of these. For instance, the environment sun has no connection with the sun dealt with in astronomy. Meat as an object either stolen or bought is not a lump of cells or tissues. The object of an act is the unity of values as well as *Sache*. Therefore, the environment is only those things whose influence one experiences. Hence, the world of values is practically experienced as something influential. Human experiences do not establish this environment. It is, instead, the ground of experiences.

Our attention is directed exclusively to environmental objects. Our concern presupposes the environment. Even our perception can register only what belongs to the environment. The contents of sensation are those partial contents constitutive of environmental objects. That Kant fails to come to grips with this sort of living environment is a weak point in his philosophy. An error arises from it, which on the one hand, fails to understand sensation within a living individual's unifying total sensory experience and tries to deal with it as something concerned with sense organs separated from this unity. And on the other, it regards a stimulus as an exertion of physical objects on the sensitive faculty. Sense organs as well as physical objects have nothing to do with acts. Concrete value objects and environmental objects prescribe it, not tissues or cells nor composites of atoms. Thus, we can say that Kant's basic error in dealing with an act lies in a one-sidedness with which he took his departure, as a result of the assumptions of the mathematical natural sciences and associational psychology prevalent in England at that time. Scheler's criticism can be said to strike a blow at Kant's most vulnerable point, that he failed to establish the world of value objects in addition to that of physical objects.

However, Scheler also completely misses another important point: that an act is, in truth, the act of *ningen*. Hence, for example, he speaks as if an act of setting fire to one's neighbor's house were intended to destroy the value attached to the house but had no connection with one's relationship with one's neighbor. Or, he says that one experiences parental affection as an environmental affair, even when they are absent.

If we conceive of an act only as what is concerned with value objects, then how do we conceive of the relations that exist among persons? This question should have come to the fore as a great difficulty, when Scheler grappled with the issue of total personality. Nevertheless, he did not actually take up this question. Even when he speaks of the activity of making a promise or of the fact (*Sachgebilde*) of entering into a contract, he does not clarify how different these are from the activities he called the *feeling of values* or from what he referred to as *life value*. However, the latter holds precisely the crux of the "act." This is the reason why Scheler's critique of the Kantian standpoint, even though it catches the weak point inherent in the latter, nevertheless loses the point of the issues surrounding an "act" to a greater extent than Kant himself.

This point is particularly evident in Scheler's account of environmental objects. He is certainly right in arguing that a meal which is likely to be stolen or bought is not a lump of cells or tissues. However, meat that is likely to be stolen or bought is also not a mere value thing. No matter how actions such as value feelings, superior or inferior value feelings, love and hatred, and so forth may be put into motion, neither "meat that is bought" nor "meat that is stolen" arise there. The former arises only on the basis of property relationships and the latter, only within economic relations. That is to say, human relationships, not action, constitute the a priori of these environmental things. All that can be said from the standpoint of action is that only "meat as a food" or "meat that looks delicious" can arise there.

But, as is claimed by Tarde and Durkheim, even food cannot arise apart from society, which is itself a set of manners of acts. A fixed manner of eating renders it possible for meat to be "food" or delicious looking. At a place where food is eaten differently or in a society in which vegetarianism is predominant, meat is neither a food nor is it delicious looking. That is to say, meat is not a valued thing. From this perspective, we see that even Scheler's so-called environmental things can be recognized only on the basis of human relationships in which some act is already presupposed. Concern with environmental things alone does not enable an act to arise for the first time.

Von Hildebrand's *The Concept of a Moral Act*,[7] which immediately follows in Scheler's steps, enlarges and makes this one-sidedness more apparent in his analysis of an act. This book analyzes the phenomenon of an act in a much more careful and detailed manner than Scheler. But here, the phenomena of an act are separated from human relationships from the outset and are grasped in their respondent relations to states of value alone. Therefore, von Hildebrand devotes his most detailed explanation to his attempts to take valuational response as an attitude-assuming decision and to distinguish it from acquiring knowledge and other claims or endeavor to submit to analysis the response of will that constitutes a special valuational response in the will. But these attempts cannot be said to be inquiries into the authentic and practical features of an act.

The characteristic features that render an act different from a valuational response, such as being pleased or becoming angry, can be recognized only in realizing some sort of matters of fact. An act of this sort, in its most typical form, is found only in the production of tools or in the creation of works of art. Von Hildebrand fails to heed this point. Although he carries on his investigation by keeping his eye on betweeness-oriented acts in human beings, he unwittingly argues this issue in accordance with the aforesaid scheme; that is, in such a way as to regard an act as a valuational response. An example of an act to which he repeatedly refers throughout the book is that of rescuing human lives courageously, which he regards as a realization of the fact of preserving human life but not as the interconnection of acts between one person and another. On hearing someone cry out to be rescued from a burning house, one must assume a definite attitude in response to this emergency. One does not desire that the other person should perish. That is, one desires that the other person's life should be preserved. According to Von Hildebrand, what is prerequisite for this decision of attitude is the consciousness of the matter of fact called *the preservation of life* and, in particular, the consciousness of value attaching to it. The attitudinal decision occurs with regard to this as a response to the value involved in it. As a result, one rushes into the house and rescues the person calling for help. This is a realization of what is called *the preservation of life*. He insists that the experiential unity of these three elements, that is, the consciousness of the matter of fact, the attitudinal decision leading to it, and the realization of this matter, is an act.

Von Hildebrand does not concern himself with the question of whether an agent who delivers a person from imminent danger is a parent, a friend, a fire fighter, or a complete stranger. But in reality this discrimination is of great importance. A parent who plunges into a house fire on hearing her child call for help performs a deed she is normally required to do as a parent and for which, therefore, she does not particularly deserve to be praised as "noble." Rather, a parent who allowed her child to die before her very eyes would be judged a parent not deserving of being a parent. The same can be said of a fire fighter who plunges into a fire without regard for his or her life. Through this deed, the fire fighter is said to have held his or her own post. By contrast, a rescue accomplished by a passerby must be thought to be something quite different. For such a person, saving a life, irrespective of whose life it is, is an act of great importance and would certainly be deemed a noble deed. But even if she had run toward an alarm to send an emergency call, not possessing the courage to plunge into the fire herself, she would not be accused of being "inhuman."

In such a case, the rescue is more than what is normally required from a passerby. In other words, even the deed that is regarded as natural for a parent is a particularly good deed for a mere passerby. From what does this distinction arise? If only the realization of what is called *the preservation of life* is of significance, then this distinction remains quite beyond our understanding. It is because what is materialized as the practical interconnection of acts within the context of a definite human relationship that the distinction arises at all. If this point is not noticed and one's focus is kept only on the realization of the preservation of life, then there is no recognizable difference between the rescue of a human life and the production of an ambulance.

This is not the whole story, however, for even the production of a tool such as an ambulance cannot be done justice to by saying that it merely realizes some state of value. In general, a tool arises as such only within certain social conditions. Hence, there is no tool which does not presuppose social characteristics inherent in value feeling. Thus, what von Hildebrand calls *the realization of a state of value* is more abstract, when compared with a human activity such as the production of a tool.

Von Hildebrand's analysis of an act can be shown to be a weak point in his phenomenology in that it departs significantly from the world of practice. But, like Scheler, he embarks upon the investigation of community in the later period of his life. He deals with this theme in his book *Metaphysics of Community*.[8] To our surprise, however, this book, whose theme centers around the contract as well as the unity between one person and another, tries to solve the problem of personal relationships by appealing not to "an act" but to "a function," and in particular to "a social function," so to speak. That is to say, such affairs as making a promise, giving an order, or making a request are, according to him, not acts but functions. His former book, which describes an act only in connection with the state of value, finally drives him into this corner. With regard to this point, there is no difference between Scheler's position and his.

From this it is easy to understand why the study of an act is almost absent in Nicolai Hartmann's voluminous work on ethics, which is said to gather together ethical theories belonging to the phenomenological school into a systematic whole. The criticism of Kant by the phenomenological school fails to catch the most excellent point in Kant's practical philosophy; that is, the point that deals with the issue of practice as subjectivity. This oversight is particularly evident in Hartmann. To speak of this in connection with an act, we can say that those critics, including Hartmann, who tried to overcome Kant, rather have taken a backward step. Cohen, who sided with Kant, must be, even here, taken into consideration with considerable respect, for he put emphasis on the issue of the subject and strongly insisted on the distinction between the unity of consciousness (*Einheit des Bewusstseins*) and of self-consciousness (*Selbstbewusstsein*), which was not yet distinctly made in Kant. Even though phenomenology became prevalent after neo-Kantianism does not deprive this insight of its value.

13   trust and truth

If we understand human action through the spatio-temporality of human existence, then we can approach the important significance of trust and truth to human existence.

First of all, what does *trust* mean? What is the ground of trust?

In the preceding chapter we referred to the fact that von Hildebrand had given the saving of a human life as a typical example of an act. According to him, the primordial element constitutive of an act is "a voice calling for help," which occasions the decision to assume an attitude, as well as to respond to a value. However, what does the phenomenon of calling for rescue mean? At a time and place where it is not anticipated that rescue could occur, there is no point in calling for rescue. Whatever danger one may find oneself in, one does not call for rescue to a stone or a tree.

In the case of a primitive person assuming such an attitude, the stone or the tree is not a mere stone or a tree but is thought to have a mystical power able to rescue this person. That is to say, this primitive person calls for rescue in a context where it can be anticipated.

Now, what are the limits within which this rescue may be anticipated? Even if a modern machine is capable of producing more than what human power can, it cannot be regarded as a human partner, to whom one calls for rescue. Generally speaking, no inanimate thing can serve as "a partner" for a human being. Even a tamed animal, which is most friendly to human beings and at times a human being is likely to call as a partner, can nevertheless not be made into a human counterpart to which one calls for rescue. One anticipates a rescue only from people, as belonging to the same species, or from a superhuman person believed to be an agent able to provide one's rescue.

Incidentally, because the superhuman person was formed or found in compliance with a human being's need for rescue, it is thought to be a part of his essential nature that this superhuman person will extend a helping hand in response to a human voice calling for rescue. This is not, however, the case with other human beings, who are not created as are those who can provide rescue. Then why does one anticipate rescue from them?

In danger, one does not necessarily call for rescue to one's parents and brothers or friends alone. One calls to other persons as well; that is, to human beings, in general. One calls to them because one places one's trust in them as helpers from the outset. They may do you an injury, as a fierce animal does, or they may be as indifferent, as a tamed animal is. In spite of this, they are trusted as agents who extend a helping hand in case of emergency. A voice calling for rescue is the expression of this trust.

If the preceding interpretation is not in error, then to hear a voice calling for rescue is at once to grasp a state of affairs in which there is need of rescue and to hear a voice of trust. Then it is that one feels the value inherent in the state of affairs called *the preservation of life*, and at the same time, one tries to respond to this trust. This is the authentic motivation that drives one to save a life. The value inherent in the preservation of life is even likely to be felt in the case of an animal in imminent danger. But this alone would not cause one to perform a courageous deed such as the saving of a human life. Only he who is able to respond to trust can perform acts such as the sacrifice of his own life. Human beings already stand in this relationship of trust to each other. This is why they anticipate rescue beforehand, in trust, and attempt to accomplish a rescue in response to a call for help.

Trust of this sort is found not only in the special case of a human life in imminent danger. It is of necessity existent whenever a human interconnection is performed in one way or another, in everyday life. When one loses one's way, one readily asks for help from a stranger on the street. Even when we have no information about who this person is and what he is likely to be prepared to do, we entirely trust that he will attempt to get us back on the right road without deceiving us. Otherwise, we would not ask him.

Of course, as a matter of fact, we might be directed to the wrong road because of having insufficient knowledge about him or we might deliberately be given the wrong direction so as to lose our way by his maliciousness. But this is only because a kind attitude, which we should naturally expect from him, is absent. Therefore, this case is unlikely to overturn our trust. Because of this, even a person who happened to have been given the wrong directions does not stop asking for directions afterward. And even a person who tells a lie out of spite is capable of performing a malicious deed through this lie, only because he takes trust for granted as the ground. If a person who asks directions did not put his trust in what is told to him, then maliciousness could not occur, no matter how much of a lie he is told.

Even a cursory glace at our everyday life is enough to show just how much trust is in evidence. This is no less the case even with life on the street, where the connection of human beings with each other is weakest, than with the intimate communal life of a family or a friendly relationship. People walk in the midst of a crowd without having to be prepared to defend themselves. Precisely because they take it on trust that strangers have no more intention of inflicting a wound on others than they themselves have, they are able to walk at ease with an unguarded attitude. Even though, in rare cases, a pickpocket or a blackmailer may threaten this unguardedness, such basic trust does not crumble. Indeed, its constancy enables a pickpocket or a blackmailer to engage in his activity. Again, on the street, one may hire a taxidriver on a definite contract, who is entirely unknown to one. Both the passenger and the driver place their trust in the belief that this contract will be observed. Each of them is in a position to inflict a wound upon the other. In spite of this, neither usually has in mind anything to fear. Immense numbers of such phenomena of trust are found on the street.

We can say, then, that human acts are, in general, based on trust of this kind. Human beings can work on one another only by trusting that other persons will not inflict harm on them whenever they please, as though they were fierce animals, rather that they are persons from whom one anticipates rescue in a crisis, that they will not tell a lie when asked directions on the street, and that they will keep a promise whenever they make one. The social position held by the agent of an act is a social expression of this trust. Just as parents are acknowledged to possess a capacity as parents, insofar as they are trusted as those who care for their children, so in advance one already anticipates acting in a manner in accordance with one's position, as when acting as a company employee, a public officer, a teacher, a student, a taxi driver, a farmer, a business person, a worker, and so forth. Of course, the trust varies in degree in accordance with differences in the social wholes that determine each position in question. Human action cannot, however, take place apart from the presence of trust to one degree or another.

What is the ground of trust? I think it possible to ascribe it, as Wilhelm Herrmann does, to the rational will inherent in each person.[1] To trust in a person is to place one's trust in the inner independence of this person. That is to say, it means to trust that this person would take hold of a definite volitional direction without thereby succumbing to a natural impulse, if he is honest with himself and, hence, obeys an unconditional *ought*. This view acknowledges the moral personality of a person, as in Kant, and tries to find in it the ground of trust. This is certainly justified in that it founds trust on the ultimate principle of morality. But what element does this principle require to make its appearance in the definite form of trust? How does acknowledging a definite volitional direction within the person, who refuses to succumb to natural impulse, turn out to be a trust relationship between human beings? It seems to me that these problems are left unclarified.

A person does not succumb to natural impulse if he is honest with himself. However this may be, it is difficult to know in advance whether or not he is honest with respect to his essence. Moreover, a prerequisite for trust is precisely the establishment of such self-honesty. If so, then the inner independence acknowledged in the conditional "if . . . honest," cannot be the ground of trust. In addition, that he is capable of independence in his relation to nature does not necessarily mean that he is worthy of trust in his relation to another *I*. Provided that an innerly independent person is stern enough to refuse to attach himself to any kind of affection and is kept at a respectful distance by others, this inner independence can be said to interrupt the trust relationship. To the contrary, even among criminals who are extremely destitute of inner independence, there can arise an intimate relationship of trust. Thus, we can assert that inner independence falls short of being the ground of trust.

However, there is some justification in Herrmann's thought that independence from natural impulse renders trust capable of being grounded. He insisted that socio-ethical reality should be looked for not in the nature of, but in the history of a human being. "We become human beings for the first time by being brought up in society."[2] Consequently, when one speaks of a human being's will, human relationships are already presupposed, in and through which natural will is progressively transformed into free will; that is, natural desire is transformed into independent will. This is the issue with which he tries to deal. He recognizes a personal authority operating within this educational relationship and comes to grasp the consciousness of the ground of this authority in the form of "trust." Therefore, we can say that he actually comes to grips with the already established laws of socio-ethical organizations. However, all he did was to glimpse these laws from a perspective that inquires into them as they develop from natural will to free will.

For a socio-ethical organization to arise, the law of negativity is already at work. But this law arises as a movement in which subjects become disrupted into and opposed to one another and then realize their unity. Therefore, this law is not concerned merely with the relation between a human being and nature. The movement of subjective negation certainly takes place as the negation of natural impulse. But ethics is not concerned just with independence from natural impulse. The ground of trust exists precisely within the society of human beings, which renders a human being capable of becoming a human being, under the guise of its laws. With this view presupposed, Herrmann was able to catch the element of negativity in a human being in the form of "freedom from natural desires."

We have inquired into the ground of trust in two directions. That is, the ultimate principle of morality and human society. In our own terms, this implies that we sought the ground of trust in the laws of *ningen sonzai*. That is to say, the ground of trust consists exactly in the movement of the multiplication/unification of subjects through the path of negation. But this is not yet enough, particularly insofar as we deal with the phenomena of trust. For trust cannot be exhausted simply by saying that the self and the other, while opposed to each other, come to have a direction of unity. A further prerequisite for trust lies in that future unity is assured in the present in advance. Hence, we have no alternative but to assert that the ground of trust will be adequately clarified only by recognizing that the movement of the multiplication/unification of subjects has a spatio-temporal structure.

Nicolai Hartmann kept his eye on the temporal element in the phenomena of trust.[3] He investigates trust by dividing it into "the capacity worthy of trust" (*Zuverlässigkeit*) and "trust in another person" (*Vertrauen*). The former he also calls *the capacity to make a promise*, which is a capacity to assure that a matter not yet realized should coincide with the utterance of specific words. Hence, the value inherent in *the capacity worthy of trust* consists of the certainty with which the act is carried on in the future. He who possesses that capacity worthy of trust, that is, who is trustworthy, does not alter his will until the matter is realized precisely as promised. He obliges himself by his

promise. Only "he who is trustworthy" can stand within the obligations or the order of social life; that is, can live within a society.

Therefore, "the capacity worthy of trust" is, at bottom, a moral
capacity of personality that is capable of prescribing one's future attitude in advance. Personality is not only the present will but aware also
of its ability to maintain itself in the future will. The identity of the will,
as well as that of the personality behind it, constitutes the ground for
being worthy of trust. Thus, Hartmann first considered trust only in
relation to the personality of an individual and then later developed,
on this basis, "the trust in other persons." On the assumption that a
person possesses the capacity of being worthy of trust, Hartmann
wastes no time in placing his trust in this person. This is what he calls
trust in another person. It is not that Hartmann trusts in him, after test-
ing whether or not he is trustworthy in the world. Accordingly, trust
is an adventure or a wager. Any human relationship, whatever it may
be, is based on trust of this sort: "trust is a capacity necessary for communal society."

Hartmann's position is that mutual trust between human beings
actually constitutes a society for the first time. The contrary argument,
that is, the argument that human society provides the ground of trust,
was denied. This is why the aforementioned second direction, in which
the ground of trust was looked for in human society, was abandoned.
Instead, the ground of trust was again pushed back to the identity of
an individual personality or to the moral value of personality. But this
is not what we wish to attend to.

Even though the ground of trust may be attributable to the identity of personality, as Hartmann argues, the crux of the matter is that
the necessity of deriving this identity lies in one's capacity to prescribe
in advance one's future will, attitude, and act. This is of much more
importance than Hartmann thought. He thought it possible to dissolve
the problem of self-anticipation simply by appealing to the identity of
personality. Hartmann remarks that "he who makes a promise will be
able to identify the present self with that subsequent to it." But in him
who broke his promise, will this self-identity disappear? No. It is on
the basis of this self-identity that one abandons a promise. No matter
what is spoken of, whether trust or distrust, obedience or betrayal, there
is no difference as regards the identity of the self. We must remark that
he committed an error in his attempt to acknowledge moral adherence
(*sittliche Beharrung*) within the identity of personality. I am convinced
that a much deeper law is at work in the contention that we are able to
prescribe in advance an act in the future. To know it, we have no alter-

native but to understand this temporal moment within the context of the law inherent in *ningen sonzai*.

The phenomenon of trust does not exist merely in placing one's trust in another person. It also means that one assumes in advance a decided attitude toward the future, which lacks definiteness with respect to the relationship between self and other. The reason we can assume this attitude is that the past we shoulder in *ningen sonzai* is, at the same time, precisely the future we are going to aim at. Our present act takes place in this identity between the past and the future. That is to say, we come back in and through an act.

Admitting that the past which the act has shouldered is, for the time being, yesterday's betweenness, we must say that this betweenness arose in our acting to do or undo something. And the act to do or undo something was likewise none other than an instantiation of the coming back movement. Hence, the past is the coming back movement, which moves on indefinitely.

Likewise, admitting that the future we aim at in the act of willing is, to begin with, tomorrow's betweenness, we must say that this betweenness will also arise in acting to do or undo something. Therefore, as the coming back movement, this process moves on indefinitely. Shouldering these movements, the present act continues to aim at them. Something that is moving through a whole series of acts is none other than the movement coming back to authenticity through negation. As a link in this movement, the present act has the dynamic structure of coming back. Therefore, the basic direction that departs from and returns to authenticity is not lost sight of, even if what is at stake here is a finite human being. The ground out of which we come is a terminus toward which we are going. On this is based the concept that one assumes in advance a definite attitude toward the future that is left undetermined.

The ground of trust lies in the spatio-temporal structure pertinent to *ningen sonzai*. That is to say, the law of *ningen sonzai*, which develops spatio-temporally, renders trust capable of existing. If this is true, then the proposition that "human relationships are based on trust," which seems to be taken for granted, actually turns the matter upside down. The ground on which human relationships stand is the law of *ningen sonzai*, which consists of spatio-temporality. And hence, this is the ground on which trust itself stands. On this ground stand human relations and trust as well. Therefore, human relations are those of trust; and at a place where human relations prevail, trust is also established.

By saying this, however, we do not mean that there is no relation such as distrust, or betrayal. These display a lack of trust, negated
from the deepest bottom of human existence, as a rebellion against
the law of *ningen sonzai*. This is why "betrayal" has been rejected as
the most abominable crime from ancient times. However, the problem is this: how is it possible for trust to be deprived? With this problem in mind, I think it possible to turn our attention to "the
truthfulness of a human being."

The truthfulness of a human being is the truth of, or the real feature of, a human being. We have traced the real feature of *ningen
sonzai* from its negative structure up to its spatio-temporal one.
Throughout this endeavor, the real feature of *ningen sonzai* cannot
be found in an individual being. Rather it is found in the individual/
social dual characteristic of a human being, that is, in the movement
of negation through which *ningen sonzai* comes back to authentic
wholeness through disruption into countless numbers of selves and
others, spatio-temporally. Hence, *ningen sonzai's* real feature or truth
occurs in the movement of a spatio-temporal coming back but has
nothing to do with what occurs nonspatially and nontemporally.
Human beings become individuals negatively in subjective space/
time and also realize their socio-ethical unity in a negative fashion.
Then, the truth of *ningen* takes place. When the movement of negation comes to a standstill, and thus the coming back movement is
interrupted, the truth of *ningen* is prevented from occurring. Instead,
what is opposed to truth, falsehood, makes its appearance.

Provided that truth occurs spatio-temporally in this way, it is an
act-oriented practical truth. That is, "truthfulness," or *makoto* in Japanese, has nothing to do with contemplative/noematic truth. What is
usually called the *correspondence* between thinking and its object in
the outer world or as that knowledge which possesses universal validity is concerned with only the latter kind of truth.

Truth of the former sort has to do with *makoto* inherent in an act,
which is a human being's truth realized only in a socio-ethical unity.
Basically speaking, a human being becomes self-aware of *makoto* only
by living his life in this *makoto* and applying it to things found in
ningen sonzai.

At this stage, truth or falsehood are spoken of in connection with
objects in the outer world. Therefore, the truth involved in the standpoint of thinking does not turn out to be truthfulness by being transmitted to the standpoint of practice, rather truthfulness turns out to be
truth by being transferred to a contemplative standpoint.

It is not my present concern to embark upon this problem in detail. But, to show that this position is not advanced arbitrarily, I would like to mention Cohen's *Ethics of Pure Will*.[4] In Cohen's opinion, ethics is based on logic, and logic as the science of "method" established knowledge on its own ground. But, in logic, the value of knowledge is expressed in terms of universality and necessity. Logic has nothing to do with what is called *truth* from the side of content. Hence, in logic such characteristics as rationality, lawfulness, universality, necessity, and so forth, prevail, but there is no truth.

Ethics adds truth there, but ethics cannot acquire truth by its own efforts alone. It can do so only in connection with logic. If truth is to be understood as the truth of knowledge then truth of this sort arises only when the two sides of reason, that is, intellect and will, connect with each other. Therefore, truth implies the coincidence of the theoretical issue with the ethical. This is the basic law of truth. Cohen takes account of truth as the truth of knowledge, and does not go so far as practical truthfulness. Truth, in the final analysis, ends up being a "pursuit of truth" and a "method." Hence, the movement of reason is of interest in the science of nature as well as that of ethics. But it has nothing to do with the real feature of act-oriented practical existence. In spite of this, truth could not be acquired only through the logic of knowledge, in Cohen's view.

Incidentally, a human being's "*makoto*" occurs in and through his spatio-temporal acts. Does this fact hold true for what is usually dealt with as a human being's *makoto* in daily life?

It is often remarked that a human being's *makoto* implies *shingon* ("true words") or *shinji* ("true things") in Japanese. From ancient times, a Chinese word *sei* (誠) has been used to denote it. It is also translatable into such words as *seijitsu* ("sincerity"), *shinjitsu* ("truthfulness"), *chujitsu* ("faithfulness"). The Chinese word *sei* means that one is pure and without falsehood in one's attitude of mind as well as in one's words and deeds. It is therefore evident that the word *sei* stands opposed to falsehood or deceit and that it is equivalent in meaning to true words and true things. The phrase *Sei is the path of Heaven, and to realize it is the path of a human being* (from *The Right Path*, one of the Chinese classics) has been popular among Japanese people from ancient times. The difference between the path of Heaven and that of a human being, as indicated in this book, lies in Heaven being truthful and without any deceit of its own and human beings should realize it in the form of truthfulness. That is to say, human beings are obliged to fulfill the task of bringing deceitfulness to nought and making

truthfulness manifest. But these remarks only repeatedly refer to truthfulness or to the lack of deceit, and say nothing about what truthfulness and deceit are actually like in the world. What kinds of affairs do
they indicate in our actual daily existence?

What is to be considered first of all with regard to this question
is the problem of whether or not a word and a fact are congruent with
one another. This problem seems to reveal the meaning of *makoto* regarded as a true word. To speak truth is none other than to make
words coincident with a given fact. The word *veracity* (*Wahrhaftigkeit*
in German) refers to this state of affairs. To make words not coincident with a given fact is a deceit or a lie. Now one ponders over the
problem of whether or not one is right in telling a lie when driven by
an apparent necessity.

If the distinction between truth and falsehood is prescribed from
the standpoint of whether or not words are coincident with a given fact
alone, we must investigate further the basic problem of what "a fact"
is in the world. If what is dealt with here is not the strictly objective
fact, but only what a person believes is a fact, then it is possible that
what he told as a lie, due to a lack of knowledge, is likely to become
more coincident with the facts. In this case, did he speak truly or tell a
lie? If the latter is the case, then it is not the coincidence between a fact
and a word but an attitude of mind of the person concerned that determines truth or falsehood.

This attitude of mind determines truth or falsehood by ponder-
ing over whether or not someone tries to deceive others but not by appealing to the relation someone bears to the real fact. Here, relations
between human beings decide the issue of truth or falsehood, not the
relation between a fact and a word.

If we grasp this point exactly, then the questions surrounding a
lie one is driven to tell disappear immediately. We often hide the reality of a disease from a patient. To tell a lie of this sort, insofar as it is
done as a result of caring about the patient's happiness, is a sort of
"truthfulness" toward the patient and, hence, is not a lie. A humane
relationship with the patient, and not the mere congruence of the fact
of the disease with the word, is the deciding factor between truth and
falsehood. Provided that a person, when threatened with danger of
death, escapes from this difficulty by telling a lie, this lie should be recognized as necessitated by the human relationship that develops from
that threat. Hence, in this case he has not deceived the other person in
the normal sense of the word. To deceive another person is a betrayal
of trust. It cannot occur at a place where there is no trust. Seen in this

light, we can say that truthfulness is decided in and through the human relation that consists in a relationship of trust. To speak truth exactly expresses this relationship.

What is considered, second, is the problem of whether or not a word is congruent with a deed. The congruence between a word and a deed seems to indicate the meaning of *makoto*, regarded as a true thing. Truthfulness or faithfulness consists of this, that a person makes his deed congruent with a word given to him. On the contrary, noncongruence is falsehood or unfaithfulness. In particular, a given word is dealt with as a promise. Such terms as *fidelity, good faith, Treue, Zuverlässigkeit,* and so forth are prescribed in the meaning of this. However, a promise is not merely a word. It is an expression of human relationships. Those who make a promise allow, already and in advance, their present being to be prescribed by those future relationships that have not yet occurred. In this way, a promise itself is already a deed based on trust. To be faithful to a promise is to realize this trust and let the real feature of human existence occur. To act contrary to a promise betrays this trust. Here we can also say that human relations determine truthfulness. There is no congruence of word with deed apart from these relations.

As was noted previously, truth and falsehood are all attributable to the relationship of trust among human beings. This is also what common sense usually understands. Time and again in our ordinary lives, we hear of parents taking their children seriously, a wife's truthful mind evidenced in her taking care of her husband, a man possessing "sincerity," a "faithful" friend, and so forth. Such occurrences refer to an attitude in which one responds by devoting oneself to intimate trust relationships such as parent and child, a husband and a wife, a pair of lovers, a pair of friends, and so forth. A parent who risks his life for the sake of his child and who devotedly endures hardships and works devotedly is said to exhibit sincerity in taking care of his child. A wife who devotes the whole of her life to her husband's benefit also reveals a truthful mind. A man who does not betray his girlfriend is judged to have sincerity. A friend who shares pain and suffering with and cares for his counterpart by abandoning egoistic attachment is said to be a sincere friend.

Common sense respects these cases, holding them as treasures difficult to obtain in a life. In such cases, *makoto* is more than the congruence of a fact with a word or of a word with a deed, even though congruence of this sort is expected as a matter of course at the place where *makato* prevails.

But *makoto*, although making its appearance in such congruent circumstances, is more than these. This commonsense understanding, I am sure, hits the mark exactly. For "an attitude one assumes in response to trust" not only makes a fact and a word as well as a word and a deed congruent each with the other in individual cases but also assumes the authority to deliberately make them incongruent, if and when occasion necessitates it. The reason why such authority is given to *makoto* lies in it being a service to others through self-abandonment or sacrifice. In other words, *makoto* as an attitude assumed in response to trust consists of the realization of socio-ethical unity via the path of negation and hence reveals the authentic feature of *ningen sonzai*. It is the same as the *makoto* of *ningen,* which was conceived of as arising spatio-temporally.

Thus, one's attempt to respond to trust in a relationship of trust and to do an act in such a way as to be worthy of that trust is precisely *makoto* in that it lets the authentic feature of *ningen sonzai* arise. Where there is no trust relationship and hence where the meaning of responding to trust is not established, *makoto* does not arise. War, where one deals with other persons as if they were fierce animals, brings the trust relationship almost to the brink of extinction, and there is almost no *makoto.*

Even though some assertion is made and then put into practice afterward or someone utters a monologue about what has just been experienced from the standpoint of detachment from human relationships, this has nothing to do with sincerity. It is always in human relationships, including trust that sincerity prevails in acts.

Incidentally, we have so far observed that all human relations involve trust to some extent. Scheler is not correct in insisting that the *Gesellschaft*-oriented relationship is originally based on distrust. It is certain that it lacks the trust relationship peculiar to *Gemeinschaft.* But a trust relationship peculiar to *Gesellschaft* exists. Otherwise, no business relations could arise. Therefore, we are allowed to insist that, in any human relationship whatsoever, *makoto* takes place in accordance with each of them.

This means, however, that the real feature of *ningen sonzai* occurs in a specific manner that corresponds to the respective trust relationship but does not mean that *makoto* takes the same shape ubiquitously.

The next chapter, which aims to subject the structures of solidarity to analysis, will examine the various names of *makoto*'s specific forms. For now, we must notice that one cannot find *makoto* at a place where the aforesaid correspondence relation is lacking. For instance, the relation one bears to people in the street has no trust relationship of the sort between family members or intimate friends. For this reason, in the context of the street, if we shared a stranger's unconfessed pain and worked on him with our full effort, we could not be said to have devoted our *makoto* to him. He would look very suspiciously at us and regard our activity as insane.

To cite another example, the relationships between passengers on a train lack an intimate community of being such as is found in the trust relationship between husband and wife. Therefore, if a woman assumed the devoted attitude toward a strange man on the train that she does towards her husband, she would not be said to have exercised *makoto* but rather would be accused of madness. There exist forms of *makoto* specifically correspondent to the relationships that hold among people in the street or among passengers, through which alone one is able to exhibit one's *makoto*.

Now, if one makes *makoto* correspond to the trust relationship, then what happens to the psychological meaning expressed by such terms as *sincerity, an honest mind, a true heart,* and so forth? According to this psychological meaning, *makoto* consists in purity of one's attitude of mind, nonfalsehood, faithfulness toward the self, and so on; that is to say, in the unchangeableness of one's attitude of mind from beginning to end. Consequently, *makoto* can be grasped as the consistency of an individual person, without thereby having recourse to the trust relationship.

Do I intend to reject this point? Not at all. What I insist on is that *magokoro* ("a true heart"), regarded here as an individual's attitude of mind, is none other than *makoto* inherent in the trust relationship as grasped from the standpoint of individual psychology. Certainly, without having recourse to the trust relationship, we are still able to investigate sincerity in individual psychology. However, this does not mean that sincerity takes place outside of the trust relationship.

It is certain that consistency and unchangeableness of mental attitude can also occur outside the trust relationship. Consider the case in which he who is fond of a particular kind of flower does not change his attitude towards this kind of flower as long as he lives. But because of this, we do not yet call him sincere. If we utter a phrase such as *honesty toward a plum flower,* it is only a personified expression. No matter how changeable one's attitude of mind toward an object may be, if it has no impact upon one's relationship toward other persons, then one is by no means said to be dishonest. On the contrary, if one who has one's affection toward another person holds this affection consistently, then one is honest, beyond a doubt. If one's affection for another person is only a moment's state of mind and one's attitude entirely lacks consistency, then one is dishonest and frivolous.

Therefore, I speak of honesty only in relation to human beings but not to things. Moreover, because human relations are at stake here, whether or not an attitude of mind is expressed gives birth to a great variety of meanings in human relations. The expression of an attitude of mind takes the shape of interconnections of acts toward other persons. Consequently, shouldering the past of a definite betweenness, it already prescribes the future relationship in advance. In other words, an expressed attitude of mind does not exist merely within the consciousness of an individual.

Even a change of a mental attitude cannot be described exhaustively merely as a change within the consciousness of an individual. It also indicates an overturn of the prescribed future betweenness. That is, it is a betrayal of trust and therefore dishonest.

However, when an attitude of mind is not expressed and, hence, the act interconnections with other persons are not shaped, the matter becomes quite different. In this case, the unchangeableness of an attitude of mind may certainly be called *honest*. But this is so only in analogy with the expressed mental attitude. The change of the unexpressed attitude of mind is merely a change within individual consciousness but has nothing to do with a betrayal of trust or dishonesty. If dishonesty does not arise, even when consistency is lacking, then honesty does not arise, even when there is consistency. Honesty, which is in question in this case, rather consists of an attitude in which one does not express one's own mind. To express one's attitude of mind such as mere caprice of the moment in human relationships means to interfere with the destiny of another person with an extremely light-minded attitude. Just because he cannot stick to his attitude of mind, he has no alternative but to fall victim to dishonesty himself. Consequently, that he does not interfere with the destiny of another person by making a firm secret of his attitude of mind only induces him to let honesty arise. Similarly, if a person is determined not to express his attitude of mind but rather restrains it precisely because this nonexpression protects his counterpart's destiny, even when this attitude is not temporary but consistent, his attitude is said to display honesty to his counterpart. In such cases, because one makes the relationship with one's counterpart honest by not expressing his mental attitude, that attitude is called honest. It is not the consistency and unchangeableness of an attitude of mind alone that makes it possible for honesty to arise.

As the real feature of *ningen sonzai*, a human being's truthfulness arises within trust relationships. Incidentally, the question of how trust can be lacking has given us occasion for paying attention to human truthfulness. Why did we do this? How does human truthfulness relate to the question of trust? The answer is simple. A human being's truthfulness may also, in turn, make clear a human being's falsity. Where there is falsehood, there is a lack of trust.

Now, what is human falsehood? In the previous attempt to investigate the meaning of the word *sei* ("honesty"), I referred to the interpretations people have given to it from ancient times in terms of such phrases as *shinjitsu mumo* ("truthfulness without 'falsehood' ") or *junitsu ni shi te itsuwari naki koto* ("purity without deceitfulness"). That is to say, when one describes *sei* from the standpoint of common sense, one already makes use of words such as *falsehood* or *deceitfulness*. On the other hand, in an attempt to define *deceitfulness,* words such as *truthfulness* or *honesty* are used, because it is precisely "truthlessness."

These concepts presuppose one another. This indicates that they are intimately related to each other. But we cannot yet say that this relationship suffices for us to come to grips with the essence of these concepts. We have tried to understand a human being's truthfulness by paying attention to the real feature of *ningen sonzai*, that is, without confronting it with falsehood.

Now, where does falsehood come from? If it is supposed that truthfulness is the real feature of *ningen sonzai*, then "truthlessness" must mean the lack of the real feature of *ningen sonzai*. This is nonsense. It may be that the real feature can certainly be hidden, but it can never be destroyed. Incidentally, the hidden real feature is a way through which it exists, but is not something that is essentially deprived of the real feature. If falsehood is precisely hidden truthfulness, it is also a manner through which truthfulness exists. Therefore, it does not have its own subsistence. Then the question must be, is this understanding of falsehood justifiable?

Human truthfulness occurs between one person and another. It does not exist ideally and statically in the form of something completed, but occurs constantly anew, as what ought to occur. Hence, it is possible that it does not occur. Kant made reference to this point precisely through his conception of *ought*. However, he emphasized this point so much that he came to insist that *ought* does not decrease its significance as *ought*, even when it is not realized at all. Therefore, he was understood as if he had insisted that practical truth is something that should be realized but actually is not yet realized.

But, truth has already occurred, is about to take place, and is now taking place. It is not something that only *should* be realized but fails to actually exist. In spite of this, it was or is possible that truth does not take place in one way or another. Here lies the significance of *ought*. Because a human being's truthfulness has the possibility of not taking place while always and already taking place, it turns out to be something that should take place. This is an *ought*-oriented characteristic of human truthfulness. This is also why falsehood arises as a manner through which truthfulness exists. I think it possible to clarify this point by considering how truthfulness does not occur.

Originally, falsehood does not have its own subsistence without truthfulness. For instance, as one example of falsehood, a lie means that a word is not congruent with a fact. But if one says a word, while clearly stating that this word is not congruent with fact, one does not tell a lie. A lie arises when one insists that a word is congruent with a fact, even though there is no congruence between them; that is, when one states something as truth, even though it is falsehood. Hence, a lie cannot arise without pretending to be truth.

This is also the case with deceit in which a word and a deed are not congruent with each other. If I make a promise, while apologizing for my intention not to put it into practice, I do not deceive another person. It is possible to deceive because one makes a promise by professing to put exactly that promise into practice, that is, by pretending to be honest. Falsehood cannot be falsehood when it discloses itself. Only when it pretends to be truthfulness can falsehood arise. This demonstrates that falsehood cannot subsist by itself. In other words, falsehood is camouflaged truthfulness, that is, a truthfulness of truthlessness, which is truthfulness in a manner of its not being truthfulness.

However this may be, truthfulness is that which always already occurs. In order that it has a manner of its not being truthfulness, it must not take place. So, truthfulness that is not truthfulness must have a characteristic such as always and already takes place and nevertheless does not take place. Insofar as falsehood takes place together with other sorts of truthfulness under the guise of camouflaged truthfulness, truthfulness is taking place. Moreover, insofar as it is camouflaged truthfulness, truthfulness is not taking place when it exists under the guise of its being in compliance with this camouflage. At a place where truthfulness does not occur at all, even camouflaged truthfulness cannot occur. So that camouflaged truthfulness may occur, that is to say, insofar as truthfulness does not occur, it must be that truthfulness is occurring. This is exactly how truthfulness does not occur.

This matter will be understood much more clearly, when we shed light on the original meaning of the fact that truthfulness occurs. This original meaning consisted of the spatio-temporal movement of *ningen sonzai*. While disrupting into countless oppositions between self and other, at the same time, *ningen* comes back to itself in a nondualistic manner. In this coming back movement, truthfulness takes place. Insofar as *ningen sonazi* is *ningen sonzai*, this movement cannot come to a halt. In other words, there is no state of affairs in which truthfulness does not occur.

What is more, in the midst of this coming back movement, that is, at a place where truthfulness occurs, this coming back movement comes to a halt and truthfulness is prevented from occurring. This halt occurs at some place and on some occasion in the countless oppositions between self and other. Such phrases as *at some place* and *on some occasion* not only refer to a determined standpoint of an individual but also to activities of an individual on a specific occasion.

Nobody can remain a mere individual on all occasions and can always practice only falsehood on all of these occasions. Even the most cunning deceiver has a part of him in which he moves with sincerity. This can be said still more of ordinary people. While always behaving honestly in the multidirectional interconnections of acts, they may fall victim to falsehood in one direction and on some occasion. While being an honest parent or an honest friend, one may well be an official who nonetheless misleads the state. While being a politician who devotes his life to the well-being of the public, one may be a dishonest husband or a dishonest friend. It is always at some place and on some occasion in the complex and inexhaustive interconnections of acts that truthfulness does not occur in *ningen sonzai*. However countless these places and occasions may be, they cannot arise except that truthfulness nevertheless takes place at bottom.

The coming back movement comes to a halt not only in a place within the standpoint of an individual, but also within the standpoint of the whole, that is to say, within a society in such a way that it becomes stiffened to traditional formalism to the extent that it imposes a strict restraint on an individual's self-awareness. In such a society, however, the need for restraint indicates that behind it is the self-awareness of an individual on the move. That traditional customs may be maintained requires that individuals who are capable of feeling these customs as oppressive have already arisen. And that these individuals have already arisen indicates at the same time that one can revolt against these customs. Even though all the revolts are crushed, through heavily controlled restraints, the strength of this oppressive force simply reflects the energy and strength involved in individual self-awareness.

We can say that, even when the coming back movement comes to a halt within the standpoint of the whole, truthfulness is occurring at bottom. Otherwise, individuals would simply be subjected to the whole as if they were cells of an organism or cogwheels of a machine. In this case, no restraint would be required nor would customs themselves bear the significance of control. This would mean that customs had perished. Then, what is here at stake is *ningen sonzai*. In other words, at a place where truthfulness does not occur at all, *ningen sonzai* perishes.

In the field where truthfulness is occurring, truthfulness does not actually occur. That is to say, the field where truthfulness does not occur is a limited place and a limited occasion. This can be adequately grasped only by recourse to the spatio-temporal structure of *ningen sonzai*.

At the end of Part II, I mentioned a standing still in the movement of negation. But now, in this section, the issue of this standing still has been described in more detail. In Part II, it was argued that this standing still was a one-sided fixation of good and evil, preventing good and evil from being transformed into each other. This fixation gives rise to evil. This has just now been disclosed as falsehood. That is to say, the fixation of evil, radical evil, consists precisely in preventing the truthfulness of *ningen sonzai* from occurring. Contrariwise, we are also able to clarify the reason why the truthfulness of *ningen* has been expounded from ancient times as the most important path taken by *ningen*.

The Greeks as well as Indians came to grips with the occurrence of truthfulness in the form of the realization of contemplative truth. The Hebrews comprehended this occurrence as the realization of God's commands in their obedience relationship to a personal God. The Chinese understood it as the realization of the path of Heaven, through which human activities put into practice the law that permeates all things. The Japanese seem to have grasped the same truthfulness of *ningen* in the form of the "self"-less pure and transparent mind. An innocent, "genuine mind" devotes itself with a pure and simple heart to the whole. It is also "truthfulness" through which one immerses oneself in the socio-ethical unity with a selfless affection. The concept of *shojiki* ("honesty"), which began to be promulgated by the Oracle of the Ise Shrine at the beginning of the Middle Ages in Japan, also refers to this selfless and transparent attitude of *ningen*. Throughout all, the truthfulness of *ningen* was precisely the authentic path of *ningen*.

14 the good and bad of *ningen:* guilt and conscience

The proposition mentioned in the preceding chapter, that radical evil consists in one's preventing truthfulness from occurring, shows us immediately what goodness is. Goodness consists of the occurence of the truthfulness of *ningen sonzai* and hence those activities of *ningen* performed in compliance with truthfulness.

However, we are now confronted by the question whether this proposition is congruent with the meaning of goodness and badness as clarified in Part II. There, it was pointed out that badness consists of the revolt against *ningen's* ground in the movement of negation and goodness, in the direction of a coming back to the ground. However, the movement by which one comes back to the ground, despite revolting against it, is nonetheless the real feature of *ningen sonzai.* Hence, even in this act of revolting against, the truthfulness of *ningen* occurs. Thus far, this revolting against cannot be. In Part II, it was remarked that badness is transformed into goodness, insofar as the negation of a revolt against constitutes the moment of the negation of negation. However, provided that the revolt against is essentially goodness as the truthfulness of *ningen,* then it does not need to be transformed into goodness yet again.

This issue is tied to the basic difficulty concerning the origin of badness. I think we are able to begin to answer this question as follows. If goodness consists in truthfulness occuring, then any advance whatsoever of the movement of negation in *ningen sonzai* is goodness. Consequently, the individualizing movement in and through the negation of something whole is also goodness. But, from this, the conclusion cannot be directly drawn that revolting against the whole is goodness, because individualization is not yet by itself a revolting against.

It is exactly the phenomenon of trust that brought this to light in the first place. The negation of something whole, that is, the self and other opposed to each other in individualization, are already anticipating the unity of the future in and through this present opposition. We recognized here the basis of trust. For this reason, from the standpoint of trust, there is no individualization that is not pierced through with the movement of coming back. So far, truthfulness is occurring in individualization, and hence, the negation of something whole is also goodness.

However, in some cases individualization loses sight of the movement of coming back that pierces it through and through. This is precisely the phenomenon of revolting against trust itself. In this instance, the revolt against wholeness and, hence, against the ground of trust comes true. Here the movement through which subjects are multiplied and then unified comes to a temporary halt. An individualized agent stops at its own individualization and prevents the coming back movement from occurring. This means that the truthfulness of *ningen sonzai* ceases to occur.

As a result, the proposition that gave occasion to the previous question, that "even on the occasion of revolting against, the truthfulness of *ningen* is occurring," is not in accordance with fact. When revolt arises as revolt, it is not the truthfulness of *ningen*. Thus, the description of goodness and badness offered in Part II is not only not in contradiction to the description offered in terms of trust and truthfulness, but also rather obtains a further detailed determination through the latter. The negation of the whole is goodness when it is pierced through by the movement of coming back but is badness in and by itself. That is to say, even something that is goodness in the incessant process of subjects' multiplication and unification can be badness in and by itself.

We think it possible to advance a step further in clarifying this point in compliance with what has already been said of the phenomenon of trust. Truthfulness occurs in human activities by the way one responds to trust. Therefore, there is no doubt that loyalty, as responding to trust is goodness, as that which lets truthfulness arise most straightforwardly. Loyalty of this sort, however, does not consist of one's subjecting oneself entirely of necessity to others without the possibility of betrayal, as is the case with cells of an organism that are subject to the whole. We do not call our hands and legs loyal because they move just as we please. When some agent that can move of its own accord, apart from, and in opposition to us nevertheless moves as we please, as if it were our own hands and legs, we term this a service *loyal* to us. In other words, when the future unity that pierces through the opposition between self and other is materialized in the present through acts, then truthfulness arises and loyalty is evident.

Perhaps the unity through this opposition cannot occur precisely by reason of its occurring in the future. Nevertheless, that it occurs is rendered possible by negating its possibility of not occurring. Hence, loyalty consists in an agent who has the capacity for betrayal becoming subordinate through the negation of this betrayal. There is no loyalty that does not imply betrayal as a sublimated moment.

By saying this, however, we do not mean that betrayal is goodness in itself. Betrayal is precisely betrayal in that it revolts against trust. Insofar as this is so, it is exactly badness because it prevents truthfulness from occurring. In spite of this, however, loyalty, which involves within itself badness as a sublimated moment, nonetheless, is entirely goodness. It is by no means contaminated with badness. In other words, while including the possibility of betrayal on every occasion, loyalty is, nevertheless, a movement that continues to reject this possibility.

This is not to say that badness is that which renders goodness possible. Clearly, betrayal is certainly badness, but insofar as it is constantly negated, it does not make its appearance as such. This movement of negation is the real feature of *ningen sonzai.* Only when the movement of negation comes to a halt does betrayal makes its appearance as such. That is to say, at the very ground where truthfulness is occurring, the fact "that truthfulness does not occur" arises as its temporary stop. Just as falsehood is possible only on the ground of truthfulness, so betrayal is rendered on the ground of trust, and badness, only on the ground of goodness. As Gogarten remarks, badness consists in the fact that goodness does not occur.

If goodness and badness are understood against the background of the trust relationship, then the various ways in which one responds to trust or betrays it vary as trust relationships differ, in all their various degrees and extents. Therefore, there is no choice but to argue that the question of what kind of act is good and what kind is bad varies accordingly as well. In a trust relationship in which only a self-sacrificial attitude is anticipated, trivial "privacy" bears the significance of betrayal. But this is entirely out of the question, so far as other trust relationships are concerned, in which only the assurance of the keeping of contracts is expected. Therefore, to separate acts from a concrete trust relationship, and to pinpoint goodness or badness only by means of external prescription is merely a pharisaic fixation. If we understand acts from inside their respective trust relationships, then, however specific that relationship may be, there is no difference with respect to the principle that an act which responds to trust is good and an act which revolts against it is bad.

We have been led to the simple proposition that one's responding to trust and rendering truthfulness capable of arising is goodness and that one's preventing it from occurring and rendering falsehood capable of appearing is badness. Is this view in accordance with the traditional conceptions of goodness and badness?

When the issue of goodness and badness is discussed in books concerned with ethics in contemporary Japan, time and again, writers define *goodness* as "something useful for achieving a specific purpose" or "something judged to be of value because it satisfies a desire." However, I do not think that the Japanese word *zen* ("goodness") is ordinarily used in this way. What those writers wish to advocate is a meaning for words such as *good, Gut, Agathon, Bonum*, which are almost equivalent to what the Japanese word *yoshi* (which means "to be good" and, at the same time, "approvable" in Japanese) signifies. *Yoki* food, *yoki* clothing, a *yoki* house, a *yoki* carpenter, *yoki* talent, *yoki* courage, and so forth are regarded as *yoshi* on the ground that they are all of use for a specific purpose and satisfy a specific desire.

However, we cannot correctly employ the word *zen* for either of these usages. *Yoki* food, *yoki* clothing, and so forth are meant to be food that tastes good and beautiful clothing, but we do not say that they are "good" food or "good" clothing. A *yoki* carpenter is a carpenter whose technique is excellent, but he is not necessarily a "good" carpenter. On the contrary, a "good" carpenter can be a carpenter whose technique is quite poor.

Therefore, the word *good* is applied to the case chosen from phenomena generally designated as *yoshi*; that is, as that which is *yoki* in the specifically moral sense of the term. Hence, when we take into account the concept of *zen*, it can be said that we have already forsaken the ethics of "*yoki* things," which is, the standpoint of *Güterethik*.

From among that which is usually called good, Kant went on to exclude good things such as a good mind, or a good capacity of judgment, good courage, or something good such as power, wealth, honor, or health, and he eventually came to accept *good will* alone as truly morally good. All the items excluded here are unlikely to be called *good*. Things such as power, wealth, honor, or health were once called *happiness* or *virtue*, but they have never been called *zen*. If we use the concept of *zen*, then Kant's care in selection becomes quite unnecessary.

Originally, *zen* was used in the same sense that such phrases as *zen nin* ("good person"), *zen ko* ("a good act"), *zen i* ("a good will") were used. This point is particularly noticeable in Japanese ethical writings. The term *Güterethik* should be translated into Japanese as "*zen* ethics," whose theme centers around the issue of "what goodness is like." Nevertheless, nobody has used the term *zen ethics* as a translation of *Güterethik*. The reason for this lies in the historical background, which reveals that the concept of *zen* in Japan is not inclusive of "happiness" or "virtue" and hence is not equivalent to "happiness."

In view of Buddhist phrases such as *good cause results in good effect*, we can say that, in the Buddhist view of the cause and effect relation, happiness, which is an effect of a good deed seems to be called *good*. Hence, within Buddhism, memorial services performed as useful for the realization of happiness after death are called *good*. But this Buddhist usage did not enter into the concept of *zen*, which is used to refer to socio-ethical relationships. Insofar as human life on earth is concerned, happiness is not goodness. Goodness is spoken of only with respect to human beings and their acts.

Then how do we judge the goodness and badness of an act? *Yosa* ("the excellence") of a *yoki* carpenter is evaluated by how well his techniques conform to the purpose of construction. Was the goodness of a good act evaluated in the same way, by how well this act conforms to the purpose of attaining happiness? This is not what history exhibits. In older society, the manner of action is, in general, prescribed by the somewhat imperative form. And this imperative had absolutely no regard for happiness. The goodness or badness of an act is determined with this imperative as the standard. How was such an authoritative imperative possible? Calculation for achieving happiness cannot possess such authority. Thus it is that the basic principle of *ningen sonzai* continues to hold sway here.

The Ten Commandments of Christianity and the Five Commandments of Buddhism are the most widely prevalent authoritative imperatives. They share the following four imperatives: do not kill, do not commit adultery, do not steal, and do not deceive. They have not lost their validity even today. Why does such an extensive convergence exist? It is because these imperatives prohibit the betrayal of a human being. As was previously discussed with regard to the "voice that cries for help," the trust one person bears for another constitutes the basis of *ningen sonzai.* Homicide revolts most conspicuously against this and fundamentally betrays human trust. On the other hand, adultery betrays the trust involved in the relationship between the sexes and hence throws into confusion that socio-ethics inherent in those relations between parents and children, husband and wife, and so forth. This is why adultery, in particular, is termed an *ethical confusion.* Again, as a betrayal of trust of the kind involved in property relationships, a thief destroys the order of *ningen sonzai.* Lies and falsehood consist, as was previously remarked, in preventing truthfulness from occurring. Consequently, these exemplary deeds are evil, just because they revolt against truthfulness and prevent it from occurring. This verdict is reached on the basis of *ningen sonzai* and therefore remains constant, in any time or place.

However, an objection has recently been raised against this viewpoint as follows. According to the history of moral thought, the evaluation of goodness and badness varies with the times, as well with the nation, and never applies universally to human beings. For instance, homicide was frequently regarded as a good deed in some primitive societies. This was not only the case with homicide as revenge. At times, as was the case with human sacrifice, even an act of murder was sanctified as a religious ritual. As a recent example, we are able to refer to a severing of the head from the body, which was prevalent among some natives in Formosa. For them, a murder was not only an act praised by the whole tribe, but was also one through which they expressed sacredness as the object of their beliefs. Not so long ago, warriors in Japan were allowed to kill others to save face. We need not turn our eyes to primitive society alone, therefore.

The prohibition of adultery is also not absolute. Recent studies of ethnology disclose that sanctified adultery in primitive religions is quite a widespread custom. In some undeveloped nations there was a custom of letting a wife of the host enter into the bedroom of a guest, to welcome him. But even here, we need not restrict our attention to primitive society. Even in a country that has the most developed civilization in the contemporary world, nobody is surprised by the fact that a wife may have a sexual relationship with another man with the same sort of freedom that a husband does with another woman.

The same may be said of theft. In Greece, not only did gods commit theft, heroes were nearly always plunderers. These plunderers were justified in depriving other persons of their possessions by means of extraordinary powers and wisdom. Furthermore, if thievery consists of plundering something not given, then an international spy must also be a thief.

Heroes of ancient times also used falsehood habitually. Excellent war lords defeated their enemies by means of falsehood. Even in the contemporary world, there are nations that take lying for granted. What is evil for these nations is rather not being able to tell a lie skillfully. From this viewpoint, it is only vacuous to say that the standard of goodness and badness does not suffer from the vicissitudes of age and place.

Affiliated with the suspicion of traditionally fixed moral thought, the preceding viewpoint seems to be more prevalent than we might suppose. But as Scheler pointed out, this view is based upon a misunderstanding through which we fail to grasp the essence of acts such as homicide, adultery, theft, and lying. We cannot exhaust the essence of homicide by saying that it deprives a person biologically or physiologically understood merely of her life. Rather, it deprives a person who has the capacity for membership in a specific society of all of her existence. In other words, to a partner who stands in a trust relationship with us and who always anticipates help from us when her life is in danger, homicide imparts the imperilment of her life. Therefore, even in a society in which the severing of the head from the body was particularly praised as good, there is no doubt that a person who killed another belonging to the same tribe would be condemned for having committed murder. The severing of the head from the body would be allowable only against those who stand outside of the tribe and outside of its trust relationship. Those who stand outside of the tribe are equivalent to wild animals and are by no means like one's compatriots.

Likewise, in a society in which human sacrifice is regarded as a sacred ritual, the nonritual killing of a member of the tribe is homicide. To approve of revenge means that it is not recognized as homicide, but this does not mean that homicide itself is not approved of. The same can be said of the custom by which the lives of common people were left to the mercy of the *samurai* during the Edo period in Japan.

Therefore, there is no difference to the extent that in no society whatsoever is homicide approved of as good. The difference lies only in the limits within which actions are thought to be instances of homicide. These limits also overlap trust relationships. In the case in which each of two persons anticipates robbing the other of her life, the one is not accused of homicide, even if she actually robbed her partner of her life. This obtains in all societies alike, whether primitive or civilized.

In a society in which revenge is said to be just, there can still be a trust relationship between bitter enemies. Hence, even if one takes vengeance, one is not said to have committed homicide. Likewise, even in the contemporary world, to kill an enemy in war is not considered homicide. But to kill a person who surrenders or is wounded, thereby ceasing to be an enemy, or who cries for help and thereby returns to a standpoint of trust is obviously homicide. A person who commits homicide is put to death as one who has swerved from the trust relationship that the state expresses. Neither is capital punishment homicide.

There is thus an overlap between the extent to which acts of killing are judged to be homicide and the existence of the trust relationship itself. Therefore, for those who try to establish a trust relationship among *all* human beings from the vantage point of universal brotherhood (as in Christianity), cases in which killing another person does not constitute homicide vanish. Consequently, war and the death penalty come to bear the significance of homicide without exception.

Buddhism extends the trust relationship to all living things. If that cow in front of us might have been our parent in a previous life, then to kill and eat that cow is no different from cannibalism. Consequently, in this context all destruction of life is prohibited. In this way, the extent of homicide varies accordingly as the trust relation is defined more widely or more narrowly. But there is no difference between any perspective in one respect: homicide itself is badness.

The same can be said of adultery. The essence of adultery does not consist in some definite physical or physiological motion but rather in the betrayal of trust inherent in the relationship between the sexes. Let us provisionally suppose that disordered sexual intercourse occurred in primitive society, but if men and women in that society did not look forward respectively to remaining faithful to only one person, then to have sexual intercourse with many persons is not adultery. However, even in such a society, an extremely strict order exists with respect to marriage. One can choose one's mate simply as one pleases. Therefore, men and women reciprocally trust that their mate does not engage in sexual intercourse with others, except within an already defined context. Adultery in primitive societies is a betrayal of this trust, and hence, the revolt against the prescribed sexual order is quite severely punished. The difference, in accordance with times or races, is concerned with the problem of how the reciprocal relationship of trust is established, but not with whether adultery itself is approved of as good or disapproved of as bad. Even though sexual relations are extremely confused in contemporary civilized societies, it is not that adultery itself is appraised as good. In this way, there is no difference in any sexual mores with regard to the fact that adultery is bad.

The same can be said of theft. The essence of theft does not consist merely in robbing another person of her possessions, but rather in betraying the trust inherent in specific relations of property. Robbing the weak of their possessions was not theft in a society in which plunder by the strong is considered righteous. The reason is that the weak did not bear trust for the strong nor were they convinced that the latter would not plunder. However, if one of the plunderers takes her booty as something private, she will obviously be expelled as a thief. As is depicted at the beginning of the *Iliad,* plunderers do expect a fair distribution of the booty among themselves, however. Where this trust is betrayed, theft arises. Therefore, even in an age in which plunder was justified, theft itself was never thought to be good. The difference in accordance with times and races is concerned only with the problem in which relations of property reciprocal trust has established.

Finally, deceit has its essence in that it is a betrayal of trust and prevents truthfulness from occurring, as already remarked on with regard to falsehood. Hence, to deceive a person who stands outside of the alleged trust relationship does not bear witness to falsehood nor tell a lie. To deceive enemies in war is "strategy," not deceit. But for one to deceive friends invites extreme hatred against oneself as a betrayal. In any society whatsoever, deceit as a betrayal of trust has never been approved of as good. Certainly, some races take lying for granted, having no doubts about its appropriateness. In the relationships by which people have reciprocal understanding that they are lying to each other, no lie can possess the meaning of betrayal. That is to say, such people are not deceived by a lie, and hence, deceit itself cannot arise.

Thus the view that the standard of goodness and badness differs in accordance with time and place is obviously false. What differs here has something to do with the extent of the trust relationship and the manner of its expression, not with the principle according to which a response to trust is good and a betrayal of trust bad. This principle has not been subject to any change throughout all societies, ranging from the most primitive to the most civilized.

However, our previous referral to those commandments prevalent in Christianity and Buddhism might lead to another strong objection. For, according to Nietzsche in his theory of ressentiment, those called *priests* and *monks* were the very persons who had turned the authentic values of goodness and badness upside down and the Ten Commandments and the Five Commandments were just a monument to this morality of ressentiment. However, we must ask whether this genealogy of morals was correct in its understanding of the history of morality? According to Nietzsche, in an authentic and healthy human life, the strong, the rich, and the noble were good, whereas the poor, the deprived, and the depressed lived bad lives. All that the weak did was give praise, have respect, and offer their services to the strong. However, among the weak, genuine knowledge about the order of values had diminished. As a result, they had not only become reluctant to offer their services to the noble but also had a tendency to become envious of, hate, and to seek revenge on the noble. This was ressentiment.

The weak tried to locate themselves above the strong by approving of their own weakness, poorness, and depression as good and by disapproving of strength, wealth, and nobility as bad. Here arose the inverted order of values, to the establishment of which priests and monks gave their utmost support and effort. Since then, the morality of love and benevolence began, and the upsurging of strong and healthy life came to be prohibited. So argues Nietzsche.

But I think that he did not do justice to the historical facts. Even though Nietzsche's view validly compares the morality of ancient Greece and that of the Jewish people, it only shows that ancient Greek society was a warrior-oriented society and Jewish society was a particularly religious-oriented one. But this has nothing to do with the genealogy of morality in general. The study of primitive societies reveals not Nietzsche's so-called lord morality but rather the herd morality. And, also, where a warrior-oriented society did arise, even after the morality of benevolence had been fully accepted, a lord morality appeared in pure form. This means that these forms of morality reflect the structure of each society, and that they have no connection with the view that the authentic order of values is either turned upside down or restored. What is more, in the moral thinking that appeared in the Greek epics and tragedies, there is no apparent difference in principle as to whether a response to trust is good or a betrayal of it is bad.

From Nietzsche's perspective, one can say as follows: the phrase *the authentic order of values* is not used historically to refer to a primitive order but rather denotes the order of values based on the will to power as the principle of the universe. This order is decided on the basis of whether the will to power is strong or weak. That moral thinking which made its appearance in history is none other than an interpretation of this authentic order by human beings. The morality of ancient Greece is a correct interpretation based on the social distinction of classes and that of the Jewish people is an inverted interpretation based on ressentiment. Just because the latter morality holds sway over contemporary Europe, it is necessary to explore the genealogy of this morality in particular.

To sum up, the problem for Nietzsche was how to restore the authentic order of values based on the will to power. This order has nothing to do with the so-called trust relationship but rather depends upon the strength of the will of a personality and the richness of a lived life. According to this view, one should tenaciously persevere in one's suffering and tell others not to worry about it, with a smile. In comparison with an attitude that cries out loudly because of suffering and asks for the sympathy and help of others, this attitude is praised for its manliness. That is, it is allegedly a good attitude. Likewise, we respect highly the person of high principles who refuses to succumb, even though tortured almost to death, as well as a person's courage in plunging without hesitation into work that has the likelihood of involving within itself the danger of death. Such a person feels the strength of her own will to be good, but is not said to respond to trust.

These objections seem, at first glance, to be justified. However, they do nothing but evaluate from the perspective of individual consciousness that which occurs inside the trust relationship. The strong/weak distinction of the will to power is concerned through and through with the distinction between strength and weakness, not with that of goodness and badness. Steadfastness of will, if it is spoken of with respect to one person only, is merely a steadfastness of will and has nothing to do with goodness.

For instance, if a person who is wounded while alone in the mountains felt ashamed of crying for help and went to her death while attempting to persevere tenaciously while in great pain, then such tenaciousness is merely surrender. She should rather have cried for help, using whatever means she could.

On the contrary, if a wounded person, while surrounded by doctors, family, and friends, went to her death by tenaciously persevering in suffering and displaying an attitude that does not appeal to others for comfort, then she is to be highly praised for her tenacity. This is because she refuses to have other people share her suffering and assumes an attitude of perseverance in them by herself. This is an attitude parents display in front of their children, at times even dashingly, even though they are ordinarily lacking in the power of will.

Therefore, tenaciously persevering in suffering obtains its value within the framework of some existing trust relationship. We can certainly investigate this attitude by itself alone, by eliminating the trust frame from it. But this does not mean that there is originally no such frame. And needless to say, tenaciously remaining faithful to one's cause such that one does not succumb to torture obtains its value from its being an attitude of responding to trust. Otherwise, it would be only stubbornness. An adventurous attitude would be akin to a violent tiger crossing a river by walking, unless it bore the meaning of responding to trust. The meaning of courage lies in defending with desperate effort one's working and living place. And one's working and living place arises as an expression of trust.

From this we can be sure that the view which maintains that one feels oneself worthy of respect only because of the strength of one's will and the richness of one's life misses the mark. Only when a person who wishes to respond to trust succeeds in doing so by virtue of the strength of will and the richness of life does this strength and richness become valuable. Therefore, when the strength of will and the richness of life become obstacles to the response of trust, they should be abandoned. The reason why tenderness and poverty are praised is attributable to ressentiment, as Nietzsche says.

Therefore, I think that the principle remains unchanged according to which goodness consists in responding to trust and giving occasion to truthfulness, no matter whether we adhere to a morality of tenderness and benevolence or one of strength and conquest. We can test this on various theories of ethics.

As was previously said, the Japanese concept of "goodness" does not involve within itself the meaning of "happiness," as is the case with concepts such as *agathon, bonum, Gut,* or *good.* Consequently, a theory of ethics that deals with "happiness" (i.e., *Güterethik*) is not here at issue. Insofar as ethical "goodness" is under consideration, there is no difference as regards the meaning that it gives occasion to truthfulness, whether goodness is thought to consist in "being in accordance with the moral law" or in "being in obedience to God's commands." In addition, goodness is itself described in various ways. For instance, goodness consists in the "realization of the ego," in one's "complying with the law inherent in the reality of the self," in "free will" itself, or in one's "belonging to the totality or to others." The difference in these descriptions, however, lies only in the manner in which we grasp the real features of *ningen sonzai.* They bear no difference regarding the point that to be in accordance with the real features of *ningen sonzai* and to give occasion to truthfulness is precisely goodness.

If goodness and badness are understood in this way, then the consciousness of badness is precisely a consciousness of betrayal. Granted this, then I think we are now able to approach the issues of guilt and conscience.

We Japanese have quite recently imported the concept of "guilt" from Europe, and no concepts used by our ancestors fit it exactly. Moreover, the word *zaiseki,* which is a Japanese word equivalent to the term *guilt,* does not denote exactly that idea the term *guilt* must indicate. The original word for *guilt* in German is *Schuld,* which means a debt or indebtedness. The term *debt* or *indebtedness* cannot express the consciousness of badness at all, which is apropos of our country. This is why *zaiseki,* which has nothing to do with *debt,* is used as a Japanese equivalent to the term *Schuld.*

But then, why is the term *Schuld,* which signifies debt, capable of denoting the consciousness of badness? To understand this more clearly, I think we must trace its meaning all the way back to the relationship between God and human beings, which the Jewish people took into consideration.

As the names of the Holy Book, the Old Testament and the New Testament, indicate, the relationship between God and human beings consists in the "covenant." God ordered the people of Israel to observe the Ten Commandments through Moses and promised to give them blessing on condition that they do so. Describing these divine laws further and in more detail, He promised that "I shall become the enemy of Thy enemies and the foe of thy foes, if Thou observest all of what I tell thou." A human being can preserve her life only by constantly observing God's commandments. Therefore, if she revolts against God's divine laws by her own will and with a clear conscience, then she cannot expect that her life will be preserved. In spite of this, if she does survive, then her life will be a life for which compensation has not yet been paid, that is to say, a life of indebtedness. This is why the conscious revolt against God can be expressed as an indebtedness. Thus, the attempt to express the idea of guilt by means of the word *debt* can be said to have originated in the genius of the Jewish people, who often display superior talent in economic affairs in particular.

The question now to be asked is whether the phenomenon that the Jewish people recognized as indebtedness exists in Japanese life. The answer is not negative. When we wish to express the awareness of the badness of our acts, we usually say *sumanai* or *sumanakatta.* [These Japanese words mean "to have no excuse for" and, at the same time, "not to have finished doing."] On the other hand, we make use of these same words for expressing our indebtedness. According to a Japanese dictionary called *Daigenkai,* because the term *sumasu* means "to pay a debt" or "to pay one's bill," the term *sumanai,* which is the negative of *sumasu*, means precisely indebtedness. Furthermore, when what should be done is completely achieved, we make use of the term *sunda*. Therefore, we can say that the word *sumanai*, which we quite ordinarily use to express an excuse, indicates something in common with the concept *Schuld*. The genius and acuteness of the Jewish people is that they came to grips with this point.

If the preceding is correct, then when we say the word *sumanai*, do we not signify in some way that we break a covenant agreement? Or does the meaning of indebtedness, or the leaving of a debt unpaid underlie this word? A little analysis of the consciousness of *sumanai* is enough to clarify this question.

The fact that we failed to do something out of weakness of will or cowardice on our part does not, by itself, give rise to the consciousness of *sumanai*. When we inflict pain on another person or give rise to a flaw in another person's existence because of our weakness or cowardice, then we feel that we cannot be excused (i.e., *sumanai*). For instance, to break the prohibition of an alcoholic drink has, by itself, nothing to do with either *sunda* or with *sumanai*. When we inflict pain on our family, cause annoyance to our friends, or leave our vocation unrealized, then there arises a situation in which we feel that we cannot be excused.

If so, then to break the law prohibiting alcoholic drinks is not a breach of contract in the sense that we revolt against the commandments of Gotama Buddha. Instead, one's family, friends, society, and so forth constitute the basis on which something like a breach of contract occurs. But we never make a contract with our family, our friends, our society, and so forth regarding alcoholic drinks. Rather, to inflict pain on one's family because of alcoholic drink is to betray the trust of one's family. That is to say, what is occasioned here is not a breach of contract but rather a betrayal of trust. By virtue of this betrayal, we fail to do for our counterpart what we should have done. Therein lies the lack of payment and so arises the meaning of indebtedness.

Insofar as the awareness of badness consists in the consciousness of a betrayal of trust, there arises the feeling of *sumanai*, which establishes the significance of a debt or guilt. The reason why the revolt against God's commandments came to be grasped as an indebtedness lay in its being a betrayal of trust at bottom. I have already mentioned that four of the Ten Commandments, which have something in common with the Buddhist Five Commandments, are concerned with the prohibition of a betrayal of trust. But there is no difference as regards the fact that even the other commandments also uphold this point.

The commandment to "honor thy father and thy mother" orders us to be faithful to our family. Needless to say, a breach of this commandment is a betrayal of familial trust. The commandment not to covet thy neighbor's house, which orders us not to covet our neighbor's wife, male and female servants, and other properties, prohibits us from betraying the trust relationships in the neighborhood community. As a "jealous God," Yahweh prohibited the Jewish people from all worship other than His own. As a commandment of devotion to the Jewish tribe as a whole, this prohibition discourages them from betraying tribal solidarity. To regard this as God's commandment is the result of a religious expression based on tribal faith and bears the particularly remarkable characteristic of a desertlike primitiveness. Consequently, the *Schuld* that derives from it, that is, the consciousness of guilt, in essence, is the consciousness of betrayal.

However this may be, this matter, although evident to us Japanese, is not necessarily evident to Europeans. People there try to understand it as a revolt against God and His laws, within individual consciousness and the will, instead of understanding it as a betrayal of the trust relationship among human beings. When philosophers come to deal with guilt as understood in this way and grasp it by eliminating God as well as His laws from it, a concept of guilt usually arises that has nothing to do with human relationships.

To take a recent example, let us examine Heidegger's concept of *Schuld*. As already mentioned in Chapter Ten of Part III, he developed what he took to be the significance of *Schuld* (indebtedness) in his fundamental ontology of *Dasein* without having recourse to the trust relationships of human beings. To begin with, he came to grips with the phenomenon of indebtedness and then clarified that it consists of "the ground of a deficiency in another person." By the way, this relationship with another person does not constitute an important element in his ontology of *Dasein*. Therefore, by eliminating the relationship with other persons from the prescription, he leaves intact only "the ground of deficiency." Indebtedness is, in general, the ground of deficiency and hence "of emptiness." Every kind of sin and responsibility is rendered possible on the ground of this basic indebtedness.

However this may be, one finds the ground of this emptiness in the ontological structure of *Dasein*. Emptiness permeates this structure, which is constituted by the three elements, that is, the thrown-forethrowing falling victim to finitude, through and through; and this is so whichever element you may choose. This means that the being of *Dasein* includes within itself death, on every occasion. That *Dasein* as such possesses indebtedness is exhaustively explained by saying that it involves emptiness at the bottom of its being, without reference either to God's laws or to another person.

Even though regarding indebtedness as the ground of emptiness, Heidegger insists that this indebtedness turns out to be the ontological condition through which morality in general is rendered possible. But I do not think that this sort of interpretation truly makes clear the consciousness of *Schuld*. To begin with, one cannot interpret the phenomenon of debt by eliminating one's partner from it. Also, the idea whereby, in general, basic guilt is held to consist of the ground of emptiness is itself dogma. Instead, the ground of every kind of "non," as absolute negativity, must be the basic capability to produce any being, whatever it may be.

In contrast with this concept of guilt that excludes human relationships, Gogarten's ethics tries to expound it completely on the basis of relations with others. In Gogarten's opinion, the issue of ethics is completely concerned with the relationship between one person and another but not with that between a human being and nature. Consequently, the place where goodness occurs is in the betweenness between human beings.

Incidentally, what Gogarten means by *a human being* is not an independent *I*. The manner through which God creates a human being lies in His creating among human beings the same relationship as obtains between God and human beings. That a human being was created by God means that a human being, despite existing in dependence on God, yet exists over against Him. Likewise, a human being, while existing in dependence on her neighbor, yet exists over against the latter. For this reason, God creates human beings as "mutually dependent and mutually opposed beings from the outset." The command to "love God as Thy Lord" and to "love thy neighbor as thou lovest thyself" combine into one. Because love lies in one's existing in dependence on one's partner while also existing over against the latter, there is no difference between the love of God and that of one's neighbor.

In this sense, the essence of *I* lies in our "being on the basis of others" (*Vom-Anderen-her-sein*), and thus *I* is subordinate to others. Hence, when *I* exists within this subordination, goodness arises. Goodness does not consist, as is usually thought, of "doing something good" (*Gutes-tun*) but in "being good." On the other hand, we are likely to revolt against others. By saying this, however, we do not mean that we shed our essence as being subordinate to others. Instead, we subordinate ourselves to others through hatred, distrust, and disobedience.

However, one who was aware of this subordination would not revolt against others. Revolt arises in one's refusing one's own essence, with the consciousness that, although being essentially subordinate to others, one is yet not subordinate, but instead belongs to oneself. This conceals the subordination of others and covers over goodness. This is "badness."

This is exactly where guilt makes its appearance. Guilt, that is, indebtedness, lies in one's subordination to others in the form of disobedience. This will become clear if one keeps one's eye on the double sense of the concept of "indebtedness." The first sense is in that which *I* owes to others (for instance, money) or which originally belonged to others. If this were not so and these things originally belonged to *I*, then even this time *I* could not be said to be indebted to others. Second, unless it came to belong to *I*, then *I* could not be said to be indebted. Because *I* takes something from the other and transforms it into *I*'s possession, *I* is indebted to the other. That is to say, indebtedness arises when something is not *I*'s possession but the other's, while it is at the same time not the other's possession but in *I*'s.

Incidentally, that for which *I* is indebted to others, in the case of my subordination to others, is not things but *I* itself. Therefore, in obedient subordination, we know that *I*'s self is not originally *I*'s possession but belongs to others. Thus far, the consciousness of indebtedness has not arisen. On the contrary, in disobedient subordination, we insist that the self belongs not to others but to *I*. However, the self of this *I* is not originally *I*'s possession. Consequently, *I* can no more be the self in front of the self than it can be in front of the other. *I* cannot live any longer. Self-loss of this sort is indebtedness; that is, the real feature of guilt. The knowledge of guilt forces us, too, to realize the emptiness of our selves.

It is clear, therefore, that Gogarten tries, in the final analysis, to expound the same view that Heidegger himself expounded. At first sight, it seems that Gogarten expounded guilt on the basis of human relations. But in reality, he developed it on the basis of the relationship between God and human beings. God, who is excluded from Heidegger's argument, appears here under the guise of the other. Disobedient subordination is indebtedness or guilt, because it is a disobedient subordination to God. This is exactly the sort of thinking in which the conscious revolt against God was expressed in terms of indebtedness.

According to my interpretation, Gogarten's thought is said, in the final analysis, to try to grasp the betrayal of trust, but has nothing to do with the emptiness of the self, as in Heidegger. And a glance at the previous description of Gogarten is enough for us to notice that he falls victim to a leap in the development of his argument, whose purpose is to lead to the emptiness of the self. In disobedient subordination, *I* insists that *I* belongs to itself alone, and hence, *I* is the self in front of the self. Just as a debt does not arise if the thing *I* owes to the other is emptiness, so indebtedness does not arise if the self that *I* owes to the other is emptiness. And, what is more, provided that the consciousness of guilt accompanies this selfhood, this is not because *I* realizes the emptiness of its self but because *I* feels hatred, distrust, disobedience and so forth to be a betrayal. If emptiness as the real feature of the self were truly realized, then self-abandonment and the practice of nonduality would immediately be there. That is to say, the practice of benevolence would arise, instead of the consciousness of guilt.

If the consciousness of badness or guilt is expounded in this way as the consciousness of betrayal, then the phenomenon of conscience takes root in this consciousness of betrayal.

In the preceding chapter, we interpreted the "voice of conscience" as a voice of absolute negativity that calls forth an individual to her source. But this voice cannot be heard when an individual occupies a standing-still contemplative viewpoint, without doing anything. For instance, in a state of mind in which one gazes rapturously on a beautiful flower, this sort of call is inaudible.

However, if this attitude of standing still carries the significance of not doing what should be done, that is, if standing still is also an act, then we will often hear this voice call to us. This indicates that the voice of conscience appears in compliance with an act of an individual. That is, it appears while the latter involving in its practical interconnection with other individuals a context that ranges from the past to the future.

Incidentally, the acts of *ningen* consist of letting truthfulness arise in response to trust and covering truthfulness in betrayal. I mentioned earlier that this brings the goodness and badness of the act to consciousness and thus gives occasion for the feeling of guilt. If so, then the reason why the voice calling forth out of the source comes to be heard on these occasions, either as the voice of concrete prohibition or accusation, will be readily understood.

We must clarify this by grasping the phenomenon of conscience just as it is. But because we already call this phenomenon *conscience*, our task is, for the time being, to investigate the meaning of this term and clarify the relation of this investigation to the phenomenon of conscience.

Mo Tse had already used the word *conscience*. But, for him, this word is identified with "the mind of benevolence and righteousness," and it literally meant to be the "good mind" in the same sense as *guter Wille.* It did not necessarily mean or indicate a capacity for distinguishing between right and wrong, or between goodness and badness.

However, in Mo Tse, we additionally find the concept of "good knowledge and good capacity." Through this capacity one already knows without studying and is capable of doing well without learning. And this concept has developed as an important one in the history of Chinese philosophy. Furthermore, in connection with this, the concept of "conscience" seems to have been understood, in Japan, as bearing the sense of mind capable of distinguishing between right and wrong, and goodness and badness, without learning. This tendency has been accelerated increasingly by the fact that the word *ryōshin* was used as the Japanese equivalent to conscience or *Gewissen.* But, I do not mean that the word *ryōshin* was completely deprived of its original conotation, signifying the mind of benevolence and righteousness. Therefore, if it is said that *ryōshin* means, in general, moral consciousness, then there occurs no shift of meaning.

The equivocalness of the word lies rather with the equivalent European words, such as conscience and *Gewissen.* Stoker discusses this equivocalness in detail in a book[1] to which Scheler paid high tribute. According to Stoker, not only do those characteristics peculiar to the phenomenon of conscience cause this equivocalness, this word came to bear a variety of meanings also because of the meaning derived from its etymological source, because of the standpoint of psychological development through which people in general, as well as poets, have used this word in various perverted ways, and finally because people transformed this word mistakenly into logic or forced it into a fixed system within the field of learning.

Etymologically speaking, words such as *Gewissen, conscientia,* or *suneidēsis,* all signify consciousness in the broad sense, a communal knowledge, and thus did not carry a particularly moral meaning. They were later transformed into words whose specific characteristic bore moral meaning. (In the French language, this transformation has not yet occurred completely. Therefore, *la conscience* means "consciousness," and *la conscience morale* means "conscience.")

Thus, those who keep their eye on words such as *Gewissen, conscientia,* and *suneidēsis* and try to give an etymological interpretation of them take notice that these words consist of two parts—that is, *ge-, con-,* and *sun-,* on the one hand, and *wissen, scientia,* and *eidēnai,* on the other—and insist that the essential feature characteristic of these words lies in the latter portion, in "knowledge." But what does the former part, that is, "together with" signify? "Together with" what do we know? Do we "know together with God," "together with other persons," or "together with our self"? About this interpreters are divided.

Yet, on reconsidering the matter, the issue of whether we attribute the source of moral consciousness to "God," to "other persons," or to "the self itself" has no connection with the original etymological meaning of words such as *Gewissen, conscientia,* and so forth. This is because, from an etymological standpoint, these words signified consciousness only in the wide sense of the word and did not bear upon moral meaning.

Likewise, that the latter parts of these words indicate "knowledge" by no means verifies that the essence of moral consciousness consists in "knowledge." When "knowledge" and "together with" have combined to give birth to these words, what is implied is consciousness in general but has nothing to do with moral consciousness in particular. Seen in this light, there is nothing here to explore from an etymological standpoint, except that the words that meant "communal knowledge" have afterward come to indicate "conscience." The word *ryōshin,* which we Japanese use as a word equivalent to conscience, has entirely no connection with the preceding exploration. But I hope I am justified in referring to the same phenomenon by means of the Japanese word *ryōshin,* as with the words *Gewissen* and *conscientia.* The only thing to be noted here is that we can by no means escape the limitation that we are incapable of literally translating *böses Gewissen* as *ashiki ryōshin* (the literal meaning of this phrase is "bad conscience"). Although the phrase *böses Gewissen* refers to "the consciousness of badness" and, hence, to the "torture of conscience," the word *ryōshin* refers to what tortures a person who has performed a bad deed and, hence, to what brings to consciousness badness as badness. These two expressions can be said to point to the same state of affairs but from different directions.

Now, what is the phenomenon called by the name *conscience* like? Conscience is moral consciousness, nay, to take the matter in the narrower sense, it is moral knowledge, even moral impulse instead of knowledge, or moral sentiment instead of either knowledge or impulse. These assertions are not so much an attempt to grasp the phenomenon of conscience as an argument concerning the concept of conscience. Therefore, we must first pay attention to the phenomenon of conscience.

First of all, the phenomenon of conscience is concerned with one's own acts. The distinguishing function of goodness and badness, or right and wrong actions of other people, is moral knowledge or moral sentiment. But we do not call this function *conscience*. For instance, when we get angry at another person's act of betrayal, we do not hear the voice of conscience.

On the contrary, when we commit an act of betrayal, we hear a tormenting voice from out of the depths of ourselves. When we attempt to commit such an act, it is obvious that "our conscience pricks us." The phenomenon we call *conscience* is thus an "accusation" or a "prick" directed to our own acts from inside ourselves. Consequently, it is not only not to be identified with moral consciousness in general, but as that which has to do with an act of our own self, it must accuse and prick us in some manner through which we have practical interconnection with others. If the functions that the self performs have entirely no connection with others (hence, if they are not acts of *ningen*), then the voice of conscience will not be heard in connection with these functions. (As a matter of fact, by saying that our functions have no connection with others, we do not mean that we commit them by ourselves alone and at a place where others are totally out of sight. Even if one robs another person's house in her absence, without being caught sight of by anybody, one commits theft nonetheless. Likewise, the motions we engage in by ourselves alone, stand mostly within those practical interconnections we share with others. The proverb that teaches us to be prudent in our activities when we are alone, refers to the view that conscience holds sway even over acts of a solitary human being.)

Second, "the voice accusing the self of its acts," which is heard from the bottom of the self, unites with the consciousness that the act was bad and, hence, with the consciousness of guilt. Only then does this "accusation" come to have the significance of "the affliction of conscience." If our acts were not brought to consciousness as "badness," then no matter how severely they inflict pain or unhappiness on us, there would not arise "the affliction of conscience." Of course, here we recognize the phenomenon of self-accusation.

For instance, let us suppose that a person who engages in a speculative enterprise suffers a fatal blow at some time due to some small degree of negligence. The person will certainly robustly accuse herself of negligence. But, insofar as this person is not conscious of this speculative enterprise as something bad, the accusation, no matter how severe it may be, does not turn out to be a torture of conscience. As a result, she soon comes to impute the responsibility for damage to destiny. This is because she does not apply the accusation of "badness" to herself. In our daily life, we repeat failures time and again due not only to negligence but also to hastiness of judgment, awkwardness of address, stupidity, misunderstanding, and so forth and thereby suffer from experiences in which regret will not mend matters. But these are not enough to give rise to the affliction of conscience.

However, when these activities do not remain restricted to damage to one's self but give rise to deficiencies of being in another person, then we feel our actions as "inexcusable" and, at the same time, genuinely suffer from the affliction of conscience. This is so even when caused by our negligence or stupidity. Still more, when we deliberately revolt against another person's trust and prevent truthfulness from occurring, the affliction of conscience presses us relentlessly. Its voice accuses us of betrayal from the deep bottom of our being.

Although the affliction of conscience accompanies the awareness of badness inherent in already accomplished acts, there corresponds to this, in the acts which one is doing or is about to do, the phenomenon described by the phrase *my conscience pricks me*. In this case, I prick myself concerning my own acts, and therefore this phenomenon does not arise when there is no awareness of the badness of these acts. The fear that a present act gives rise to some sort of unhappiness or pain or the anxiety that an act one is about to perform will result in such and such a failure are only "worries for the future" and have nothing to do with pricks of conscience per se. Conscience pricks only when these acts constitute a revolt against trust and prevent truthfulness from occurring; that is, when these acts have the intention of betrayal or are carrying out betrayal. Even when no one else can perceive this sort of betrayal, the performer herself is conscious of it. Then it is that her conscience pricks her.

Third, in the phenomenon of conscience, an accuser and the accused stand opposed to one another. The accused is the acting *I*. But the question of what an accuser is cannot be immediately answered. The accuser is thought to be "conscience," in the phrase *the affliction of conscience*. When it is said that the "mind pricks," then the accuser is the "mind." From the standpoint in which the performer is regarded as the empirical ego, the accuser is thought to be "the ideal ego" or "the noumenal ego." But when the voice of conscience is grasped as God's voice or the voice of a demon, then the accuser is thought to be "God" or "demon" as standing opposed to us. Furthermore, an accuser may be "the public," "a church," or "the state."

For instance, instead of saying that the "mind pricks," one might worry about punishment, as described in such phrases as these: *when disclosed, I will be reproached by the public, or I will be excommuni-cated from the church, or I will receive a penalty.*

From this we can conclude that it is not necessarily clear that the accuser is the same *I* as the performer. But no matter exactly who or what the accuser may be, there is no difference in opinion regarding the view that the accusing voice is always heard from the bottom of the self's heart. With this in mind, we looked for the source of the ac-cusing voice in the origin of *ningen sonzai.*

Whether we regard the source as *I,* or God, or society, these are all mere interpretations concerning the origin of *ningen sonzai.* It is common in the philosophical world in particular to regard it as *I.* But an acting *I* is never merely the empirical ego. Kant had already emphati-cally insisted that the subject of an act has another side as well, which is noumenal. Consequently, the voice of the noumenal cannot be the voice of that *I* which stands opposed to an acting *I* but must be a voice heard from the bottom of an acting *I.* We hear this voice calling, through the medium by means of which we are able to approach the noumenal.

Therefore, what we call into question regarding the phenomenon of conscience is not so much the opposition between an accuser and the accused as that between an accusing voice and the accused. Because an accusing voice is heard from the bottom of the accused, only the agent of an act will be able to hear it. She can confront this voice by herself alone, without being interfered with by another person.

Of course, it is possible not to listen to this voice. In the case of one's assuming this attitude in a positive way, one wages war against and offers resistance to this voice. But we cannot do away with this voice as if it were a corporeal enemy. It may seize the opportunity to be heard at any time. One must subordinate this voice within oneself by persuasion or let it sleep. In the former case, we build up theories defending our own acts against the complaint of an accusing voice and search for agreement with a third party by appealing to that third party. Theories whose purpose it is to decrease the authority of conscience were constructed time and again in this way. In the latter case, a method of self-deception is employed, through which a person, even though she does not actually listen to the accusing voice, acts as if she listened to it. For example, Bernard Shaw dramatizes through words placed in Napoleon's mouth that Englishmen are geniuses of such self-deceit.

One may assume a negative attitude in such a way that one wants to listen to an accusing voice but nonetheless cannot stop performing bad acts. St. Paul says in the Christian Bible that "I do not do what I want, but I do the very thing I hate."[2] Here the accusing voice appears under the guise of self-hatred, self-ridicule, shame, and so forth.

In the second case, in which one confronts an accusing voice, we listen to this voice obediently. When we assume this attitude in a positive way, we suffer contentedly from the affliction of conscience, repent for the badness of our acts, and try to compensate for the damage for which we are liable to the greatest extent possible. Or, as our mind pricks us, we immediately bring our present activity to a halt and cease doing what we want to do. In these cases, there is a heartful respect for the accusing voice, by listening to which we also come to respect ourselves.

But a listening attitude also makes its appearance in a negative way as well. Even though we do not desire to listen to an accusing voice wholeheartedly, we nonetheless obey it due to a kind of timidity. In such a case, we fall victim to self-ridicule. When we refrain from doing an act because our mind pricks us, we hear a condemning voice to the effect that "you cannot do such a thing; what a coward you are!" This self-condemnation and resistance toward the accusing voice are two sides of the same coin.

Incidentally, an accusing voice accuses and pricks betrayal. Hence, to oppose this voice is to approve of betrayal and to listen to it restores trust. The former consists in fixating the direction of revolt against the source and the latter, in moving back to the source. Therefore, the difference of attitude toward an accusing voice depends, in the final analysis, on whether or not we listen to the voice that calls to us out of the source.

If we suppose that behind an accusing voice are specific accusing agents, for instance God, the church, the state, the public, or some specific individual, then an accusing voice, even though heard from the bottom of our heart, is felt as if it were an overwhelming power from the outside. Consequently, opposition to this voice is a defense of the independence and dignity of the self and listening to it transforms the self into a slave. In this case, the authority of conscience falls to the ground.

What emerges next is the endeavor to grasp conscience not as an accusing voice but as the certainty of the independent self. *Gewissen* is *Gewissheit*; that is, the feeling of the self as certain. The awareness that an act of the self is righteous and good arises immediately out of the source of the self.

The preceding conception of conscience cannot be said to be strictly loyal to the phenomenon of conscience. To feel that one "is not ashamed of one's conscience" is to have conviction of the rightness of one's own acts. This means that one's acts are not blameworthy, but does not alter that conscience is an accusing agent through and through. And when it is said that "her work is conscientious," this means that she has no deceptive trick and truly puts into practice the endeavor to be done, but this does not imply that the work is done with confidence. Confidence or approval of one's own acts often results in one's falling victim to a sense of self-sufficiency. To support this self-sufficiency, one will necessarily come to self-deceit.

Contrary to the phrase the "mind pricks," this self-approving attitude of mind is expressed in terms of the Japanese phrase, *ki o ou* ("to be indebted to mind"). An act in which one is indebted to one's mind is usually rather unconscientious because of one's subjective distortion of it.

Hegel deals with this state of affairs in his theory of conscience. According to him, conscience as the certainty of the self, gives too much importance to subjectivity and thus stands as the possibility of badness, on the brink of being transformed into badness. To carry it a step further, it turns out to be hypocrisy to others and self-satisfaction to oneself. This is why authentic conscience was thought by Hegel to be an attitude of mind in which one desires to achieve goodness in accordance with objective prescriptions and specific obligations in one's socioethical relationships. We should remark that this suggests that the phenomena of conscience are to be submitted to reconsideration from a socio-ethical perspective.

If the phenomena of conscience are just what we have thus far found them to be, then they can be fundamentally clarified only on the basis of the spatio-temporal structure of *ningen sonzai. Ningen sonzai* consists of the movement through which human beings come back to the original totality through a disruption into self and other, spatially as well as temporally. Here arose the significance of the act of *ningen* as practical interconnectedness, and it was found to be the reason why the act is a response to trust, a letting of truthfulness occur. When one betrays trust and does damage to truthfulness, the consciousness of badness or of guilt appears, through which a voice calling forth from authenticity is heard.

As was said before, Stoker described conscience in such a way that it is "that through which the badness of an individual is disclosed substantially and innerly." This description deals with one hearing conscience from the bottom of one's heart only through the consciousness of badness and guilt. I am convinced, however, that this point must be taken a step further to refer to the revolt against authenticity in a betrayal of trust, as well as to a voice calling forth to a rebel from authenticity. Only then can we understand the opposition that exists between an accusing voice and an acting *I* and the mysterious authority inherent in that accusing voice.

The standpoint of an acting *I* consists of the disruption of self and other and thus is established in the direction of negating authenticity. Precisely because that authenticity is so negated, it turns out to be a voice calling forth an acting *I*. What is more, just because it is a voice coming from the authentic totality, it has the authority to accuse, overwhelm and awe the self, even though it is heard from the bottom of the self.

It is said that, in the voice of conscience, the authentic self is disclosed. In other words, this voice is a manifestation in the self of authentic totality. It is not the case, however, that the authentic is the "self." Because we grasp authentic totality as God, this voice is attributed to God. The spatio-temporal structure of *ningen sonzai* most clearly discloses the context in which the calling voice comes to be heard as the awareness of the badness of our selves.

In Chapter Ten I made it clear just how intimately Heidegger's interpretation of temporality is connected with indebtedness and the voice of conscience. And in Chapter Eleven, I criticized how mere temporality, which does not comply with spatiality, falls short of an adequate clarification of the phenomena of indebtedness and conscience. However this may be, it is worthy of the attempt to relate the significance of indebtedness and conscience to the temporality of *ningen sonzai*. Temporality is the basic structure of *ningen sonzai*, and the voice of conscience comes to be heard from the source of this *sonzai*. It is certainly a tribute to Heidegger that he grasped conscience in this basic way. But, because his temporality was not linked to spatiality, he could not grasp the structure of *ningen sonzai* except in a one-sided way, and hence, he failed to correctly deal with the significance of conscience. By offsetting this fault, I am convinced that we can advance a step further his endeavor, which tried to investigate conscience in a fundamental way.

Heidegger's endeavor aims at interpreting the phenomenon of conscience as taking root in layers of being much deeper than consciousness. Therefore, it seems to be quite different from traditional endeavors, which consist in solving the issue of conscience only from inside consciousness itself. Even these endeavors include many instances in which we cannot solve the issue of conscience, unless they eventually trace it back to some metaphysical ground of consciousness.

For instance, let us consider the case of Höffding, who tried to build ethics on the basis of empirical psychology and sociology. To investigate conscience, he traced back to the basic structure of consciousness and relied upon the relationship of the genuine ego over against the empirical ego. This genuine ego is, in the final analysis, akin to Kant's concept of the authentic ego or of practical reason.

Yet, even in a standpoint that rejects this tendency deliberately and tries to expound conscience on the basis of experience, problems are only left unsolved. For instance, Bentham explained that conscience arose through punishment. But punishment presupposes the social group that exercises it, and further, that the group exists in the socio-ethical order alone. The problem was only switched to punishment and its socio-ethical ground. And if we pursue these problems, we come upon the question concerning the basic structure of *ningen sonzai.*

When it comes to the latter question, we cannot simply do away with the issue of whether or not conscience precedes punishment. In the developing process of individual consciousness in which a child is trained to listen to the voice of conscience, certainly the parents' punishments give occasion for the emergence of conscience on the part of a child. On the other hand, the parents themselves follow the voice of conscience. To scold a child at random is not enough for conscience to be cultivated. The business of cultivation lies within society itself, which builds up punishments objectively. Society prescribes specific ways of action and imposes punishments on whoever deviates from them.

Incidentally, the ways of action cannot take a definite shape unless individual members listen to the voice of conscience. And apart from specific kinds of action, social punishments could not arise. Seen in this way, the phenomenon of conscience already exists at a place where the socio-ethical order, in whatever form, prevails.

However, we have no intention of continuing to investigate traditional theories of conscience, one after another. There is some reason to attempt to understand conscience as moral consciousness, as moral knowledge, as moral impulse, or as moral sentiment. It is not my intention to entirely deny these attempts. What I wanted to say is only that they cannot solve the phenomenon of conscience in a fundamental way. My view only clarifies the fact that the phenomenon of conscience, which makes its appearance in the form of knowledge, impulse, and sentiment, has its basis in the spatio-temporal structure of *ningen sonzai.*

We cannot exhaust the problems to be solved with regard to the spatio-temporal structure of *ningen sonzai.* Among the issues I set up at the end of Part II, the question of freedom is so important that we cannot overlook it here. Insofar as freedom consists in the freedom of *ningen,* it is not only the movement of negation but must also be a movement that unfolds spatially and temporally. On the other hand, freedom that is regarded somewhat as an emancipation of an individual from the whole is freedom strictly determined by the past bondage from which it is emancipated. The significance of freedom differs, depending on whether this emancipation is from one's family, the church, or the state.

Likewise, the past detachment with which the individual ego is burdened determines the autonomous freedom that arises as the restraint of the total ego over against the individual ego. Hence, freedom of this sort operates in such a way as to build up the socio-ethical relations variously and in accordance with the respective burden. To concretely investigate the issue of freedom in compliance with these various states of affairs, it will be a prerequisite to analyze the structure of solidarity inherent in *ningen sonzai* and come to grips with the genuine meaning of *personality*.

From this standpoint, I think it better to reserve this question for a future part. There, we will see that freedom operates not only to form the various structures of solidarity, but also constitutes the principle of the unifying layers of these forms.

In addition, I think that problems such as justice, benevolence, human love, courage, prudence, and so forth need also to be considered there. Just as Socrates investigated justice as "the virtue of a citizen of the polis," so we think it appropriate to probe into these questions in accordance with the concrete socio-ethical systems. Paul Natorp found in the Kantian principle of humanity the principle of justice and love as well. Consequently, in Natorp, supreme justice was love and supreme love was justice. Justice and love in these senses, in general, belong to *ningen sonzai* and are not confined to an individual structure of solidarity. But I think it possible to comprehend their meaning so much better, if and after we investigate issues ranging from family love or friendship, to their loss.

appendix: correspondence with Yuasa Yasuo[^1]

Desirous of entering into a conversation with Watsuji's most outstanding student, now an eminent philosopher both in Japan and internationally, I sent my *interpretive essay* to him, followed by subsequent inquiries about the role of Shintō in Watsuji's thought and his relationship to Heidegger and European thought. Professor Yuasa replied at length, addressing these matters with insight and wisdom. His replies follow.

Correspondence with Professor Yuasa Yasuo

February 16, 1995

Dear Professor Carter,

I have read your "Introduction to Watsuji Tetsurō's *Rinrigaku.*" Your interpretation and evaluation of Watsuji's ethical system is correct and appropriate. It is certainly true that his concept of *aidagara*, or "betweenness," was influenced by Nishida's concept of *basho* (*zettai-mujun no jiko dōitsu*). However, as LaFleur has said, Watsuji confined Nishida's *basho* solely to the level of our daily experience.

It is my view that the point of departure for Watsuji's philosophical thinking is to be found in his observations regarding the differences between the Eastern and Western, artistic sensibilities. Prior to his employment at Kyoto University where he was in charge of the Ethics Section, he was working at several private universities in Tokyo, and during this time, he was conducting research on aesthetics and theories regarding Japanese culture. Although it had not been his hope to be put in charge of an Ethics Section, he did, upon Nishida's enthusiastic request, move to Kyoto University and shift his focus to the study of ethics. Watsuji's "Theory of Art" (*Geijutsu-ron*), which he wrote during this period, was not published at that time, but it has recently been included in a supplementary volume to the *Watsuji Tetsurō Zenshū* (Collected Works of Watsuji Tetsurō) that I compiled and edited. In his "Theory of Art," Watsuji pays careful attention to the art of China, especially the paintings of the Tang and Sung, and he attempts a comparative analysis of these works and the paintings of the West. According to Watsuji, in comparison with Western paintings, the most outstanding trait to be found in the "sensibility" of these Chinese paintings is the manner in which the natural landscape or scenery is perceived or conveyed.

The last section of *Climate and Culture: a Philosophical Study* (*Fūdo*) is devoted almost entirely to observations regarding artistic and aesthetic theories. (This portion has not been translated into English.) In this section, Watsuji stresses that in the arts there are differences based on "time/temporality" and differences resulting from "place" (region). Watsuji discusses Herder, the "geographical philosopher," as a Western thinker to whom we should pay particular attention. In sum, observations regarding the differences between Western and Eastern artistic sensibilities constituted the earliest point of departure for Watsuji's philosophy.

In comparison to the West, one can see a strong affection for nature in the artistic traditions of the East. *Sumi-e* paintings and landscape work by such artists as Hokusai and Hiroshige serve as examples of this. Although the West began depicting landscapes around the time of Cézanne and the Impressionist movement, this occurred largely under the influence of the *Ukiyoe* paintings. The differences between the Western and Eastern ways of feeling toward nature served as the starting point for Watsuji's thinking.

While Watsuji's sensitivity to art and culture was clearly of an exceptionally high order, it seems to me that he was a man largely incapable of understanding religion. Following the war, he served as a member of the Cultural Properties Protection Committee for Hōryūji, and while in that capacity, he set forth the proposal that all of the temples be placed under the administration of the state. This suggestion met with violent opposition by Hōryūji's monks and as a result of this was dropped. In Watsuji's mind, religion was nothing more than a single aspect of ethnic culture.

As for Watsuji's research into early Buddhism, the section addressing epistemological questions seems to me to be extremely well done. The basis for Watsuji's approach in this section is to be found in Husserl's phenomenology. His interpretation of *engisetsu*, however, is incorrect. The experiential foundation for *engisetsu* is to be found in the meditative practices that strive for Nirvāṇa. This Watsuji ignores.

Concerning Watsuji's relationship to the politics associated with the philosophy of the Kyoto school during the war years, Heisig's approach seems convincing to me. It should be noted that, among those connected to that philosophical circle, Nishida and Watsuji were the most anxious about the future of the Japanese nation.

Directly following Japan's defeat, Watsuji initiated a counter attack in response to the attack launched by the left against the Imperial system in which he strongly urged the Japanese people to support that system. This act is the primary reason why Watsuji came to be seen as a conservative who could not be easily reclaimed by the liberal intellectuals with whom he had been associated. To my mind, Watsuji's basic temperament was that of a moderate liberal. Following the war, at the request of Koisumi Shinzō, then president of Keiō University and educational advisor to the crown prince, he gave lectures for quite a long time to our present emperor, who was then the crown prince, on the historical tradition of both Japanese culture and thought.

Watsuji's reason for defending the Imperial system is to be found in the institution's service as a unifying force between Japan's ethnic culture and its intellectual tradition for the 2,000 years prior to the modern period. In contrast to this, Japan's modern nation-state had been able to keep the Imperial system in its possession for at most the last 150 years. Watsuji was well aware that the Pacific war had been a tragic failure for Japan. Nonetheless, he wanted to protect and preserve the value of Japan's long history and culture.

Some time around 1920, Watsuji became close friends with the famous folklore scholar Yanagita Kunio. Following the First World War, Yanagita served on the United Nations' League of Nations in Geneva. During this time he became familiar with French literature, and he encouraged Watsuji to read Anatole France's novel *Sur La Pierre Blanche*. France was well known for being a pacifist. In this particular novel, is a scene in which a group of French and Italians are discussing the Russo-Japanese War (1904–1905). The focus of their discussion is on whether Japan or Russia will win the war. The reason he gives is that the Asian race lies somewhere between humans and monkeys. In response to this, someone else retorts, "we Westerners say that the modern world is being oppressed by the 'Yellow Peril,' but from the Asian's position, don't you think that they might well be feeling that the modern world is being oppressed by a 'White Peril'?" For many years after this, Watsuji continued to discuss the strong impression he received from this novel.

Modern Japanese liberals have been in great sympathy with the intellectual institutions of democracy and individualism that Japan received from the West. However, they have also felt a deep resentment toward the racial discrimination that the West has held against Asians. For this reason they came to view the Pacific war as a conflict that would free the various Asian people who had been colonized under Western imperialism. In this context they remained silent concerning Japan's control of Korea and China. Though the modern Japanese state was also an imperialist nation like the advanced nations of the West, modern Japanese liberals did not view the war in this context, but rather saw it as an essentially racial conflict fought between the white and colored races.

This approach to an understanding of the Pacific war is in line with the views expressed by Christopher Thorne in his study, *The Issue of War: State, Societies and the Far Eastern Conflict of 1941–1945.*[2] Thorne asserts that the Second World War should not be viewed as a single historical event, but that the German conflict, which took place in Europe, and the Japanese war, which took place in the Pacific, were entirely different in terms of their historical significance. These wars are similar in that they both were conducted between imperialist nations, but in the case of the European war, the problems associated with the colonization of various regions throughout the world is ignored. Thorne stresses that the Pacific war was fundamentally a racial conflict between the Japanese and Western imperialism that had been occurring since the nineteenth century and of which England stands as a representative participant. That this system of colonization collapsed in concert with Japan's defeat in the Pacific war seems highly significant for the modern world.

Watsuji's study *Fūdo*, in its initial draft, was entitled "Observations on National Character." This work aimed to provide a comparative analysis on the specific psychological characteristics of ethnic groups from different regions based upon the particular traits of the natural phenomenon in various locals throughout the world. Directly on his return from Europe, Watsuji gave a series of lectures at Kyoto University on what was to be the basic content of this study (I have included the draft in the supplementary volume to the *Collected Works of Watsuji Tetsurō*). He was then beginning to formulate the overall design for his ethical system (*rinrigaku*). *Ningen* and *aidagara* were to be the fundamental principles for that system. Watsuji saw *fūdo* as the arena or place in which those principles were expressed in a concrete fashion. For Watsuji, *fūdo* was naturally the same as "mores" and thus could be considered equal to ethics (*rinri*).

Only a fragment of Watsuji's plan for this ethical system remains
with us today. Within it, however, is a memorandum regarding the
historical position of modern Japan. In this memorandum Watsuji
discusses the Russo-Japanese War and its possible historical
significance in world history from that point onward. During this
period, Watsuji felt great sympathy with Anatole France's pacifism
and wrote a paper critical of Japan's imperialistic stance since the
Russo-Japanese War. Despite this, as the world situation changed in
the years that followed, his thinking did tend to support in certain
fundamental ways the course being taken by Japan. That Watsuji's
ethical system, in its completed state, attributes the ultimate standard
of value to the state is just as Bellah and other American scholars have
pointed out.

Although I do recognize that something is exceptionally
valuable in Watsuji's ethics, I have some doubts about the position he
ascribes to the state. What troubles me is the manner in which the true
nature or essence of religion is included within the general category of
culture and positioned as something subordinate to the state. In
addition, he draws no distinction whatsoever between the state
(*kokka*) and the nation (ethnicity) (*minzoku*). Having said this, it
should be noted that the problem of race or ethnicity is something we
are only now starting to become aware of, fifty years after the end of
the Second World War. I wonder whether we have the right to
criticize Watsuji in this regard.

In conclusion, I would like to share an anecdote that I have
heard. This is a story for which there is no clear proof, but it is one
that has been asserted by a number of scholars. The thesis is that the
model for one of the characters in Natsume Sōseki's novel *Kokoro* is
Watsuji Tetsurō. I believe that the narrative of the novel has *Sensei*,
who is modeled after Sōseke himself, turn to the *watakushi* character
(the character referred to as *I*) and confess his past before committing
suicide. What this group of scholars assert is that Watsuji was this *I*
character, the student disciple of the *Sensei*.

It seems to me that, in the plot line of this novel, there are some
places that are somewhat forced. It is said that the idea for *Sensei's*
suicide was suggested to Sōseki by General Nōgi's own ritual suicide,
done to follow the Emperor Meiji to the grave. For the Japanese of
Sōseki's generation, Emperor Meiji was the symbol of Japan itself.
Sōseki must have felt that in the death of Emperor Meiji something of
importance in the Japanese tradition had also died. Sōseki had studied
as an exchange student in England and throughout his life he was
continually conscious of the various contradictions that had been set

in place within modern Japan. In his work the themes he engaged always involved the contradictions between the individual and human relationships (*ningen kankei*). In *Kokoro*, "Sensei" is a person forever plagued by a sense of guilt resulting because, while a young man, he betrayed a close friend and stole from that friend the woman he loved. I wonder if Sōseki, in his novel, is not in fact addressing his own young disciples who loved and respected him, and telling them the story of what Japan lost when the Meiji era came to a close.

Sincerely yours,
Yuasa Yasuo

Regarding the Tradition of Shintō in Japanese Intellectual History and Watsuji's Interpretation of That Tradition:

March 20, 1995

1.) The earliest beginnings of Shintō are to be found in the various beliefs of the Japanese people during the mythological or archaic age. What is unusual in the case of Japan is that this tradition of mythological beliefs has continued to exist for an exceptionally long period of time. Even after Buddhism had entered the country, such beliefs did not die out. Buddhism began to establish a foothold in Japan in the ninth century with the introduction of Esoteric Buddhism. In Japan, however, Esoteric Buddhism was to take on the form of what is referred to as *Shinbutso Shūgo* (the syncretism of Buddhism and Shintō). Under this formulation, Buddhism developed based largely on a belief in nature worship. This particular manifestation of Buddhism is referred to as *Shūgendō*. This religion requires its practitioners to enter into a mountainous region and conduct there various rituals with the aim of self-cultivation. Folk customs such as those expressed in the *Shūgendō* tradition have exercised a great influence on the Japanese people. Even though Buddhism and Shintō were officially separated at the time of the Meiji restoration, these beliefs remain alive even today. For example, in Japan, exceptionally old shrines are said to possess a history that dates back to the mythological age. At present, in mountainous regions throughout Japan, there stand shrines built on land once considered sacred ground during the mythological age. Up until the Meiji period, the majority of these shrines were connected to Buddhist temples. I think it could be said that, from a psychological point of view, Shintō beliefs, which originated in the mythological age, have become an integral part of the Japanese people's collective unconscious.

Lafcadio Hearn (Kiozumi Yakumo) investigated Japanese folk customs in the Meiji period and came to the conclusion that the foundation of the Japanese people's religious beliefs was to be found in Shintō.

When the anthropologist Lévy-Strauss came to Japan, he conducted research on the folk beliefs of the various artisans residing in a number of fishing and mountain villages. As a result of his work, he concluded that Japan was the last of the highly industrialized societies in which animism continued to have a strong presence. Animism is the belief that views nature or the natural world as replete with the spirits of the gods (*kami-gami*).

2.) One of the outstanding characteristics of Japanese Buddhism is that it is connected with ancestor worship. Buddhism in Southeast Asia, by contrast, has no relation whatsoever to ancestor worship. And in China and Korea, Confucianism has come to bear a connection with ancestor worship. Within Japan, however, from the medieval period on (that is, since the Kamakura period in the thirteenth century) Buddhism developed by focusing primarily on rituals that paid homage to dead ancestors. This folk custom was started in large part by members of the warrior (*Bushi*) class. Although these warriors were followers of both Shintō and Buddhism, they treated their regional or local beliefs with greater importance, and as a result of this, they built a large number of Shintō shrines (one example of this being the Tsurugaoka Hachiman Shrine in Kamakura).

In ancient times, Japanese people believed that the spirits of the dead lived within the mountains. This belief came to be connected with Buddhism and subsequently gave birth to the particular form of Buddhism I have been discussing here, which is grounded in ancestor worship.

3.) In his study of Watsuji Tetsurō, Robert Bellah states that the Japanese Imperial system is a living remnant of a bronze age monarchy. *Bronze age* should be understood as referring to the mythological or archaic age. As Bellah explains it, according to the history of the human race, during ancient times there were a large number of bronze age monarchies throughout the world. With the appearance of the historic type of monarchy, these monarchies were completely destroyed. The monarchies of ancient Egypt, Rome, and China are examples of this historic type. The history of the human race has been constructed by these particular monarchies. In Japan, however, it can be said that not until the modern period did the Japanese people come under the rule of this type of grand monarchy. As a consequence of this, the beliefs associated with a bronze age monarchy remained intact right up until the modern period. The Japanese Imperial system has functioned to convey the traditional set of beliefs associated with the mythological age. I think it can be said that the psychology of the Japanese people's collective unconscious has permitted the Imperial system to continue to exist along side Shintō. It seems to me that Watsuji supported the Imperial system precisely because he saw it as integral to the set of cultural and religious beliefs that the Japanese people had embraced for many centuries.

4.) However, in the research that I have conducted it has become apparent to me that Watsuji's particular interpretation of Shintō does carry with it rather strong political connotations. The tendency to view Shintō primarily from a political point of view began in the Edo period (some time during the eighteenth century) when *Kokugaku* or National Learning scholars like Motoori Norinaga undertook studies related to Japanese antiquity. Watsuji's own understanding of Shintō was influenced by Norinaga's work. National Learning also exerted substantial philosophical influence on the specific theories that the *Bakumatsu* embraced regarding respect for the emperor. Based on such theories, those behind the Meiji Restoration were later able to bring down the Tokugawa Bakufu and reinsert the emperor into the political equation. Japan's modern history begins with this act.

Folklore scholars such as Yanagita Kunio and Origuchi Shinobu did not adopt such a political perspective in their considerations of Shintō. Instead they attached importance to Shintō as a religious practice firmly rooted in the daily customs of the Japanese people. Up until the medieval period (thirteenth–sixteenth centuries), the political aspect of Shintō and the cultural or folk aspect of Shintō were not separated. However, after the warrior class gained exclusive possession of the country's political power during the Edo period and subsequently excluded the emperor from politics, the way of looking at Shintō began to change. (Herman Oomes in his *Tokugawa Ideology* draws attention to Tokugawa Bakufu adopting a policy of linking Shintō to the Bakufū's government. For example, the Toshōgu Shrine in Nikkō was constructed as a place where Tokugawa Ieyasu would be worshipped as one of the gods or *kami* in the Shintō pantheon. We can find no such example during the medieval period.) In short, since the seventeenth century the tendency emerged within Japan to connect Shintō with the political body ruling the country. However, I think we can also say that, despite this, the folk beliefs of the general populace have continued to exist fundamentally unchanged.

I have come to feel that when considering the problem of modern Japanese nationalism, the manner in which one views this particular issue, that is, the relationship between and differentiation of Shintō's political nature and its folk nature, is of critical importance.

Sincerely yours,
Yuasa Yasuo

On Heidegger and Watsuji's Manner of Dealing with European Philosophers

April 1, 1995

Watsuji went to Europe in 1927, when Heidegger's *Sein und Zeit* was published. Watsuji confessed that he got this book in Berlin and read it through. In Germany, he had stayed in Berlin for the most part and seems to have made fewer trips than he was supposed to. It was to Italy that he mainly travelled. The purpose of his Italian travel was to appreciate works of art there.

Watsuji said that he had read Heidegger with great interest, but he seems to have taken a critical view of him, to some extent. Two reasons for this are given. One is concerned with Heidegger's attempt to put emphasis on temporality in conceiving of *Dasein* as being in the world. Watsuji concerns himself with this problem because of his contention that, in an attempt to grasp a human being, one should pay more emphasis to space than to time. To speak the matter more concretely, what is here meant in terms of space is *fūdo* (climate), that is, nature. I think that Watsuji's manner of perceiving things consists in the view that the concern with nature (*fūdo*) is of primary importance for pursuing a human being's mode of being. This may probably be the case with a manner of perceiving things peculiar to Japanese or Asian peoples.

The other objection Watsuji raised against Heidegger has to do with the latter's view on understanding Being (*Seinsverstandniss*) on the level of a human being's everyday life. Heidegger characterizes the being together (*Mitsein*) by means of *das Man* and describes this state in terms of *Verfallen*. Here we can get a glimpse of the influence Kierkegaard exercised on the formation of Heidegger's thought. This is why Heidegger was at that time regarded as an existentialism-oriented thinker. On the other hand, for Watsuji, the being together arising on the scene of everyday life is something connected with the state of his so-called betweenness, which was of great significance for his philosophy.

In his adolescent period, in which he had devoted much of his time to literature, he had favored the study of Nietzsche and Kierkegaard. After turning out to be a philosopher, however, he had almost no sympathy for the existentialist movement. When I was a student, Sartre had been in vogue. But Watsuji had a negative opinion of him.

In my view, Heidegger, in his later stage, seems rather to have been interested in the issues of nature and climate. Therefore, I hold the view that Heidegger's concern with existentialism seems to have been accidentally occasioned by a sort of "journalistic interpretation from the audience."

In my opinion, Watsuji had no sympathy for German idealism such as that expounded by Kant. His favorite European philosophers were, first of all, Herder in Germany and then Vico and Lamprecht. He evaluated Herder highly in his book *Climate and Culture*. This is because Herder pursued the relationship between geography and a human being. So far as history is concerned, Watsuji did not take sides with Hegel, who explored history by means of idealistic logic. Instead, he searched for historical studies. As to Vico, Watsuji once published a short biographical essay about him.

So far as my knowledge extends, his favorite of German philosophers seems to have been Dilthey. In his lectures on the history of Japanese thought, Watsuji referred to Dilthey many times.

The following is one of the episodes I happen to recall. When he was awarded a cultural medal, he had the occasion to explain his own philosophical works to the late emperor of Showa. I once asked him about this episode. He summarized what he had told the emperor as follows: "A philosophical study is in need of both theoretical and historical research. I think that Japanese philosophers have thus far succeeded in bringing about achievements in theoretical research to a great extent, but have failed to give heed to the history of philosophical thought. I devoted my research activities to this field, and regard it as an important aspect of my work at this time."

What he had in mind with the phrase *the history of philosophical thought* is not the philosophy prevalent in the West but rather the history of Japanese thought. I am convinced that he had a pride in being a Japanese philosopher from beginning to end. Ordinary Japanese philosophers are not so much interested in the philosophical tradition of Japan as one might expect them to be, because they are under the overwhelming influence of European philosophy. In this regard, it is probably right to say that Watsuji was a cultural nationalist, so to speak.

Incidentally, when he listened to lectures in philosophy at Berlin University, Wertheimer, a psychologist, took charge of giving those lectures. Watsuji seemed to have taken an interest in this fact. I recall having heard this many times. He said, "Something funny is implied in speaking of a specialist in philosophy, because philosophy consists, originally, in *allgemeine Bildung*."

The idiosyncrasy of Japan concerning the relationship between state and race is well known. More than 1,000 years would pass before Japan was modernized, having had no connection with foreign cultures or races because of the geological condition of being isolated. As I wrote to you the other day, I think it appropriate for Bellah to declare that the Imperial system of Japan is a survival of the monarchy that existed in the bronze age. For this reason, we can go so far as to say that the Japanese people have passed their lives without being able to distinguish between state and race.

Because the term *nation* was derived from historical science, it has nothing to do with the distinction between state and ethnicity. In Japanese, the term *nation* is translated into either *min-zoku* or *kokumin*. But essentially, these two terms are to be distinguished from each other. The term *kokumin* refers to people as members of a political state and, therefore, has nothing to do with race or ethnicity. For this reason, the term *nationalism*, in Japanese, is translated into various words such as *kokkashugi*, *kokuminshugi*, and *minzoku-shugi*. But these Japanese words are slightly different from each other in their connotation.

At any rate, it is obvious that the Japanese people are unable to realize that a state is constituted by a variety of races. As a result, Japanese people have an increasing penchant for confounding ethnic identity with the institutional system of the state.

I completely agree with Professor Reischauer as to why Japan was so smoothly modernized in the nineteenth century. He referred to a similarity between the feudal systems in the West and in Japan and regarded this similarity as the driving force of Japanese modernization. The feudal system in Japan had been held under the sway of *samurai* swordsmen, whereas the feudal systems of China and Korea were entirely different. The ruling class in these latter countries was composed of civilians chosen on the basis of the system of civil service examinations affiliated with Confucianism. They were called *mandarins*, who were recruited from the landlord and merchant groups. On the other hand, most of the *samurai* swordsmen did not own their own lands nor did they have anything to do with merchant activities. In this respect, there seems to have been a big difference between Japan and China, as well as Korea. That is to say, the merchants, the lowest class in Japan at that time, held real economic power in the feudal age. The *samurai* swordsmen, the governing class, were said to be poor from an economic point of view.

As to the feudal system in the West, it can be said that the power of the king was comparatively weak, whereas the nobles (i.e., nobles as similar to the *samurai* swordsmen in that they wore swords) were in possession of lots of land. This is quite similar to the system of *bakufu* in Japan. In other countries in Asia, the ruling class affiliated with the emperor or king was overwhelming in its power and, therefore, was not susceptible to reforms from within. This is the point Professor Reischauer focused on.

The emperor in Japan had no connection with politics for a long time and was associated only with religion, culture, the arts, and so forth. However, in the nineteenth century, the emperor was forced to emerge suddenly to the center of power politics, because of the existing international situation. This was the result of the historical conditions characteristic of Japan. For about 1,000 years, emperors had been agents with nothing to do with military power, but as a result of the Meiji Restoration, which was caused by the *samurai* swordsmen, the emperor was placed in a position about the military. From a historical standpoint, this is a characteristic of Japanese nationalism.

It is now well known, thanks to historical study, that the Emperor Meiji had an extreme distaste for military affairs. As for the Showa emperor, because he was greatly influenced in the formation of his thought by the Meiji emperor, it can be said that he was placed in an extremely contradictory position. In my opinion, the situation with the emperors can be made intelligible in recalling that the traditional Imperial system of Japan originally had nothing to do with the exercise of military power. That the emperor had become the symbol of modern nationalism seems to have been an incident that could be described as an irony of history. I maintain the view that the course of events was a sort of destiny, the result of the rise of the specific relationship between state and race inherent in the history of the Japanese people.

Yours sincerely,
Yuasa Yasuo

interpretive essay: strands of influence

Robert E. Carter

Japan's political and cultural isolationism over a significant part of its history stands in sharp contrast to its remarkable openness to foreign religious, cultural, and philosophical influences. There have been intolerant times, but the Japanese ability to assimilate and transform outside cultural influences is striking. William LaFleur cites Watsuji's *Zoku Nihon seishishi kenkyū* ("Continued Research on Japan's Intellectual History") of 1926, in which Watsuji coined the term *jūsōsei* ("the quality of being stratified or laminated") to graphically indicate that Japanese culture consists of layers of influence from various traditions, "much of it from abroad," which together with Japan's own indigenous culture, shaped Japan.[1] Shintōism, Confucianism, Taoism, Chinese (and Indian) Buddhism, neo-Confucianism, Christianity, and the numerous strands of Western philosophy and culture have all contributed to the Japan of today. LaFleur attributes to Watsuji the view that Buddhism is "the principal cohesive factor in Asian civilization."[2] And there is little doubt that Buddhism occupies a central position in Watsuji's interpretation of the workings of Japanese social and ethical relationships. Yet Shintō and Confucian ideas need to be recognized as important as well. Indeed, Yuasa Yasuo writes of Shintō as having become "an integral part of the Japanese people's collective unconscious."[3]

Shintō is an instinctive stance in Japan, an attitudinal predisposition, unconsciously or nonconsciously ingested in much the same way that language and so many subtle forms of social behavior simply appear, without seemingly having been taught at all. Even though Shintō has no scripture, no creed, and no explicit code of ethics, an implicit code may be extracted from a scrutiny of its encouragement of a "way" of walking in the world. *Michi* is character, or integrity and includes an awareness of one's connection with the All and the sense of flowing in accordance with its development and progress. Also Purity

325

(harai) is achieved symbolically by washing out the mouth and scrubbing one's hands before entering the shrine or its grounds and by salt, which is sprinkled on doorsteps and elsewhere. But an inward purity of the heart is sought, and this is achieved by acting in accordance with several virtues, including *michi*. A third virtue, which Watsuji makes much of, is *makoto* or sincerity. Whether one reads Chinese texts or Japanese texts, Confucianism, Taoism, Chinese Buddhism, or any of the Japanese sources, sincerity is always front and center. Sincerity means that one's words will become deeds, that what one says one will do, that one will put one's money where one's mouth is, and so on. Watsuji writes of *makoto* as being the root of truthfulness, honesty, and trustworthiness, an interactively open attitude of mutual trust on which all other human relationships are based. Sincerity demands one's entire commitment, putting one's heart, mind, soul and body into one's commitment to whatever one does. It is genuine piety, which results from having a sense of the divine and in displaying real benevolence toward children and those one loves, faithfulness toward friends, loyalty toward those to whom one owes or is expected to show loyalty, and love toward one's neighbors.[4] Sincerity is the careful avoidance of error in word or deed and the fastidiousness to keep one's soul unsullied by the grime of selfish desire, hatred, ill will, or materialism. *Makoto* leads to *wa* or group harmony. It implies solidarity, a solidarity of community feeling that manifests itself as peacefulness, good will, and happiness. *Akaki* means cheerfulness of heart and is another virtue, as well as evidence of the presence of *makoto* and *wa*.

More virtues could be listed as integral to the Shintō way, but perhaps enough has been said to suggest that much of what is central to Shintō is also central in Confucianism and much of Buddhism. Whether the virtues were already "Japanese" before the encounter with nonindigenous cultures occurred or whether the virtues were so evident that they easily slipped into a developing Japanese culture is impossible to say. Whatever the case, the Japanese emphasis on shame can be seen to have arisen from the promulgation of virtues such as these. If one falls significantly short of any of these virtuous attitudes or ways of walking with others in the world, one brings *dishonor* to oneself and to one's family and to the groups with which one is associated. Nitobe concluded that "honor is the only tie that binds the Japanese to the ethical world"[5] and is a powerful alternative for the more traditional Western goad of *sin*. One brings shame upon oneself and upon others if one misses the mark and comes up short.

Tradition has it that Confucianism was introduced into Japan from Korea in 404 A.D., but as Warren W. Smith writes, "it remained for about two hundred years after this little more than a name associated with Japanese efforts to learn to read and write Chinese."[6] The key to living and to its obligations, consisted of a right ordering of things under heaven in accordance with the laws of heaven. The goal was an establishing of a harmony, which resulted when the laws above and below bore a one-to-one correspondence. The microcosm of human life perfectly reiterates the macrocosm of heaven. The "five obligations"—between sovereign and minister, father and son, husband and wife, elder brother and younger, and those having to do with friendship—together with the three virtues of wisdom, compassion, and courage were the ideal moral qualities of people.[7] These relational rules and virtues had as their purpose the creation of a social environment in which human beings could interact with a high degree of comfort, encouraging self-development and peaceful social interaction needed for the creation and maintenance of a harmonious society. Emphasis was places on the spirit of respect, reverence, loyalty, sincerity or integrity, and honesty and truthfulness as the virtues of a developed Confucian.

The importance of *li*, or ritual, particularly the *li* of filial piety cannot be overstated. The actions of truly filial sons represent those attitudes and virtues that ought to typify the ideal society: "Ceremonial acts in this connection symbolize desirable behavioral patterns. To respect the old and to honor the dead is to show special concern for the common origin of all."[8] What is more, respect for one's ancestors "brings forth communal identity and social solidarity. Society so conceived is not an adversary system consisting of pressure groups but a fiduciary community based on mutual trust."[9] Mutual trust, social solidarity, the sense of being a member of one large family extending from the humblest peasant to the emperor, on the one hand, and from generations yet to be born through generations of ancestors who have come before, from whose shoulders we stride forth to try our own hand at life, is the ground of that relatedness which comprehends the importance of the interconnectedness of lives. *Ch'eng*, or sincerity, we read in the Chung-yung (*Doctrine of the Mean*), is "the Way of Heaven" itself, for "to think how to be sincere is the Way of man. He who is sincere is one who hits upon what is right without effort and apprehends without thinking."[10] Even though it does refer to one's own integrity or truthfulness with oneself, it also points to Heaven as sincere. Human beings who give expression to their "heavenly" qualities, who have discovered their own authentic humanity have the power to charismatically transform others. We are all potentially authentic persons, but we become distracted by the details of living and the power of our unbridled desires and egoistic yearnings. An encounter with a "sage," however, is irresistible, for it awakens us to what we ought to be like: "its brilliance radiates. As a result, the person who possesses *ch'eng* moves, changes, and transforms others."[11]

When Confucianism came to Japan in 404, it was welcomed rather than resisted. In significant respects, it provided precisely what Shintō lacked: specificity of behavioral pattern in an organized and written form. It was not thought of as a new religion to be taken in but rather was understood to be a systematic account and perhaps a deepening of what was already actively Japanese: a profound belief in the importance of showing respect for one's ancestors, a sense of the vital importance of filial piety, an existing practice of rituals and ceremonies, and a codification of an acute ethical sensitivity.[12] Precisely as Nakamura Hajime argues, Confucianism, as with other foreign cultures was "adopted as a constituent element of the Japanese culture."[13] They adapted from it whatever "value is recognized as a helpful means to Japan's progress."[14] The two virtues the Japanese took to be the most important Confucian virtues were loyalty and filial piety. These are essential virtues of the family and, at the same time, the essential virtues of the political realm. Writes Watsuji, "the virtue that is called filial piety from the aspect of the household becomes loyalty from the standpoint of the state. So filial piety and loyalty are essentially identical, the virtue prescribing the individual in accordance with the interests of the whole."[15] Loyalty was to be shown to one's lord, and eventually to the imperial house, and well as to those with whom one was in one of the various specified relationships. Filial piety is shown foremost through one's reverence and respect toward the imperial family, but insofar as Japan was thought of as one big household or family, then filial piety was to be shown in one's sense of proper relationships. Writes Smith of modern times, "loyalty and filial piety were constantly extolled as basic to family life, harmony in society, and the carrying out of one's duties to the Emperor."[16] Smith quotes the ultranationalist Okawa Shumei, whose history of Japan (published in 1940) urged that Japan was the only country in the world where Confucian doctrines were still alive: "We Japanese first had contact with Chinese thought and culture and we made it our own. . . . These teachings remain alive in Japan, but have died in China . . . Confucianism has raised the level of virtue of the Japanese people."[17] In this century, not only had Confucianism come to be seen as a part of the Japanese mentality, it was even claimed that both loyalty and filial piety were uniquely Japanese virtues and descriptive of the essence of Japan.

This brief sketch of the virtues advanced by Shintō and Confucian thought and practice provides but a glimpse at the background perspective Watsuji attempted to crystallize in his study of Japanese ethics. It is evident that the emphasis is on relationships, and it need hardly be pointed out that, for the Japanese, nothing in life is more important than personal and societal relationships. What Watsuji's study makes evident, with a considerable degree of success, is just how the Japanese have come to envision these relational patterns in their day-to-day living. He has provided a relational map of the proper and harmonious interactions of a people in their everyday lives.

Watsuji and Western Individualism

Watsuji's objection to the ethics of the individual, which he associates with virtually all Western thinkers to some degree, is that it loses touch completely with the vast network of interconnections that serves to make us what we are, as individuals inescapably immersed in the space/time of a world, together with others. Furthermore, without taking into consideration this network of social interconnections, ethics is impossible. Individual persons, if conceived of in isolation from their various social contexts, do not and cannot exist except as abstractions (p. 101). Even a solitary writer (pp. 49–50), writes for a possible audience, although there may be no expectation that what is written will be published. Still, the writing is done as though others were looking over one's shoulder and in a language accessible to others. One does not write in a unique, private language, to ensure that others will never be able to break the code. Writing is communication, if only potentially, and communication requires that there be at least one other, at least implicitly, to whom what is written may be communicated—perhaps one's God or one's dead father or mother. It is theoretically possible, nonetheless, to conjure up a reason for intentionally solitary coded writing—perhaps to remind oneself of one's own history, one's private autobiography that dealt with certain perverse and sordid sexual fantasies, for example. It is more likely, however, that one writes down such reflections and observations as being of possible interest to others at some point or at least to *preserve* them for some vague reason.

Indeed, one's sense of historical connectedness, which involves the lifelong showing of "respect" for one's ancestors, is an essential ingredient in one's own awareness of existence (*sonzai*) as a human being (*ningen*). We may choose not to bring to the surface of consciousness all of those influences that have come to us out of the historical and prehistorical past of our own coming to existence, but they will be present nonetheless. Our way of being in the world is an expression of countless people and countless actions in a particular "climate," which together have shaped us as we are. Respect for one's ancestors is an acceptance of this and an attempt to make our history our own, through a proper awareness of a communal solidarity that extends far beyond our birth and will extend far beyond our physical death. Culture and history continue to play out our actions and our influence long after we are gone. As such, we are already on our way to being the ancestors of generations to come. In Watsuji's words, "it is never inappropriate to grasp *ningen sonzai* as the unified structure of past, present, and future. To put this another way, the structural unity of *ningen sonzai* 'comes to the home ground in the present' " (p. 190). Each of us is, then, the intersection of past and future, in the present "now."

There is no possibility, then, of the isolation of the ego, and yet many write as though there were. They are able to make a case of it, in part, because they ignore the spatiality of *ningen* and focus on *ningen's* temporality. For Watsuji, whereas it is easier to consider a human being as strictly individual when viewed temporally (i.e., through an introspective series that need not involve another, as with Descartes' *cogito*), it is much more difficult to do so when one thinks of an individual spatially. Spatially, we move in a common field, and that field is cultural in that it is criss-crossed by roads and paths and even by forms of communication such as messenger services, postal routes, newspapers, flyers, and broadcasts over great distances, in addition to ordinary polite conversation. Even Robinson Crusoe continued to be culturally connected, continuing to speak an inherited language, and improvising housing, food, and clothing based on past social experience and, no doubt, continuing to hope, however dimly, for rescue at the hands of unknown others!

Thus, the spatiality Watsuji insists upon is a "subjective spatiality," and this subjective spatiality is conceived of as a field or *basho* and is that spatio-temporality of possibility Watsuji termed *betweenness*. He is not concerned merely with physical space, for physical space, too, is an abstraction (by the sciences, for the purposes of science). Real, lived space is both subjective and objective, and in time as well, as a field or place where the various strands of cultural and social interconnection play back and forth. Subjective space is already humanized; that is, it must be understood or grasped from the vantage point of human purposes, as already shaped and defined by one's cultural and social history. Such space is akin to Heidegger's "wood paths," to use an example *not* used by Watsuji, wherein one finds that even the meandering paths of the wood collector, which although leading nowhere at all because that is not their function, nevertheless record the history of the wood collector's journey into the uncharted forest to collect the day's firewood. And firewood represents a socialization built on the discovery of fire in the unhistorical past, the designing and building of fireplaces and stoves, the designing of dwellings that can be heated, a change in indoor clothing from the presumed skins of prehistoric times, and all of the social and cultural changes that permanent dwellings imply, such as a community, a division of labor, stores, roads, manufacturing, and of course that collection of sensitivities which make it possible for people to live together well; namely, morality. All groups have a morality; that is, possess some way of distinguishing between the good and the bad, the social and the antisocial. And even though these sensitivities may differ greatly in content, what Watsuji seeks to explain is what they all share in common as moralities. It is not so much that he is seeking a common set of rules but rather a common outlook on the basis of which all possible ethics is both necessarily and justifiably founded.

What is of particular interest to Western readers is that his assumptions are quite different from those which Western thinkers have more or less taken for granted. That is to say, whereas most ethical theorists in the West have based their pronouncements on the assumption that human beings are, foremost, individuals, who then set about establishing community, Watsuji argues that we are foremost *both* social *and* individual and that ethics is established, in its true sense, as a unity of these two, which leads to an emptiness, a selflessness, a nonduality that expresses itself as benevolence or compassion (p. 226). Let me elaborate.

Double Negation: Individual and Group

One becomes an individual by *negating* the social group or by rebelling against various social expectations or requirements. To be an individual demands that one negate the group. On the other hand, to envision oneself as a member of a group is to negate one's individuality. From the Western perspective, of course, this is an instance of poor logic! One can remain an individual and as such join as many groups as one wishes. Or one can think of oneself as an individual and yet as a parent, a worker, an artist, a theater goer, and so forth. Watsuji understands this, but he argues that it is possible to think in this way only if one has already granted logical priority to the individual *qua* individual. Whatever group one belongs to, one belongs to it as an individual, and this individuality is not quenchable, except through death (Heidegger,

Sartre, de Beauvoir, etc.), by inauthenticity (Heidegger, Sartre, de Beauvoir, etc.), or by bad faith (Sartre). One can reject one's individuality, but even then one denies one's freedom freely, as an individual, if only potentially.

However, Watsuji's conception of the *negation of negation* has another dimension. To extricate ourselves from one or another socio-cultural inheritance, say the acceptance of the Shintō religion, one has to rebel against this socio-cultural form by affirming one's individuality in such a way as to negate its overt influence on oneself. This is to negate an aspect of one's history by affirming one's individuality. But the *second* negation occurs when one becomes a truly ethical human being and one negates one's individual separateness by abandoning one's individual independence from others (p. 134), and from the deeper meaning of a tradition. This is the true meaning of goodness, for Watsuji and I suspect for most Eastern thinkers. True morality is the forgetting of the self, as Dogen urges, which yields a "selfless morality" (p. 225). True *authenticity* is not the asserting of one's individuality, as with the Existentialists, but an annihilation of the self such that one is now identified with others in a nondualistic merging of self and other. Now there is only the authenticity of benevolence or compassion, which is the "authentic countenance" of *ningen* (p. 146). The absolute wholeness of which Watsuji writes consists of the nonduality of the self and other, which he associates with the Zen Buddhist *koan* that asks what one's face or countenance was like even before the birth of one's own parents (p. 187). The answer is that we, and all other things, already were as that faceless, distinctionless, thingless *nothingness* out of which all things as distinct emerge and that is the ground of all distinctions, yet that itself is without distinction. This is our "authentic home ground," but it is a home ground few Western thinkers would be willing to call their own. Why not?

As with Western mystical traditions, the greatest stumbling block to the acceptance of mystical teachings concerns the annihilation of the self or the absorption of the self in the undifferentiated sea of the Absolute, the Ground of Being, or God. The "ultimate ground out of which we come is the ultimate *terminus ad quem* to which we return. . . . The temporal structure of *ningen sonzai* [human existence] is, in the final analysis, the exhibition of this authenticity" (p. 187). Of course, in one's everydayness, one operates and acts in the field of betweenness, where one encounters others. But ethics demands, for Watsuji, that the individual, who has obtained individuality precisely through the negation of community, recognize that independent subsistence is impossible.

Even to negate one's community is to recognize implicitly that other individuals exist, from whom one has distanced oneself (p. 187). Given this standing opposed to others as an individual, there is, nonetheless, recognition that others are also not without connection. In fact, they are individuals in that they are now relative to each other as individuals. This distance is, therefore, "at the same time, a field in which the movement of the connection as well as the unification of subjects, takes place" (p. 187). Thus, as individuals, we also incessantly look for connections between the self and other in the betweenness between us. Why? Because we wish to return to *authenticity*. To look for connection, is to look for one's own absolute wholeness, one's own authenticity in one's home ground (p. 188). Thus, we act as individuals to achieve a greater sense of community, if we are truly moral, and out of this develops our true authenticity. Our true authenticity is "the ground out of which" we have "come forth" (p. 188), and to which we may return, ethically speaking. All truly ethical actions are attempts to return to one's home ground; and this is the second negation, the negation of self as individual.

For Watsuji, the individual is always already socially immersed, and so it is inconceivable that an individual decides whether or not to join a group. One can decide to join a specific group, of course, but one is already historically connected with one's ancestors (pp. 88–89), with a common language, with a common network of transportation and communication, with common residential and workplace architecture and supporting services, with common culinary tastes, with a common family and community structure, and with a common morality that makes possible the distinction between goodness and badness in such a way as to make group existence both possible and pleasant. To deny such interconnection makes about as much sense as to deny that, as ethical beings, we have bodies with which to act in morally acceptable or unacceptable ways. In fact, the denial of spatiality and the dominance of temporality in ethical analysis is tantamount to just such a denial. Although thoughts may be temporal alone, actions are necessarily spatial and usually involve others.

Encounter with Heidegger and Phenomenology

What Watsuji wrote about climate in his 1943 Preface to *Climate and Culture*, applies as well to his approach to ethics: when we consider the relationship between the natural and human "climate," on the one hand, and actual human life, on the other, "the latter is already objectified, with the result that we find ourselves examining the relation between object and object, and there is no link with subjective human existence."[18] Instead, Watsuji announces that it is his purpose to treat the phenomena of climate as expressions of subjective human existence. Having been exposed to Heidegger, Husserl, and others in the increasingly influential phenomenological movement, Watsuji interpreted the central notion of *intentionality* as supportive of Japanese approaches to the understanding of the flow of lived life. Intentionality is that doctrine which maintains that all human experience is experience *of* something. All experience *intends* some object. One may intend a unicorn as an imaginative object, Napoleon as an historical object, an electron as a scientific object, and sexual pleasure as an object of lived experience. But even though many kinds of claims are made about the existential status of an object of consciousness, all objects are objects for and *in* some consciousness (for some subject). No one is ever aware of anything that is not *in* consciousness, and therefore, all objectivity is objectivity *for* some consciousness (subjectivity). If taken in this way, then all possible claims about the real world, necessarily involve human consciousness. But they are not merely subjective. One encounters, in the intentionality of experience, a real, "objective" world as well, and it is peopled by *others*.

The scientific and perhaps the typically Western understanding of *objectivity* is a *dualistic* separation of object from subject. Objectivity demands that we eliminate subjectivity, and to be objective for a Westerner is to let the external facts speak for themselves. Although the West has occasioned an eclipse of the self, the East, and Japan in particular, has kept alive the seeds that may help to provide a rebirth of the self. Ironically, the understanding of the self in much Eastern thought culminates in a forgetting of the self, with a resultant "selflessness" that seems to contradict the possibility of a rebirth. Yet, the loss of the self is, in fact, a gaining of a new sense of self as related. When we truly love another, we step outside of ourselves, so to speak, and in some sense, metaphorical or real, we merge with the beloved person. We speak of losing ourselves in nature, as when D. T. Suzuki urges that "the real flower is enjoyed only when the poet-artist lives with it, in it; and when even a sense of identity is no longer here."[19] This results in an opening of self to a sense of relatedness—intimate relatedness—with a greater whole, whether it be that of people in love or that of family, group, nation, or even some sense of cosmic consciousness. In any case, what arises is quite a different sense of self, that of the self as expanded and in a considerably wider relationship. This awareness of the importance of relationship characterizes Watsuji's philosophy.

Relationship is ever present, linking subjectivity and objectivity, individual and social, nature and self, and even time and space. Watsuji was among the very first to read Heidegger's *Zein und Seit* in 1927, just as it reached the booksellers during his sojourn in Europe. He was impressed by the book, but surprised that Heidegger's emphasis was on the *temporality* of human existence, with less emphasis on *spatiality*. Coupled with this emphasis on temporality was an exaggerated and one-sided emphasis on individuality and individual moral conscious- ness, and a blindness to the importance of social relationships. Watsuji notes that, ever since Descartes and probably as far back in Western foundational history as we could go, a priority was given to the mind over the body. The mind, as Descartes made utterly "clear and distinct," was absolutely never extended in space and therefore absolutely never a spatial thing. It is a thinking thing and only extended things are in space, and these absolutely never think. Thus, the dualism of mind and body readily leads to the dualistic exclusion of time and space. It is less easy to see how social relationship is more spatial and less temporal, nor is it clear how individualism is more temporal and less spatial, al- though it is obvious that the act of contemplating one's relationship with one's God in much of Christianity is a solitary act. In this contempla- tion time is important, but one's spatiality is relatively insignificant. Social acts, by contrast, require some place and some physical struc- ture: families live in homes, organizations have buildings or factories, nation-states occupy territory, and one's relationship with the environ- ment is global. What Watsuji tries to show is that even the acts per- formed by an individual are drenched in social relations of various sorts. As individuals, we pray to our God, whose conception is itself a socio-cultural phenomenon, as is the language we use. When we walk alone, we walk on roads and paths carved by generations of others, and our purpose in walking is inevitably socially linked in some way with others. Communication in any form is a network of social relationships. Transportation in any form relies on a network of social relationships. Thus, individuality is an abstraction, and a misleading one at that.

The "later" Heidegger, particularly his emphasis on the "thrownness" (*Geworfenheit*) of life, Yuasa writes of as "the self . . . *thrown* into the world-space."[20] Indeed, the "turn," which refers to the transition from earlier to later forms of theorizing for Heidegger, Yuasa refers to as "a turn from temporal life to spatial life."[21] But even though one might argue that the later Heidegger was already implicit in the earlier, *Being and Time* nonetheless had a very different agenda from that of reconnecting the spatial with the temporal, and the individual with the social. Watsuji's "difference" was not only cross-culturally significant, but it also helped him to formulate what was distinctive about Japanese ethics. The Japanese were ethical in a cultural and geographical context, already interconnected in many ways in a spatial *betweenness* already etched by the lives and footprints of generations past and anticipating those who would follow in the future.

Climate, Culture and *Ningen*

In his discussion of climate in *Climate and Culture*, Watsuji understood climate to be a geographical/cultural/social clustering of attitudes and expectations that relate to a specific region of the earth, populated by a particular people who share a great deal in common. If properly understood, climate in this broad sense "does not exist apart from history, nor history apart from climate."[22] Climate is correspondent with spaciality, whereas history is correspondent with temporality. Climate and human social history are mutually determining. They form one of the many identities of self-contradiction that abound in the work of Watsuji. The notion of self-contradictory identity he borrowed from Nishida, and we shall examine this remarkable notion in more detail shortly. First, however, it is necessary to begin at the beginning, to explore Watsuji's claim that human being is itself an identity of self-contradiction: "it is in climate that man apprehends himself. The activity of man's self-apprehension, man, that is, in his dual character of individual and social being, is at the same time of a historical nature."[23] *Human being* is both a product of the environment and a shaper of that environment. We are individuals, and yet we are in society. As Furukawa deftly writes, "Man [human being] here means not a mere individual, nor mere society, but Man [human being] as an entity dialectically synthesizing the Individual and the World."[24] Thus, it is our nature to be environmentally conditioned and yet to condition our environment to be individuals and yet to be members of many groups. To the extent that we are environmentally conditioned, we are not shapers of our environment. To the extent that we are shapers of our environment, we are not environmentally conditioned. Although the affirmation of the one is a denial of the other, the one cannot exist apart from the other. This is exactly what Nishida (see p. 338) speaks of in terms of the identity of self-contradiction. Hence, to look from either side of this contradictory/identity, the affirmation of the one is a denial of the other. Similarly, to the extent that we are individuals, we are not (merely) determined by our social relationships. To the extent that we are socially related, we are not (merely) individuals. Again, to look from either side of this contradictory/identity, the affirmation of the one is a denial of the other. The *identity* of self-contradiction, however, demands that we look at both sides at once, or at least that we remember that one side implies the existence of the other and vice versa. And the great advantage of this both-sided requirement is that we are alerted to the dynamic interaction between the two. It is not that we are statically both individual and social but that we temper our social interconnections by reaffirming our individuality and we temper our excessive individuality by reaffirming our social interconnectedness. There is a give and take, a flowing from one to the other, a rebalancing of our *dual* nature.

The Japanese word for the sense of human being that Watsuji discusses is *ningen*. *Ningen* is usually translated as "human being," "man," or "person." It is composed of two characters, the first, *nin*, meaning "human being" or "person", and the second, *gen*, meaning "space" or "between", as in the betweenness between human beings. Watsuji makes much of this notion of "betweenness", and he uses the term *aidagara*, which refers to the space or place in which people are located, to make this "trace" ingredient in *ningen* even more explicit. Yuasa Yasuo observes that "this betweenness consists of the various human relationships of our life-world. To put it simply, it is the network which provides humanity with a social meaning, for example, one's being an inhabitant of this or that town or a member of a certain business firm. To live as a person means, in this instance, to exist in such betweenness."[25] Watsuji's philosophical etymology makes abundantly clear that "human being" in Japanese refers to a dual nature: we are individuals and we have individual personalities and unique histories, *and yet*, we are inextricably connected to many, relationally, for we exist communally. We cannot be separated from social relationships except for the one-sided purposes of abstract thinking, for as individuals we use a common language, walk along common paths and roads, eat food grown and prepared by others, and so on. We are private and public beings at the same time. We enter the world already within a *network* of relationships and obligations, not unlike the network of roads, railways, and communication facilities that we share. We are, at one time or another, children and parents, cousins and friends, students and teachers, consumers and merchants, laborers and vacationers, patients in need of care and caregivers, and we gossip and are the subjects of gossip, offer praise and are occasionally praised by others. Betweenness refers specifically to the human relationships of our everyday world. The network of social relationships exists in this betweenness,

and the Japanese live their lives within such a relational network."[26]
Betweenness (*aidagara*) implies spatial distance separating thing and
thing (*aida*), indicating *both* that we *can* come to meet in the between
and that we are at a distance from one another. Once again a self-
contradictory tension exists. *Aida* indicates that betweenness is spatial,
whatever else it might be, and so we exist within a definite space, a
spatial *basho* or "place." Therefore, to exist in space is an evident fact
of human existence, to be added to our evident temporality.

Ningen, Yuasa reminds us, was originally a Buddhist term, and
signifies "the human world as contrasted with the worlds of beasts and
of heavenly beings."[27] In modern usage, *ningen* expresses some sense
of exemplary character; and when one is less than fully human in not
displaying human virtues, then one is more like a beast, one is *chikusho*.
Such a one is disgraced and is clearly less than human; that is, is an
underachiever in virtue or perhaps morally impaired! At the other end
of the scale, and with an obviously Zen Buddhist implication, a realized human being, an overachiever, is *satori ningen*.

The dual nature of *ningen* as both individual and social being, as
both temporal and spatial, as interconnected in a betweenness which
is both "close up" and intimate, and yet is "distant," points to a basic
contradictoriness. Nonetheless, this contradictoriness coheres as a unity,
as a person or self. Indeed *sonzai*, a term that means "existence,"
Watsuji further analyzes to again show that it is composed of two characters, one emphasizing temporal existence and the other spatial existence. *Ningen sonzai* is doubly dual in nature and therefore doubly
self-contradictory, referring to human existence as individual and social, in time and in space.

Watsuji, Nishida, and the Kyoto School

Several of the key notions found in Watsuji's philosophy were "in the
air" during the first half of this century, and it might be useful to look
more carefully at the intellectual climate of Watsuji's own spatio-
temporal "betweenness." At the focal point of that intellectual climate
was Nishida Kitarō (1870–1945), who was the founder and leader of
what came to be called the *Kyoto School*. Even though Watsuji was certainly never a member of the "inner circle" of that school and even now
it is a matter of contention whether he ought to be included in any account of the Kyoto school, the influence of that developing tradition
on Watsuji is evident. Watsuji "is usually considered to have been a
thinker who occupied a position somewhere on the periphery of the

Kyoto School."[28] As well, insofar as he took up a position at Tokyo Imperial University in 1934, he was physically removed from the spatial center of the Kyoto movement. Finally, he was never a student of Nishida, as he was a younger contemporary of Nishida's, nor was his project avowedly religious, as was Nishida's. Watsuji was a philosopher of culture, and his interests increasingly and singlemindedly became ethical ones. Nonetheless, he was one of those at the very center of the intellectual ferment within Japanese intellectual circles during the first half of the present century, and his own distinctive system discusses many of the same issues the other member of the Kyoto school discussed, and indeed, his interest in such notions as the identity of self-contradiction, the negation of negation, absolute negativity, and nothingness or emptiness was no doubt the result of his interaction with Nishida's philosophy. Indeed, it seems to me that the application of what appears to be Nishida's pivotal notion of the identity of self-contradiction is the underlying skeletal structure of Watsuji's ethical theory. In this sense, he was clearly greatly influenced by and no doubt an influence on the development of the Kyoto philosophy. Of course, there is no actual Kyoto "school" in which one is given membership, in any case, but merely a more or less rough and ready classification of Japanese philosophers based on their similarity of conception to that of Nishida.

Be that as it may, a pivotal notion in Nishida's philosophy and an equally central one in Watsuji's account of Japanese ethics is the identity of self-contradiction. Although emphasis is placed on the self-contradictory quality of experience, it is not to be assumed that Nishida, Watsuji, and the Japanese generally are illogical because of this. Rather, what is being stressed is that some judgments of logical contradiction are at best penultimate judgments, which may point us in the direction of a more comprehensive and accurate understanding of our experience. A more profound understanding would reach below the surface level of contradiction and comprehend that opposites are necessarily opposites within some context. To use a Nishidan example, to be able to say that white is a color means that, to distinguish between white and black, one must have already grasped that white and black are located within a developed *system of colors*. White is located within a system of colors; and even though the distinction or contradiction of white and black is the primary judgment, it rests on what is in fact the real subject, the system of colors that makes distinction possible and unifies all colors into a single system identity—a unity of opposites or an identity of self-contradiction. Similarly, Watsuji refers to *wakaru* ("to understand"), which is derived from *wakeru* ("to divide"); and in order to *wakeru,* one must already have presupposed something whole, that is to say, a system or unity. For example, in self-reflection, we make our own self, *other.* Yet the distinction reveals the original unity, for the self *is* other as objectified and of course is divided from the originally unified self. Such a unity in division may be expressed in the propositional form, "S *is* P." Thus, in Watsuji's words, "a statement separates and yet brings the original unity to awareness. What is divided is connected by means of *is*" (p. 35). And again, "the term 'is' is nothing more than an indication of the unity that has come to awareness by the disruption" [of an original unity]. To recapitulate, now in Nishida's own words, "to think of one thing is to distinguish it from the other. In order for the distinction to be possible, it must originally have something in common with the other."[29] Thus, to emphasize the contradiction is to plunge into the world as many; to emphasize the context, or background, or matrix is to plunge into the world as one.

For example, the one is self-contradictorily composed of the many, and the many are self-contradictorily one. The world can be viewed from two distinct vantage points—this allows us to apprehend the world of experience as though through a sort of double aperture—and its unity is not a unity of mere oneness, but of self-contradiction. The logical formulation for this is that A is A; and A is not-A; therefore, A is A. There is a double negation in evidence here: an individual is an individual, and yet an individual is not individual unless one stands opposed to other individuals. That an individual stands opposed to others means that one is related to others, that is to say, is a member of a group. In order that an individual may be an individual, one must negate one's being a member of a group. Otherwise, one cannot affirm oneself to be oneself. On the other hand, one must therefore negate this negation, because one cannot be an individual unless one is a member of a group. But because an individual is a member of a group, one is both a *member* (as an individual) of a group *and* lost in the *group.* Each of us is both one and many, both an individual as isolated *and* inextricably interconnected with others in some community or other. As *ningen,* we negate our individuality to the extent that we are communally connected, and we negate our communality to the extent that we express our individuality. We are both, in *mutual* interactive negation, as well as being determined by the group or community, *and* determining and shaping the community. As such, we are living self-contradictions and therefore living identities of self-contradiction, or unities of opposites, in mutual interactive negation. And for Nishida, this emphasis on context is an emphasis on place, on *basho*. For Watsuji, the *unity* of self-contradiction arises in the *betweenness*. It is a logic of place as a matrix or as a network of relationships in which individuals *face* each other. The self-contradictory identity of the human being as individual and social in dynamic interaction is well articulated by Watsuji on pages 14 and 15, the conclusion to which account reads: "oneself and the other are absolutely separated from each other but, nevertheless, become one in the relationship of communal existence. Individuals are basically different from society and yet dissolve themselves into the latter. *Ningen* denotes the unity of these contradictories. Without this dialectical structure in mind, we cannot understand the essence of *ningen*."

Ningen (human being) does not mean merely an individual nor mere society but both together in a mutually negating and incessantly ongoing negation of the one by the other, which also constitutes their interconnected union. Ethics is concerned with those problems that arise between persons, as individuals and as members of society.

The Japanese word for *ethics* is *rinri*, composed of *rin* and *ri*. *Rin* means "fellows," "company," or *nakama*, which refers to a system of relations guiding human association or to one's communitarian relationships with and attitude toward others. *Ri* means "reason" or "principle," the rational ordering of human relationships. Furukawa suggests that *ri* "means literally the order or principle that enables men [human beings] to live in friendly community."[30] Watsuji refers to ancient Confucianism, which specified the precise and appropriate relational interactions between "parent and child, lord and vassal, husband and wife, young and old, friend and friend, and so forth . . ." (p. 11). *Aidagara* or "betweenness" refers to those relationships that connect us, as they occur in the place and space or *basho* between us and in which we associatively interact properly or appropriately. Therefore, *rinri*, or ethics, "is nothing else than the order or the way through which the communal existence of human beings is rendered possible. In other words, ethics consists of the laws of social existence" (p. 11).

Please note, however, that the double negation, in Watsuji, Nishida, and others in the Eastern way of looking at things, is not a complete negation that obliterates that which is negated. The identity of self-contradiction makes clear that that which is negated *is preserved*, else there would be no self-contradiction. Hegel moves to a synthesis, by apparently eliminating the thesis and the antithesis or, to be more precise, by blending them into a new synthesis. It is claimed that this blend preserves the original elements, and in some sense it surely does. But it does not preserve them *in the sense in which Watsuji and Nishida preserve them.* This different sense of preservation is a preservation without blending, without the creation of something new composed of the active ingredients of each. What is preserved is precisely the thesis as it is and the antithesis as it is, without transformation of any kind. What is added is the idea that the two together are needed to give a full(er) account of the experiential reality that is being described. Thus, it is not that *ningen* becomes some third thing, which blends individuality and sociality, but rather that *ningen* is individual *and* social *and* both of these rest on a deeper ground, which itself is neither individual nor social, but is that out of which both the individual and the social arise; namely, *nothingness.* For Nishida, nothingness is a determinative factor without "being" something determinant, because it is *not* "being," but nothingness. Hegel's concept of synthesis seems to be based on the concept of being; that is, on absolute being. For Nishida, nothingness is the realm of nonduality. Nonduality is that out of which the dualism of individual and social, the self and other arise. It is the face before the individual and social, the self and other are born, so to speak.

Nothingness as "Home Ground"

What is the significance of this rather abstract and certainly formless *nothingness* for ethics? The annihilation of the self, as the negation of negation "constitutes the basis of every selfless morality since ancient times" (p. 225). The losing of self, for Watsuji, is a returning to one's authenticity, to one's home ground, whereas a losing of self in Heidegger's negative sense, is an abandonment of self to mass consciousness and, hence, is inauthenticity. Whether the individual faces becoming a victim of the masses or a victim of death itself, Watsuji asks how this focus on the individual is supposed to enable us to understand what is required of morality (p. 226). Morality is not a concern of the individual, but one that of necessity involves at least one other. The preoccupation with one's own death is by itself insignificant, unless one includes the implication of one's death for others or for society at large. Hence, "only in the relationship between self and other that the preparedness for death gives full play to its genuine significance. As a spontaneous abandonment of the self, it paves the way for the nondual relation between the self and other and terminates in the activity of benevolence" (p. 226). The ethics of benevolence is the development of the capacity to embrace others as oneself or, more precisely, to forget one's self such that the distinction between the self and other does not arise in this nondualistic awareness. One has now abandoned one's self, one's individuality, and become the authentic ground of the self and other as the realization of absolute totality. Ethics is now a matter of spontaneous compassion, spontaneous caring, concern for the whole. This is the birth of selfless morality, for which the only counterparts in the West are the mystical traditions and perhaps some forms of religiosity in which it is God who moves in us, and not we ourselves.

Morality, for Watsuji is a coming back to authentic unity through an initial opposition between the self and other as the negation of betweenness and then a re-establishing of that betweenness ideally culminating in a nondualistic connection between the self and others that actually negates any trace of opposition. This is the negation of negation, and it occurs in both time and space. It is not simply a matter of enlightenment as a private, individual experience, calling one to awareness of the interconnectedness of all things. Rather, it is a spatio-temporal series of interconnected actions, occurring in the betweenness between us, which leads us to an awareness of betweenness that ultimately eliminates the self and other, but of course, only from within a nondualistic perspective. Dualistically comprehended, both the self and other are preserved. What is left is betweenness itself in which (human) actions occur. In this sense, betweenness is nothingness, and nothingness is betweenness. Betweenness is the place where compassion arises and is acted out selflessly in the spatio-temporal theater of the world. In LaFleur's words, emptiness is not "something metaphysical called 'non-being' but . . . [that which] operates to make possible a series of relationships and reciprocities."[31]

However, there is a significant difference in the ideal of betweenness as nothingness, and the everydayness where most of us live, where we hope to gain some glimpse of a morality that effectively assists us in living our lives well. Those concerned with ethics wish to find some guidance that will enable them to know what it means to be good or bad. What quickly becomes clear is that the structure of existence (*sonzai*) appropriate to human beings (*ningen*) is a mutuality of coexistence that expects and depends on *truth and trust* in human relationships. Trust and truth are not intellectual demands made from a purely theoretical interest, but are to be found in the actions of human beings through and by which they are connected with one another. Truth and trust occur spatio-temporally; that is, in the world in which we live, as living, breathing, self-conscious bodies. And even those who act in such a way as to reject truthfulness or trustworthiness in their relations with others—those who lie and cheat, break promises, and do physical harm

344 WATSUJI TETSURŌ'S RINRIGAKU

to the persons and property of others—nevertheless rely on the expectation of others that they will act truthfully and in a loyal and trustworthy manner to carry out their nefarious deeds. The very fabric of social interaction of civilization, in any of its forms, is based on that network of trusting relationships and truth telling without which our lives together would be nasty, brutish, and short. But there is no state of nature, as Hobbes may have argued, from which we emerge as individuals slowly making our way to a contractual society for the first time. There never was a time nor could there have been when we were not always already immersed in a network of social interconnection. And all such social interconnection is inescapably based on some sense of trustworthiness and the expectation that one will tell the truth. We are always already public, as well as private, social as well as individual, and the state of nature is but an abstraction that will simply not pass serious examination.

Watsuji is bothered by all such "desert island" constructions. Hobbes imagines a state of nature in which we are radically discrete individuals, a time before significant social interconnections have been established. And Kant employed a series of examples in an attempt to demonstrate his ethical maxim that whatever is morally acceptable must necessarily be self-consistent. It may need to be more, as well, but it cannot be less. Any maxim of action that is internally inconsistent, cannot be correct. For Watsuji, however, all ethical maxims are *contextual.* The consistency of an action is not just a matter of examining a maxim in sublime isolation from the interrelationships of an everyday life in a real society. To begin, Watsuji warns that even the notion of self-consistency is open to question, for in the East, the logic of the identity of self-contradiction actually resolves seeming inconsistencies by placing them in a broader context. We are both individual and social beings when we are understood as *ningen.* Furthermore, even admonitions such as Kant's that suicide is always wrong is rejected by Watsuji on the grounds that whether or not suicide is in any way an acceptable form of behavior is not merely a matter of abstract principle but also heavily dependent on the norms and patterns of relationship already within society. And even though he does not argue that suicide *is* sometimes correct, he does point out that, if it is morally wrong, "the real act of suicide is usually committed with an awareness of the bankruptcy of life, because suicide cannot be based on a principle. Accordingly, a suicide note is filled with excuses offered to one's family, friends, and sometimes, to the nation as a whole" (p. 251). Thus, whether suicide is judged right or wrong is dependent on its relation to a network of social expectations, demands, concerns, and support.

Similarly, Watsuji's rejection of Kant's demonstration that a swindler acts wrongly—stealing cannot be taken to be a universal law because it is self-contradictory—is achieved by observing in a pointedly Japanese way that, before one succumbs to being a swindler, one's poverty "will be discussed among one's relatives and friends, and eventually various forms of assistance will be offered" (p. 252). In other words, one determines whether an action ought to be done not by comparing the maxim of an action with a universal law, but in the context of one's social web of interconnectedness, in the betweenness between us where we already exist as social beings. Social considerations alone cannot suffice to tell us how to act morally, neither can they be ignored in our attempt to decide what is right and what is wrong. In Japanese society, there simply are other alternatives. And, even though such reflections are not enough to determine the rightness or wrongness of an action, they do make evident that the Japanese approach to moral decision making is not via abstract principles alone but must take account of the social, contextual, and circumstantial elements in a particular instance, as well. Japanese *contextualism* is too engrained for Kantian principled morality to seem at all adequate or accurate.

What is demanded is a system of social ethics grounded in a communal sense of the connectedness of one person with another. The state as a merely legal structure is not enough to express the demands of *ningen sonzai* (human existence). To be truly ethical, there must be a sense of community and solidarity that arises from a sense of shared history and an interconnection of social and cultural activities expressed in the real space/time world. In other words, "the solidarity expressed legally falls short of expressing the way of *ningen*, if it is not backed up by the community of *sonzai*," that is, by a heartfelt awareness and appreciation of an intense web of human connectedness, stretching back into history, and reaching toward the future in the form of common goals and aspirations (p. 26). Even learning itself is the exploration of our betweenness (p. 29). Betweenness is communality, and communality is a mutuality wherein each individual may affect every other individual and thereby affect the community; and the community, as an historical expression of the whole may affect each individual. This mutuality is an essential characteristic of the identity of self-contradiction. Things stand in contradictory opposition only in the sense that each pole of the opposition may affect the other in the betweenness between them. Their relationship is a *mutuality* of interconnection.

Social ethics for Watsuji is the negation of negation as the self-returning and self-realizing of that absolute totality or home ground (pp. 21–24). Social ethics requires *both* the establishment of the individual and the negation of individuality through the recognition of an absolute totality as ideal, and yet the negated individual does not thereby perish but exists by negating the social aspect or dimension. The negation is double, and the relation is one of mutuality: the self as individual is negated for the social to emerge, and the social is negated for the individual aspect to remain. This mutuality is not one of *priority* in any sense. Neither temporally nor logically does one aspect exist or make its appearance before the other. Rather, the very notion "individual" implies society, and "society" already implies and requires the existence of individuals. In true Buddhist fashion, they originate codependently; that is, the sense of relationship here is that of codependent origination.[32] Let me emphasize, on Watsuji's behalf, that "apart from the self-awareness of an individual, there is no social ethics" (p. 23). Facile criticisms of Watsuji in particular and the Far East in general as having submerged the individual in a collectivity of mass consciousness are largely in error. Nonetheless, the emphasis on absolute totality does suggest that part of what might have been won is partially lost all the same. That is to say, although individuality is a necessary moment on the way to the realization of absolute totality, the notion of absolute totality itself is a submerging of the individual in the collectivism of the greater whole. And to the extent to which Watsuji, at times, associated absolute totality with the political state instead of with Zen Buddhist nothingness, matters become worse still. On the other hand, LaFleur remarks that "the notion of '*absolute* negation' is not functionally significant in Watsuji's thought."[33] And while he does use the term, his emphasis is on *nothingness* as immanent in society and in the individual, not as *absolute* in Nishida's sense of a transcendent *as well as an immanent* nothingness. I think Nishida would have insisted that Watsuji's nothingness was a "relative" nothingness, one that would make of "self and others/not two,"[34] within a harmonious and unifying socio-politico-cultural state, but not a metaphysical one that eliminated all distinctions in an absolute state of nondistinction. After all, for betweenness to operate as a place of relation, the self and other, individual and social, and other seemingly self-contradictory opposites must continue to exist. And yet, self-contradictorily, they must also negate one another. Rather, Watsuji wanted to maintain the tension: "Watsuji, it should be noted, takes pains to point out that he is not describing some kind of experiential process in which particularity and multiplicity are simply cancelled out in favour of merger and undifferentiated unity. This would involve the error of assuming that some higher reality lies in the one behind multiform existence."[35]

Nishida's approach was to cancel out the distinctions, nondualistically understood, and to envision the "final *basho*," or place, or emptiness as beyond *all distinction, and yet* to retain them all as relatively absolute; that is, as the only way in which logic, words, and all experience except the experience of enlightenment could grasp them, as a mutuality of self-contradictory tension. But the tension is *both* horizontal, between the individual and society, the many and the one, and so forth, and vertical, between relative nothingness and absolute nothingness. This latter vertical self-contradictory tension is between a relative oneness in which distinctions are preserved, yet at the same time negated in a relative unity, and absolute oneness, in which all distinctions vanish. Watsuji appears not to have taken this last step in such a way as to make it functionally integrated into his system of understanding.

The Self, East and West

In a fascinating article by Alasdair MacIntyre, "Individual and Social Morality in Japan and the United States: Rival Conceptions of the Self," an attempt is made to show that there is no such thing as a "culturally neutral conception of the distinction between *the social* and *the individual*."[36] What is focal in this article is MacIntyre's allegation that there is an important difference in the conception of *self* in America and in Japan. The American self is (first) able to "abstract itself from the particular social role which it happens to inhabit, and indeed from the whole social order of which that role is a constitutive part, so as to reflect upon itself as an individual *qua* individual, rather than *qua* family member or member of this or that social group."[37] There is a self, indeed a primary sense of self, which is apart from and independent of all social roles, capable even of escaping from all past history and influence. A second aspect of the American conception of self is "dominated by standards of acquisition and competition," whereby we are evaluated by others and are almost victimized by that role or vocation society has inflicted upon us.[38] A third sense of self in America, argues MacIntyre, is "the self which looks to institutionalized human relationships, defined in terms of what remains of inherited religious and moral norms. . ."[39] The result is an incommensurability, leading to divided selves in inner conflict. The old notion of *psyche*, or soul, "which could achieve its own good only in and through its participation in forms of community in which allegiance to the good of the community" and leading toward "a supreme good transcending the good of the human community" is long since lost.[40]

By contrast, in Japan there seems to have been a consistency of conception of self throughout its history, and there has never been "any place for the substantial *psyche*."[41] Furthermore, "this constancy seems to be bound up with a mode of organization of the self in which the European and American contrasts and antitheses between individual and society, whether in the older form of a soul whose good transcends as well as includes its social good, or in the new forms of modern individualism, find no place."[42] For the Japanese, there is that in the self which is manifest and that which is concealed. That which is manifest is both individual and social, and the "outer aspects of the individual *are* the social order."[43] There is also that which is unspoken and concealed, that which belongs to the heart, but the overt self is manifestly individual and social. MacIntyre adds, "the individual without and apart from his or her social role is not yet complete, is a set of potentialities waiting to be achieved, just as the social role is empty until brought into actuality by a particular person's self-completion through it."[44] This is an accurate and independent account of Watsuji's own insistence that *ningen* is not only both individual and social, and mutually interactive as such, but further, an *identity* embraces the self-contradictions that are ever present. That identity is, I think, an expression of the nondivided self that is part of the strength of Japanese culture. However, perhaps it would be more accurate to claim that it is a divided yet not divided self or a self that divides by not dividing and that not divides by dividing. In other words, it is an identity of self-contradiction. As well, MacIntyre captures well the implication that a self is *incomplete* without and apart from its social roles. Part of what it means to be *ningen*, to be *human*, is both to realize and to accept one's inextricable connection with others. And this interconnection is normatively prescribed, at least in general Confucian-like relationships, and culminates in the eradication of individualistic and egoistic conceptions of self and their replacement with a sense of self that is individualistic in relationship and relational as individual. Again, there is an identity of self-contradiction with an unusual degree of emphasis on the social interconnectedness of an individual, culminating in the whole as the state, or in that nondualistic awareness that transcends both the individual and the relational and serves as that *emptiness* out of which these and all other self-contradictory distinctions arise. Apart from our social roles and our normative social relationships, we are considerably less than human, having only partially actualized our human potentiality.

Watsuji writes of nothingness as that final place or context in which all distinctions disappear, and yet from which they emerge.

Nothingness is also a foundational notion in Nishida, but he pushes the reader past relative context or place, after relatively wider and more enveloping contexts or places, until reaching a final or "absolute" *basho*/place/matrix. This is *absolute nothingness*. But Watsuji's final version of *nothingness* seems distinctly different. The Buddhist influence is apparent in both Watsuji and Nishida, but for Nishida it was an ultimate religious vision, whereas for Watsuji it has more of an epistemological and an ontological status and function. The difference is subtle and may well be captured in a disagreement between William Lafleur and David Dilworth, which appears in the literature.

Cosmic-Oriented Humanism

Lafleur objects to Dilworth's conclusion that, although Watsuji makes use of Buddhist ideas, "it should be stressed that Watsuji's position was not essentially a Buddhistic or religious one such as worked out in the Kyoto school . . . [and he seems] to have refused, at least philosophically and methodologically, to embrace the solution of religion."[45] By contrast, Lafleur concludes that, "not only does Watsuji embrace a religious solution but he does so, I think, philosophically and methodologically."[46] The details of the debate I will leave for the reader to search out and ponder, but what is of particular interest here is Lafleur's conclusion that, for Watsuji, "it was in the Buddhist notion of emptiness that Watsuji found *the* principle that gives his system . . . coherence."[47] Watsuji's subject matter is ethics, but his pivotal principle is emptiness, or nothingness! Lafleur goes on to argue that Watsuji's conception of religion and its place in culture is quite different from Nishida's. Writes Lafleur: "it is not that Nishida pursued a religious solution whereas Watsuji did not. Rather, each had a different understanding of religion."[48] For Watsuji, religion is a cultural phenomenon, like communication and transportation, the arts, and such, whereas for Nishida, religion transcended culture. I think, as well, that for Nishida, religion was much more of an individualistic phenomenon, whereas for Watsuji it was yet another communality. Watsuji studied religion as an aspect of the "climate" that causally influenced geographic regions and racial groups to understand the world and to act in it as they do. For Nishida, religion was the driving force behind his philosophical and social analysis. For Watsuji, religion was but a part of the network of human interaction. In this sense, Watsuji is perhaps too much the sociologist and religious anthropologist and too little a practitioner with an experiential basis for his views on religion.

Watsuji placed a heavy emphasis on communality, and as Lafleur notes, this communality took the form of classical Confucianism, where the five basic relationships were taken to be all important: husband and wife, parents and child, elder child to younger child, and so forth. But, as Lafleur also observes, Watsuji's interpretive emphasis is on the *mutuality* of these relationships, and this emphasis is much more Buddhist than Confucian. Lafleur writes, "his emphasis upon a finely balanced *mutuality of dependence* is decidedly not Confucian; nor is his dismissal of priority as being philosophically unimportant."[49] *Priority* has to do with the necessity that both sides of a relationship should exist simultaneously, for example, a parent cannot be a parent unless there is a child, and a child could not be counted as a child unless it was born of parents and was being nurtured by parents, in some sense. "Therefore, the notion of priority is undercut and production is always mutual. . . . The point is that a son, by being born, makes a 'parent' of his father and in that sense 'produces' his parent. Mutuality is always characteristic of production; priority is an illusion."[50] Lafleur goes on to observe that this rejection of priority in causal production can be traced back to Nāgārjuna, a view that has come to be identified as at the very heart of Buddhism, the notion of emptiness as codependent origination.[51]

The Buddhist notion of *pratītya-samutpāda*, or "dependent co-origination," "relationality," "conditioned coproduction," "dependent coarising," or "codependent origination" implies that everything is "empty"; that is to say, that everything is deprived of its substantiality, nothing exists independently, everything is related to everything else, nothing ranks as a first cause, and even the *self* is but a delusory construction.[52] The delusion of independent individuality can be overcome by recognizing our radical relational interconnectedness. At the same time, the negation must be negated, and so our radical relational interconnectedness is possible only because true individuals have created a network in the betweenness between them. Lafleur summarizes Watsuji's position: "the social side of human existence 'empties' the individuated side of any possible priority or autonomy and the individuated side does something exactly the same and exactly proportionate to and for the social side. There can be no doubt, I think, that for Watsuji emptiness is the key to it all."[53]

Abe Masao provides the Buddhist background to this, in his remarkably clear summary of Nāgārjuna's position on emptiness:

> . . . it was Nāgārjuna who explicitly developed the notion of "Emptiness" implicit in the Buddha's doctrine of dependent

co-origination. He set forth the theory of dependent co-origination in terms of the Eightfold Negation—neither origination nor cessation; neither permanence nor impermanence; neither unity nor diversity; neither coming nor going. Nāgārjuna not only repudiated the eternalist view, which takes phenomena to be real just as they are and essentially unchangeable; he also rejected as illusory the opposite nihilistic view which emphasizes emptiness and non-being as the true reality. This double negation in terms of "neither . . . nor" is the pivotal point for the realization of Mahayana Emptiness which is never a sheer emptiness but rather Fullness. For "neither . . . nor" *in this case* refers to the two opposing and conversion from the absolute negation (negation of both affirmation and negation, that is, "Emptiness") into the absolute affirmation (affirmation of both affirmation and negation, that is, "Fullness").[54]

Watsuji's "fullness" is less an object of religious worship or ecstasy and more an epistemological recognition that contradictions are mutually negated in a tension that allows a truer understanding of human being as individual and social, with each pole mutually interactive in negating the other. That is the flux of life experience, the tension of body/mind existence in a physical/cultural climate.

The religious passion connected with nothingness or emptiness for Nishida is not present in Watsuji's more strictly epistemological and ontological account. Nishida writes of abandoning one's "self-power" (*jiriki*) of independent egohood and living in accordance with the "other-power" (*tariki*) of faith.[55] Watsuji's emptiness is more a recognition of underlying relatedness, a "mutuality which exists in spite of differences between hard and soft, great and small, observer and observed, etc."[56] It manifests as a place, a *basho* that is the dynamic and creative origination of all relationships and all networks of interactions. And even when Watsuji uses religious language (as in "it is a religious ecstasy of the great emptiness")[57] that ecstasy is not a mystical-like insight into one's union or unity with God or the Absolute or a recognition of floating in "other-power" but a relational union of those persons involved in some communal forms, eventually culminating with the state. In other words, it is an ethical, or political, or communal ecstasy and not a religious identification with a transcendent Other. Watsuji gives no evidence of religiosity but expresses a profound and sometimes ecstatic ethical humanism. This ethical humanism is heavily Buddhist in its conception. In this sense, perhaps Dilworth and Lafleur are themselves involved in a dialectical tension, each correctly recognizing an aspect of Watsuji's own intellectual heritage and focus and, when taken together, provide a perspective that comes considerably closer to an accurate and comprehensive account of the distinctiveness and originality of Watsuji's position.

Transcendence as Immanence

Still, the difference is perhaps overstated in the preceding, in part because of what I take to be a suspiciously Western interpretation of emptiness as a discrete "transcendent other," an object standing over and above us, and above the world, as a divinely created "other." Again, Abe makes very clear that Buddhism, and by implication Nishida, is unlikely to have turned "emptiness" into an "other" with an independent existence, with an ontological and valuational priority. Summarizing the "Middle Way" of Buddhism as dependent co-origination, Abe offers three points that make abundantly clear why caution must be exercised in interpreting any proposed "transcendence":

1. In the Buddhist notion of dependent co-origination, there is *nothing* whatsoever "more real" . . . which lies beyond or behind the interdependence of everything in the universe.

2. But this "nothingness" should not be taken as nothingness which is distinguished from "somethingness". If so, we are involved in another duality, a duality between "nothingness" and "somethingness". "Nothingness" realized behind the interdependence of everything is not "relative nothingness" in contrast to "somethingness" but the "absolute Nothingness" which is beyond the duality of nothingness and somethingness.

3. When one says that there is absolutely nothing "more real" behind the interdependence of everything, one means that its interdependence is determined and limited *by itself* without any outside principle of determination and limitation.[58]

For Watsuji, emptiness is realized in the betweenness of natural space in the phenomenal world, here and now. Moral laws arise only as a result of the negation of the self and recognition of one's subsequent communality that culminates in one's taking one's place in the whole of the state. Recognition of the emptiness of the self (*ku*) is essential if one is to reach that absolute totality which is beyond individual awareness. As Piovesana remarks, "society, formed as it is of individuals, is but a dialectical development of self-denying units toward the great void which is social totality."[59] This incredible emphasis on the nation state was the major source of postwar allegations that Watsuji played into the hands of militant Japanese nationalists during the war. Watsuji toned down this emphasis in his books subsequently, as a result of such criticism. Bellah summarizes Watsuji's 1943 lecture and essay, "The Way of the Subject in Japan," in which he finds affirmations (which he paraphrases) such as, "for Watsuji the core of ethical value in the Japanese tradition and the reason for its superiority to other traditions lies in the Way of Reverence for the Emperor."[60] Or again, "that which relates men to their deepest and most basic absolute is only actualized truly and concretely in a human relational structure, most fully in the state,"[61] or that "the state is the highest ethical structure."[62] Even more to the point, Bellah writes, "for Watsuji, the state is the expression of the absolute whole which is the same as absolute negativity or absolute emptiness."[63]

Such assertions, if unqualified, would make Watsuji's position less an ethical humanism, and more a "totalitarian state-ethics," as Piovesana suggests.[64] It is impossible to dismiss this conclusion as farfetched, but it is equally impossible to evaluate the entire flow and thrust of Watsuji's clearly humanistic/ethical writings from such a narrow nationalistic viewpoint. James W. Heisig, in confronting precisely this issue in the writings of Nishida, Tanabe, and Nishitani of the Kyoto school, but not specifically including Watsuji, concludes that, although he does "not mean to claim that the Kyoto philosophers are as innocent as, say, Nietzsche was, of the way his thought was twisted to the ends of patriotic nationalism; but only that what guilt there is does not belong among the fundamental inspirations of these three thinkers."[65] I think that something like this applies as well to Watsuji, although his wartime writings may well tarnish him with a greater degree of personal guilt. Nevertheless, Heisig's conclusion is apt here as well: "The irony is that in a sense, the failure of Japan's nationalist aims was a victory for the true aims of the Kyoto philosophers, calling them less to a laundering of their image than to a return to their fundamental inspirations."[66] Indeed Bellah, who takes Watsuji to task for not actually coming out in opposition to the Japanese involvement in the Second World War, nevertheless remarks that "Watsuji turns the tables on those who would hold Shintō to be inferior because primitive," for even though Shintō emphasized the singular importance of the emperor, the emperor was not absolute, but could be thought of as one instantiation of the sacred on earth, and therefore "from this there developed the broad ideal of taking the best from all countries."[67] In other words, from a standpoint higher than any manifestation of the sacred, many religions could be thought to contribute to Japan and Shintō and could be taken in by the Japanese culture and accepted by the emperor. Were other religions and states to do the same, there could emerge a syncretic religiosity that would affirm unity within difference. Nonetheless, Yuasa remarks that Japan's special mission was to overthrow the capitalistic and aggressively militaristic Western powers, to "liberate the oppressed races in Asia."[68] Yuasa continues that Japan's defeat "was a severe shock to him. He had to reconcile himself to the fact that the historical mission of Japan in the contemporary age had ended in failure."[69]

Watsuji's fundamental inspiration and focal project was to redress the imbalance of undue emphasis on human individuality and egoity that predominates in the West, by reintroducing a vivial sense of our communitarian interconnectedness, and our spatial and bodily place in the betweenness between us, where we meet, love, and strive to live ethical lives together, as one and yet as individuals. This is a noble redressing and one that the contemporary West is desperately in need of discovering and enacting. Increasingly, the same may be said of contemporary Japan as well, for as the past recedes, the future is increasingly colored by Western ways of being in the world. Remarkably, Watsuji may be more relevant to both East and West than he was when he lived and wrote his epic-making *Rinrigaku*.

notes

Foreword

1. Robert N. Bellah, "Japan's Cultural Identity: Some Reflections on the Work of Watsuji Tetsurō," *The Journal of Asian Studies* 24:4 (August, 1965), pp. 573–594.

2. Watsuji had been granted funds and went to Germany in February of 1927 for what was supposed to have been three years of study, especially with Heidegger, whose reputation then had already reached Japan. Watsuji appears not to have been much taken either with Heidegger or with Germany; it was, in fact, in Italy that he spent much of what would turn out to be less than a year and one-half in Europe. Very soon after his return to Japan, during the summer of 1928, he published the germinal form of *A Climate* as an essay. That work, comprised largely of his travel journals puffed out into a problematic theory about climate and cultures, may have been offered in some haste to the public to show at least *something* for the time spent away from Japan studying in Europe.

3. I relate that history and offer my own criticism of this work in "An Ethic of As-Is: State and Society in the *Rinrigaku* of Watsuji Tetsurō," in Léon Vandermeersch, ed., *La société civile face à l'État dans les traditions chinoise, japonaise, coréenne et vietnamienne* (Paris: École française d'Extrême-Orient, 1994), pp. 453–464.

4. Yuasa Yasuo, *Watsuji Tetsurō: Shisō no unmei* (1981).

5. It also served as a catalyst for a number of important studies, notably *Watsuji Tetsurō* by Sakabe Megumi (1986), *Watsuji Tetsurōron* by Yamada Kō (1987), *Watsuji Tetsurō no menboku* by Yoshizawa Denzaburō (1994), and *Hikari no ryōgaku: Watsuji Tetsurō* by Karube Tadashi (1995).

Introduction

1. Watsuji Tetsurō, *Climate and Culture: A Philosophical Study*, trans. Geoffrey Bownas, (Tokyo: The Hokuseido Press, Ministry of Education, 1961), p. 217.

2. Furukawa Tetsushi, "Watsuji Tetsurō, the Man and His Work" (pp. 209–235), in ibid., p. 218.

3. Ibid., p. 219.

4. David Dilworth, "Watsuji Tetsurō (1889–1960): Cultural Phenomenologist and Ethician," *Philosophy East and West* 24, no. 1 (Jan. 1974): 5.

5. Ibid., p. 8.

6. Furukawa, "Watsuji Tetsurō, the Man and His Work," p. 226.

7. Gino K. Piovesana, *Contemporary Japanese Philosophical Thought*, Asian Philosophical Studies No. 4 (New York: St. John's University Press, 1969), p. 132.

8. William R. LaFleur, "A Turning in Taishō: Asia and Europe in the Early Writings of Watsuji Tetsurō," in J. Thomas Rimer, ed., *Culture and Identity: Japanese Intellectuals During the Interwar Years* (Princeton, N.J.: Princeton University Press, 1990), pp. 234–256.

9. Ibid., p. 243.

10. Ibid., p. 249.

11. Furukawa, "Watsuji Tetsurō, the Man and His Work," p. 226.

12. Ibid.

13. Piovesana, *Contemporary Japanese Philosophical Thought*, p. 134.

14. Dilworth, "Watsuji Tetsurō," pp. 5–6.

15. Yuasa Yasuo, "The Encounter of Modern Japanese Philosophy with Heidegger," in Graham Parkes, ed., *Heidegger and Asian Thought* (Honolulu: University of Hawaii Press, 1987), p. 156.

16. Watsuji, *Climate and Culture*, p. vi.

17. Ibid.

18. Yuasa Yasuo, "The Encounter of Modern Japanese Philosophy with Heidegger," in Parkes, ed., *Heidegger and Asian Thought*, p. 168.

Chapter One. The Significance of Ethics as the Study of *Ningen*

1. The Japanese word *ningen* is usually translated as "human being," "person," or "man." But it also means the *betweenness* of human beings. The customary English translation does not carry both senses of *ningen* (Rober E. Carter).

2. Darmstadt: Otto Reichel Verlag, 1930, 5. 30.

3. *Philosophische Weltanschauung* (Bonn: F. Cohen), 1929. Chapter 2, "*Mensch und Geschichte*."

4. Karl Löwith, *Das individuum in der rolle des mitmenschen* (Munich: Drei Masken Verlag, 1928).

5. The authentic significance of what is called an *act* consists of the mutual connections between subjective persons who cannot be objectified by any means. People have so far have attempted to grasp it only in the relation between person and nature, without giving heed to these interpersonal connections. In this sense, an act was characterized as the bodily movement of a human being (1) with clear-cut aims or motives and who self-consciously strives to realize these aims (2) through deliberation, selection, and decision. But, if this is the case, then all that we can say is that it is only someone's activity, but not necessarily a personal act, or the "act" of a human being. For instance, take the case of someone throwing a

stone, aiming at some mark on the riverside. If you perform the same activity within the campus of a school, aiming at the window glass, then that turns out to be an act. Why? Because the notion of aim here is already connected with other persons or with the group. Such processes as deliberation, selection, and decision are here made as attitude-assuming decisions in the preceding connection. That is to say, the notions of aim, deliberation, selection, and decision here rest on their subjective connections with others. It is here that the significance of an "act" appears. This problem will be discussed in detail in the second chapter.

Chapter Four.   Individual Moments Making Up Human Existence

1. Watsuji here refers to licensed quarters, which were completely abolished many years ago.

2. Max Scheler, *Wesen und formen der Sympathie: der "Phaenomemologie und Theorie der Sympathiegefuehle,"* 5 vols. (Frankfurt am Main: Schulte-Bulmke, 1948), p. 6.

3. Max Scheler, *Der Formalismus in der Ethik und die materiale Wertethik* (Halle: Max Niemeyer, 1913–16), pp. 413 ff.

4. Theodor Litt, *Individuum und Gemeinschaft* (Leipzig: B. G. Teubner, 1924), pp. 51 ff.

5. Johann Gottlieb Fichte, *Das System der Sittenlehre nach den Principien der Wissenschaftslehre* (Jena: Christian Ernst Gabler, 1798), p. 22.

6. Max Scheler, *Der Formalismus*, pp. 340 ff.

7. Ibid., pp. 585 ff.

8. George Wilhelm Friedrich Hegel, *Die Philosophie des Rechts: die Mitschriften*, Wannenmann (Heidelberg, 1817–18) and Homeyer (Berlin, 1818–19), sec. 158.

9. Karl Marx, *Zur Kritik der Politischen Öekonomie*, ed. Karl Kautsky (Stuttgard: J. H. W. Dietz, 1897) p. xiv.

10. Ludwig Gumplowicz, *Grundiss der Soziologie*, 2nd ed. (Vienna: Manzsche K.u.K. Hof-Verlags and University Bookstore), 1905; new edition ed. Gottfried Salomon (Innsbruck: Wagner, 1926).

Chapter Five.   The Element of the Whole in a Human Being

1. Max Scheler, *Der Formalismus*, p. 544.

2. Ibid., pp. 542–543.

3. Ibid., p. 543.

4. Ibid., p. 555.

5. Ibid., p. 544: "*In der Person selbst also scheidet sich Einzelperson und Gesamtperson.*"

6. Ibid., p. 555: *"Die Einheit selbstständiger, geistiger, individueller Einzelpersonen in einer selbstständigen, geistigen, individuellen Gesamtperson."*

7. Ibid., p. 411.

8. Ibid., p. 413.

9. Ibid., p. 518.

10. Ibid., p. 542.

11. Ibid., p. 412.

Chapter Six. The Negative Structure of a Human Being

1. Gabriel Tarde, *The Laws of Imitation*, trans. Elsie Clews Parsons (New York: Holt, 1903), pp. 14, 68, 70; *Les lois de l'imitation*, 6. ed., Paris: F. Alcan, 1911, pp. 15–16, 73, 75, 85.

2. Gabriel Tarde, *Les lois sociales*, 6. ed., Paris: F. Alcan, 1910; *Social Laws: An Outline of Sociology* (New York: Arno Press, 1899).

3. George Simmel, *Soziologie: Untersuchungen über die Formen der Vergesellschaftung* (Munich and Leipzig: Ducker and Humblot, 1922), pp. 14 ff: *" . . . des . . . interindividuellen Lebens . . . zwischen den Atomen der Gesellschaft."*

4. Ibid., p. 4.

5. Ibid., pp. 21 ff.

6. Ibid., p. 24.

7. Alfred Vierkandt, *Gesellschaftslehre: Hauptprobleme der philosophischen Soziologie* (Stuttgart: F. Enke, 1923), pp. 4 f., p. 28.

8. Leopold von Wiese, *Allgemeine soziologie als lehre von den beziehungen und beziehungsgebilden der menschen* (Munich and Leipzig: Duncker and Humblot, 1924–29), Part II, pp. 2f.

9. Ibid., pp. 74 ff.

10. Ibid., p. 73

11. Émile Durkheim, *Les règles de la méthode sociologique* (Paris: F. Alean, 1912), 6th ed., pp. 5 f; *Die Methode der Soziologie* (Leipzig: A Kröner, 1908), p. 26 ff.

12. Ibid., p. 19.

13. In ibid., p. 138.

14. Ibid., pp. 128, 140.

Chapter Seven. The Fundamental Law of a Human Being (The Basic Principle of Ethics)

1. Alfred Edward Taylor, *The Problem of Conduct: A study in the Phenomenology of Ethics* (London: Macmillan, 1901), pp. 89 ff.

2. Max Scheler, *Der Formalismus*, p. 21.

3. Ibid., p. 22.

4. Ibid., p. 23.

5. Ibid., p. 24.

Chapter Nine. The Spatiality of a Human Being

1. English edition, trans. William E. Naff (Honolulu: University of Hawaii Press, 1987).

2. In Japanese, *koto* means a "word," as well as the thing signified.

3. Franz Brentano, *Psychologie vom empirischen Standpunkt*, 2 vols. (Leipzig: F. Meiner, 1924–25), vol. 2, pp. 262 ff; 111 ff; *Vom Dasein Gottes*, Leipzic: Kastil, 1929, pp. 102 ff.

4. Anton Marty, *Raum und Zeit* (Halle: Niemeyer, 1916).

5. Henri Bergson, *Materie und Gedächtnis, Essays zur Beziehung zwischen Körper und Geist* (Jena: E. Diederichs, 1908), pp. 185 ff.

6. Martin Heidegger, *Sein und Zeit*, in *Jahrbuch für Philosophie und Phänomenologische Forschung* 8 (1927): 1–438; also published in book form (Halle: Max Niemeyer, 1927).

7. Max Scheler, *Idealismus-Realismus*, Philosophischer Anzeiger, no. 2 (Bonn: Verlag Friedrich Cohen, 1927), p. 311.

8. Theodor Litt, *Individuum und Gemeinschaft: Grundlegung der Kulturphilosophie*, 2 vols. (Leipzig: B. G. Teubner, 1924).

9. Oskar Becker, "Beiträge zur phänomenologischen Begründung der Geometrie und ihrer physikalischen Anwendungen," *Jahrbuch Jr. f. Philosophie und Phanomenologiche Forschung* (19 Halle: M. Niemeyer, 1913): 454 ff.

Chapter Ten. The Temporality of *Ningen Sonzai*

1. This word is an English translation of the original Japanese word *shin* or *tayori* (信頼), which means in Japanese correspondence as well as fidelity. See p. 160.

2. Toan Tejima, *Collection of Practical Ethics,* in *Collected Works [Tejima Toan zenshu]* (Osaka: Seibundo, 1973; originally published by Iwanami Press), p. 99.

3. The Japanese term *mirai* ("the future") means "not yet come."

4. Aristotle, *Physica*, chaps. 10–14 (217b 29–224a 17). See Heidegger, *Sein und Zeit*, pp. 426 f.

5. Ibid., chap. 11, 219b 1.

6. Ibid., 219a 11, 219b 23.

7. Henri Bergson, *Schöperische Entwicklung* (Jena: E. Diederichs, 1921), pp. 339 ff.

8. Bergson, *Schöpferische*, pp. 308 ff.

9. See Heidegger, *Sein und Zeit*, pp. 421 f.

10. Immanuel Kant, *Critique of Pure Reason*, 1787, B. 49–51.

11. Franz Brentano, . . . *Vom Dasein Gottes* (Leipzig: F. Meiner, 1929), pp. 102 ff. See also, Franz Brentano, *Psychologie vom empirischen Standpunkt* (Leipzig: F. Meiner, 1924–25), vol. 2, pp. 271 f.

12. *Psychologie*, vol. 2, pp. 142 ff.

13. Ibid., p. 111: "*Vom sinnlichen und noetischen Bewusstsein,*" pp. 38 f.

14. A. Marty, *Raum und Zeit*, p. 20.

15. Ibid., pp. 239 ff.

16. Bergson, *Schöpferische*, pp. 8–14.

17. Henri Bergson, *Les deux sources de la morale et de la religion* (Paris: F. Alcan, 1932). *Die Beiden Quellen der Moral und der Religion*, trans. Eugen Lerch (Jena: Diederichs, 1933). *The Two Sources of Morality and Religion*, trans. Ashley Audra and Cloudesley Brereton (Garden City, N.Y.: Doubleday, 1935).

18. Ibid., *Two Sources*, p. 98.

19. *Edmund Husserl's Vorlesungen zur Phänomenologie des inneren Zeitbewusstseins*, ed. Martin Heidegger (Halle: M. Niemeyer, 1928).

20. Ibid., p. 436.

21. See Satomi Takahasi, "Time and the Stream-of-Consciousness in Husserl," *The Point of View of the Whole [Zentai no tachiba]* (Tokyo: Iwanami Shoten, 1932).

22. Heidegger, *Sein und Zeit*, pp. 191 ff.

Chapter Eleven. The Mutual Relation of Spatiality and Temporality

1. "*Die lebendige Seele der Totalität,*" in Georg Wilhelm Friedrick Hegel, *Encyklopädie der philosophischen Wissenschaften im Grndrisse* (Heidelberg: A. Oswald, 1817), p. 149.

Chapter Twelve. The Acts of *Ningen*

1. Immanuel Kant, *Grundlegung zür Metaphysik der Sitten* (Leipzig: F. Meiner, 1947).

2. Hermann Cohen, *Ethik des reinen Willens* (Berlin: B. Cassirer, 1921), p. 184.

3. Ibid., p. 191.

4. A. E. Taylor, *The Problem of Conduct*, p. 44.

5. Max Scheler, *Der Formalismus*, pp. 120 f.

6. Ibid., p. 127

7. Dietrich von Hildebrand, *Die Idee der sittlichen Handlung*, in Husserl's *Jahrbuch für Philosophie und phanomenologische Forschung* 3 (1916): 126–251.

8. Dietrich von Hildebrand, *Metaphysik der Gemeinschaft* (Stuttgart: Kohlhammer, 1930).

Chapter Thirteen. Trust and Truth

1. Wilhelm Herrmann, *Ethik* (Tübingen and Leipzig: J. C. B. Mohr, 1901), pp. 38 ff.

2. Ibid., p. 37.

3. Nicolai Hartmann, *Ethik* (Berlin: De Gruyter, 1926), pp. 422 ff.

4. Hermann Cohen, *Ethik des reinen Willens* (Berlin: B. Cassirer, 1921), chap. 1.

Chapter Fourteen. The Good and Bad of *Ningen:* Guilt and Conscience

1. H. G. Stoker, *Das Gewissen: Erscheinungsformen und Theorien* (Bonn: Cohen, 1925).

2. The actual scriptural passage to which Watsuji refers is *Romans 7*, and continues by pointedly observing that ". . . if I do what I do not want, I agree that the law is good. So then it is no longer I that do it, but sin which dwells within me. For I know that nothing good dwells within me, that is, in my flesh. I can will what is right, but I cannot do it. For I do not do the good I want, but the evil I do not want is what I do (Robert E. Carter)."

Appendix: Correspondence with Yuasa Yasuo

1. Yuaso Yasuo is the author of *The Body: Toward an Eastern Mind-Body Theory,* ed. T. P. Kasulis, trans. T. P. Kasulis and Nagatomo Shigenori (Albany: State University of New York Press, 1987) and a student of Watsuji Tetsurō.

2. London: Hamish Hamilton, 1985.

Interpretive Essay: Strands of Influence

1. William R. LaFleur, "A Turning in Taishō: Asia and Europe in the Early Writings of Watsuji Tetsurō," in J. Thomas Rimer, ed., *Culture and Identity: Japanese Intellectuals During the Interwar Years* (Princeton, N. J.: Princeton University Press, 1990), p. 254.

2. Ibid., p. 243.

3. Yuasa Yasuo, in a letter to me dated March 20, 1995, entitled "Regarding the Tradition of Shintō in Japanese Intellectual History and Watsuji's Interpretation of That Tradition."

4. Jean Herbert, *Shintō: At the Fountain-head of Japan* (London: George Allen and Unwin Ltd., 1967), p. 72.

5. Quoted in ibid., p. 76. Herbert's reference is to Hori Hidenari, *Shin-mei-kō* [*research into the Names of Kami*] (Tokyo, 1909), pp. 99 ff., but because the statement is attributed to Nitobe, it is either an oral recollection or from Nitobe Inazō's *Bushido: The Moral Ideals of Japan* (London: Heinemann, 1904).

6. Warren W. Smith, *Confucianism in Modern Japan: A Study of Conservatism in Japanese Intellectual History* (Tokyo: Hokuseido Press, 1973), p. 6.

7. Confucius, *Chung-yung* (*Doctrine of the Mean*), chap. 20, 8, trans. James Legge, as *The Confucian Classics*, 2nd ed. (Oxford: Clarendon Press, 1893), vol. 1, p. 406.

8. Tu Wei-Ming, *Centrality and Commonality: An Essay on Confucian Religiousness* (Albany: State University of New York Press, 1989), p. 48.

9. Ibid.

10. Confucius, *Chung-yung* (*Doctrine of the Mean*), chap. 20, 18.

11. Tu Wei-Ming, *Centrality and Commonality*, p. 79.

12. Genpei Ninomiya, "Ethical Backgrounds in Japan and Their Bearing upon the Rise of Social Consciousness of Japan," M.A. thesis, University of Chicago, 1927, p. 56.

13. Nakamura Hajime, *Ways of Thinking of Eastern Peoples: India-China-Tibet-Japan* (Honolulu: East-West Center Press, 1964), p. 401.

14. Ibid.

15. Watsuji Tetsurō, *Climate and Culture: A Philosophical Study* (Tokyo: The Hokuseido Press, Ministry of Education, 1961), p. 148.

16. Smith, *Confucianism*, p. 160.

17. Ibid., p. 158. The quotation is from Ōkawa Shūmei, *Shintei Nippon nissen roppyakunen shi* (*The Two Thousand Six Hundred Year History of Japan, Newly Revised*), 21st ed. (Tokyo: Daichi Shobō, 1940), pp. 22–23.

18. Watsuji, *Climate and Culture*, p. v.

19. Daisetz T. Suzuki, *Zen and Japanese Culture*, Bollingen Series 64 (Princeton, N.J.: Princeton University Press, 1959), p. 355.

20. Yuasa Yasuo, "The Encounter of Modern Japanese Philosophy with Heidegger," in *Heidegger and Asian Thought*, ed. Graham Parkes (Honolulu: University of Hawaii Press, 1987), p. 173.

21. Ibid.

22. Watsuji, *Climate and Culture*, p. 8.

23. Ibid.

24. Furukawa Tetsushi, "Watsuji Tetsurō, the Man and His Work," in Watsuji Tetsurō, *Climate and Culture*, p. 228. Furukawa goes on to add that "We find our ethical problems not in the consciousness of the individual in isolation, but in the relations between man [human being] and man [human being]."

25. Yuasa Yasuo, *The Body: Toward an Eastern Mind-Body Theory*, SUNY Series in Buddhist Studies (Albany: State University of New York Press, 1987) p. 37.

26. Ibid.

27. Ibid. According to Buddhism, every living thing, including human beings, transmigrate six worlds; that is, hell, the realm of hungry ghosts, beasts, *ningen* (the human world per se), the Asuras (a realm of frightening and sometimes merciless beings, who, at other times, are protectors), and heaven or gods.

28. William R. Lafleur, "Buddhist Emptiness in the Ethics and Aesthetics of Watsuji Tetsurō," *Religious Studies* 14: 237.

29. Michiko Yusa, 'Persona Originalis': 'Jinkaku' and 'Personne,' According to the Philosophies of Nishida Kitarō and Jacques Maritain, Ph.D. dissertation, University of California at Santa Barbara, 1983, p. 58. From Nishida's *Collected Works*, vol. 9, p. 73.

30. Furukawa Tetsushi, "Watsuji Tetsurō, the Man and His Work," p. 228.

31. LaFleur, "Buddhist Emptiness," p. 247.

32. An excellent discussion of codependent origination is to be found in Abe Masao, "Non-Being and *Mu*—the Metaphysical Nature of Negativity in the East and the West," in Abe Masao, *Zen and Western Thought*, ed. William R. LaFleur (Honolulu: University of Hawaii Press, 1985): "That everything is impermanent, having no eternal selfhood (self-being) and no unchangeable substance, is one of the basic principles of Buddhism. That everything is dependent on something else, that nothing is independent and self-existing, is another basic Buddhist principle. This is termed *pratītya-samutpāda*, which can be translated as dependent origination, relationality, relational origination, or dependent co-arising. The realization that everything is impermanent and dependently originating must be applied to things not only *in* the universe but also *beyond* the universe" (pp. 125–126).

It seems to be that Watsuji does not take the step beyond the universe or at least that he does not do so in such a way as to make clear that he intends to utilize the sense of transcendent emptiness in a way which is at all similar to that of Nishida.

33. LaFleur, "Buddhist Emptiness," p. 250.

34. Ibid., p. 249.

35. Ibid.

36. Alasdair MacIntyre, "Individual and Social Morality in Japan and the United States: Rival Conceptions of the Self," *Philosophy East and West* 40, no. 4 (October 1990): 489.

37. Ibid., p. 491.

38. Ibid.

39. Ibid.

40. Ibid.

41. Ibid., p. 493.

42. Ibid.

43. Ibid.

44. Ibid., pp. 493–494.

45. David Dilworth, "Watsuji Tetsurō" (1889–1960): Cultural Phenomonologist and Ethician," *Philosophy East and West* 24, no. 1 (January 1974): 17; and William R. LaFleur, "Buddhist Emptiness," p. 238.

46. Ibid.

47. Ibid., p. 239.

48. Ibid.

49. Ibid., p. 244

50. Ibid., p. 245

51. Ibid. What Nāgārjuna demonstrates is that concepts, and the words and propositions that express them, are incapable of capturing that alleged reality which they attempt to state. All words and all concepts are intrinsically dualistic; that is, they divide the world into what is stated and by implication into its opposite—for example, night/day, up/down, one/many, cause/effect. Thus, all philosophical distinctions are relative and logically interdependent. Therefore, to state the cause, one implies the effect; and because a cause can also be an effect, the matter is worse still. The only escape is to recognize the emptiness of concepts and words, understanding that distinctions have no extralinguistic reality. They are mere conventions, and all that they refer to is other words and sets of words.

This recognition can be instrumental in leading us to accept the interdependence of all things, causally, so that everything is understood to be the cause of everything else and also the effect of everything else. Because everything (including ourselves, having no substantiality) is empty, everything is but a temporary intersection of causal influences, which will persist only so long as those influences continue in sufficient ways and quantities to keep us and things in existence.

Wisdom (*prajñā*) is that state of realization which comprehends the emptiness of all things and that verbal distinctions do not name anything. Ultimate truth is *beyond* all such distinctions not in that it is another *thing* of another *kind*, but in that it is a dissolving of all graspings after conceptualizations, all systems, all "ultimates." "Emptiness," then, is simply without objective referent. At most, it is that state of awareness which recognizes that all "things" are infinitely interconnected.

52. Abe Masao, "Mahayana Buddhism and Whitehead," in Abe, *Zen and Western Thought*, p. 153. Abe gives this series of alternative translations in his helpful essay comparing Mahayana Buddhist thought and Whitehead's philosophy.

53. William R. Lafleur, "Buddhist Emptiness," p. 250.

54. Masao Abe, *Zen and Western Thought*, p. 159.

55. Robert E. Carter, *The Nothingness Beyond God: An Introduction to the Philosophy of Nishida Kitarō* (New York: Paragon House, 1989), p. 98.

56. William R. Lafleur, "Buddhist Emptiness," p. 247.

57. Ibid., p. 249.

58. Abe Masao, *Zen and Western Thought*, p. 158.

59. Gino K. Piovesana, *Contemporary Japanese Philosophical Thought*, Asian Philosophical Studies, No. 4 (New York: St. John's University Press, 1969), p. 143.

60. Robert N. Bellah, "Japan's Cultural Identity: Some Reflections on the Work of Watsuji Tetsurō," *Journal of Asian Studies* 24, no. 4 (August 1965): 579.

61. Ibid., p. 580.

62. Ibid., p. 581.

63. Ibid. But I do not think that "the state is the expression of the absolute whole" in some different sense than would equally apply to people or mountains, except that the state is the highest ethical structure or organization thus far reached. Bellah is certainly right in equating the absolute whole of the state with absolute emptiness. And he is right in identifying the state with the highest ethical structure yet created. And Watsuji did hold, at least during the war, that the Imperial system in Japan was the highest achievement of any state thus far in human history. This is not the end, but the early beginnings of what human attempts to return to their "home ground" might create in the world, over a considerable period of evolutionary historical time. It is not that the state itself *is* the highest possible ethical organization nor that the Japanese political system *is* the best organization possible, but only that the state *is thus far* the highest expression of communality as a negation of the individual, while at the same time preserving the individual through the identity of self-contradiction; and, that the Japanese system is the most effective form of collective solidarity thus far achieved, because it rests on mutual good-will, as in a family, is held together by mutual respect and reverence, and operates on the basis of trust and truthfulness, at least at its best. Nonetheless, the evolution of the state as the highest form of solidarity is still in progress, and the real possibility of our journey to our home ground taking us well beyond the state as it presently exists cannot be ruled out and probably ought to be anticipated. Watsuji's historical sense makes abundantly clear that the evolution of institutions, like that of species and of the individuals that make them up, is a never ending process.

64. Gino K. Piovesana, *Contemporary Japanese Philosophical Thought*, p. 143.

65. James W. Heisig, "The Religious Philosophy of the Kyoto School—An Overview," *Journal of Religious Studies* 17, no. 1 (1990): 54.

66. Ibid., p. 54.

67. Bellah, "Japan's Cultural Identity," p. 580.

68. Yuasa, "The Encounter of Modern Japanese Philosophy with Heidegger," p. 168.

69. Ibid., p. 169.

glossary of japanese terms

決リ	*kimari*—agreement
誠	*makoto*—sincerity
眞心	*magokoro*—true heart
身持	*mimochi*—the way in which one behaves oneself
人間	*ningen*—human beings
仲間	*nakama*—fellows
中	*naka*—in
仲違いする	*naka tagai suru*—to break up relations
人間存在	*ningen sonzai*—human existence
仲良し	*naka yoshi*—a good friend
行い	*okonai*—personal doings
訪れ	*otozure*—correspondence and visitation
倫理	*rinri*—ethics
連中	*renchū*—a party
良心	*ryōshin*—conscience
郎党	*rotō*—a group
済まない	*sumanai*—to have no excuse for and at the same time not to have finished doing
済ます	*sumasu*—to finish doing and at the same time, to pay a debt
済んだ	*sunda*—to have finished doing
武士	*samurai*—warriors
済まなかた	*sumanakatta*—a past tense of *sumani*
世間	*seken*—the public
世	*yo*—a generation and at the same time a society
存在	*sonzai*—being

存身	*sonshin*—the survival of the body
存命	*sonmei*—the survival of life
存錄	*sonroku*—the survival of records
存亡	*sonbō*—maintenance and loss
正直	*shōjiki*—honesty
晴天	*seiten*—fine weather
眞実	*shinjitsu*—truthfulness
眞言	*shingon*—true words
眞事	*shinji*—true things
誠実	*seijitsu*—sincerity
友達	*tomodachi*—friends
問う	*tou*—to ask
太陽	*taiyo*—the sun
態度	*taido*—attitudes
賴り	*tayori*—news and at the same time reliance
天下	*tenka*—the world
世中	*yononaka*—the public
夜明	*yoake*—daybreak
夕暮	*yūgure*—evening
夜	*yoru*—night
良し	*yoshi*—to be good and at the same time to be approvable
良さ	*yosa*—excellence
在宿	*zai shuku*—to stay at an inn
在室	*zai shitsu*—to stay at home
在世	*zai sei*—to remain in this world
善	*zen*—goodness
善人	*zen nin*—a good person
善行	*zen kō*—a good act
善意	*zen i*—a good will
罪責	*zai seki*—guilt
若衆	*waka shu*—young fellows

分	*wake*—meaning or reason
分けられる	*wakerareru*—to be divided
分かる	*wakaru*—to understand
分ける	*wakeru*—to divide

bibliography of works about watsuji

Arima, Tatsuo. *The Failure of Freedom: A Portrait of Modern Japanese Intellectuals*. Cambridge, Mass.: Harvard University Press, 1969.

Bellah, Robert N. "Japan's Cultural Identity: Some Reflections on the Work of Watsuji Tetsurō." *The Journal of Asian Studies* 24, no. 4 (1965): 573–594.

Berque, Augustin. "Milieu et logique du lieu chez Watsuji." *Revue de Philosophique Louvain* 92, no. 4 (November 1994): 495–507.

———. *Vivre l'Espace au Japon*. Paris: Presses Universitaires de France, 1982.

Dilworth, David A. "Watsuji Tetsurō (1889–1960): Cultural Phenomenologist and Ethician." *Philosophy East and West* 24, no. 1 (January 1974).

Furukawa, Tetsushi. "Watsuji Tetsurō, the Man and His Work." In Watsuji Tetsurō, *Climate and Culture: A Philosophical Study*, 1961. pp. 209–235. Tokyo: The Hokuseido Press, Ministry of Education, 1961.

LaFleur, William R. "A Turning in Taishō: Asia and Europe in the Early Writings of Watsuji Tetsurō." In J. Thomas Rimer, ed., *Culture and Identity: Japanese Intellectuals During the Interwar Years*, pp. 234–256. Princeton, N.J.: Princeton University Press, 1990.

———. "An Ethic of As-Is: State and Society in the *Rinrigaku* of Watsuji Tetsurō." In Léon Vandermeersch, ed., *La société civile face à l'État dans les traditions chinoïse, japonaise, coréenne et vietnamienne*. Paris: Études thématiques 3, École française d'Extrême-Orient, 1994, pp. 453–464.

———. "Buddhist Emptiness in the Ethics and Aesthetics of Watsuji Tetsurō." *Religious Studies* 14 (1978): 237–250.

Nagami, Isamu. "The Ontological Foundations in Tetsurō Watsuji's Philosophy: *Kū* and Human Existence." *Philosophy East and West* 31, no. 3 (July 1981).

Najita, Tetsuo, and Harootunian, H. D. "Japanese Revolt Against the West: Political and Cultural Criticism in the Twentieth Century." In Peter Duus, ed., *The Twentieth Century: The Cambridge History of Japan*. New York/ Cambridge: Cambridge University Press, 1988, vol. 6, pp. 711–774.

Odin, Steve. "The Japanese Concept of Nature in Relation to the Environmental Ethics and Conservation Aesthetics of Aldo Leopold." *Environmental Ethics* 13, no. 4 (Winter 1991).

———. "The Social Self in Japanese Philosophy and American Pragmatism: A Comparative Study of Watsuji Tetsurō and George Herbert Mead." *Philosophy East and West* 42, no. 3 (July 1992): 475–501.

Piovesana, Gino K. *Contemporary Japanese Philosophical Thought.* New York: St. John's University Press, 1969.

Sakai, Naoki. "Return to the West/Return to the East: Watsuji Tetsurō's Anthropology and Discussions of Authenticity." In Masao Miyoshi, *Japan and the World*, a special issue of *Boundary 2* [Duke University Press] (Fall 1991): 157–190.

Yuasa, Yasuo. *The Body: Toward an Eastern Mind-Body Theory*, ed. T. P. Kasulis, trans. Nagatomo Shigenori and T. P. Kasulis. Albany: State University of New York Press, 1987.

———. "The Encounter of Modern Japanese Philosophy with Heidegger." In *Heidegger and Asian Thought*, ed. Graham Parkes, pp. 155–174. Honolulu: University of Hawaii Press, 1987.

index

morality 11, 236, 295, 299; of *Dasein*
217; Kantian 126, 139–49, 259;
Nietzsche's view of 292; *ningen* 37,
227–28, 269–70; obligation 245;
selfless 236; social 86, 121, 205
mores 314
motivation 242–43, 254–55, 267
mysticism 122

naka-tagai-suru 仲違いする 18
nakama 仲間 10, 12, 15
nakayoshi 仲良し 134
nation 26–7, 74, 79, 94, 113, 121–22,
125–27, 138, 148–50, 161, 171, 182,
191, 251, 289, 290
natura naturans 167–68
negation 36, 142, 283, 310–11; and authenticity 82, 101, 187–89, 223–30,
272; of community 23, 80–1, 85, 98,
102, 108, 115, 117, 120, 123, 137,
145, 235; ethical 116, 118, 121, 129–
33, 233, 277; individual 22–4, 93–8;
spatio-temporal 16, 124, 178, 229–
33, 270, 273; truth 270, 284–86; of
the whole 99, 285
New Testament 296
Nichitigkeit 216–17
negation of negation 23, 117–18, 121,
135, 137, 139, 224, 228–33, 284
ningen 人間 332, 336–38, 340–44, 348;
acts of 24, 233, 244, 300, 303; as authenticity 225, 228; as betweenness
14; and common sense 38–9; consciousness of 30–1; dual characteristics of 16, 22, 165, 175–77, 228; as
expression 36; holistic structure of
32; as individual 15–6, 19; manner
of existence 133; *makoto* of 276;
meaning of 12–5, 145; paths of 24;
as public 14–6, 199; question of 30–
1; as self 231; and spaciality 329–
30; study of 9–10, 14, 27, 29; structure of 229; as subject 32; as subjective 43, 230, 232; totality of 26,
224–25, 22; and transportation
183–84; 7; and truthfulness 283–84;

as unity of contradictories 15–6, 19
ningen sonzai 人間存在 305, 345; as
authenticity 188–89, 225, 229; basic
principle of 287–88; climatic character of 39; and ethics 29, 37; as expression 37–40, 44–5, 49; as ground
220; as questioning 31; and
Heidegger 219–21, 223–299; and
history 43–5; as interconnection of
acts 235; laws of 248, 252, 269, 271–
72; and negation 283, 285; as
nondualistic 281–82; spatiality of
177, 181, 224, 239–40, 243, 307–10;
as self 231; structure of 185–87,
190, 223; temporality of 182–83,
186–87, 190, 220–21, 228, 307–10,
332; and trust 276, 279–82; and
truthfulness 278–82, 294
nirvāṇa 312
non-dual(ity) 34, 187–90, 223–28, 231–
33, 281, 300, 341–43
nothingness 19, 216–17, 223, 342–43,
346–49
noumenal ego 38
noumenon 32

okonai 行い 236–37
ontology 19–20, 68, 176, 196, 297
organism 59–60, 85, 89, 113, 153, 282,
284
otozure 訪れ 162

person: total 93; finite 95
personality-as-a-whole 79
phenomenology 16, 33, 68, 125, 128,
199–200, 203, 207, 211–12, 219, 292–
93
physiology 59–60, 238
point of individuality 77, 107–08
preparedness 217–18, 220, 228, 245,
256–57
privacy 25
privatus 146
psychology 70, 136; associational 351;
body/mind 199; and communication 244; and consciousness 199,

NAMES